THE OTHER SIDE OF THE ERROR TERM

Aging and Development as Model Systems in Cognitive Neuroscience

edited by

Naftali RAZ

Department of Psychology
The University of Memphis
Memphis, TN, USA

1998

ELSEVIER
Amsterdam – Lausanne – New York – Oxford – Shannon – Singapore – Tokyo

NORTH-HOLLAND
ELSEVIER SCIENCE B.V.
Sara Burgerhartstraat 25
P.O. Box 211, 1000 AE Amsterdam, The Netherlands

Library of Congress Cataloging-in-Publication Data

The other side of the error term : aging and development as model systems in cognitive neuroscience / Naftali Raz, editor.
p. cm. -- (Advances in psychology ; 125)
Includes bibliographical references and index.
ISBN 0-444-82522-3
1. Cognitive neuroscience--Research--Methodology.
2. Developmental neurobiology. 3. Dyslexia--Animal models.
I. Raz, Naftali. II. Series: Advances in psychology (Amsterdam, Netherlands) ; 125.
QP360.5.086 1998
612.8'2--dc21 98-3180
CIP

ISBN: 0 444 82522 3

This book is printed on acid-free paper.

Transferred to digital printing 2006

THE OTHER SIDE OF THE ERROR TERM
Aging and Development as Model Systems in Cognitive Neuroscience

ADVANCES IN PSYCHOLOGY

125

Editor:

G. E. STELMACH

ELSEVIER
Amsterdam – Lausanne – New York – Oxford – Shannon – Singapore – Tokyo

LIST OF CONTRIBUTORS

Theodore Bashore
University of Northern Colorado,
Greeley, CO 80631
USA

Nelson Cowan
Department of Psychology,
University of Missouri,
Columbia, MO 65211
USA

Jennifer Dorfman
Section of Cognitive Neuroscience
Rush-Presbyterian-St. Luke's
Medical Center
1645 W. Jackson, Suite 450
Chicago, IL 60612
USA

Steven W. Gangestad
Department of Psychology,
University of New Mexico,
Albuquerque, NM 87131
USA

Elizabeth L. Glisky
Department of Psychology,
University of Arizona,
Tucson, AZ 85721
USA

Dennis L. Molfese
Department of Psychology,
Southern Illinois University ,
Carbondale, IL 62901-6502
USA

Maurits van der Mollen,
University of Amsterdam,
Department of Developmental
Psychology,
Roetersstraat 15,
1018 WB Amsterdam,
the Netherlands

K. Richard Ridderinkhof,
University of Amsterdam,
Department of Developmental
Psychology,
Roetersstraat 15,
1018 WB Amsterdam,
the Netherlands

Glenn D. Rosen
Department of Neurology,
Beth Israel Hospital,
330 Brookline Ave.
Boston, MA 02215
USA

J. Scott Saults
Department of Psychology,
University of Missouri,
Columbia, MO 65211
USA

Patricia Tun
Volen National Center for Complex
Systems, MS 013,
Brandeis University,
P.O. Box 9110,
Waltham, MA 02254-9110
USA

Gloria Waters
Neuropsychology Laboratory,
Massachusetts General Hospital
32 Fruit St.

Boston, MA02114
USA

Arthur Wingfield
Volen National Center for Complex
Systems, MS 013,
Brandeis University,
P.O. Box 9110,
Waltham, MA 02254-9110
USA

Ronald A. Yeo
Department of Psychology,
University of New Mexico,
Albuquerque, NM 87131
USA

CONTENTS

INTRODUCTION

To study any aspect of human condition, one must contend with an issue of substantial inter-individual variability and heterogeneity that are apparent in structure and function alike. In pursuit of general laws of behavior and general neural mechanisms of cognition, it is tempting to treat individual variability as a source of bothersome noise that obscures a valuable message.

Nevertheless, clichés aside, one man's trash is another man's treasure, or in terms of the trade, one person's error term is another person's main effect. The same unwanted sources of variability that seem to obscure the general laws of cognition become the focus of investigation for a scholar seeking to explain the individuality of human behavior. For such a researcher subjects' characteristics and the unique nature of the sample come into focus and become the goal in itself. Developmental psychologists are interested in infants, children, and adolescents for what these subjects are; gerontologists are concerned with the elderly rather than "young controls;" for psychopathologists understanding of the peculiarities of psychoses is the main goal; educational psychologists labor on finding new and better ways of educating the gifted, the learning-disabled, and the mentally retarded.

The universal practical appeal of such stances hardly needs an elaborate justification. All these disciplines have emerged and progressed with an eye on their target populations, yet every good study in any of these domains inevitably has another important dimension. This additional dimension is just as obvious as the primary avenue of exploration. Whenever a study is designed to turn a spotlight to some special population, the light is also shed on the mainstream from which the target group deviates. As a matter of fact, even the most recent history of cognitive neuroscience yields fine examples of such collateral gains. For instance, the distinction between implicit and explicit memory originated from and rests largely on the differential response of these mnemonic functions to specific brain pathology, their order of emergence in the course of development, and their heterosynchonous decline at the end of the life span. Many insights into the general laws of language came from research on peculiarities of child development and aphasias in stroke victims. Understanding basic principles of executive management of behavior and use of inhibitory control in cognitive operations is impossible without careful study of their development and decline from infancy to senium, and their alterations in neuro- and psychopathology. The list can go on.

This book is designed as an expanded version of this list. Its objective is to examine what we can learn about general and universal phenomena and laws of cognition, and about the brain substrates of cognition by examining the odd, the rare, the transient, and the exceptional. Although many exceptional examples and accidents of nature can be recruited for the sake of exploration of the general phenomenon, in this volume, we will restrict our attention to the discussions inspired by normal development and aging.

The first four chapters are devoted to the insights that developmental models of cognition provide into cognitive phenomena and their neural foundation. We start with what can serve as a meta-theory to all models based on exceptionality. In Chapter 1, Yeo and Gangestad develop the notion of developmental instability as the foundation of a wide variety of exceptional and pathological conditions. By examining behavioral and neural correlates of the extremes of DI, the authors demonstrate how inclusion of exceptional individuals in the sample contributes to understanding of not only individual differences but general trends in evolution of brain organization and behavior.

Moving to the level of the whole organism and the central nervous system, Rosen (Chapter 2) explores the role of exceptional animals (ectopic mice) in building models of complex human functions such as reading and speech processing. This approach makes a strong case for two-tier modeling in which animal model addresses a pathological aspect of human behavior which in turn may enlighten our understanding of universal cognitive phenomena. Animals with known cytoarchitectonic defects are used to study nonlinguistic behaviors that are associated with reading deficits in humans. Rosen shows, how understanding of these nonlinguistic deficits centered on temporal information processing, may elucidate the mechanism of reading deficits, which in turn will shed light on the basic processes underlying a complex and probably uniquely human ability - comprehension of written language.

Molfese (Chapter 3) addresses the mechanisms of language comprehension by examining phonetic perception in infants and children. He demonstrates how the results of this developmental model challenge the dogma of exclusive left-hemispheric localization of language and advance the understanding of the mechanisms responsible for recovery of linguistic skills after brain damage.

In the final chapter devoted to developmental studies, Saults and Cowan (Chapter 4) summarize a research program based on application of individual differences methodology to search for mechanism of memory, and specifically, to the theories of working memory. They take Baddeley's model of working memory which was initially developed in the traditional realm of cognitive research, and put it to a test under conditions of maturation and development. By imposing developmental constraints, Saults and Cowan reveal the breaking points of the venerable theory. The authors show, for example, how understanding of the phonological loop mechanisms must be revised in light of the finding that both output and rehearsal processes must be taken into account to explain the performance of young children. They argue that ostensibly automatic processes such as rehearsal in a phonological loop, may still require attentional resources. When it comes to *bona fide* effortful processes as exemplified by the working memory performance in complex span tasks, Saults and Cowan show that the role of inhibition in WM capacity became clear only due to studies of development and aging.

The next four chapters deal with the insights drawn from studying of normal aging and age-associated diseases and conditions. Aging presents an interesting model system for investigating brain correlates and mechanisms of cognitive functions that require executive control over multiple processes rather than faithful execution of a single and circumscribe function. Bridging early developmental studies and investigations of older adults, Bashore, Riderinkhoff & van der Mollen (Chapter 5) tackle a thorny issue of speed of information processing, and its role in cognition. The authors demonstrate how under scrutiny of psychophysiological methods in the context of life-span development a seemingly uniform landscape of human cognition reveals significant peaks and troughs, and how process-specific differentiation may be a rule and not an exception in human information processing.

Glisky (Chapter 6) uses evidence from studies on normal aging and focal lesions to draw a distinction between two major brain systems underpinning memory functions: the limbic/diencephalic and the prefrontal. Although theorizing about these two systems is abundant, Glisky presents an organized account of experimental findings that favors the distinction. Differential aging of the brain shows a predilection for prefrontal cortex, whereas age-related dementia of Alzheimer type targets mesolimbic areas at its early stages. These circumstances make cognitive aging studies especially relevant to testing the plausibility of the two-system account.

Wingfield, Waters, & Tun (Chapter 7) use normal aging, age-associated diseases, and focal lesions as model systems in their examination of one of the hotly debated questions in psycholinguistics: Is language comprehension critically limited by the working memory capacity? Their analysis shows that a received wisdom of working memory being the bottleneck of linguistic comprehension may be wrong. The use of aging as a model showing the breaking point of the working memory-comprehension association is especially illustrative. This chapter presents an interesting analysis of another age-related phenomenon - experience by capacity interaction. It is apparent that older adults who are skilled in comprehension of language and have a life-long experience in that area may find ways around their moderately impaired working memory capacity. As the mechanisms allowing such circumvention are revealed, we gain more insights into the mechanics of language comprehension than would be possible should we restrict our interest to college-age adults.

In the final chapter (Chapter 8), Dorfman sketches a strategic approach to a complex and multidimensional subject - problem solving. With growing evidence for the importance of inhibition in insight problem-solving, computer models that lack that important feature appear increasingly inadequate. Human model systems with prominent variability in inhibitory control are needed to account for fundamental phenomena of problem solving such as incubation. Dorfman proposes to use aging with its selective impact on the prefrontal cortex and frontostriatal loops and its prominent failures of inhibition as a powerful tool for testing hypotheses about brain substrates of problem solving skills.

By design, this book is a diverse collection of articles and it was not meant to present an integrative view. It is hoped, however, that it will reinforce and promote the interest in exploring human diversity at the service of furthering the understanding of universal phenomena of cognition.

Naftali Raz,

Memphis, October 1997

ACKNOWLEDGMENT

The editor gratefully acknowledges the support provided to him in preparation of this book by the National Institutes of Health (grant R01-AG11230) and the State of Tennessee (Center of Excellence grant). This book was formatted and edited with the Word Perfect 6.1 and Sigmaplot 4.0 software.

The Other Side of the Error Term - N. Raz (Editor)

Chapter 1

DEVELOPMENTAL INSTABILITY AND PHENOTYPIC VARIATION IN NEURAL ORGANIZATION

Ronald A. Yeo

Steven W. Gangestad

University of New Mexico

ABSTRACT

Developmental instability (DI), the imprecise expression of the genetic plan for development due to the introduction of developmental noise, appears to contribute substantially to individual variations in handedness, functional hemispheric asymmetries for cognitive tasks, and cortical asymmetries, including atypical asymmetry of the planum temporale. The nature of the genetic and environmental factors underlying developmental instability provides insights into the selection factors that maintain population genetic diversity related to individual variation in functional and anatomic asymmetry. The DI perspective helps account for associations between atypical asymmetries and neurodevelopmental disorders, and more generally, offers a genetic and evolutionary framework for understanding individual variation in human brain organization.

Each and every member of our species has been conferred an extraordinarily expensive inheritance -- our genes. These genes have, over the course of millions of years, proven valuable in helping our ancestors survive and procreate. The successes and failures in the lives of untold millions of our direct ancestors and their relatives have served to provide us with a genetic wisdom almost beyond imagination, a wisdom as to how to deal with the range of social and environmental situations typically encountered by members of our species. Further, the genes passed down have proven able to work together effectively, representing adapted aggregations.

Remarkably, there are important differences amongst us in our ability to capitalize upon this inheritance, to express accurately in ontogeny the wisdom of our genes. To varying degrees, each of us "squanders" our inheritance by failing to faithfully execute our genetic program. Noise creeps into development, leading to imprecise expression of the genetic plan for the growth and function of the body and brain, as we shall detail shortly. Why would this be so? Why do we fail to utilize fully the hard-wrought legacy of our ancestors? And specifically, what are the effects of developmental noise on the brain? In this chapter we will attempt to answer these questions, and hopefully, provide some insight into fundamental issues regarding human nature and the origins of important dimensions of psychological and biological differences amongst us. We shall first review genetic causes of maladaptation and introduce the concept of developmental instability (DI). The impact of DI on reproductive fitness and mating behaviors in humans will be discussed briefly. We then review in some detail the impact of DI on human brain function and anatomy.

Maladaptation in Organisms

It has sometimes been assumed that individual members of a species will be near-equally fit genetically (e.g., Kirkpatrick, 1986). Selection drives out maladaptive variants and, hence, it's been thought individuals should have essentially the same basic genetic inheritance equipping them to survive and reproduce. Recently, this view has begun to give sway to an alternative: A view that maladaptive variants persist in populations despite selection.

The view that selection drives and keeps out maladaptive variants depends upon the assumption that both populations and the environments they live in are static. In fact, however, both populations and environments change, such that, in absence of selection, the fitness of populations degrades. First, mutations, which usually result in maladaptive outcomes, occur. Because humans probably average one or two fresh deleterious mutations (Charlesworth, 1990), each of which may compromise fitness (as indicated by survival and fertility) by up to a couple of percent (e.g., Rice, 1988, and references therein on empirical studies of maladaptive effects of mutations), the effect of mutations on fitness in human populations may be considerable. Second, environments themselves change, resulting in an increasing lack of fitness of a population that doesn't change. (Just as the Red Queen in *Alice in Wonderland* finds she must run to stay in the same place, a population must evolve simply to maintain its fitness; Fisher, 1958). Changes in the environment that occur in a short time interval can create the greatest incompatibility between organisms and their environments. Historically, the most rapid changes are probably changes in other organisms with which we are in conflict and, the shorter-lived the organism, the more rapid the change. Pathogens and parasites evolve over time in ways that are to their benefit and our loss; to maintain fitness, we must evolve in response to their changes (i.e., hosts and parasites "coevolve"; e.g., Anderson & May, 1982; Hamilton, 1982). More recently, we are increasingly exposed to toxins in our environment to which we are not adapted -- environmental changes of our own making.

Because changes that degrade fitness are one step ahead of selection that can compensate for them, populations are constantly burdened with some level of maladaptation. Thus, for instance, Rice (1988) used a quantitative model to estimate that, due to deleterious mutations alone (the "genetic load"), *Drosophila melanogaster* (fruit flies) on average have only about 75% of the fitness of a fruit fly free of mutations. In principle, maladaptation due to pathogens and parasites could be of similar magnitude (see Charleworth, 1990).

As it turns out, not only do changing environments and mutations maintain maladaptation in populations; these processes also inevitably maintain individual *variation* in fitness. Thus, once again, due to mutations alone, the most fit and least fit Drosophila are expected to vary in fitness by a factor of over 1.5 (Rice, 1988). Similarly, variation in fitness is theoretically expected to be maintained by environmental changes that occur through host-parasite evolution. Hence, contrary to some previous claims, populations can have substantial genetic variance in fitness. Indeed, recent reviews of the empirical literature indicate that fitness components (e.g., longevity, fecundity) have genetic coefficients of variation (additive genetic variation standardized by the mean) much greater than those of ordinary morphological traits under stabilizing selection (e.g., Houle, 1992; Pomiankowski & Møller, 1995).

Maladaptation and the Evolution of Sex

The fact that maladaptation persists in populations despite selection may have had tremendously important implications for the evolution of organisms. Indeed, recent theories of the evolution of sex attribute it to this fact. Genomes in a line of asexually reproducing organisms cannot readily be cleansed of deleterious mutations or adapt to quickly changing environments. A fundamental effect of sex is that, by shuffling genes, it increases variance of offspring. Thus, a parent who has a number of mutations produces some gametes that have many mutations and some that have very few. Similarly, a parent who has some alleles that work against current pathogens and some that do not produces some gametes offering less resistance to current pathogens and some gametes offering more. Mathematical models indicate that, when the rate of newly introduced maladaptation either through mutation of environmental changes is sufficiently great, sexual reproduction can be advantaged over asexual reproduction due to its ability to eliminate quickly maladaptive forms (see, for instance, Charlesworth, 1990; Hamilton, 1982; Kondrashov, 1988). In so doing, however, sex does not produce only adaptive offspring. Rather, according to these models, sex evolved only *because* it results in differences in genetic fitness across offspring.

Developmental Instability

A key theoretical question is how disadvantaged genes adversely affect fitness. Recently, biologists have taken great interest in one potential pathway: developmental imprecision. This process can perhaps best be understood in terms of an analogy. Microcircuitry of a computer must be manufactured in an extremely clean, dust-free environment. Only in such an environment can the "design" of the microcircuitry be actualized. Dust that enters the environment and inadvertently becomes "part" of the chip can affect the functioning of the circuitry in random ways. In so much as the computer chip is designed to do perform certain tasks near-optimally under constraints of size and expense, any random departure from the chip's design is almost certain to result in poorer performance. Similarly, mutations (slight departures from near-optimal DNA structure), pathogens, and toxins can act as "dust" in the environment in which genes and epigenetic processes "manufacture" a organism's phenotype, introducing random deviations from design selected through natural selection. Slight departures from design caused by the random effects of mutations, pathogens, and toxins nearly always result in a phenotype that performs more poorly than the phenotype specified by "design." Biologists refer to organisms' inability to keep their development error-free *developmental instability.*

Biologists have studied variations in developmental instability using a couple of indicators. One is fluctuating asymmetry or FA. FA is departure from perfect symmetry on bilateral traits that are symmetrical at the population level, with deviations being near-normally distributed. Asymmetry of this sort is thought to be due to the accumulation of random errors in the development of the two sides of the body. A second measure is phenodeviance, an unusual phenotypic form of a character due to developmental disruption. In 1954 Lerner coined the term "phenodeviant" to designate the sporadic occurrence of abnormal morphological traits associated with inbreeding, such as crooked toes in chickens. Of course, we are especially interested in human beings, and the most widely studied equivalents of crooked toes are "minor physical anomalies" (Waldrop & Halverson, 1971). Such features as wide-spaced eyes or low-seated ears reflect abnormally slow development at a particular time in the first or second trimester of fetal development.

Many studies have examined the association between fluctuating asymmetry and components of fitness and health in natural populations of a large variety of organisms. Recent meta-analyses and non-quantitative reviews of the literature reveal that, within populations, FA negatively predicts longevity (Møller, in press), fecundity (Møller, in press), fitness traits (Leung & Forbes, in press; Møller, in press), health (Thornhill & Møller, in press), and mating success (Møller & Thornhill, submitted). Although the size of these relationships may not appear large (correlations of approximately -.2 to -.3 on average; e.g., Leung & Forbes, in press; Møller & Thornhill, submitted), much of the variance in FA is merely random error not relating to individual differences in developmental instability. In light of the small proportion of variance in FA estimated to be due to individual differences in developmental instability, the size of the association between these individual differences and fitness components is in fact probably very large (Gangestad & Thornhill, submitted).[1] Studies of the heritability of FA also indicate that underlying individual differences in developmental instability is substantially attributable to genetic variation (Møller & Thornhill, in press). Thus, a significant and perhaps substantial proportion of genetic variance in fitness may be due to developmental instability.

Causes of Developmental Instability

As noted above, major causes of maladaptation in organisms include

---

[1] Evidence suggests that asymmetry itself generally doesn't cause loss of fitness, so that the variance in associated with fitness traits must be largely contained within the variance in FA due to underlying individual differences in developmental instability (Gangestad & Thornhill, submitted).

mutations and environmental stressors novel to the organism, either because of coevolutionary processes (e.g, parasites) or recent introduction (e.g., toxins). These too are probably major causes of developmental instability (see, for instance, Møller, 1996a, on the effect of parasites on fluctuating asymmetry). Two other possible genetic contributions to developmental instability are protein homozygosity and lack of genic coadaptation.

A number of studies in diverse species suggest that protein homozygosity compromises growth rates and fitness (for reviews, see Mitton & Grant, 1984; Møller & Swaddle, 1997). Recent meta-analysis of the literature suggests that the observed effects are real but weak (though underlying effects of heterozygosity may be highly underestimated because of the very minimal sampling of heterozygous alleles in any single study). How heterozygosity affects fitness is not fully understood, but it appears to be partly due to a relationship between heterozygosity and metabolic efficiency (see Mitton & Grant, 1984), which in turn may have to do with differential costs of protein turnover in heterozygotes and homozygotes (Mitton, 1993). Many proteins have a short half-life and require replacement daily. The cost of replacement appears to be greater in homozygotes (who must replace much of a single protein coded for by a genetic locus) than heterozygotes (who replace smaller amounts of two functionally redundant proteins coded for by the same locus). Protein replacement costs are greatest for those proteins centrally involved in metabolic processes and, hence, Mitton (1993) suggests that the impact of heterozygosity on fitness is probably restricted to certain key loci.

If protein homozygosity compromises metabolic efficiency and thereby deters growth, perhaps it also detracts from developmental precision. Associations between protein homozygosity and fluctuating asymmetry have been reported in a variety of species, but so too have null or negative associations (see

Møller & Swaddle, 1997, for a review). A meta-analysis of all studies suggests that protein homozygosity predicts fluctuating asymmetry across populations, but that, within-populations, the association is on average small or non-existent (Møller & Swaddle, 1997). As the former result may have more to do with the effects of inbreeding depression than the effects of protein homozygosity *per se*, the literature reveals no clear link between protein homozygosity and increased developmental error. Nonetheless, an important role for protein homozygosity cannot be ruled out for a couple of reasons. First, perhaps only homozygosity at particular loci (weakly represented in studies to date) is crucial. Second, if overall genomic homozygosity is crucial, homozygosity at the few loci measured in individual studies probably cannot measure this property accurately and, hence, predict its outcomes (Møller & Swaddle, 1997).

Genes complexes tend to be co-adapted; the individual genes tend to work well together as a unit. Hybridization splits up coadapted gene complexes and, more often than not, results in a loss of fitness and developmental stability (e.g., Clarke, 1993). Increased developmental instability due to hybridization may occur because of loss of appropriate timing, imbalances of crucial enzymes, or increased instability of the genome (see Møller & Swaddle, 1997, for a review).

FA, Fitness Components, and Mating Behaviors in Humans

As noted, developmental instability predicts lower longevity and fecundity in many species (e.g., Møller, in press). Because humans in Westernized countries live in environments very different than those in which we evolved (e.g., ones in which antibiotics and effective contraception are abundant), there is no reason to necessarily expect similar associations in humans. Few studies have examined these relationships (though see Møller, Soler, & Thornhill, 1995, on the association between female breast asymmetry and fertility).

Developmental instability similarly predicts mating success in many species (Møller & Thornhill, submitted). These relationships purportedly are due to two processes. First, individuals whose development has been more precise are better able to compete for mates. Second (and perhaps relatedly), individuals whose development has been more precise possess phenotypic features that are more attractive to potential mates (in theory, due to evolved mating preferences that were favored because they led to mating with individuals providing genetic or other benefits to offspring). A number of studies indicate that these mating phenomena similarly exist in humans. Men who are lower in developmental instability (as indexed by low FA) tend to be perceived more physically attractive (Gangestad, Thornhill, & Yeo, 1994; Grammer & Thornhill, 1994; Perrett et al., submitted; Thornhill & Gangestad, 1994), have more sex partners (Thornhill & Gangestad, 1994; Gangestad & Thornhill, submitted), have more sex partners outside of a relationship (Gangestad & Thornhill, in press), and are more often chosen as a sex partner outside of a mate's relationship (Gangestad & Thornhill, in press).

Developmental instability in humans: the neural consequences

The preference for mates with relatively less DI may reflect, at least in part, the fact that their offspring may have greater developmental precision. Such precision could be manifest in diverse organ systems, including the nervous system. Our attempt to apply the construct of DI to individual variation in cerebral lateralization began with an interest in handedness. Asymmetric hand preference and skill is intriguing for many reasons, most notably the fact that it is unique to our species. While individual members of other species may show characteristic hand or paw preference, at a population level no other species shows either the extent of asymmetry shown in humans (90 % of people are right-handed; Gilbert & Wysocki, 1991) or the wide range of tasks for which a preference is exhibited. Importantly, variations in handedness are at least in part under genetic control (McManus & Bryden, 1992). Every culture ever studied shows a marked right-hand preference. Further, the incidence of left-handedness appears to be stable over time. Coren and Porac (1977) studied depictions of hand use in works of art and found no change in the proportion of left-handedness over a 5,000 year time span. But of specific interest to us was this puzzle about handedness: left-handers seem to have reduced reproductive fitness, yet left-handedness seems to be maintained at a stable incidence in the population over time.

Though an extraordinary number of adverse conditions have been linked with left-handedness, including alcoholism (London, 1990), immune disorders (Bryden, McManus, & Bulman-Fleming, 1994), neural tube defects (Fraser, 1983), neurodevelopmental disorders (Bishop, 1990), and low birth weight (O'Callaghan, Tudehope, Dugdale, Mohay, Burns, & Cook, 1987), among others (Coren, 1991), the most compelling evidence for reduced reproductive fitness is that left-handers tend to have fewer children. We recently conducted a study in which 664 individuals who had volunteered as blood donors were mailed a handedness questionnaire, to which we appended questions regarding the number of offspring of each individual (Gangestad, Yeo, Shaw, Thoma, Daniel, & Korthank, 1996). After controlling for the effects of sex, age, age squared, ethnic background, and several interactions (sex and ethnic background with age and age squared) we found that left-handedness was significantly associated with having fewer offspring. Whereas right-handers were expected to have 2.03 children by age 45, left-handers were expected to have 1.62. McManus and Bryden (1992) reviewed a number of studies in which handedness of both parents and offspring were assessed. Though the major focus of these studies was of familial resemblance in direction of handedness, they also provided data on the number of offspring as a function of handedness. Left-handers had significantly fewer children, though the effect size varied across studies.

The reasons why left-handers have fewer children are not known, though the available literature offers a few suggestions. Some studies have found that left-handedness may be associated with a homosexual orientation (e.g., Halpern & Cass, 1994; Lindsay, 1987) and a recent epidemiological investigation found that left-handed men and women were less to have ever been married (Stellman, Wynder, DeRose, & Muscat, 1997). As described below, left-handers are more apt to possess the DR3 human leukocyte antigen (HLA) allele (Gangestad et al., 1996), an allele associated with recurrent spontaneous abortions (Christiansen, Pedersen, Mathiesen, Husth, & Grunnet, 1996).

If left-handers have fewer children, and variations in handedness are partly heritable, how is it that the population incidence of left-handedness is not decreasing? This situation cannot be understood from a Mendelian perspective in which specific alleles code directly for variations in handedness. Genetic diversity can be maintained in a population through various means, including neutral selection, frequency dependent selection, diversifying selection, new mutations and heterozygote selection. The purported association of polygenic homozygosity with fluctuating asymmetry (e.g., Leary, Allendorf, & Knudsen, 1983) suggested a particular hypothesis. Perhaps variations from typical asymmetry in hand skill (i.e., moderate right-handedness) reflect the influence of developmental instability. Just as fluctuating asymmetry in pectoral fins in rainbow trout reflect DI (Leary, Allendorf, & Knudsen, 1983) so too may variations in hand skill, in either direction from the species-typical norm reflect DI. Note though, that handedness and some other aspects of brain function are typically asymmetric, as opposed many other human body characteristics or the fins of trout. Thus, phenotypic variation occurs around a specific degree of directional asymmetry. In each case though, whether a given body character demonstrates fluctuating or directional asymmetry, phenotypic variation around the population norm may reflect DI. We proposed "that there is little or no variability in the direct genetic coding for the neurobiologic substrate of handedness. Individuals differ only in genes that determine the precision with which a design for moderate left hemisphere dominance is expressed" (Yeo & Gangestad, 1993, p. 288).

To test this basic idea that DI underlies variations in handedness we have analyzed the relationship between classic markers of DI, fluctuating asymmetry (FA), and minor physical anomalies (MPA's), and measures of handedness. Though we have used both handedness preference questionnaires and measures of relative hand skill, the latter are more central to our work. Questionnaires of preference are not very good at discriminating between someone of moderate right-hand skill and someone much more skilled with their right-hand, as each will show a strong and consistent right-hand preference. We predicted that all individuals deviating from the norm in relative hand skill, either toward left-handedness or extreme right-handedness, would show increased DI. Annett's pegboard task (1985), which requires one to place a series of wooden pegs in small holes, one hand at a time, provided a measure of relative hand skill.

Three studies of the relationship between relative hand skill and DI have now been completed (Yeo, Gangestad, & Daniel, 1993; Yeo et al., under review). We have combined the data from these three studies in order to provide the most reliable characterization of the overall relationship (N = 348). Our assessment of DI included measurements of MPA's (Waldrop & Halverson, 1971), several body FA variables (foot, ankle, hands, wrist and elbow widths, and ear length and breadth), and asymmetry of the atd angle, a dermatoglyphic FA. In Figure 1, relative hand skill is plotted against a composite measure of DI. This composite was created by summing individual FA measures to get a total, then standardizing that total, and adding it to the sum of the individual MPA's, which was also standardized. We rounded relative hand performance scores on the peg moving task to the nearest .1 second and then for each subject in that interval averaged the DI composite scores. Towards the ends of the distribution we combined several intervals to have at least nine subjects in each. To reduce irregularities in the function due to sampling variability we then smoothed the function using procedures described by Tukey (1970).

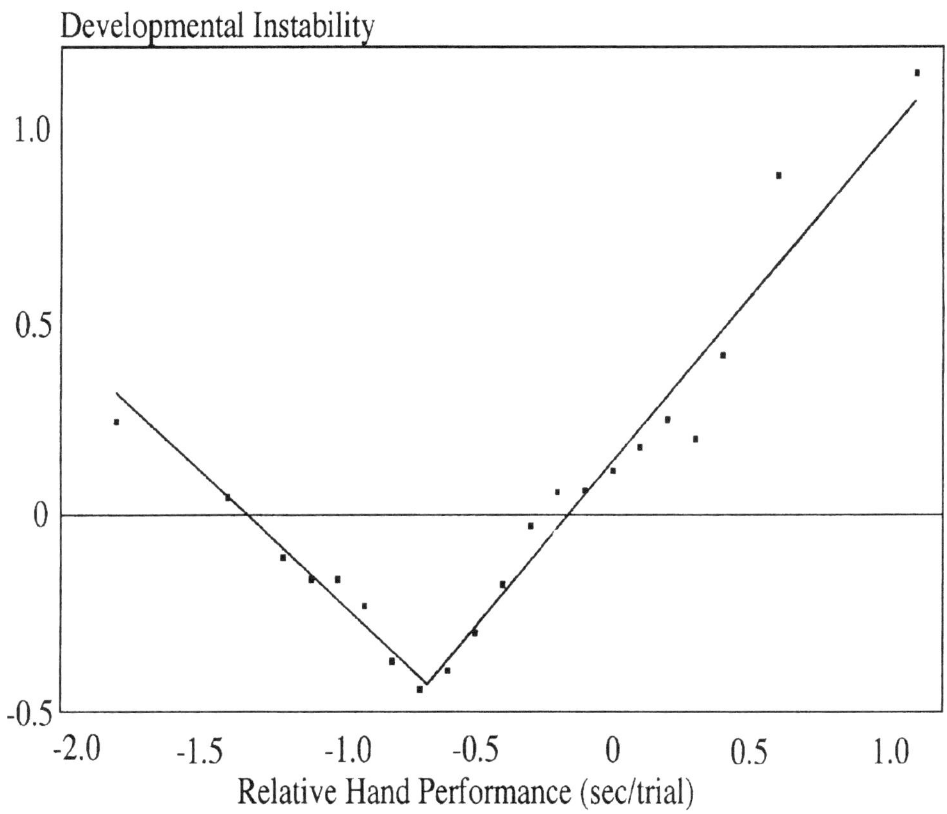

Figure 1. The non-linear relationship between relative hand skill and developmental instability.

The observed relationship is fairly straightforward. The value of relative hand performance associated with minimal DI (-.67 sec) is near the median value of relative hand skill. As one deviates from this value, observed DI increases. This function is not predicted by other genetic models of variation in hand skill, such as those of Annett (1985) or McManus (1985).

The relative importance of the FA and MPA components of the DI composite is of some interest because these two components may have two distinct developmental windows. MPA's are thought to be formed at the end of the first trimester or during the second trimester of fetal development (Waldrop & Halverson, 1971; Waldrop, Halverson & Shetterly, 1989). The asymmetry of the atd angle is also determined prenatally (Penrose, 1954). In contrast, FA increases over the life span (Thornhill & Gangestad, 1994). We found that MPA's and asymmetry of the atd angle are more predictive of variations in relative hand skill than FA. This pattern suggests that variations in handedness are likely determined quite early in neural development. Consistent with this formulation is the observation that 92% of fetuses observed to suck their thumb on ultrasound scans sucked their right thumb (Hepper et al., 1991).

Familial Resemblance and Specific Genetic Factors

The DI model of individual variation in handedness makes different predictions than the single gene models of Annett (1985) or McManus (1985) regarding the relationship between parental and offspring handedness. We predict that it is the tendency to deviate that is heritable, rather than a specific directional tendency. While the predictions of the DI and single gene models are the same for left-handed parents -- they should produce more left-handed children, the DI model additionally predicts that, because they possess genotypes predisposing to developmental instability, left-handers should also produce more extreme right-handed offspring. Single gene models predict that left-handed parents will produce relatively few extremely right-handed offspring.

We tested this hypothesis in a sample of 234 individuals from whom we obtained data on the peg moving task and reports of parental hand preference (right or left). Parental handedness was treated as a continuous variable with three levels: 0 = no left-handed parents, 1 = one left-handed parent, and 2 = two left-handed parents. As can be seen in Figure 2, a significant curvilinear effect emerged.

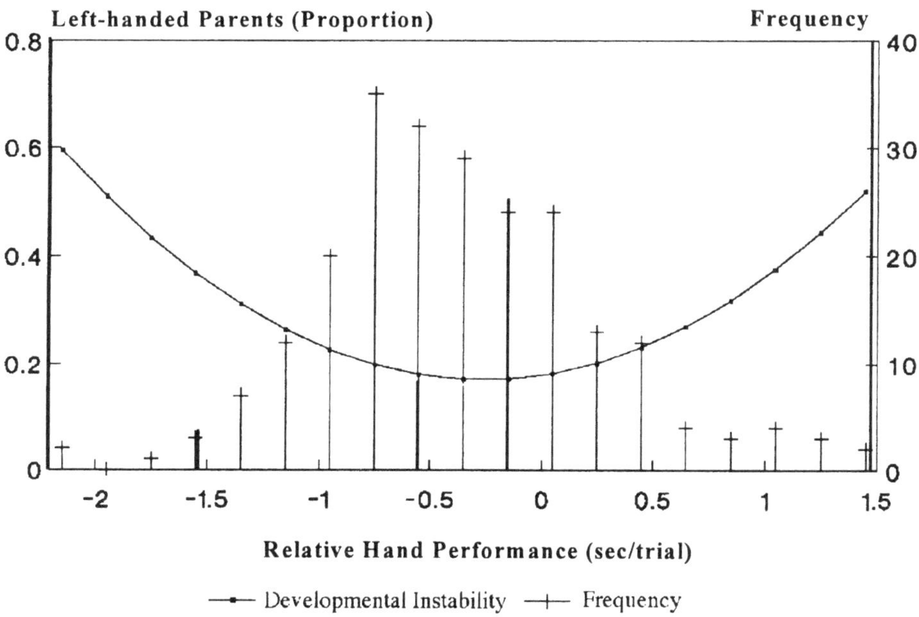

Figure 2. Parental hand preference and relative hand skill in offspring.

Both left-handers and extreme right-handers were more likely to have left-handed parents, supporting the DI model of handedness. This result is consistent with studies of paw preference in mice, where the direction of preference is not heritable, though the extent of deviation is (Collins, 1985). Further, polygenic homozygosity in mice has been linked with greater nondirectional deviation in preference (Collins, Sargent, & Neumann, 1993).

Thus, the factors underlying individual variability in lateral preference may be the same for mice and man; we suggest that the major difference across species lies in the fact that among humans there is a universal, species-wide, directional bias toward the left hemisphere for motor control, and hence, the right hand. We believe this hypothesis is more parsimonious than the explanations offered by Annett (1985) or McManus (1985). In essence they suggest that there is a source of variance beyond fluctuating asymmetry, unique to humans, that leads to inter-individual variation. In our proposal, the sources of variability are the same across species, reflecting the fact that selection pressures related to pathogen resistance are essentially the same across long-lived animals, and all organisms are subject to mutations. What is unique to our species is not the source of inter-individual variability, but something about our brain -- a directional bias. Collins et al.'s (1993) study of paw preference in mice utilized genetic analyses of multiple loci to quantify polygenic homozygosity. No similar studies are available for humans, but we have attempted to obtain indirect measures of polygenic homozygosity. We took advantage of the known relationship between polygenic homozygosity and phenotypic variability in traits characterized by substantial additive genetic variance. Individuals who are relatively more homozygous across many loci are more apt to demonstrate "extreme" phenotypes. For example, consider the simple situation in which height is determined by the additive actions of two alleles at a given locus, a "T" allele conferring great height and a "t" allele conferring short stature. The population characterized by homozygosity (TT *and* tt) will exhibit greater variability (extremity) than the heterozygous population (Tt and tT).

Our measure of extremity was constructed from the individual measurements of the two sides of the body that provided the FA measures. We averaged the measures for the two sides of the body for a given trait (for men and women separately, N = 118) and then squared the deviation of each individual's size from the appropriate mean. To obtain a measure of overall extremity, we averaged these squared deviations across the seven measures for each individual. This measure possessed a curvilinear relationship with relative hand performance (see Figure 3). Individuals with extreme relative hand skill scores, in either direction, tended to possess extreme phenotypes, and perhaps, relatively greater polygenic homozygosity. It must also be noted that a greater incidence of mutations might also produce this curvilinear relationship.

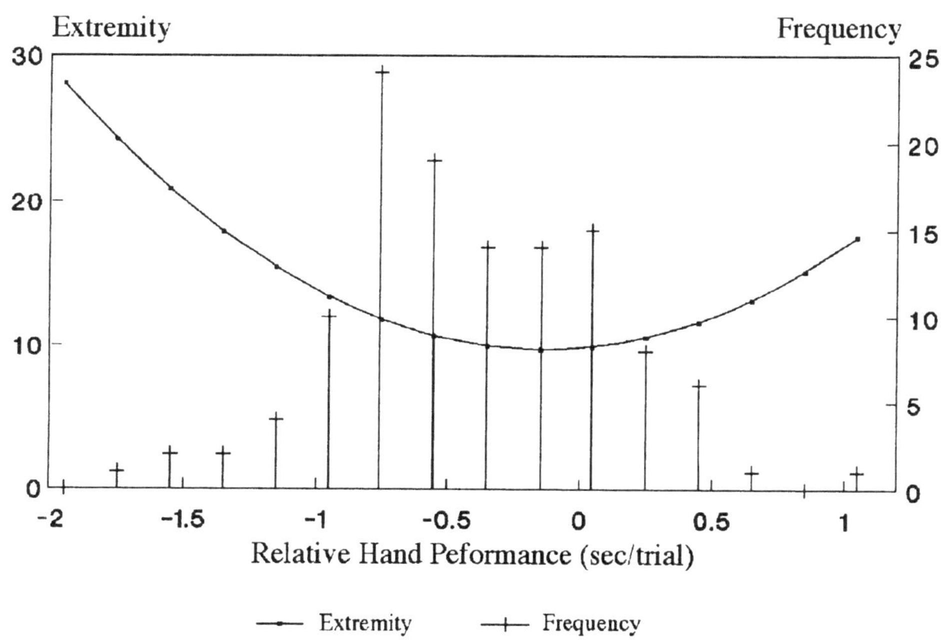

Figure 3. Physical "extremity" and relative hand skill (see text for explanation).

Any negative consequence of polygenic homozygosity may represent the price to be paid for a general heterozygote advantage. As discussed earlier, polygenic heterozygosity may be advantaged in terms of pathogen resistance. But there are other strategies organisms use to fight off pathogens that also involve maintaining genetic variation. In particular, there seems to be constant pressure on the human leukocyte antigen (HLA) system, due to the everchanging nature of constantly evolving pathogens (Hill, Allsops, Kwiatkowski, et al., 1991). The HLA system may be subject to frequency dependent selection, a mechanism that maintains genetic diversity. That is, the adaptive value of a given HLA allele is at least in part a function of its historical frequency in the population. The longer it has been around, and the more prevalent its distribution, the greater opportunity pathogens have had to evolve ways to counter that allele's biochemical properties. Hence, that allele becomes less adaptive. As this occurs, its frequency in the population diminishes, until it becomes sufficiently rare that pathogens have had little exposure to it. At this point, its adaptive value may increase (Anderson & May, 1982; Hamilton, 1982).

Thus, both individual variation in polygenic homozygosity and in HLA alleles may result from pathogen-induced selection pressures. Just as one cost of polygenic homozygosity may be increased DI, so too may certain HLA alleles be linked with increased DI. Of interest in this regard is the fact that left-handedness, one consequence of DI, has been associated with particular immune disorders, and these immune disorders are associated with the same set of HLA alleles. In a recent study we sought to determine whether variations in handedness might be associated with these same HLA alleles (Gangestad, Yeo, Shaw, Thoma, Daniel, & Korthank, 1996).

Bryden, McManus, & Bulman-Fleming (1994) recently conducted a meta-analysis that found left-handedness to be associated with autoimmune disorders of the thyroid (Graves' disease and Hashimoto's thyroiditis), autoimmune diseases of the gut (celiac disease and Crohn's disease), and systemic lupus erythematosus. Each of these diseases is related to the same set of HLA markers: A1, B8, and DR3 (Gangestad, Yeo, Shaw, et al., 1996; Tiwari & Terasaki, 1985). These alleles are in linkage disequilibrium and thus correlate with one another. Based on these associations of diseases with handedness we predicted that the three alleles associated with these diseases would be more common in left- than right-handers. In a sample of 664 blood donors data were available for the A and B loci, though only a subset of the group had information on the DR locus. These individuals were mailed Annett's Handedness Questionnaire, which provided a measure of hand preference. Unfortunately, given the study methodology, we could not obtain hand performance data. Left-handers were significantly more likely than right-handers to possess the B8 and DR3 alleles, as well as the A1/B8 haplotype. They were also more likely to possess the A1 allele, though this effect did not reach significance. To our knowledge this is the first study to suggest specific genes being related to left-handedness. It is possible that a measure of relative hand skill would show even stronger relationships, as we would predict that extreme right-handers, who in this study were lumped in with moderate right-handers, would resemble left-handers.

The manner in which these alleles influence handedness is uncertain. Indeed, it may not be these particular alleles, but rather some others in linkage disequilibrium, that are responsible for the association. Our best guess, however, is that these alleles may adversely affect either the mother's or the infant's immune response to pathogenic threats to fetal development, and thereby influence developmental stability of the fetus, ultimately producing atypical handedness. In support of this view, Livshits and colleagues (Livshits, Davadi, Kobylianski, Ben-Amatal, Levy, & Merlob, 1988) have reported that maternal infections increase FA in offspring. Further, in our study the B8 allele and the

A1/B8 haplotypes were associated with having fewer offspring, and the A1 allele showed a marginal effect.

Extension of the model to other lateralized skills

Handedness is but one of a great many brain functions characterized by lateral asymmetry. Language production, facial perception, spatial processing, musical skill and sustained attention are other examples, and each of these shows substantial individual variability. What factors determine variation from species-typical asymmetries for these functions? Much less is known of the sources of variance underlying these sorts of cognitive skills than is known about handedness. This state of affairs may reflect the fact that hand asymmetry is so readily observable and the easily assessed.

Annett's and McManus' models suggest that alleles at a single locus affect left hemisphere dominance for language, and secondarily, handedness. But it is difficult to see how they might be extended to encompass other cerebral asymmetries. The fundamental problem they face is that different asymmetries are essentially uncorrelated. Boles (1991) demonstrated that correlations among various laterality scores, computed from such procedures as dichotic listening or tachistoscopic presentation, typically are not high. The same is true for anatomic cortical asymmetries, as recently demonstrated by Habib and colleagues (Habib, Robicho, Levrier, Khalil, & Solamon, 1995). Were a single developmental process, stemming from a single gene and influencing hemispheric asymmetry rather broadly, to affect a wide variety of functional asymmetries, different asymmetry scores should correlate substantially.

In theory, DI might account for individual variation in diverse aspects of functional asymmetry, not just handedness. Indeed, FA of different body characteristics generally show very weak or no correlation with each other, yet DI seems to underlie these variations (Palmer & Strobeck, 1986). In a recent study we have attempted to evaluate this possibility by collecting information on a variety of functional cerebral asymmetries, along with our conventional DI measures (Yeo, Gangestad, Thoma, Shaw, & Repa, in press). The specific laterality tasks were chosen to reflect very different cognitive skills. We used the Fused Rhymed Word Dichotic Listening task (Repp, 1977, which assessed language lateralization, two measures tapping emotional processing of faces, Levy's Chimeric Faces Test (Levy, Heller, Banich, & Burton, 1983) and Carlson and Harris' (1985) Cartoon Faces Test, along with the line bisection test (Manning, Halligan, & Marshall, 1990), which assesses asymmetry of spatial processing. Our major interest was whether DI accounts for variation in lateralized cognitive tests in general, so the most direct and powerful way to test this hypothesis with a single analysis was to develop a composite atypical asymmetry score. Laterality scores from each test were first standardized, and then to derive a measure of nondirectional atypicality, the absolute values of these standardized scores were derived. We then averaged these absolute value scores across the tasks to produce a composite measure of atypical lateralization.

Results supported the DI model. The atypical lateralization composite was correlated with our DI composite, $r = .28$, $p < .001$. In a separate regression analysis we controlled for directional laterality scores from each test, entering each of these before the atypical lateralization composite score. None of the individual tests significantly predicted the DI composite, though again, the atypical lateralization composite did, beta = .32, $t(121) = 3.53$, $p < .0005$. As with relative hand skill, the extent of deviation from the population norm, but not the direction of deviation, was predicted by DI.

The DI model thus may offer a parsimonious account of individual variation in functional asymmetries, without the need to invoke different mechanisms (i.e., genes) for variation in each individual asymmetry. In contrast to our analysis of handedness, however, the FA component of DI proved more related to atypical cognitive asymmetry than measures of MPA's or dermatoglyphic asymmetries, which tend to be the product of events in the first or early part of the second trimester of fetal development (Smith, 1970). Thus, developmental noise occurring postnatally may well be relatively more important for these cognitive asymmetries than manual asymmetries. This is consistent with the known timetables for brain development. The development and specialization of the cortex certainly continues beyond birth. Yet at the time at which Hepper and colleagues (1991) noted right thumb sucking in fetuses, around 12 weeks gestational age, cortical development is minimal. It may be that asymmetrical thumb sucking reflects asymmetrical basal ganglia development, which occurs earlier than cortical development (Finlay & Darlington, 1995). If so, given the relatively greater role of the basal ganglia in motor initiation than fine motor coordination, the primary motor asymmetry may be better conceptualized as involving "preference" than "performance", supporting the suggestion of McManus et al. (1992).

Brain anatomy and physiology

Function emerges from structure, so if DI is related to variations in functional cerebral asymmetry, it should also be related to variation in brain anatomy. We have explored this possibility in a recent magnetic resonance imaging (MRI) and magnetic source imaging (MSI) study (Thoma, Yeo, Gangestad, & Lewine, 1996; Thoma, Yeo, Gangestad, & Lewine, under review). Since our focus was on cortical anatomy, and FA seems to predict variation in cortical function more than MPAs or dermatoglyphic asymmetries, DI was assessed solely with our composite FA measure.

Several aspects of MRI scans were quantified using CEMAX VIP software running on a SUN workstation. Left and right hemisphere volumes were determined from a series of 128 1mm thick T1-weighted slices using the CEMAX autodraw function. We also determined gray and white matter volumes of the cerebral hemispheres through semi-automated thresholding procedures. The area of the left and right planum temporale were also computed, utilizing procedures adapted from Steinmetz (1989). The left planum is typically quite a bit larger than the right, an asymmetry thought to partly underlie left hemisphere language dominance (Geschwind & Levitsky, 1968). Finally, on the midsagittal slice we measured the total area of the corpus callosum, the major fiber tract connecting the two cerebral hemispheres. Callosal area was further broken down into seven subregions, utilizing Witelson's (1989) procedures. Of special interest was the area of the isthmus, that region connecting the two plana and adjacent cortical areas.

A total measure of atypical brain asymmetry was calculated from left and right total hemisphere volumes, gray matter volumes, white matter volumes, and planum areas. Since these brain features might well be asymmetric at the population level (the planum certainly is) calculation of atypical asymmetry differed slightly from that of body characteristics that are symmetric at the population level. Though atypical brain asymmetries are conceptually similar to FA of body characteristics, the presence of some directional asymmetry means that the term "FA" is probably not appropriate (Palmer & Strobeck, 1994). For each participant, each FA index was calculated as following: First, the median directional (r-l) asymmetry for the entire sample was determined; second, we computed the absolute value of the difference between the individual FA (r-l) and the sample median directional asymmetry score; and finally we divided this absolute value by the average size of the individual character, defined as one half of the sum of the right and left values. To increase the reliability of the index and subsequently to improve the likelihood of detecting a relationship between atypical brain asymmetry and FA, the four measures of atypical brain asymmetry were summed to produce a total atypical brain asymmetry measure (Weiner, Brown & Micheals, 1991). Because brain parameters may differ as a function of gender and body size, we partialed out of all correlations sex, height, and frame size (by summing the widths of feet, ankles, wrists, and elbows). One-tailed significance tests were used because directional predictions were made.

In support of our hypothesis, body FA significantly covaried with the atypical brain asymmetry score, partial $r = .48$, $p = .008$, (N = 28). Figure 4 shows the scatter plot of this relationship. Body FA correlated most strongly with planum temporale asymmetry, $r = .45$, $p = .012$, followed by gray matter asymmetry, $r = .34$, $p = .048$. No directional brain asymmetries were significantly related to body FA. Based on the shared variance of the body FA composite and the atypical brain asymmetry composite, these two measures were summed to provide a more reliable measure of DI, and this overall measure was then correlated with measures of callosal size. A significant relationship was observed ($r = .33$, $p = .033$).

Given the significant relationship of planum asymmetry to body FA, and the importance of the planum for language, we also examined the correlation of this same overall measure with the area of the isthmus. This correlation was also significant, $r = -.47$, $p = .008$ (see Figure 5). Finally, we related this same overall measure (body FA plus atypical brain asymmetry) to total cerebral volume, as many other studies of FA have found an inverse relationship between FA and average size of the character (Møller & Swaddle, 1996). A nonsignificant trend was noted, $r = .28$, $p < .10$. These results suggest that DI generally influences aspects of cerebral anatomic asymmetry in the same manner in which it influences functional cerebral asymmetry and body asymmetry.

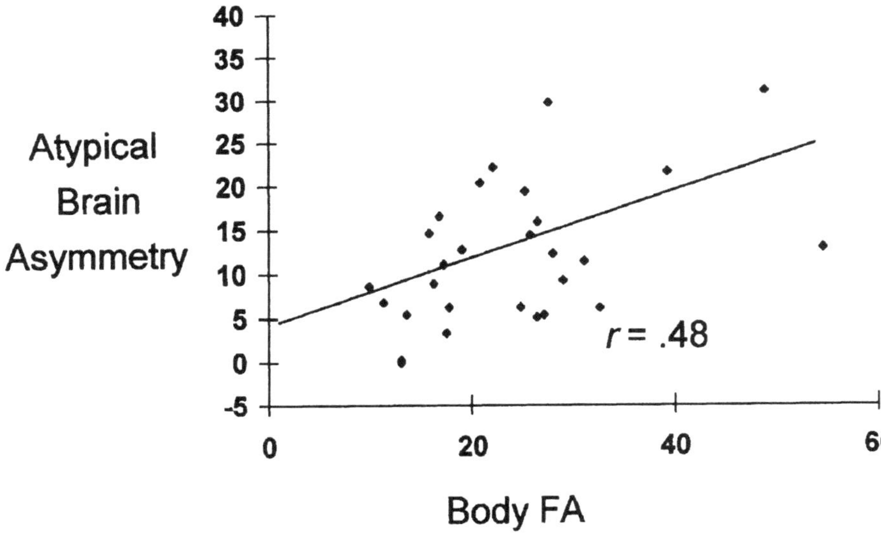

Figure 4. Scatter plot of the relationship between body FA and atypical brain asymmetry.

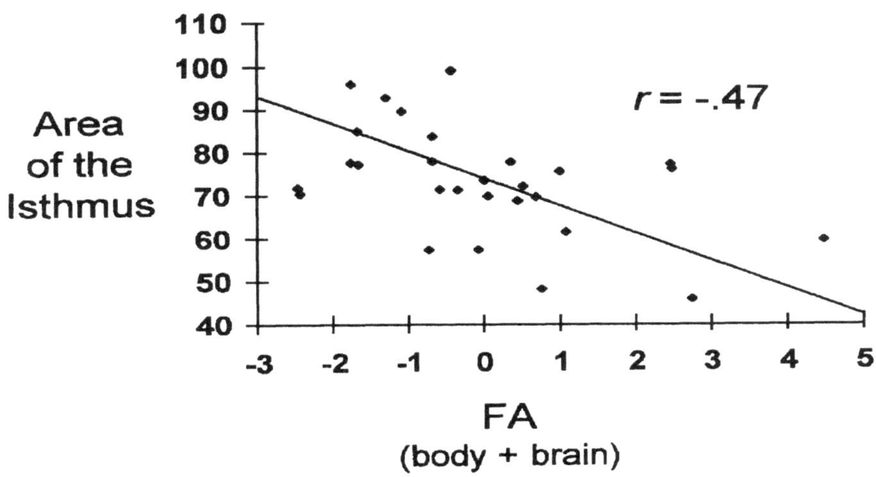

Figure 5. Scatter plot of the relationship between combined body and brain FA and area of the isthmus portion of the corpus callosum.

A subset of these participants (N = 9) underwent analysis of magnetic source imaging (MSI). This method combines magnetoencephalographic procedures for locating source dipoles for functional activity with anatomic information from MRI, providing precise localization of the detected dipoles (Lewine & Orrison, 1996). These data were collected with a large array biomagnetometer (Bti) equipped with 37 first-order, axial gradiometers. We first attempted to map the size of the somatosensory representation of each hand. In four test blocks subjects made 150 self-paced movements of the left and right thumbs and little fingers. Dipoles were fit for each finger movement and the distances between the two dipoles in each hemisphere were computed, providing a linear estimate of the size of the somatosensory representation of the hand for each hemisphere. Relative hand skill was assessed at a different time with the Annett pegboard task we have used in prior studies.

A striking relationship was observed between relative hand skill (left minus right) and the asymmetry (left minus right) of the two linear measures of somatosensory size of the hand, $r = .81$, $p = .01$. This demonstrates that individual variation in hand skill is highly related to individual variation in cortical mappings of the somatosensory strip. Since we have demonstrated that relative hand skill asymmetry is related to DI, so too should be its putative anatomical substrate. The combined brain and body FA measure predicted atypical asymmetry of the size of the somatosensory representations (calculated as above), $r = .63$, $p = .033$. As these analyses are based on a very small sample, they certainly need replication. Nonetheless, they offer support for the DI model of individual variation in cerebral asymmetry.

The relationship between DI and atypical functional and anatomic asymmetries has implications for the manner in which brain structure-function relationships are typically examined (Yeo, 1996). A major methodological concern of such studies, whether they attempt to relate variations in structure size or physiologic activity to cognitive performance, is minimizing individual variability. The typical approach to this problem is to study only right-handers. Our work clearly shows the limitations of this strategy. Variations among right-handers are meaningful. An alternative strategy, which could be applied across studies of different cognitive domains, would be to study individuals low in DI, as they are most apt to be "typical" for a variety of lateralized functions.

If we knew the specific cytological features associated with variation in species-typical symmetry (or asymmetry, for such structures as the planum), we would have an important clue as to the precise manner in which DI influences neural development. There are a number of possibilities as to the neuronal differences related to atypical asymmetry, including variations in cell size, cell packing density, and cell number. In Broca's area there appear to be more very large pyramidal cells than in the homologous portion of the right hemisphere (Hayes & Lewis, 1993), though it is not known whether this asymmetry predicts the gross morphological asymmetry in the region (Foundas, Leonard, Gilmore, Fennell, & Heilman, 1996). Witelson (1995) has described sex differences in packing density in the Wernicke's area, and women may show less asymmetry of the planum (Kulynich, Vladar, Jones, & Weinberger, 1994), though it is not known if sex differences in packing density relates to variations in asymmetry in the planum. However, at least in the rat's visual cortex, asymmetry in packing density is unrelated to asymmetry of architectonic volume (Galaburda, Aboitiz, Rosen, & Sherman, 1986).

The most likely candidate for producing atypical gross anatomic asymmetries is probably lateral variation in neuron number. In the rat's visual cortex, variations in cell number have been found to predict variation in gross asymmetry (Galaburda, Aboitiz, Rosen, & Sherman, 1986). As Rosen (this volume) points out, differences in cell number could arise from asymmetries occurring in the germinal zone, in proliferation, or in pruning. Results from a [^{3}H] thymidine labeling study of the visual cortex suggested that asymmetries in progenitor cell proliferation were more apt to contribute to asymmetries than later developmental events. However, planum asymmetry may increase with age during childhood and early adolescence (Leonard, Lombardino, Breier, et al., 1994) implicating later neurodevelopmental events, such as dendritic growth (Scheibel, Conrad, Perdue, Tomiyasu, & Wechsler, 1990) or axonal and synaptic pruning, which continue postnatally (Rakic, 1995). Our data are also consistent with this possibility. We have found that it is the FA component of DI, rather than the MPA component, that predicts atypical anatomical and functional cerebral asymmetries. FA tends to increase over the lifetime (Thornhill & Gangestad, 1994), but may nonetheless be the consequence of events relatively early in ontogeny (Møller, 1996b). MPA's, in contrast, are produced early in fetal development. Animal studies relating FA to features of brain morphology and development would prove invaluable in illuminating these issues.

Evolutionary Implications

By studying individual variation in cerebral lateralization, its causes and correlates, we have perhaps learned not only about "phenodeviants", but also, perhaps, something about human nature. Our work suggests that there is a universal "plan" for cerebral lateralization in our species. Though there certainly are differences among us, stemming in part from genetic differences, these differences may be conceptualized as "concomitants of parasite-driven selection for biochemical individuality" (Tooby & Cosmides, 1990, p.17) and also mutation load. Thus, the modal pattern of cerebral asymmetry may be one facet of "human nature". But does this modal pattern represent an adaptation? And if so, what selection pressures led to its development? These are tough, but important, questions. We offer only one set of speculations concerning the possible benefits of a neurodevelopmental design culminating in modal asymmetry.

Let us assume that cortical function is massively parallel in architecture, and that, at best, only a vague "protomap" exists to specify cortical localization of function (see Elman, Bates, Johnson et al., [1996] for a recent review). Genetic influences on cortical development are likely to code for rather broad "self-organizing" strategies, rather than the fates of specific cells or cell assemblies. Whatever these strategies may be, they need eventuate in a design that is efficient and flexible enough to work effectively across the broad range of environments in which humans may be expected to develop (e.g., an English or Mandarin linguistic environment).

Some clues as to the design features allowing efficiency may be gleaned from the principles governing massively parallel computers. Marr (1976) noted that modularity (in the "weak" sense) is an efficient design principle, for both brains and computers, allowing efficient "debugging". Nelson and Bower (1990) describe two fundamental sources of computational inefficiency in parallel computers and brains. "Load imbalance" refers to "how uniformly the computational workload is distributed among the available processors. Since the speed of the parallel computation is limited by the speed of the slowest processor, unduly burdening even a single processor can dramatically deplete the overall performance (p. 404)." Nelson and Bower define communication overhead as "the cost of communicating information between processors... this overhead is primarily associated with the time-cost for exchanging information between processors [and] the physical space taken up by connections between processors (p. 404)."

Putting together the virtues of modularity and the costs of communication overhead and load imbalance, two principles of efficient cortical design emerge:

(1) modules should be equally distributed across the two hemispheres (limiting load imbalance); and (2) modules that interact frequently should develop in close physical proximity (limiting communication overhead). We suggest that the neurodevelopmental plan to implement these principles culminates in modal laterality. A specific pattern of hand or language dominance is not the goal of this plan, but rather a by-product. Specifically, we suggest that the mechanism to implement this plan is an alternating sequence of asymmetric hemispheric growth rates. The best data for such a "dialectic" pattern of development comes from Thatcher's (1992) study of EEG changes across childhood, though there is also evidence for asymmetric prenatal growth rates of cortical gyri (Chi, Dooling, & Gilles, 1983) and for asymmetric dendritic growth rates (Scheibel et al., 1990). As long as the duration of growth spurts are approximately equal for each hemisphere, this developmental plan distributes modules equally over the two hemispheres. Thus, load imbalance is minimized. That portion of the brain (or hemisphere) developing most rapidly at a given point in time will be maximally influenced by prevalent environmental inputs and behaviors. Since the life skills to be learned through childhood are somewhat age-specific (e.g., language vs. peer relations), those modules related to a given skill are likely to develop in close physical proximity. Thus, communication overhead is limited.

Thatcher (1992) notes that only particular portions of each hemisphere may show a growth spurt during a given phase (e.g., right faster or left faster). Thus, the time frame during which a given asymmetry is established will differ according to the developmental trajectory of the specific cortical substrate. The direction of a given functional asymmetry is determined by the phase (i.e., which hemisphere is developing most rapidly). We assume that species-wide directional asymmetries reflect chance events in our distant phylogenetic history. That is, there is no computational advantage for the species-typical directional asymmetries, such as left hemisphere dominance for language, as compared to its mirror image.

This perspective suggests that the proposed "universal neurodevelopmental dialectic", which culminates in typical cerebral lateralization, was selected as a means to ensure computational efficiency. Other strategies may well be more desireable in species for which postnatal adaptation to particular environmental circumstances is less important than in our own. Two predictions follow. Greater lateralization of function across species should be associated with greater computational efficiency. This is a difficult hypothesis to test directly, in large part because it is far from clear exactly how "computational efficiency" should be operationalized for cross-species comparisons, but it seems at least broadly consistent with available laterality data across species. Also, variations from typical brain asymmetry should predict lower computational efficiency within members of our species. For the sake of simplicity, let us consider "intelligence" as a proxy for computational efficiency. Unfortunately, most studies potentially able to shed some light on this matter have examined only directional asymmetries. From our perspective the key relationships would be between nondirectional measures of atypicality in lateralization and such global measures of computational efficiency as IQ. (Variations in handedness may be less revealing than atypical cognitive asymmetries, as the latter are likely more cortical in origin.)

In partial support of this hypothesis, relatively greater body FA, which we have linked with atypical brain asymmetry (Yeo et al., in press), predicts lower IQ (Furlow, Armijo-Prewitt, Gangestad, & Thornhill, 1997). This association raises the possibility that at least some of the genetic variation underlying IQ emerges from the genomic influences leading to DI, as opposed to genetic loci coding directly for variation in intelligence itself. One might suspect that measures of atypical brain asymmetry might show an even stronger relationship with IQ than body FA measures. A related observation is the negative correlation between splenium area and intelligence (Strauss, Wada, & Hunter, 1994); recall that we have shown that the splenium is smaller in high DI subjects (Thoma et al., submitted).

Individual Differences in Environmental Sensitivity

FA and MPA's represent one particular type of outcome of DI. Disruptions of growth rates, due to both genetic susceptibility to DI and environmental stress, produce both the anatomic asymmetries leading to FA and the slowed rate of development leading to MPA's. But the organism characterized by relatively greater DI may also show other types of atypical responses to environmental stresses. In this section we would like to discuss two such possibilities. First, individuals characterized by high DI may be more influenced by the "environment", broadly conceived as non-genetic influences, biological or social. Second, we consider that high DI individuals may show exaggerated responses to a specific, acute environmental stressor.

Rose and colleagues (Rose, Reed, & Bogle, 1987) have analyzed a MZ twin sample in which each pair was characterized as having either high or low relative DI, based on a single dermatoglyphic feature, asymmetry of the AB ridgecount across the left and right palms. The AB ridgecount is the number of dermal ridges between the A triaradius (under the index finger) and the B triradius (under the middle finger). On several scales from the Minnesota Multiphasic Personality Inventory (MMPI), an omnibus personality test, twin pairs characterized by high DI resembled each other less than members of twin pairs characterized by low DI. This same group (Bogle, Reed, and Rose; 1994) recently replicated these observations. They also found that high DI twin pairs (again, as determined from the asymmetry of the AB ridgecount) showed greater temporal variability in several MMPI scores than low DI twin pairs. That is, over a period of four to five years, high DI individuals showed greater change in their MMPI scores. Since all twin pairs in these studies were genetically identical, it appears that some genotypes are simply less well canalized than others. Results from these two MMPI studies raise the intriguing possibility that there are important individual differences in the extent to which personality variables are shaped by the environment. Unfortunately, we know of no similar studies of intellectual functioning.

The possibility that some genetic influences on personality may be nondirectional, as seems to be the case for functional and anatomic hemispheric asymmetry, may shed some light on behavior genetic studies of personality. Directional genetic influences are ubiquitous; heritability (h^2) is never nonzero. More controversial is the nature of the environmental influences. Two classes of environmental factors are typically distinguished, "shared" and "unique" factors. Shared environmental factors can be thought of as those shared by children in the same family (e.g., socioeconomic status, parental intelligence, religion), whereas unique factors are those that distinguish one child from another (e.g., a charismatic third grade teacher, or getting dropped on your head at birth). Across a great many studies (e.g., Dunn & Plomin, 1990), unique environmental effects seem to be much more important. Indeed, it is sometimes difficult to demonstrate that shared effects are significant. Despite their importance, the nature of these unique effects have proven exceedingly difficult to identify.

Nondirectional genetic influences, such as those associated with DI, would fall into the "unique environment" category of variance in most behavior genetic analyses, though this is not typically recognized. Thus, at least part of what has typically been considered a type of environmental variance may acutally represent a gene x environment interaction (Molenaar, Boorsma, & Dolan, 1993;

Yeo, Gangestad, & Turkheimer, 1995).

Might DI also be associated with responses to acute stressors? A couple of studies suggest this possibility. Irwin (1985) reported that left-handers, individuals relatively high in DI, showed greater EEG responses than right-handers to a wide variety of psychoactive drugs. Also, among schizophrenic patients being treated with antipsychotic medications, those with relatively more MPA's suffer more tardive dyskinesia, a debilitating side effect to these medications (Waddington, O'Callaghan, Buckley, et al., 1995).

We have recently attempted to evaluate whether DI might mediate responses to a specific psychoactive drug, caffeine (Jung, Yeo, & Gangestad, submitted). Caffeine exerts its effects on the CNS largely as an antagonist to adenosine, a CNS sedative (Fredholm & Dinwiddie, 1988). Many studies have shown that caffeine can affect various aspects of attention, short-term memory, and long-term memory. Our study investigated effects on verbal list learning. Terry and Dhifer (1986) found that caffeine had an adverse effect on long-term recall of word lists, a result replicated in pilot work in our lab. We used the two alternate forms of the Rey Auditory Verbal Learning Test (Lezak, 1995), each of which consist of 15 words read to participants over five separate trials. Participants were first administered one of two versions of the test, then 3 mg caffeine per kg bodyweight, then given the alternate form (counterbalanced). MPAs and FA were also assessed. We did not include a placebo control group because prior studies have shown that subjects can reliably estimate the amount of caffeine ingested, even in the absence of olfactory or gustatory cues (Blount & Cox, 1985). Further, due to the slow metabolism of caffeine in the body it was impractical to counterbalance the off-drug, on-drug order of memory testing used.

Across the entire sample (N = 100), caffeine had the expected adverse effect on the two dependent variables, reducing recall on trial one, and reducing the sum of words recalled over the five trials. DI was unrelated to performance measures in the off-drug condition. To test our main hypothesis, we correlated DI with difference scores (off-drug minus on-drug conditions) for the two memory variables. The DI composite predicted the difference score for trial one, $r = -.38$, $p < .001$, and the difference score for the sum of trials one through five, $r = -.30$, $p < .01$. Thus, relatively greater DI predicted more adverse effects of caffeine on verbal memory. The specific mechanisms underlying this relationship are uncertain. High DI individuals may show exaggerated adenosine inhibition, less efficient clearance of caffeine by the liver, or some other effect. However, there is no reason to believe that caffeine effects are uniquely associated with DI. Only future research will clarify the range of drug effects potentially moderated by DI.

Neurodevelopmental disorders

If DI is related to atypical brain organization and function, it may well be related to the etiology of neurodevelopmental disorders. There is substantial evidence that this is so. First, an elevated incidence of MPA's has been described in many different disorders, including Down Syndrome (Down, 1866), schizophrenia (e.g., Green et al., 1994; Gualtieri et al, 1982; Guy et al., 1989), autism (Campbell et al., 1978), hyperactivity (Gualtieri et al., 1982; Quinn & Rapoport, 1974; Rapoport & Quinn, 1975; Waldrop & Halverson, 1971), and dyslexia (Cummings, Flynn, & Preuss, 1982; Steg & Rapoport, 1975; Von Hilsheimer & Kurko, 1979). FA has been less frequently studied, but has also been related to schizophrenia (Markow & Gottesman, 1989; Markow & Wandler, 1986; Mellor, 1992) and dyslexia (Sorenson, 1989). Left-handedness, which we have demonstrated to be linked with DI, also appears at an elevated incidence in many neurodevelopmental disorders, including autism (Boucher, 1977; Colby & Parkinson, 1977), stuttering (Bishop, 1990), schizophrenia (Lishman & McMeekan, 1976), and psychopathy (Ellis, 1990). These handedness studies, however, being based on measures of hand preference, did not distinguish between moderate and extreme right-handedness, and hence may not fully capture the shared variance between atypical handedness and neurodevelopmental disorders. Some studies have associated a smaller corpus callosum (Cemrud-Clikeman et al., 1994; Hynd et al., 1995) and atypical asymmetry of the planum temporale (Galaburda, 1993) with neurodevelopmental disorders, two aspects of brain anatomy we have correlated with DI. Thus, neurodevelopmental disorders seem to be characterized by an elevated incidence of the known markers of DI.

We have speculated that DI may represent a "vulnerability" factor in the etiology of neurodevelopmental disorders (Yeo, Hodde-Vargas, Hendren, Vargas, Brooks, Ford, Gangestad, & Hart, submitted). Given its association with "reduced buffering" or "reduced canalization", the presence of relatively greater DI may constitute a permissive early neurodevelopmental environment, allowing disorder-specific etiologic factors to have an especially adverse effect. Consider, for example, schizophrenia, which is commonly conceptualized as a neurodevelopmental disorder with its roots in fetal development (e.g., Weinberger, 1987). Whatever may be the unique (environmental or genetic) etiologic factor distinguishing schizophrenia from, say, dyslexia, these adverse influences may have a greater effect on neural anatomy and function in a high DI individual, whose ability to get back on the species-typical track for neural development is relatively reduced. This may help us understand the observation that obstetric complications are most strongly related to schizophrenia in affected individuals who have a schizophrenic parent, i.e., a parent most likely above average in terms of DI (Mednick, Cannon, & Barr, 1991). Strong support for the hypothesis that DI is related to schizophrenia comes from a recent study of dermatoglyphic FA (Fananas, Gutierrez, Meral, & Bertranpetit, 1994). Dermatoglyphic FA was elevated in schizophrenics, and further, was associated with relatively greater homozygosity as determined from seven blood polymorphisms.

If this perspective has merit, then analysis of DI may be a valuable tool in the study of neurodevelopmental disorders. For example, one might hypothesize that the unique abnormalities associated with each disorder might be better discerned in studies of affected individuals relatively low in DI, or when DI has been statistically covaried. Affected individuals high in DI might be expected to have more "mixed" conditions from a diagnostic perspective and a greater familial incidence of neurodevelopmental disorders other than their own.

Conclusions

The single most important dimension of individual differences among people may well lie in our ability to faithfully execute our ontogenetic program for development. The genetic features determining this program have proven successful over many thousands of generations. We ignore this collective wisdom at our peril. Individuals with high developmental instability, i.e. imprecise expression of the genetic plan for development, may show a broad range of phenotypic deviance, including less reproductive and sexual success, atypical brain asymmetry, lower intelligence, and neurodevelopmental disorders. Though we have emphasized the genetic variation underlying the ability to be buffered from environmental noise during development, individual differences in exposure to environmental stressors are undoubtedly important. Environmental stressors occurring during fetal development and early life appear to be most influential, clearly indicating the importance of good pre- and perinatal health care.

The concept of developmental instability provides a framework for understanding the associations among phenotypic variations, for example, the co-occurrence of atypical asymmetry and neurodevelopmental disorders. It also provides some insight into the vexing question of why genetic variation associated with adverse outcomes is maintained in the population. The vulnerability of DNA to mutation is one of "the facts of life" for species on our planet. Another fact of life is the rapid evolution of pathogens and parasites, and DI may be a consequence of the strategies selected to deal with this constant threat.

References

Anderson, R. M., & May, R. M. (1982). Coevolution of hosts and parasites. *Parasitology, 10*, 411-426.

Annett, M. (1971). A classification of hand preference by association analysis.*British Journal of Psychology, 61*, 303-321.

Annett, M. (1985). *Left, right, hand, and brain: The right shift theory.* Hillsdale, NJ: Erlbaum.

Bishop. D. V. M. (1990). *Handedness and Developmental Disorders.* Blackwell Scientific Publishing, Oxford.

Blount,J. P., & Cox, W. M. (1985). perception of caffeine and its effects: Laboratory and everyday abilities. *Perception and Psychophysics, 38*, 55-62.

Bogle, A. C., Reed, T., & Rose, R. J. (1994). Replication of asymmetry of *a-b* ridge count and behavioral discordance in monozygotic twins. *Behavior Genetics, 24*, 65-72.

Boles, D. B. (1991). Factor analysis and the cerebral hemispheres: Pilot study and parietal functions. *Neuropsychologia, 29*, 59-91.

Boucher, J. (1977). Hand preference in autistic children and their parents. *Journal of Autism and Childhood Schizophrenia, 7*, 177-187.

Bryden, M. P., McManus, I. C., Bulman-Fleming, M.B. (1994). Evaluating the empirical support for the Geschwind-Behan-Galaburda model of cerebral lateralization. *Brain and Cognition, 26,* 103-165.

Campbell, M., Geller, B., Small, A. M., Petti, T. A., & Perris, S. H. (1978). Minor physical anomalies in young psychotic children. *American Journal of Psychiatry, 135,* 573-575.

Carlson, D. F., & Harris, L. J. (1985). Perception of positive and negative emotion in face viewing of asymmetrical faces: Sex and handedness effects. Paper presented at the 13th annual meeting of the International

Neuropsychological Society, San Diego, CA.

Cemrud-Clikeman, M., Filipek, P.A., Bierderman, J., Steingard, R., Kennedy, D., Renshaw, P., & Bekken, K. (1994). Attention-deficit hyperactivity disorder: Magnetic resonance imaging morphometric analysis of the corpus callosum. *Journal of the American Academy of Child and Adolescent Psychiatry, 33*, 875-881.

Charlesworth, B. (1990). Mutation-selection balance and the evolutionary advantage of sex and recombination. *Genetical Research*, *55*, 817-820.

Chi, J. C., Dooling, E. C., & Gilles, F. H. (1977). Gyral development of the human brain. *Annals of Neurology, 1*, 86-93.

Clarke, G. M., Oldroyd, B. P., & Hunt, P. (1992). The genetic basis of developmental stability in *Apsis mellifera*: Heterozygosity versus genic imbalance. *Evolution, 46*, 753-762.

Colby, K. M., & Parkinson, C. (1977). Handedness in autistic children. *Journal of Autism and Childhood Schizophrenia, 7,* 3-9.

Collins, R. L. (1985). On the inheritance of direction and degree of asymmetry. In Glick, S. D. (Ed.), *Cerebral Lateralization in Non-human Species,* Academic Press, New York, pp. 41-71.

Collins, R. L., Sargent, E. E., & Neumann, P. E. (1993). Genetic and behavioral tests of the McManus hypothesis relating response to selection for lateralization of handedness in mice to degree of heterozygosity. *Behavior Genetics, 23*, 413-421.

Coren, S. (Ed.). (1990). *Left-handedness. Behavioral Implications and Anomalies*. Elsevier Publishers: New York.

Coren, S., & Porac, C. (1977). Fifty centuries of right-handedness: The historical record. *Science, 198,* 631-632.

Christiansen, O. B., Pedersen, B., Mathiesen, O., Husth, M., & Grunnet,

N. Maternal HLA class-II alleles predispose to pregnancy loss in Danish women with recurrent spontaneous abortions and their female relatives. *American Journal of Reproductive Immunology, 35*, 239-244.

Cummings, C., Flynn, D., & Preuss, M. (1982). Increased morphological variants in children with learning disabilities. *Journal of Autism and Childhood Schizophrenia, 12,*17-23.

Down, J. L. H. (1866). Observations on an ethnic classification of idiots. *London Hospital and Lecture Reports, 3*, 259-262.

Dunn, J., & Plomin, R. (1990). *Separate Lives: Why Siblings are So Different.*New York: Basic Books.

Ellis, L. (1990). Left- and mixed handedness and criminality: Explanations for a probable relationship. In S. Coren (Ed.), *Left-handedness: Behavioral implications and anomalies.* Elsevier, New York, pp. 485-508..

Elman, J. L., Bates, E., Johnson, M. H., Karmiloff-Smith, A., Parisi, D., & Plunkett, K. (1996). *Rethinking Innateness. A Connectionist Perspective on Development.* Cambridge, MIT Press.

Fananas, L., Gutierrez, B., Moral, P., & Bertranpetit, J. (1994). Fluctuating asymmetry, heterozygosity of genetic polymorphisms, and severity in schizophrenic patients. *Behavior Genetics, 24*, 511.

Finlay, B. L., & Darlington, R. B. (1995). Linked regularities in the development and evolution of mammalian brains. *Science, 268,* 1578-1584.

Fisher, R. A. (1958). *The Genetical Theory of Natural Selection.* Dover, New York.

Foundas, A. L., Leonard, C. M., Gilmore, R., Fennell, E., Heilman, K. M. (1996). Pars triangularis asymmetry and language dominance. *Proceedings of the National Academy of Sciences, 93,* 719-722.

Fraser, F. C. (1983). Neural tube defects and parental

nonrighthandedness. *American Journal of Human Genetics, 35*, 89.

Fredholm, B. B., & Dunwiddie, T. V. (1988). How does adenosine inhibit transmitter release? *TIPS, 9*, 130-135.

Furlow, F. B., Armijo-Prewitt, T., Gangestad, S. W., & Thornhill, R. (1997). Fluctuating asymmetry and psychometric intelligence. *Proceedings of the Royal Society, London B, 264*, 823-830..

Galaburda, A. M. (1990). The testosterone hypothesis: Assessment since Geschwind and Behan, 1982. *Annals of Dyslexia, 40*, 18-37.

Galaburda, A.M. (1993). The planum temporale. *Archives of Neurology, 50*, 457.

Galaburda, A. M., Aboitiz, F., Rosen, G. D., & Sherman, G. F. (1986). Histological asymmetry in the primary visual cortex of the rat: Implications for mechanisms of cerebral asymmetry. *Cortex, 22*, 151-160.

Gangestad, S. W., & Thornhill, R. (in press). The evolutionary psychology of extrapair sex: The role of fluctuating asymmetry. *Evolution and Human Behavior.*

Gangestad, S. W., & Thornhill, R. (submitted). Individual differences in developmental imprecision and fluctuating asymmetry: A model and its implications.

Gangestad, S. W., Thornhill, R., & Yeo, R. A. (1994). Facial attractiveness and fluctuating anatomic asymmetries. *Ethology and Sociobiology*, 15, 73-85.

Gangestad, S. W., & Yeo, R. A. (1994). Parental handedness and relative hand skill: A test of the developmental instability hypothesis. *Neuropsychology, 8*, 572-578.

Gangestad, S. W., Yeo, R. A., Shaw, P. K., Thoma, R., Daniel, W. F., & Korthank, A. (1996). Human leukocyte antigens and hand preference:

Preliminary observations. *Neuropsychology, 10*, 423-428.

Geschwind, N. & Levitsky, W. (1968). Human brain: Left-right asymmetries in the temporal speech region. *Science, 161,* 186-187.

Gilbert, A. N., & Wysocki, C. J. (1992). Hand preference and age in the United States. *Neuropsychologia, 30,* 601-608.

Grammer, K. & Thornhill, R. (1994). Human facial attractiveness and sexual selection: The role of symmetry and averageness. *Journal of Comparative Psychology, 108,* 233-242.

Grimshaw, G. M., McManus, I. C., & Bryden, M. P. (1994). Controlling for stimulus dominance in dichotic listening tasks. *Neuropsychology, 8*, 278-283.

Gualtieri, T., Adams, T. A., Shen, C. D., & Loiselle, D. (1982). Minor physical anomalies in alcoholic and schizophrenic adults and hyperactive and schizophrenic children. *American Journal of Psychiatry, 139,* 640-643.

Guy, S. D., L. V. Majurski, Wallace, C. J., & Guy, M. P. (1989). The incidence of minor physical anomalies in adult male schizophrenics. *Schizophrenia Bulletin, 39,* 571-582.

Habib, M., Robichon, F., Levrier, O., Khalil, R., & Solamon, G. (1995). Diverging asymmetries of the tempero-parietal cortical areas: A re-appraisal of the Geschwind/Galaburda theory. *Brain and Language, 48*, 238-258.

Halpern, D. F., & Cass, M. (1994). Laterality, sexual orientation, and immune system functioning: Is there a relationship? *International Journal of Neuroscience, 77,* 167-180.

Hamilton, W. D. (1982). Pathogens as causes of genetic diversity in their host populations. In R. M. Anderson & R. M. May (Eds.), *Population Biology of Infectious Diseases* (pp. 269-296). Springer-Verlag, New York.

Hayes, T. L., & Lewis, D. A., Hemispheric differences in layer III pyramidal neurons of the anterior language area. *Archives of Neurology, 50,* 501-505.

Hepper, P. G., Shahidullah, S., & White, R. (1991). Handedness in the human fetus. *Neuropsychologia, 28*, 1107-1111.

Hill, A. V. S., Allsop, C. E. M., Kwiatkowski, D., Anstey, N. M., Twumasi, P., Rowe, P. A., Bennet, S., Brewster, D., McMichael, A. J., & Greenwood, B. M. (1991). Common West African HLA antigens are associated with protection from severe malaria. *Nature, 352,* 595-600.

Houle, D. (1992). Comparing evolvability and variability of traits. *Genetics, 130*, 195-204.

Huttenlocher, P. R. (1994). Synaptogenesis in the human cerebral cortex. In G. Dawson & K. W. Fischer (Eds.), *Human Behavior and the Developing Brain*, pp. 137-152, Guilford Press, NY.

Hynd, G.W., Hall, J., Nover, E.S., Eliopulos, D., Black, K., Gonzalez, J.J., Edmonds, J.E., Riccio, C., and Cohen, M. (1995). Dyslexia and corpus callosum morphology. *Archives of Neurology*, 52:32-38, 1995.

Kulynich, J. J., Vladar, K., Jones, D. W., & Weinberger, D. R. (1994). Z-score differences in the normal lateralization of the supratemporal cortex: MRI surface-rendering morphometry of Heschl's gyrus and the planum temporale. *Cerebral Cortex*, *4*, 107-118.

Irwin, P. (1985). Greater brain response of left-handers to drugs. *Neuropsychologia, 23,* 61-67.

Jung, R., Yeo, R. A., & Gangestad, S. W. (submitted). Developmental instability predicts individual differences in responce to caffeine on a verbal memory test.

Leonard, C. M., Lombardino, L. J., Mercado, L., Breier, J. I., Foundas, A. L., Browd, S. R., Agee, O. F., & Heilman, K. M. (1994). Increased asymmetry of the planum temporale parallels improved phonological conceptualization in childhood. *Society for Neuroscience Abstracts, 20*, 1423.

Leary, R. F., Allendorf, F. W., & Knudsen, K. L. (1983). Developmental instability and enzyme heterozygosity in rainbow trout. *Nature, 301*, 71-72.

Lerner, I. M. (1954). *Genetic Homeostasis*. John Wiley & Sons: New York.

Levy, J., Heller, W., Banich, M., & Burton, L. (1983). Asymmetry of perception in free viewing of chimeric faces. *Brain and Cognition, 2*, 404-419.

Lewine, J. D., & Orrison, W. W. (1995). Magnetoencephalography. In Orrison, W. W., Lewine, J. D., Sanders, J. A., & Hartshorne, M. F. (Eds.), *Functional Brain Imaging,* Mosby, St. Louis.

Lishman, W. A., & McMeekan, E. R. L. (1976). Hand preference patterns in psychiatric patients. *British Journal of Psychiatry, 129,* 158-166.

Livshits, G., Davadi, L., Kobyliansky, E., Ben-Amatal, D., Levy, Y., & Merlob, P. (1988). Decreased developmental stability as assessed by fluctuating asymmetry of morphometric traits in preterm infants. *American Journal of Human Genetics, 29*, 793-805.

London, W. P. (1990). Left-handedness and alcoholism. In S. Coren (Ed.,), *Left-handedness: Behavioral Implications and Anomalies,* pp. 457-484. Elsevier, NY.

Lyndsay, J. (1987). Laterality shift in homosexual men. *Neuropsychologia, 25,* 965-969.

Manning, L., Halligan, P. W., & Marshall, J. C. (1990). Individual variation in line bisection: A study of normal subjects with application to the interpretation of visual neglect. *Neuropsychologia, 28*, 647-655.

Markow, T. A. (1992). Human handedness and the concept of developmental instability. *Genetica, 87*, 87-94.

Markow, T. A. (1994). *Developmental Instability: Its Origins and Evolutionary Implications.* Dordrecht: Kluwer Academic Publishers.

Markow, T. A., & Gottesman, I. I. (1989). Fluctuating dermatoglyphic asymmetry in psychotic twins. *Psychiatry Research, 19*, 37-43.

Markow, T. A., & Wandler, K. (1986). Fluctuating asymmetry and the genetics of liability to schizophrenia. *Psychiatry Research, 19,* 323-328.

Marr, D. (1976). Early processing of visual information. *Philosophical Transactions of the Royal Society* (London), *B290,* 199-218.

McManus, I. C. (1985). Handedness, language dominance, and aphasia: A genetic model. *Psychological Medicine (Monograph Supplement 8)*, Cambridge: Cambridge University Press.

McManus, I. C., & Bryden, M. P. (1992). The genetics of handedness, cerebral dominance, and lateralization. In I. Rapin & S. Segalowitz (Eds.), *Handbook of Neuropsychology: Sect.10. Developmental Neuropsychology* (pp. 115-144). Amsterdam: Elsevier Press.

McManus, I. C., Murray, B., Doyle, K., & Baron-Cohen, S. (1992). Handedness in autism shows a dissociation of skill and performance. *Cortex, 28,* 373-381.

Mednick, S. A., Cannon, T. D., & Barr, C. E. (1991). Obstetric events and adult schizophrenia. In S. A. Mednick, T. D. Cannon, C. E. Barr, & M. Lyon, (Eds.) *Fetal Neural Development and Adult Schizophrenia*, Cambridge:

Mellor. C. S. (1992). Dermatoglyphic evidence for fluctuating asymmetry in schizophrenia. *British Journal of Psychiatry, 160*, 467-472.

Mitton, J. B., & Grant, M. C. (1984). Associations among protein heterozygosity, growth rate, and developmental homeostasis. *Annual Review of Ecology and Systematics, 15*, 479-499.

Molinaar, P. C. M., Boorsma, D. I., & Dolan, C. V. (1993). A third source of developmental differences. *Behavior Genetics, 23,* 519-524.

Møller, A. P. (in press). Developmental stability and fitness: A review. *American Naturalist.*

Møller, A. P. (1996a). Parasitism and developmental stability in hosts: A review. *Oikos, 77,* 189-196.

Møller, A. P. (1996b). Development of fluctuating asymmetry in tail feathers of the barn swallow *Hirundo rustica. Journal of Evolutionary Biology, 9*, 677-694.

Møller, A. P. Soler, M., & Thornhill, R. (1995). Breast asymmetry, sexual selection, and human reproductive success. *Ethology and Sociobiology, 16,* 207-219.

Møller, A. P., & Swaddle, J. P. (1997). *Developmental Stability and Evolution*, Oxford University Press.

Møller, A. P., & Thornhill, R. (submitted). Bilateral symmetry and sexual selection: A meta-analysis.

Nelson, M. E., & Bower, J. M. (1990). Brain maps and parallel computers. *TINS, 13,* 403-409.

O'Callaghan, M. J., Tudehope, D. I., Dugdale, A. E., Mohay, H., Burns, Y., & Cook, F. Handedness in children with birthweights below 1000g. *Lancet, 7,* 1155.

Olkin, I., & Finn, J. (1990). Testing correlated correlations. *Psychological Bulletin, 108*, 330-333.

Palmer, A. R., & Strobeck, C. (1986). Fluctuating asymmetry: Measurement, analysis, patterns. *Annual Review of Ecology and Systematics, 17,* 391-421.

Penrose, L. S. (1954). The distal triradius t on the hands of parents and sibs of mongol imbeciles.*Annals of Human Genetics, 19,* 10-38.

Perrett, D. I., Burt, D. M., Lee, L. J., & Rowland, P. A.. (submitted). Fluctuating asymmetry in human faces: Symmetry is beautiful.

Pomiankowski, A. & Moller, A. P. (1995). A resolution of the lek paradox.

Proceedings of the Royal Society of London B, 260, 21-29.

Quinn, P. O., & Rapoport, J. L. (1974) Minor physical anomalies and neurologic status in hyperactive boys. *Pediatrics, 53*, 742-747.

Rakic, P. (1995). Corticogenesis in human and nonhuman primates. In M. S. Gazzaniga, (Ed.), *The Cognitive Neurosciences,* Cambridge, MA, MIT Press.

Rapoport, J. L., & Quinn, P. O. (1975). Minor physical anomalies and early developmental deviation: A major subgroup of hyperactive children. *International Journal of Mental Health, 4*, 29-44.

Repp, B. H. (1977). Measuring laterality effects in dichotic listening. *Journal of the Acoustical Society of America, 48*, 720-736.

Rice, W. R. (1988). Heritable variation in fitness as a prerequisite for adaptive female choice: The effect of mutation-selection balance. *Evolution, 42,* 817-820.

Rose, R. J., Reed, T., & Bogle, A. (1987). Asymmetry of the a-b ridgecount and behavioral discordance of monozygotic twins. *Behavior Genetics, 17*, 125-140.

Satz, P. (1972). Pathological left-handedness: An explanatory model. *Cortex, 8*, 121-135.

Scheibel, A. B., Conrad, T., Perdue, S., Tomiyasu, U., & Wechsler, A. (1990). A quantitative study of dedritic complexity in selected areas of the human cerebral cortex. *Brain and Cognition, 12*, 85-101.

Smith, D. W. (1970). *Recognizable Patterns of Human Malformation.* Saunders, Philadelphia.

Sorenson Jamison, C. (1990). Palmar dermatoglyphics of dyslexia. *American Journal of Physical Anthropology, 76*, 505-513.

Steg, J. P., & Rapoport, J. L. (1975). Minor physical anomalies in neurotic, learning disabled, and severely disturbed children. *Journal of Autism and*

Childhood Schizophrenia, 5, 299-307.

Stellman, S. D., Wynder, E. L., DeRose, D. J., & Muscat, J. E. (1997). The epidemiology of left-handedness in a hospital population. *Annals of Epidemiology, 7,* 167-171.

Strauss, E., Hunter, M., & Wada, J. (1993). Wisconsin Card Sorting Performance: Effects of age of onset of damage and laterality of dysfunction. *Journal of Clinical and Experimental Neuropsychology, 15,* 896-902.

Terry, W. S., & Phifer, B., (1986). Caffeine and memory performance on the AVLT. *Journal of Clinical Psychology, 42,*860-863.

Thatcher, R. W. (1992). Cyclic cortical reorganization during early childhood. *Brain and Cognition, 20*, 24-50.

Thoma, R. Yeo, R. A., Gangestad, S. W., Lewine, J. D., & Davis, J. (submitted). Fluctuating asymmetry and the human brain.

Thornhill, R., & Gangestad, S. W. (1994). Human fluctuating asymmetry and sexual behavior. *Psychological Science, 5*, 297-302.

Thornhill, R., & Møller, A. P. (in press). Developmental stability, disease, and medicine. *Biological Reviews.*

Tiwari, J. L., & Terasaki, P. I. (1987). *HLA and disease associations*. New York: Springer-Verlag.

Tooby, J. (1982). Pathogens, polymorphism and the evolution of sex. *Journal of Theoretical Biology, 97*, 557-576.

Tooby, J., & Cosmides, L. (1990). On the universality of human nature and the uniqueness of the individual: The role of genetics and adaptation. *Journal of Personality, 58*, 17-67.

Tukey, J. W. (1970). *Exploratory Data Analysis*. Reading, MA: Addison-Wesley.

Van Valen, L. (1962). A study of fluctuating asymmetry. *Evolution, 16,*

125-142.

Von Hilsheimer, E., & Kurko, J. (1979). Minor physical anomalies in exceptional children. *Journal of Learning Disabilities, 12,* 462-469.

Waddington, J. L., O'Callaghan, E., Buckley, P., Madigan, C., Stack, J. P., Kinsella, A., Larkin, C., & Ennis, J. T. (1995). Tardive dyskinesia in schizophrenia. Relationship to minor physical anomalies, frontal lobe dysfunction, and cerebral structure on magnetic resonance imaging. *British Journal of Psychiatry, 167,* 41-44.

Waldrop, M. F., & Halverson, C. F. (1971). Minor physical anomalies and hyperactive behavior in children. In I. J. Helmuth (Ed.), *Exceptional Infant: Studies in Abnormality* (pp. 343-380), New York: Bruner-Mazel.

Waldrop, M. F., Halverson, C. F., & Shetterly, K. (1989). *Manual for Assessing Minor Physical Anomalies (Rev. Ed.).* Unpublished manuscript, University of Georgia, Athens.

Weinberger, D. R. (1987). Implications for normal brain development for the pathogenesis of schizophrenia. *Archives of General Psychiatry, 44*, 660-669.

Weiner, B. J., Brown, D. R., & Micheals, K. M. (1991). *Statistical Principles in Experimental Design, (3rd ed.).* McGraw, New York.

Wexler, B. E., & Halwes, T. (1984). Increasing the power of dichotic methods: The fused rhymed words test. *Neuropsychologia, 21*, 59-66.

Witelson, S. F., Glezer, I. I., & Kigar, D. L. (1995). Women have greater density of neurons in posterior temporal cortex. *Journal of Neuroscience, 15*, 3418-3428.

Yeo, R. A. (1996). Neuroimaging and biology: Concluding remarks. In E. D. Bigler (Ed.), *Neuroimaging II. Clinical Applications* (pp. 351-357), New York: Plenum Press.

Yeo, R. A., Hodde-Vargas, J., Hendren, R. L., Vargas, L. A., Brooks, W.

M., Ford, C. C., Gangestad, S. W., Hart, B. F. (submitted). Brain abnormalities in schizophrenia-spectrum children: Implications for the etiology of adult schizophrenia.

Yeo, R. A., & Gangestad, S. W. (1993). Developmental origins of variation in human hand preference. *Genetica, 89*, 281-296.

Yeo, R. A., Gangestad, S. W., & Daniel, W. F. (1993). Hand preference and developmental instability. *Psychobiology, 21*, 161-168.

Yeo, R. A., Gangestad, S. W., Thoma, R., Shaw, P., & Repa, K. (in press). Developmental instability and cerebral lateralization. *Neuropsychology*.

Yeo, R. A., Gangestad, S. W., & Turkheimer, E. (1995). Non-directional genetic influences on development. Paper presented at the 1995 meeting of the Society for Research in Child Development.

The Other Side of the Error Term - N. Raz (Editor)

Chapter 2
ANIMAL MODELS OF DEVELOPMENTAL DYSLEXIA: LESSONS FROM DEVELOPMENTAL AND COGNITIVE NEUROSCIENCE

Glenn D. Rosen
Harvard University and Beth Israel Hospital

ABSTRACT

Developmental dyslexia, a potentially crippling problem in a literate society, has attracted considerable research interest over the past 20 years. In addition to investigating its target problems, this research effort has yielded results that bear on our general understanding of brain-behavior relationships. Thus, three differences between the brains of dyslexic and non-dyslexic individuals have been noted: (1) Symmetry of normally asymmetric brain regions; (2) The appearance of focal minor neocortical malformations; and (3) Defects in the fast processing of auditory and visual information. It is hypothesized that injury during late neocortical migration underlies these differences. Using rats, we have studied the morphological, cellular, developmental, and connectional aspects of cerebral asymmetry. Immune-disordered mice, such as New Zealand Black (NZB) and BXSB strains, spontaneously develop focal neocortical malformations and we can induce similar disorders in otherwise normal rodents, thus enabling further study of the anatomic and behavioral sequelae. Animals with induced malformations (but not their unlesioned counterparts) have difficulties in the fast processing of auditory information. Taken together, this research suggests that focal injury to developing cortical plate can have widespread anatomical and cognitive consequences, and that these outcomes can be successfully modeled in non-human animals.

While the use of laboratory animals to model cognitive behavior is common in the psychological literature, the notion that this type of research could be helpful in understanding purportedly unique human characteristics such as language has been considered to be difficult at best — the existence of language in non-human higher primates is not universally accepted, and there is certainly no evidence of any type of linguistic behavior in any other non-human species. Given this particular nature of language in humans, the notion that one could study developmental language disorders in rodents could be considered highly suspect. Despite these caveats, neuroscience- and cognitive science-based investigations into the underlying substrates of developmental dyslexia has uncovered a variety of distinct characteristics which characterize this disorder. Moreover, it is these basic findings which have proven themselves to be amenable to further examination using non-human subjects.

In this chapter, then, I will review some of the work, from our laboratory and others, that describes the examination of the biological and behavioral substrates underlying developmental dyslexia using animal models. I will first discuss some of the neurobiological and behavioral findings associated with developmental dyslexia, and them move to a discussion of the animal models that have proven useful in our understanding of some of the basic problems underlying this complex developmental disorder.

Developmental Dyslexia - Behavioral Phenotype

The definition of developmental dyslexia has proved to be quite controversial since the disorder was first described by Morgan (1896), Hishelwood (1917), and Orton (1925). The Orton Dyslexia Society has arrived at an "operational" definition which has been endorsed by NIH and was introduced into the literature by Shaywitz, Fletcher & Shaywitz (1994):

> Dyslexia is one of several distinct learning disabilities. It is a specific language-based disorder of constitutional origin characterized by difficulties in single word decoding, usually reflecting insufficient phonological processing abilities. These difficulties in single word decoding are often unexpected in relation to age and other cognitive and academic abilities; they are not the result of generalized developmental disability or sensory impairment.

Dyslexia is manifested by variable difficulty with different forms of language, often including, in addition to problems reading, a conspicuous problem with acquiring proficiency in writing and spelling (Lyon, 1995). In practice, dyslexics are usually diagnosed by a discrepancy between their expected and actual reading level. This is not to say the developmental dyslexia is simply a disorder of reading, as there is much evidence to support the notion that dyslexics have problems processing information from a variety of modalities. For example, dyslexics are deficient in phonological awareness (Shankweiler & Crain, 1986; Siegel & Ryan, 1988; Liberman, Shankweiler, & Liberman, 1989; Olson, Wise, Conners, Rack, &

Fulker, 1989; Crain & Shankweiler, 1990; Crain, Shankweiler, Macaruso, & Bar-Shalom, 1990; Brady, 1991; Crain, 1991; Torgesen, 1991; Shankweiler, et al., 1995). In addition, dyslexics have an impaired verbal working memory system, and this is true whether the material is presented in visual or auditory form (Mann, Liberman, & Shankweiler, 1980; Jorm, 1983; Shankweiler & Crain, 1986; Siegel & Ryan, 1988; Liberman, et al., 1989; Siegel & Ryan, 1989; Smith, Macaruso, Shankweiler, & Crain, 1989; Swanson, Cochran, & Ewers, 1989; Crain & Shankweiler, 1990; Crain, et al., 1990; Brady, 1991; Torgesen, 1991; Swanson, 1993). Interestingly, among the deaf, those with better working memories are also better readers (Liberman & Mattingly, 1989; Hanson, 1991). That being said, defects in phonological skills occur more frequently and are more strongly correlated with reading deficits than are verbal working memory deficits (Siegel & Ryan, 1988; Brady, 1991; Shankweiler, et al., 1995).

Importantly, not all the differences seen between dyslexics and controls favor those who acquire reading in a standard fashion. Dyslexics are significantly better than normal reading controls in orthographic skills (Olson, et al., 1989; Siegel, Share, & Esther, 1995); and visuospatial measures, including the WISC Block Design (Gordon, 1980; Harness, Epstein, & Gordon, 1984; Gordon, 1988).

Developmental Dyslexia - Anatomy and Physiology

From the earliest writings on the subject, researchers had believed that there was bound to be neural substrate underlying developmental dyslexia (Orton, 1925), but it was not until relatively recently that researchers began to systematically examine this issue. Drake (1968) reported a small corpus callosum as well as “excessive gyration” in the brain of post-mortem dyslexic, but that work was not continued in greater depth. Beginning the late 1970’s, Galaburda and colleagues began a systematic post-mortem study of the brains of dyslexics. From these experiments, they have identified three key anatomical differences: (1) the absence of the typical expression of asymmetry in a language-related region of the neocortex,

(2) the presence of developmental anomalies in the cerebral cortex, and (3) defects in primary sensory systems. These will be discussed below in greater detail.

Asymmetry

The *planum temporale* is an auditory region which lies on the superior surface of the temporal lobe and contains a portion of what is classically known as Wernicke's area. In normal readers the planum is larger on the left side of the brain in about two-thirds of cases and is symmetric in another quarter (Geschwind & Levitsky, 1968; Teszner, Tzavaras, Gruner, & Hécaen, 1972; Witelson & Pallie, 1973; Wada, Clarke, & Hamm, 1975). In dyslexics, however, the planum was symmetric in all consecutively studied male (n=5) and female (n=3) dyslexic brains examined at autopsy (Galaburda & Kemper, 1979; Galaburda, Sherman, Rosen, Aboitiz, & Geschwind, 1985; Humphreys, Kaufmann, & Galaburda, 1990). MRI scans of living dyslexics has further documented the symmetry of this region (Larsen, Høein, Lundberg, & Ødegaard, 1990). Since 25% of normals have symmetry of this structure, however, it is not sufficient for the production of dyslexia, although it may relate to a decrease in reading skills in non-dyslexics.

Minor Malformations of the Cerebral Cortex

Microscopic examination of human dyslexic brains has revealed several related forms of developmental neuropathologic lesions (Galaburda & Kemper, 1979; Galaburda, et al., 1985; Humphreys, et al., 1990). Principally, consecutively-studied male dyslexics and two of three female dyslexics have foci of cerebrocortical microdysgenesis consisting of (1) neuronal ectopias in neocortical layer I, (2) subjacent laminar dysplasia, (3) focal microgyria, and (4) microvascular anomalies. These abnormalities range in number from 30 to 150 focal lesions per brain, tend to be located in perisylvian regions, affect the anterior vascular borderzone, and usually involve the left more than the right hemisphere. In female brains, ectopias are relatively uncommon. Instead, these brains have large numbers of focal, myelinated glial scars that are located in the same distribution as the ectopias

(Humphreys, et al., 1990). Such scarring represents the same pathogenetic mechanisms as that of the ectopias, but acts on the developing brain somewhat later, after completion of neuronal migration, when the brain is no longer able to react by producing ectopias or microgyria. By contrast, the types of pathology described above are substantially less frequent, and when present less severe, in normative brains from comparable studies (Kaufmann & Galaburda, 1989). Together, the different types of developmental neuropathology implicate a developmental window beginning early during the second half of pregnancy and terminating by the end of the second year of postnatal life (see Fig. 1).

Fast Processing Deficits

There is also evidence that fundamental, sublinguistic mechanisms may play a role in the pathogenesis of language disorders. Tallal and collaborators have shown that developmentally language impaired children suffered from temporal processing deficits affecting even non-linguistic sounds, which suggested that the language deficits were a consequence of this auditory processing anomaly rather than primary (Tallal & Piercy, 1973; Tallal, Miller, & Fitch, 1993). Workers in the visual system also showed subcognitive deficits in dyslexics affecting temporal processing of fundamental visual stimuli, indicating that multiple sensory systems were involved (Lovegrove, Garzia, & Nicholson, 1990; Williams & Lecluyse, 1990; Livingstone, Rosen, Drislane, & Galaburda, 1991; Chase & Jenner, 1993; Slaghuis, Lovegrove, & Davidson, 1993; Williams, May, Solman, & Zhou, 1995). Livingstone et al (1991), for example, found that the magnocellular component of the visual system, which is responsible for processing fast, low-contrast information, is impaired in dyslexics. The physiologic response of this system is slowed in comparison to controls and in addition, the magnocellular neurons of the lateral geniculate nucleus are smaller than in normals (Livingstone, et al., 1991).

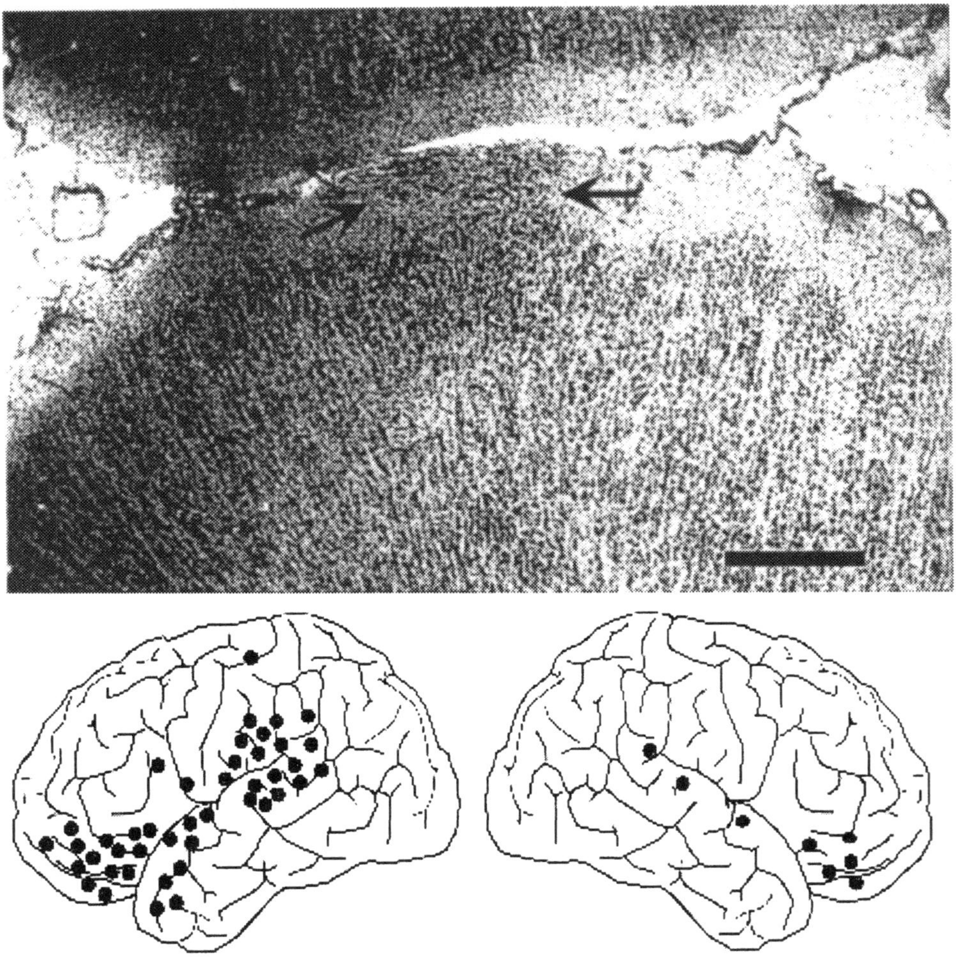

Figure 1. Top: Photomicrograph of molecular layer ectopia in layer one of a human dyslexic (arrows). Note the paucity of cells in the outermost layer of the adjacent cortex. Bar = 500 μm. Bottom: Schematic demonstrating typical locations of molecular layer ectopias in the left and right hemispheres.

The authors speculated that this visual processing disturbance could interfere with normal reading and that similar deficits in other sensory pathways, such as the auditory system, could interfere with the normal acquisition of phonological skills that also would contribute to the detriment in language processing and reading ability. Toward that end, the cell size in the left medial geniculate nucleus (the primary thalamic auditory nucleus; MGN) was found to be smaller than those on the right in dyslexics, whereas there was no difference in cell size in controls. Further, there were more small neurons and fewer large neurons in the left dyslexic MGN (Galaburda, Menard, & Rosen, 1994). These findings complement previous reports of anomalies in the dyslexic MGN (Galaburda & Eidelberg, 1982), and are consistent with reported behavioral findings of a left hemisphere-based phonological defect in dyslexic individuals (Schwartz & Tallal, 1980; Ortiz Alonso, Navarro, & vila Abad, 1990).

Hypotheses

At present there is agreement about the fact that dyslexia is a complex behavioral syndrome that includes at least disordered language processing, namely phonological deficits, and low level, perceptual deficits, namely slowed visual and auditory temporal processing of low level stimuli. One implication in the current scientific dialogue is that the cognitive problems (linguistic and non-linguistic) are the consequence of low level processing problems. Specifically, if high level centers do not receive the "correct type" of information from low level centers during development, high level function cannot develop normally. An alternative explanation of the data may be that low level processing deficits are not the cause, but rather the consequence of high level dysfunction. Namely, if high level processing areas do not develop properly, they may not reinforce development of low level processing areas for some functions, say fast temporal processing, because they are incapable of processing those stimuli further. A third possibility, not negligible in developmental disorders, is that pathology is acquired at multiple levels at the same time. An example of the latter mechanism is a form of cerebral palsy in which circulatory deficiencies early in life lead to injury to the cortex as well as to subcortical gray masses (Lyon & Robain, 1967; Friede, 1975).

In the remainder of this chapter, I will discuss our work involving rodent models of the differences that we've seen in the brains of dyslexics. These models have proven to be useful in helping to sort through the various scenarios outlined above. We have used the rat to study some of the biological substrates of anatomic asymmetry in the hopes of better understanding the differences between symmetric and asymmetric brains. Following the discussion of asymmetry, I will describe two models of minor malformations of the cortex — one spontaneous and one induced — and further explore how these models may help us to answer some of the issues discussed in above.

Animal Models of Developmental Dyslexia - Asymmetry

It is generally accepted that in humans the left hemisphere is specialized for the processing of some aspects of language while the right hemisphere dominates over many spatial, emotional, and musical functions (c.f., Springer & Deutsch, 1993; but see also Schlaug, Jäncke, Huang, Staiger, & Steinmetz, 1995; Schlaug, Jäncke, Huang, & Steinmetz, 1995) Because of the obvious lateralization of speech and language, the search for its biological substrates and has mostly centered around the classical language areas. As discussed above, a number of researchers have found the left planum temporale — a region on the posterior portion of the superior temporal sulcus which contains auditory association areas — to be larger in the left hemisphere than the right in a majority of cases (c.f., Teszner, et al., 1972; Witelson & Pallie, 1973; Wada, et al., 1975; Rubens, Mahowald, & Hutton, 1976; Chi, Dooling, & Gilles, 1977; Pieniadz & Naeser, 1984; Steinmetz, et al., 1989; Steinmetz, Volkmann, Jäncke, & Freund, 1991; Aboitiz, Scheibel, & Zaidel, 1992; Witelson & Kigar, 1992). Cytoarchitectonic areas Tpt (an auditory association cortex located partially within the planum temporale) and PG are larger on the left, and their asymmetry directly relates to planum asymmetry (Galaburda, Sanides, & Geschwind, 1978; Eidelberg & Galaburda, 1984).

Lateralization of function and anatomic asymmetry are not limited to humans, however (see Denenberg, 1981 for review). Passerine birds produce song predominantly with their left hemisphere (Nottebohm, 1971; Nottebohm, 1972; Nottebohm, 1976; Nottebohm & Nottebohm, 1976), and Japanese macaques have a right ear advantage for the processing of species-specific vocalizations (Petersen, Beecher, Zoloth, Moody, & Stebbins, 1978). In the rat, the right hemisphere is purported to be dominant for the processing of spatial information (Denenberg, Garbanati, Sherman, Yutzey, & Kaplan, 1978; Sherman, Garbanati, Rosen, Yutzey, & Denenberg, 1980; Denenberg, 1981), and the left hemisphere seems to process auditory information preferentially (Fitch, Brown, O'Connor, & Tallal, 1993). Anatomic asymmetries have been found in species ranging from reptiles (Engbretson, Reiner, & Brecha, 1981) to amphibians (Braitenberg & Kemali, 1971; Kemali, 1983; Kemali, Guglielmotti, & Fiorino, 1990; Vota-Pinardi & Kemali, 1990), to birds (DeVoogd, Pyskaty, & Nottebohm, 1991), to rodents (Diamond, Johnson, & Ingham, 1975; Diamond, Young, Singh, & Johnson, 1981; Kolb, Sutherland, Nonneman, & Whishaw, 1982; Fleming, Anderson, Rhees, Kinghorn, & Bakaitis, 1986; Stewart & Kolb, 1988), to primates (Yeni-Komshian & Benson, 1976; Cain & Wada, 1979; Gilissen, 1992).

As discussed above, we have found symmetry of the *planum temporale* in all 8 cases of dyslexic brains that we've examined. In the hopes of better understanding the processes that distinguish symmetric and asymmetric brains, we have conducted research on human and rat brains. We hypothesized that asymmetric regions function differently than their symmetric counterparts because of fundamental differences in the cellular, connectional, and probably also subcellular and molecular make-up. We therefore conducted a series of experiments, outlined below, which attempted to address these questions.

Characteristics of gross anatomic asymmetry

With respect to asymmetric brain regions, symmetry can result developmentally from either an increase in the normally smaller side, a decrease in the usually larger side, or a combination of the two processes. In the first case, the measure of total brain area of symmetric brain regions would be larger than their asymmetric counterparts whereas the opposite would be true in the second case. Brain areas would be similar if the third scenario were true.

To test these alternatives, we examined the same photographs of the 100 brains used by Geschwind and Levitsky (1968) and measured the total planum area in the left and right sides (Galaburda, Corsiglia, Rosen, & Sherman, 1987). Similar to their findings, we found a leftward asymmetry in the majority of cases. When we plotted the total planum area (right + left) against a measure of directionless asymmetry, we found a significant negative correlation, indicating that as asymmetry increased, the total planum area decreased. These results demonstrated that symmetric brains were larger than their asymmetric counterparts and, further, support the hypothesis that asymmetry is the result of the production of a small side rather than the production of a large side.

Cell density or cell number?

The architectonic volume of a region is determined by two factors: the numbers and packing density of the cells contained within the region. The differences between asymmetric and symmetric brains regions may be therefore explained by: (1) a difference in cell numbers without any change in cell-packing density, (2) changes in cell-packing density without differences in cell numbers, or (3) a combination of changes in both cell-packing density and cell number.

We measured the volume of cortical area 17 (the primary visual cortex) of the rat and found a negative correlation between the total volume of area 17 and degree of asymmetry indicating that in rats, as in humans, symmetric brain regions are larger. This having been established, we estimated cell packing densities of each hemisphere and found that there was no correlation between its asymmetry and asymmetry of architectonic volume. On the other hand, we found a highly positive correlation between cell number asymmetry and volume asymmetry, indicating that there were greater number of cells in the larger of the two hemispheres. We concluded, therefore, that architectonic areal asymmetry must be due to changes in total numbers of neurons (Galaburda, Aboitiz, Rosen, & Sherman, 1986).

Despite these findings, it could be that specific neuronal subtypes might be differentially concentrated in symmetric and asymmetric brains. In order to investigate this issue, we counted parvalbumin- and vasoactive intestinal peptide- (VIP) immunoreactive neurons in the somatosensory/somatomotor region (SM1) of the left and right hemispheres of rats (Rosen, Sherman, & Galaburda, 1993). We found a significant negative correlation between total volume and volumetric asymmetry of SM1 — a replication of previous findings. There was a significant positive correlation between SM1 volume asymmetry and both parvalbumin and VIP cell number asymmetry, which indicated that there are greater numbers of each of these types of cells in the larger SM1. Interestingly, while there was no significant relationship between asymmetry of VIP neuronal density and SM1 volume asymmetry, there was a greater cell packing density of parvalbumin neurons in the larger, as opposed to the smaller side. Thus, the processing capacity of the larger of two asymmetric homologous regions may be greater because it has more neurons. In addition, the increased concentration of parvalbumin-immunoreactive neurons in the large side may indicate qualitative differences in connectivity.

Development of anatomic asymmetry

In the previous section, evidence was presented that neuronal numbers were an important determinant of volumetric asymmetry. Because asymmetries in some areas of the human brain are visible shortly after the middle of gestation (Fontes, 1944) , it is likely that the production of cerebrocortical asymmetry depends on early developmental factors that determine neuronal numbers in the cerebral cortex. As outlined by Rakic (1988) these are: (a) the number of early progenitor cell divisions, which affects the number of proliferative neuroblasts in the germinal zone; (b) the number of divisions of neuroblasts occurring after the birth of the first neuron; and (c) ontogenetic neuronal death, which can occur either early (in the germinal zone) or late (after the birth of the first neuron). Thus, volume asymmetry of cytoarchitectonic areas could be the result of side differences (1) occurring in the germinal zone, (2) in proliferation. or (3) in cell loss, either in the germinal zone or later in ontogenesis. We determined the contribution of proliferation to the production of asymmetry of neuronal numbers in asymmetric architectonic regions by labeling with [^{3}H]thymidine those neurons undergoing their last mitosis. After neuronal migration and postmigrational ontogenetic neuronal death, the number of heavily labeled neurons present in a cortical region would reflect those neurons that were born at the time of injection minus those that died or were otherwise lost to neighboring architectonic areas by tangential movement (c.f. Walsh & Cepko, 1992; Walsh & Cepko, 1993) or fluctuations in boundary placement (Rakic, 1988). Changes in the ratio of labeled to unlabeled neurons (labeling ratio) between architectonic regions would therefore reflect differences in production of neurons during the late phase of corticogenesis, while postmigrational neuronal loss of neurons would have no effect on this measure, since both labeled and unlabeled cells would be equally affected. Furthermore, early proliferative cell division, which takes place before the injection of thymidine would likewise have no effect on this ratio. Therefore, assuming appropriate sampling over the course of neurogenesis, any differences in the labeling ratio between two cortical regions must reflect differences in late neuroblast division.

If the lengths of the cell cycles differ in two cortical areas after pulse injections of thymidine, then a substantial difference in neuronal production could occur without changing the labeling ratio. A shorter cycle can lead to more cells being produced by a radial unit over time, which, if it does not grow in radial length, must result in increased cell-packing density. We assessed potential cell cycle differences by estimating and comparing cell-packing densities and the numbers of labeled neurons between two sides of symmetric and asymmetric cases.

We injected pregnant rats with [^{3}H]thymidine at various embryonic days representing the range of cortical neuronal birthdates and their pups were sacrificed postnatally. The neocortical architectonic boundaries of primary visual area 17 and visual association area 18a were determined, their volumes computed in both the right and left hemispheres, and the numbers of labeled and unlabeled neurons were counted within these cytoarchitectonic regions.

There were no hemispheric differences in labeling ratios between the hemispheres, regardless of degree of asymmetry. This indicated that later neuroblast division doesn't play a significant role in the production of asymmetry. There were, however, differences in the labeling ratios of architectonic areas 17 and 18a, thus demonstrating that architectonic specification can be explained, at least in part, by areal differences in late neuronal production. This finding has since been replicated in monkeys (Dehay, Giroud, Berland, Smart, & Kennedy, 1993).

There was no difference in cell cycles between the hemispheres in areas 18a or 17, as assessed by labeled cell-packing density and radial extent. On the other hand, we found significant differences in labeled cell-packing densities between area 17 and area 18a. Thus, cell cycle length appears not to differ between homologous areas, asymmetric or not, but differs between non-homologous cytoarchitectonic areas.

We are then left with the suggestion that events occurring early in corticogenesis — specifically during the period of progenitor cell proliferation and/or death (before the birth of the first neuron) — are important for the formation of asymmetric cortical areas such that division and death of progenitor cells changes the number of neuroblasts on the two sides. We found no evidence that late neuronal production or postmigrational neuronal death plays a significant role (Rosen, Sherman, & Galaburda, 1991). It therefore appears to be the case that anatomic asymmetry is present at the earliest stages of cortical development.

Callosal connections and asymmetry

It has long been speculated that the mechanism for cerebral dominance might lie in the callosal connectivity—that the dominant hemisphere exerts control over its homologue through the corpus callosum (Weiskrantz, 1977). By this reasoning, one might expect that the larger, dominant brain region, which has more cells than its homologue, sends more (and different?) projections across the corpus callosum. Alternatively, it could be the case that symmetric and asymmetric brains differ in the number and pattern of connections.

We sought to investigate the latter question by severing the corpus callosum of the rat and looking at the pattern of axonal terminal degeneration with reference to asymmetry in the callosally related regions (Rosen, Sherman, & Galaburda, 1989). Specifically, we parceled SM1 and determined the percent of callosal terminal degeneration (callosal ratio). As previously reported for other brain regions (see above), we again found a negative correlation between the degree of asymmetry and total (right+left) volume of SM1 indicating that as the degree of asymmetry of the architectonic region increased, the total volume of the region decreased. In addition, there was a significant inverse relationship between asymmetry coefficient and callosal ratio. This indicated that in symmetric regions a greater percentage of SM1 received callosal terminations than in asymmetric regions.

Because callosal projections in the rat segregate into patches of termination, these results suggest a number of possible interpretations. It could be that there are more patches of termination in symmetric brain regions as compared to asymmetric. Alternatively, if there were similar numbers of patches of degeneration in symmetric and asymmetric regions, the width of these patches would be greater in the symmetric cases. A third possibility is that there are more patches of callosal termination in asymmetric brains but that these patches in symmetric regions occupy a greater proportion of the region.

In order distinguish among these possibilities, we counted the number of patches of callosal termination and found a negative relationship between them and the asymmetry coefficient indicating that there are more patches of callosal termination in the symmetric, as opposed to asymmetric, brain regions. It would appear then, that more symmetric brains have relatively greater numbers of callosal fibers and that there are more patches of termination in symmetric brains.

If the detailed architecture of connections, as well as their number, affects functional capacity, symmetric and asymmetric brains may differ in their preferred cognitive strategies as well as in their extent of hemispheric lateralization. For example, researchers have demonstrated a difference in the midsagittal area of the corpus callosum between left and right handers whereby left handers, whose brains may be more likely to be symmetric (LeMay & Culebras, 1972; but see also Steinmetz, et al., 1991), had larger midsagittal corpus callosum areas (the result of more and/or thicker fibers) than did their right-handed counterparts (Witelson, 1985; Witelson, 1989; Denenberg, Kertesz, & Cowell, 1991). It is possible that the greater cross-sectional area of the corpus callosum in left handers reflects cerebral symmetry.

Because asymmetric areas have fewer neurons than symmetric areas, and since some of these neurons may be callosally connected, it is reasonable to suggest that asymmetric areas could have fewer callosal connections (Witelson & Nowakowski, 1991). But, according to this reasoning, it is not expected that the callosal ratio would differ, since both neurons and axons would be proportionately reduced. Instead, callosal axons diminish out of proportion to cell numbers and this relative deficit of callosal connections must mean that with increasing asymmetry, some neurons withdraw their callosal axons during development while they maintain intrahemispheric connections. Supporting this notion is the finding, described above, that the density of long connecting parvalbumin-immunoreactive cells is decreased in the smaller of the two sides in asymmetric cases (Rosen, et al., 1993). Alternatively, there could be a disproportionate loss of callosally related, as compared to noncallosal cells in the asymmetric case. On the other hand, others have shown that neuronal death is not a major factor in the development of callosal projections in SM1 (O'Leary, Stanfield, & Cowan, 1981; Ivy & Killackey, 1982). The resolution of these findings awaits further research.

Summary

We have found that as asymmetry increases, the total area of the region decreases, suggesting that when a brain is symmetric, it is the result of two large sides rather than two small sides. Also, these volume differences are caused by changes in the overall number of cells, not changes in cell-packing density, although there are differences in cell packing density in certain neuronal subtypes. The ontogenetic basis for this difference in cell numbers likely relates to events that occur quite early in corticogenesis before final mitosis of proliferative units, but definitive proof is lacking. Finally, the pattern and degree of callosal connections differ between symmetric and asymmetric brains, with differential axonal pruning being implicated as the likely mechanism.

What implication do these findings have to the study of developmental dyslexia? It must first be pointed out that the relationship of anatomic asymmetry to functional lateralization is still far from being understood. What is clear, however, is that simple phrenological notions of the relationship between functional lateralization and anatomic asymmetry do not explain the variety of differences we've demonstrated. Thus, when considering the symmetric *planum temporale* in dyslexics, it could be somewhat simplistically thought that the "extra" language-related cortex somehow interfered with normal language development. What this research suggests instead is that there may be fundamental differences in organization of symmetric and asymmetric brain regions, especially in terms of connectivity, that might lead to a more instructive ways of viewing the cognitive deficit. Further, the evidence which suggests that the development of symmetric and asymmetric brain regions occurs early in gestation can serve as a solid foundation from which to examine the effects of early neocortical damage on asymmetry and connectivity as discussed below.

Animal Models of Developmental Dyslexia - Minor Malformations of the Cortex

Spontaneous malformations

In the early 1980's, Geschwind and Behan published a series of papers relating dyslexia, left-handedness, and auto-immune disease (Geschwind & Behan, 1982; Geschwind & Behan, 1984). Specifically, they found a higher incidence of both auto-immune disorders and dyslexia in left-handers as opposed to right handers. Continuing interest in the Geschwind hypothesis has led to several papers in recent years, and whether the hypothesis generated by this work as spelled out by Geschwind and Galaburda (Geschwind & Galaburda, 1985a; Geschwind & Galaburda, 1985b; Geschwind & Galaburda, 1985c; Geschwind & Galaburda, 1987) is correct is a matter of intense debate (McManus & Bryden, 1991; Bryden, McManus, & Bulman-Fleming, 1994). The hypothesis is of interest to the present discussion because it led to the finding of anatomic anomalies in the brains of immune-disordered mice that are similar in appearance to those seen in dyslexics. Specifically, in a series of studies, Sherman and colleagues (Sherman, Galaburda, & Geschwind, 1985; Sherman, Galaburda, Behan, & Rosen, 1987; Sherman, Morrison, Rosen, Behan, & Galaburda, 1990) have described molecular layer ectopias appearing in a number of strains of autoimmune mice, including New Zealand Black (NZB) and BXSB. In addition to these "ectopias," these mice also have cell-free, gliotic punched out lesions in the cortical plate (Fig. 2).

Overall about 40% of the NZB and BXSB mice have ectopias. Typically, only one ectopic nest is seen in each affected brain, although up to 25% of the affected brains have multiple ectopias. In these mice the ectopias are usually single and varied in location according to strain. In NZB mice they affect SM1, while in BXSBs the frontal cortex is involved

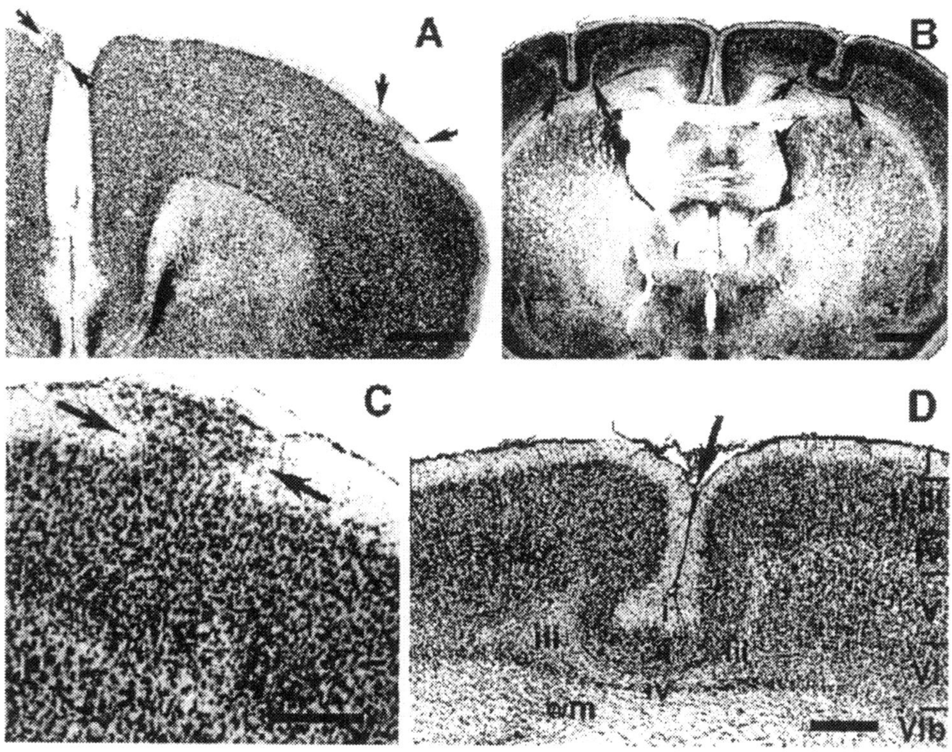

Figure 2. A. Photomicrograph of two molecular ectopias in a single immune-disordered mouse (arrows). Bar = 500 μm. B. Photomicrograph of rat with two induced microgyria (arrows). Bar = 1 mm. C. Higher power photomicrograph of a molecular layer ectopia (arrows). Bar = 250 μm. D. Higher power photomicrograph of microgyrus. Arrow indicates microsulcus. Lower case roman numerals indicate the four layers of the microgyric cortex. Upper case roman numerals indicate six layers of adjacent, normal cortex. Abbreviation: wm = white matter. Bar = 500 μm.

Gender differences are sometimes present in samples, with more affected males than females (Sherman, Rosen, & Galaburda, 1988). Interestingly, especially with respect to the discussion above, mice with ectopias displayed alterations of patterns of cerebral asymmetry, changing the rules by which asymmetry relates to volumes of architectonic areas (Rosen, Sherman, Mehler, Emsbo, & Galaburda, 1989).

Development

Examination of the brains of fetal NZB mice showed that the earliest ectopias were present by embryonic day (E) 15 and like the newborn (gestation is 19 days in the mouse) are associated with a disorganization of radial glial fibers and a breach (which is suspected to be caused by an injurious process) in the external glial limiting membrane (Sherman, Rosen, Stone, Press, & Galaburda, 1992). A subsequent study used the S-phase marker 5-bromo-2'-deoxyuridine (BrdU) to determine the fetal birthdates of neurons contained within the cortical ectopias (Sherman, et al., 1992). Early injections of BrdU (E11-13) resulted in labeling of cells in the lower layers of the adult neocortex and later injections (E14-18) resulted in staining of cells in the upper layers. Darkly-labeled neurons were first seen in the layer I ectopias after E12-13 injections. BrdU injections from E14-18 also resulted in labeling of neurons in ectopias, although at E18 fewer cells in the ectopias were BrdU positive. This indicated that the small, focal breach in the external limiting membrane is created before E12 (the mechanism is unknown) and migrating neurons born during the period covering E12-18 migrate through this break (or are pushed through by later migrating neurons) leading to the formation of ectopias.

Several studies addressed the relationship between cortical anomalies and immune status, but none could be found. Specifically, embryos from BXSB mice were transplanted at the 8 cell stage into the uteruses of control mice. There were significant effects on behavior and immune status, but there was no effect on the incidence of the malformations (Denenberg, et al., 1991), suggesting the possibility of a genetic influence on the formation of the ectopias. Further research has pointed to ectopias being linked to a single gene recessive trait with incomplete penetrance (Sherman, Stone, Denenberg, & Beier, 1994)

Neuroanatomical characteristics

In adulthood ectopias exhibit abnormal patterns of connectional- and chemo-architecture. Neurofilament staining of the ectopias show striking distortion of neuronal fibers and dendrites within and below the ectopias, consistent with disturbances of the local neuropil and connectivity (Sherman, Stone, Press, Rosen, & Galaburda, 1990). Abnormal bundles of neurofilament-containing processes were occasionally traced to the corpus callosum, which suggested that the ectopic nests projected to and/or from the opposite hemisphere. VIP, NPY, GABA and somatostatin containing neurons staining are seen in a small number of neurons within the ectopias in the NZB mouse (Sherman, Stone, Rosen, & Galaburda, 1990). VIP and somatostatin are present in the largest numbers. Further, there was an increase in the total number of VIP neurons in the hemispheres with ectopias as opposed to those without ectopias. This difference was accounted for by more VIP neurons in the columns containing ectopias than in those in the homologous areas of the opposite hemispheres, as well as by more VIP neurons in located medial to the ectopias. This indicated that the ectopias may represent not only inappropriately placed neurons, but also a problem with the regulation of their numbers. Subtle abnormalities are also seen in the hippocampus (Nowakowski & Sekiguchi, 1987), and recently the cerebellum of the NZB was found to be unusual in a number of anatomical characteristics (Sekiguchi, Shimai, Mariya, & Nowakowski, 1991).

Ectopia-Associated Behaviors

NZB mice with ectopias learn differently than those NZB mice without ectopias (Denenberg, Sherman, Schrott, Rosen, & Galaburda, 1991; Schrott, et al., 1992). Thus, ectopias depress performance of black-white discrimination in a swimming T-maze, increase the time necessary to find a hidden platform in the Morris maze (Schrott, et al., 1992), and interact with pawedness to affect performance on a spatial water escape task (Denenberg, et al., 1991). Importantly, post-weaning enriched environment ameliorates the decrements seen in the discrimination learning task and the Morris maze. Thus, following a relatively short period of environmental enrichment, the behavior of animals with ectopias was indistinguishable from that of controls. This suggests the possibility that early experience can compensate for early brain injury (Schrott, et al., 1992; Boehm, et al., 1996).

There are also tasks where ectopic mice perform in a superior manner to their non-ectopic counterparts. In the Morris maze, for example, ectopic mice take less time to find a platform and are faster swimmers than non-ectopics (Denenberg, et al., 1996). This group also studied mice that were embryo transferred to hybrid non-autoimmune mothers. Here, too, ectopic mice were better than non-ectopics on the Morris maze, suggesting that non-genetic maternal/uterine factors do not influence the behavioral consequences of these anomalies. Ectopic mice also have superior long-term retention of a water escape task (Boehm, et al., 1996).

Recent work by Denenberg and colleagues has pointed to some interesting parallels between the working memory deficits seen in dyslexics and those seen in mice with ectopias. Working memory requires an animal to disregard part of the information it has acquired on previous training trials and focus upon new information presented in the immediate trial. In a delayed-matching-to-sample task (DMTS) on a water maze, non-ectopic mice took less time and swam a lesser distance to find the platform on trial 2 than did ectopic mice (Waters, Sherman, Rosen, Galaburda, & Denenberg, in press). In a recently developed water version of the radial arm maze (Hyde, Sherman, & Denenberg, 1996), ectopic BXSB mice made significantly more working memory errors.

Summary

A number of mouse strains that were bred to develop immune disorders have shown cerebral cortical malformations similar to those seen in dyslexia. These anomalies appear to be caused by injury during the early stages of cortical development. The etiology of this injury remains unknown, but it has been shown not to be related to the autoimmune disease, but rather to be under genetic control. These ectopias have both positive and negative behavioral effects, and some of latter can be ameliorated by early experience. What is not yet known is how these small focal anomalies can have such widespread effects on behavior, although the possibility of changes in cerebrocortical connectivity is a possibility.

In the following section, a complimentary animal model is introduced which involves the induction of cortical malformations.

Induced malformations

In order to study further the effects of neocortical malformations, we wished to develop a model where lesion location and severity could be controlled. Moreover, it was desirable to separate the other biological associations (e.g., immune-disorders) from the anatomy. Toward that end, we have modified and developed techniques for inducing cerebrocortical microgyria in otherwise normal rats.

Polymicrogyria (micropolygyria, microgyria), has been associated with a wide variety human of neuropathologic disorders including porencephaly, (Levine, Fisher, & Caviness, 1974) thanatophoric dysplasia (Ho, Chang, Yang, & Chason, 1984), microencephaly (Norman, 1980), parabiotic twin syndrome (Barth & van der Harten, 1985), and developmental dyslexia (Galaburda & Kemper, 1979; Galaburda, et al., 1985). The abnormality can be very focal and associated with no cognitive or neurologic deficits, or can involve a major portion of the cerebral convexity and result in profound retardation and neurologic impairment. There are two types of microgyria: four-layered and unlayered. Four-layered microgyria, the most common type, is the type that is modeled here.

P0 Lesion

Dvorák and colleagues (Dvorák & Feit, 1977; Dvorák, Feit, & Juránková, 1978) first described a method for inducing focal microgyria in the rat. They placed a freezing probe on the skulls of newborn rats for approximately 2-3 seconds. They found that they could induce malformations of the cerebral cortex that resembled four-layered microgyria in humans. They subsequently found, using [^{3}H]Thymidine labeling, that layer II of the microgyria was formed by neurons (normally destined to be in layer II-III) migrating through the area of necrosis. The morphology of these neurons appeared normal by Golgi staining.

We have replicated and extended these findings by inducing cerebrocortical microgyria by placement of a freezing probe (cooled to ≈ -70°C) directly on the skull of P0 or P1 rat and mouse pups for 5 seconds (Humphreys, Rosen, Press, Sherman, & Galaburda, 1991). Neuronal necrosis can be observed as soon as 1.5 h after the freezing injury. At that point, most radial glial fibers in the area are beginning to be lost and there are a few reactive astrocytes in the area of the lesion. Interestingly, the pial surface is intact. One day after the lesion, there is complete tissue necrosis of the cortical plate, sparing only layer VIb (or subplate) neurons. Radial glial fibers have completely withdrawn from the area of damage, but their cell bodies appear to be intact. Macrophages begin to appear in excess in the damaged area and there is a dramatic increase in the number of astrocytes. Three days post-lesion, radial glial fibers regrow though a region of intense astrogliosis, and neurons begin to migrate through that area. There is a marked increase in the number of macrophages present and the area of tissue necrosis decreases. The beginning of the formation of a microgyria can clearly be seen by day 5, starting primarily at the periphery of the lesion, where radial glial fibers are continuing their regrowth through the damaged area. The microgyria gain their adult appearance by P15 at which time radial glial fibers can still be seen in the area of damage, although not elsewhere. These results suggest that the formation of microgyria is the result of basic brain repair mechanisms occurring during the end of the period of neuronal migration (Suzuki & Choi, 1991; Rosen, Press, Sherman, & Galaburda, 1992).

In its mature state, the lesions consist of a large area of selective neuronal loss and the presence of glial nuclei involving layers IV, V, and VIa while Layer VIb is usually preserved. There is a characteristic infolding of the superficial cortical layers to form a microsulcus with opposed, fused pial surfaces which varies in depth from 10-95% of the thickness of the neocortex. The molecular layer (I) follows the microsulcus in its entirety, although layer thickness varies. Layers II and III are invariably preserved in their whole or in part, and swept downward toward the region of neuronal loss, following the course of the microsulcus. The anterior-posterior extent of this type of lesion is 1.8-2.1 mm. In some cases, the freezing injury leads to two diverging microsulci which, in appropriate sections produces a true microgyrus sandwiched between the microsulci. Effectively, this type of freezing injury recreated a microgyric four-layer cortex comprising (i) a molecular layer, (ii) a superficial (infolded) neuronal layer (corresponding to ordinary layers II, III but less layered), (iii) a neuron-free zone (necrotic area), (iv) a deep neuronal layer (corresponding to ordinary layer VIb; Fig 2).

P10 Lesion

In contrast to the freezing injury at P0 or P1, placing a freezing probe on the skull of P10 rats for up to 20 seconds does not result in the formation of microgyria. After this type of injury, a zone of neuronal loss is often seen extending from 10 - 75% of the thickness of the cortex with no formation of a microsulcus. The appearance of the cortex on either side of the damaged area is perfectly normal with no evidence of distortion or absence of fiber staining as revealed by neurofilament and glutamate staining. This confirms earlier reports (Dvorák & Feit, 1977; Dvorák, et al., 1978) that microgyria can only be formed by injury occurring before the end of neocortical neuronal migration.

Strength of Lesion

In addition to the differential effects of lesion timing, we have also found that lesions of different strengths yield very different forms of cerebrocortical microdysgenesis. These results suggest that a single etiologic event can cause a wide variety of malformations (Rosen & Galaburda, 1995). We exposed rats to either one lesion or two adjacent lesions of durations ranging from 2- 20 sec. Rats with a single 2 sec freezing lesion had very minor damage, with molecular layer ectopias occasionally appearing. When microgyria were present, they were rather shallow in depth and extent. As the length of time of the freezing probe and the number of freezing lesions increased, the resultant microdysgenetic cortex became proportionally more severe. These lesions were microgyric in appearance, with the more severe lesions having deeper and more microsulci. The most severe lesion occurred when animals were exposed to the freezing probe for two 20 sec lesions. These animals almost uniformly demonstrated porencephalic cysts and other gross distortions of cytoarchitecture (Rosen & Galaburda, 1995).

Cortical puncture and ectopias

Although occasional layer I ectopias arose in P0 and P10-lesioned animals, they were of a qualitatively different type from those seen in immune-disordered mice. The collections of neurons in ectopias always reach the pial surface and they generally have a contained, "mushroom-like" appearance, whereas the induced anomalies tend not to reach the pial surface and are more dispersed. Based on the finding of a breach in the external limiting membrane overlying areas of spontaneous ectopias (Sherman, et al., 1992), we created a small focal area of damage of the external limiting membrane by puncture wound of the neocortex. This resulted in ectopic collections of neurons in layer I of the neocortex comparable to those seen in spontaneous ectopias of humans and mice (Rosen, Sherman, Richman, Stone, & Galaburda, 1992).

Behavior

Nonimmune-disordered animals with induced ectopias and microgyria have behavioral deficits which are, in some ways, quite similar to those seen in immune-disrodered mice with spontaneous ectopias. Lesioned mice (irrespective of hemisphere or type of damage) performed poorly when compared to sham-operated animals in discrimination learning, in a spatial Match-to-Sample task, and in a Lashley Type III maze. In shuttlebox avoidance conditioning, where immunological disorder compromises behavioral performance, there was no difference between lesioned and sham animals. These results reveal the similarities to the behavioral effects of spontaneous and induced neocortical malformations (Rosen, Waters,

Galaburda, & Denenberg, 1995).

Summary

In the previous two sections two different but related models of the anatomic malformations seen in the dyslexic brain have been presented. From this work, we have been able to glean a wealth of information that would not necessarily be amenable to study in the humans. We have evidence, for example, that these malformations are the result of injury occurring early in gestation and that they have a genetic component. This latter fact, combined with evidence from the human dyslexic suggesting a link with chromosomes 6 and 15 may yield more insights into the etiology of this disorder.

The parallels between the dyslexic and these animal models extend to behavior as well. Thus, while it is impossible to test animals for the phonological defects exhibited by dyslexics, these animals have measurable deficits in working memory — a difficulty also encountered in developmental dyselxics. In the following section, we present evidence suggesting that animals with induced malformations also have difficulties with fast processing of auditory information

Animal Models of Developmental Dyslexia - Fast Processing Defects

As described above, minor developmental cortical malformations, including microgyria, are seen in the brains of dyslexics and in our animal models. Concomitant studies have shown that language-impaired (LI) children, a large subset of whom are dyslexic, exhibit severe deficits in the discrimination of rapidly presented auditory stimuli, including phonological and non-verbal stimuli (i.e., sequential tones), specifically when total stimulus durations falls below 350 ms (Tallal & Piercy, 1973). This two tone sequence discrimination task which elicited these significant differences between LI and control children was adapted to an operant conditioning go-no go target identification paradigm for rats. Male rats had significantly better discrimination of tone sequences with the right as compared to the left ear, suggesting left hemisphere specialization for this function (Fitch, et al.,

1993). Male rats were also found to exhibit a significantly stronger right ear advantage (REA) than females, a sex difference which may relate to evidence of a stronger right ear advantage for verbal processing in men as compared to women.

We sought to develop an animal model for impaired auditory temporal processing by exploiting the functional parallels between rats and humans in two tone discrimination, and our ability to model some of the neuroanatomic anomalies seen in dyslexia. Toward that end, adult male rats with neonatally induced microgyria were tested in an operant paradigm for auditory discrimination of stimuli consisting of two sequential tones (Fitch, Tallal, Brown, Galaburda, & Rosen, 1994). Subjects were shaped to perform a go-no go target identification, using water reinforcement. Stimuli were reduced in duration from 540 to 249 ms across 24 days of testing. Discrimination indices were calculated from the difference, in msec, between mean latencies to respond to the target (hits) versus non-targets (false-alarms) for each subject across days. Results showed that all subjects were able to discriminate at longer stimulus durations. However, lesioned subjects showed specific impairment at stimulus durations of 332 ms or less, and were significantly depressed in comparison to shams. These results suggest a possible link between the neuropathologic anomalies observed in some LI brains, and the auditory temporal processing deficits reported for LI subjects. More recent studies have shown that female rats, unlike males, successfully perform the auditory discrimination task at all conditions, irrespective of whether or not they have induced microgyria (Fitch, Brown, Tallal, & Rosen, 1997). In addition, animals who had a freezing injury and then were immediately treated with a neuroprotective agent behaved identically to their unlesioned littermates. Specifically, not only did the neuroprotective treatment significantly decrease the size of the malformation, but it also ameliorated the behavior deficit (Fig. 3).

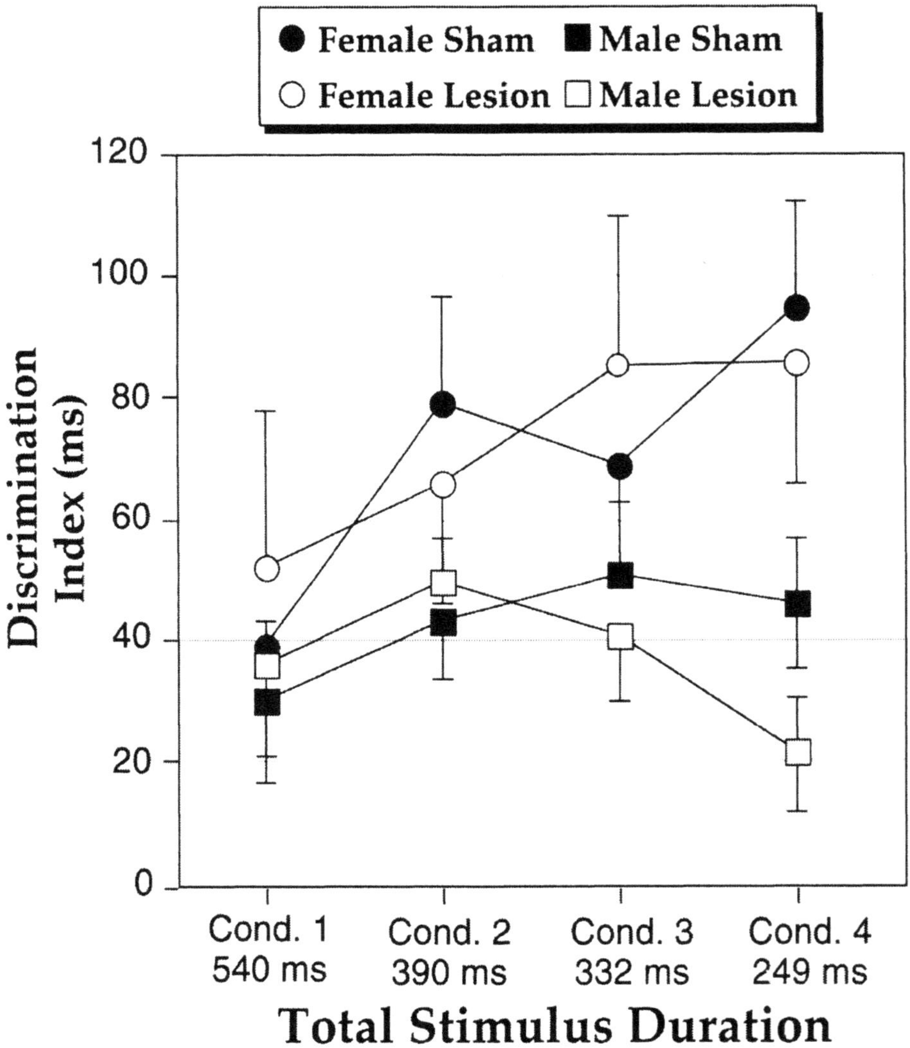

Figure 3. Mean discrimination index for male (square) and female (circle) lesioned (filled) and sham (open) groups at the 4 stimulus duration conditions. Discrimination indices are mean scores over 6 days of testing at each condition. The numbers under each condition are total stimulus time (pre-tone/ISI/post-tone). From Fitch et al. (1997). Reprinted with permission of the American Psychological Association ©1997.

In both these studies, however, microgyria were induced in somatosensory (and to a lesser extent in frontal) cortex, brain regions that do not normally directly mediate auditory functions. It was hypothesized that injury to the developing neocortex, irrespective of location, could propagate along transient or anomalous connections leading to changes in areas important for low level auditory processing, even if several synapses away. Furthermore, the finding that male and females show different behavioral effects after lesioning suggest that, with the latter hypothesis in mind, propagating (plasticity) effects are different in the two sexes. We further hypothesized that these changes might be reflected, as they are in the dyslexic, by changes in cell sizes in the primary auditory thalamic nucleus, the MGN (Galaburda, et al., 1994). We therefore measured MGN cell size, packing-density, and number in male and female rats with induced frontal, occipital, or parietal microgyria who were also tested for auditory discrimination learning.

Changes in Thalamic Neuronal Size

Behaviorally, as mentioned above, males with microgyria were unable to perform the fast auditory discriminations. Females, on the other hand, were significantly better than males, and there was no difference between lesioned and unlesioned females at any condition. When we looked at the MGN, we found that in the males, there were more small and fewer large cells in the lesioned animals. In contrast, there were no differences in MGN cell size distribution in the females. Moreover, MGN cell size predicted behavior in males but not females. We had hypothesized that after injury causes these ectopias, reorganization of the cerebral cortex leads to propagation of effects throughout the brain in a top-down manner, to explain the changes in the thalamus. The current findings lend some support to this hypothesis.

One conduit for propagation of changes could be neuronal connections. Connections between the injured area and the thalamic target could be (1) direct, (2) developmentally transient, (3) polysynaptic, or (4) new connections produced by the injury. Developmentally, there are transient connections between somatosensory cortex and the MGN. In fact, unilateral removal of facial whiskers in newborn rats results in the maintenance of this transient cross-modal projection (Nicolelis, Chapin, & Lin, 1991). Maintenance of otherwise transient projections also follows the induction of microgyria in cats by injection of ibotenic acid into the developing visual cortex (Innocenti & Berbel, 1991b; Innocenti & Berbel, 1991a). Furthermore, widespread brain reorganization has been reported following a variety of developmental injuries. In hamsters, for example, neonatal lesions of the superior colliculus result in altered retinal projections (Finlay, Wilson, & Schneider, 1979; Schneider, 1979; Schneider, 1981). Neonatal ischemia, induced by bilateral carotid ligation in cats, results in an excess of callosal projections from visual areas 17 and 18 (Miller, et al., 1993). Thus, in summary, hypoxic-ischemic insults that result in microgyria may disrupt standard patterns of neuronal connectivity by maintenance of transient projections (Innocenti & Berbel, 1991b; Nicolelis, et al., 1991), or from the invasion of vacated terminal space by axons from undamaged regions (e.g., Schneider, 1981).

It is possible, therefore, that early freezing injury produces microgyria with normal and abnormal efferent and afferent connectivity, which could provide the conduits for the propagation of cascading effects on structures thus connected to this region. The abnormal connectivity could theoretically be the result of the pathological maintenance of normally transient connections or the formation of novel connections. Although propagation of changes along standard connections would be easily traced, changes propagated via transient or anomalous connections require special experimental demonstration.

In the following section, some recent investigations of the effects of cortical malformations on cerebrocortical connectivity are discussed.

Connectional Differences

Connectional abnormalities in ectopic mice

As discussed above, immunohistochemical studies have shown an increased density of neurofilament-immunoreactive fibers radially oriented underlying ectopias (Sherman, et al., 1990). A follow-up DiI (a lipophilic tracer) study was designed to show definitively that these bundles contained afferent and efferent fibers from neurons in the ectopias. Small crystals of DiI were placed in the middle of an ectopia and the projections from the ectopia traced (Jenner, Galaburda, & Sherman, 1995). In all cases there was a distinctive bundle of labeled fibers extending from the ectopic cells through the deeper layers of the cortex. This bundle of fibers then either entered the corpus callosum, the internal capsule or both. Depending on the location of the ectopia within the somatosensory cortex, labeling was seen in appropriate thalamic nuclei. Cortico-cortical connections were also seen between ectopias in barrel cortex and both secondary somatosensory and primary motor cortices. Rarely was there any visible connections in the contralateral cortex.

The DiI labeling from non-ectopic cortex showed a distinctly different pattern of connectivity. In no case was there labeling of fiber bundles under the injection site in the controls. In comparison to the ectopias the non-ectopic cortex seemed to have less intense staining of the thalamic nuclei. The non-ectopic placements showed more fibers crossing the corpus callosum with distinctive patterns of connections in the contralateral cortex. These DiI studies provide the first conclusive evidence that the neurons within the ectopias are connected both to other cortical areas and to thalamic nuclei and preliminary evidence that the ectopias are associated with abnormal connectivity.

Changes in connectivity with microgyria

Disturbed interhemispheric connectivity has been associated with a spontaneously occurring microgyrus in the rat (Rosen, et al., 1989). Because spontaneously occurring microgyria are rare in experimental animal species, we severed the corpus callosum of rats with induced microgyria and examined their brains for the patterns of degenerating axon terminals. The most obvious changes in the patterns of callosal axonal terminations occurred in and around the areas of the neocortical microgyria. In all cases, there were increases in the density of callosal terminations in the microgyrus when the latter was located in an area that normally received callosal terminations. Exuberant patches of callosal termination were found immediately medial or lateral to the region of microdysgenesis which were either not seen in homologous regions of control brains or were gross distortions of patches that were normally present. There was a decrease in the pattern of axonal terminations in the entire contralateral hemisphere, either when compared to controls or to the patterns of termination within the ipsilateral hemisphere. Areas lateral to the homologous regions also showed a relative decrease in axonal degeneration, although there was relative preservation of callosal terminations in areas medial to the homologous area.

In order to confirm these changes in callosal connectivity, we injected *in vivo* tracers into the microgyria of adult animals. Specifically, we injected biotinylated dextran amine (BDA) into microgyric and matched control cases. Animals with microgyria in their parietal cortices (Par1) show patterns of interhemispheric connectivity consistent with the results reported above. In comparison to controls, there was a decrease in efferent projections from the microgyric cortex to the opposite hemisphere. Par1 microgyria had abnormal efferent connections to secondary somatosensory cortex (Par2) of the opposite hemisphere. Although cortico-thalamic projections appeared normal, thalamo-cortical projections were markedly decreased. Injection of BDA into the homologous area of the undamaged hemisphere highlighted aberrant projections into frontal and Par2 cortex of the affected hemisphere (Rosen & Galaburda, 1996). Thus, connectional abnormalities are seen in both the case of the spontaneous and induced malformations.

Sex Differences

While lesioned males had more small and fewer large cells than their unlesioned counterparts, there was no difference between lesioned and unlesioned females. This sex difference is of particular interest in light of the estimate that dyslexia is up to three times more common in males than females (Finucci, Isaacs, Whitehouse, & Childs, 1983; Liederman & Flannery, 1993) but see, c.f., Shaywitz et al., (1990). In fact, evidence indicates that males are preferentially afflicted with virtually every neurodevelopmental and psychiatric disorder of childhood, including mental retardation, autism, hyperactivity, dyslexia, epilepsy, and cerebral palsy (Gualtieri & Hicks, 1985).

It could be that the female brain is more resistant to injurious agents. In animal studies, for example, it has been shown that female gerbils show less injury from ischemic challenges than males (Hall, Pazara, & Linseman, 1991). We found, however, no difference in lesion size between males and females, indicating an equivalent response to the injury, at least acutely. It could be argued, then, that males and females have a different delayed response to the lesion. For example, females are less susceptible behaviorally to the effects of early neocortical damage (Raz, Lauterbach, Hopkins, Glogowski, & Porter, 1995). Alternatively, the possibility exists that sex differences in maturation and/or plasticity timing of brain regions could play a role. Thus, Goldman et al. (1974) reported that male monkeys whose orbital prefrontal cortex had been removed in infancy were impaired at an object discrimination reversal task at two and a half months of age, while lesioned females did not show a behavioral deficit until approximately 1 year later. They hypothesized that sex differences in the development of cortical regions could have implications not only for the acquisition of behavioral and cognitive skills, but also for the higher incidence of developmental disorders in males.

One other possibility that deserves consideration is that the presence of circulating testosterone during the time of injury in the male rats exacerbates cerebral plasticity such that there is an enhanced re-organization of the brain. Thus, research has shown that estrogen, which is the product of aromatization of testosterone, acts to regulate various neurotrophic receptors (Sohrabji, Greene, Miranda, & Toran-Allerand, 1994; Sohrabji, Miranda, & Toran-Allerand, 1994). These findings suggest the possibility that the male brain is "hyper-plastic" and therefore reacts to early injury to a greater extent —with perhaps more deleterious effects — than does the female brain. Further empirical research will help resolve these issues.

Summary

Previous research had indicated that freezing injury to the presumptive somatosensory cortices of rats induces cerebrocortical microgyria and was associated with a defect in fast auditory processing (Fitch, et al., 1994). What remained unexplained in that study was how this cortical damage could affect auditory discrimination as there is no evidence that these cortices play a significant role in auditory processing in this animal.

We have demonstrated that freezing injury to the cortical plate in males significantly affects the distribution of cell sizes in the MGN. Specifically, microgyric males have more small and fewer large neurons in the MGN than their unlesioned counterparts, and lesion location played no role on this measure. Further, lesioned males were significantly impaired in their ability to perform a fast auditory discrimination in comparison with their sham littermates, and MGN cell size correlated with behavior at the fastest condition. In contrast, lesioned females did not differ from sham littermates in either anatomy or behavior. We hypothesize (and have some empirical evidence to support it) that early injury to the cortical plate causes histological changes at distant sites, explained by propagation along connectional pathways, some of which may be only transient connections, others anomalous connections. Further, there may be gender factors that separate males and females in this response.

Conclusions

The work discussed in this chapter has pointed to a number of areas where research into the biological substrates of developmental dyslexia has been aided by the use of animal models. Examination of the brains of dyslexic individuals revealed differences in three different domains, each of which has been successfully modeled in rodents. Thus, we have gained insight into the differences between symmetric and asymmetric brain regions by examining their gross morphometric, cellular, developmental, and connectional aspects. We know that symmetric brain regions are larger, have more cells, and have greater proportions of interhemispheric connections than their asymmetric counterparts. In addition, whether a brain is symmetric or asymmetric appears to be the result of events that occur quite early in development. From examination of animals with either induced or spontaneous malformations, we have learned more about their etiology and their effects on brain organization. In addition, behavioral testing has pointed to some intriguing parallels with the non-linguistic deficits seen in dyslexia and other language impairments. In the case of the spontaneous malformations, for example, there is evidence that ectopic animals have working memory deficits. Animals with induced microgyria, like language-impaired individuals, have problems with the fast processing of auditory information.

Perhaps most important, however, is that the examination of these animal models has enabled us to link together the three main differences found in the study of developmental dyslexic: symmetry of a language-related region, presence of neocortical malformations, and defects in fast processing. For example, we know that the presence of cortical malformations disturbs the normal relationship between asymmetry and volume. Specifically, whereas the correlation between asymmetry and volume of a region has been shown for every species examined, there is no correlation in mice with ectopias. This suggests that the presence of the ectopias somehow disrupts the normal development of asymmetry (Rosen, et al., 1989). We also know that the induction of a microgyria into an otherwise normal cortex profoundly disturbs the ability of that animal to process auditory information when it is presented in a fast manner. This supports the notion that this defect in fast processing may be caused by a top-down disruption of cerebral architecture induced by the early injury. The mechanisms for this disruption are hypothesized to the result of connectional reorganization — an hypothesis that is supported by some of our preliminary research.

Although there are obvious and important limits to the types of questions that we can ask non-human animals with respect to developmental dyslexia, there are similarities in the basic biological substrates that may underlie this disorder that allow and encourage the use of animal models. It is hoped that as we learn more about the basic anatomical, behavioral, and cognitive aspects of this disorder that other similarities will become evident and allow researchers to converge on a more complete understanding of this disorder.

Acknowledgments

This work was supported, in part, by PHS grants NS27119 and HD20806, by a grant from the New England Branch of the Orton Dyslexia Society. This work was performed collaboratively primarily with Drs. Albert M. Galaburda, Gordon F. Sherman, Victor H. Denenberg, R. Holly Fitch, and Lisa M. Schrott and the author thanks them for all their input. Other collaborators included Drs. Francisco Aboitiz, Joan Corsiglia, Claudia Mehler, and Kari Emsbo as well as my students Amy Herman and Alex Carter. Acknowledgments also go to Antis Zalkalns, Lisa Stone Garcia, and Heinz Windzio for technical assistance.

References

Aboitiz, F., Scheibel, A. B., & Zaidel, E. (1992). Morphometry of the sylvian fissure and the corpus callosum, with emphasis on sex differences. *Brain, 115*, 1521-1541.

Barth, P. G., & van der Harten, J. J. (1985). Parabiotic twin syndrome with topical isocortical disruption and gastroschisis. *Acta Neuropathologica, 67*, 345-349.

Boehm, G. W., Sherman, G. F., Hoplight, B. J., Hyde, L. A., Waters, N. S., Bradway, D. M., Galaburda, A. M., & Denenberg, V. H. (1996). Learning and memory in the autoimmune BXSB mouse: Effects of neocortical ectopias and environmental enrichment. *Brain Research, 726*, 11-22.

Brady, S. A. (1991). The role of working memory in reading disability. In S. A. Brady, & D. P. Shankweiler (Ed.), *Phonological Processes in Literacy- A Tribute to Isabelle Y. Liberman* (pp. 125-151). Hillsdale: Lawrence Erlbaum Associates, Publishers.

Braitenberg, V., & Kemali, N. (1971). Exceptions to bilateral symmetry in the epithalamus of lower vertebrates. *Journal of Comparative Neuro*logy, *138,* 137-146.

Bryden, M. P., McManus, I. C., & Bulman-Fleming, M. B. (1994). Evaluating the empirical support for the Geschwind-Behan-Galaburda model of cerebral lateralization. *Brain and Cognition, 26*, 103-167.

Cain, D. P., & Wada, J. A. (1979). An anatomical asymmetry in the baboon brain. *Brain, Behavior, and Evolution, 16*, 222-226.

Chase, C., & Jenner, A. (1993). Magnocellular visual deficits affect temporal processing of dyslexics. In P. Tallal, A. M. Galaburda, R. Llinas, & C. von Euler (Ed.), *Temporal Information Processing in the Nervous System, with Special Reference to Dyslexia and Dysphasia* New York: New York Academy of Sciences.

Chi, J. G., Dooling, E. C., & Gilles, F. H. (1977). Gyral development of the human brain. *Annals of Neurology*, 1, 86-93.

Crain, S. (1991). Language acquisition in the absence of experience. *Behavioral and Brain Science*, 14, 597-650.

Crain, S., & Shankweiler, D. (1990). Explaining failures in spoken language comprehension by children with reading disabilities. In D. A. Balota, G. B. Flores d'Arcais, & K. Rayner (Ed.), *Comprehension Processes in Reading* (pp. 539-555). Hillsdale, NJ: Lawrence Erlbaum Associates.

Crain, S., Shankweiler, D., Macaruso, P., & Bar-Shalom, E. (1990). Working memory and comprehension of spoken sentences: Investigation of children with reading disorder. In G. Vallar, & T. Shallice (Ed.), *Neuropsychological impairments of short-term memory* (pp. 477-508). Cambridge: Cambridge University Press.

Dehay, C., Giroud, P., Berland, M., Smart, I., & Kennedy, H. (1993). Modulation of the cell cycle contributes to the parcellation of the primate visual cortex. *Nature*, 366(6454), 464-466.

Denenberg, V. H. (1981). Hemispheric laterality in animals and the effects of early experience. *Behavioral and Brain Science*, 4, 1-49.

Denenberg, V. H., Garbanati, J., Sherman, G., Yutzey, D. A., & Kaplan, R. (1978). Infantile stimulation induces brain lateralization in rats. *Science*, 201, 1150-1152.

Denenberg, V. H., Kertesz, A., & Cowell, P. E. (1991). A factor analysis of the human's corpus callosum. *Brain Research*, 548(1-2), 126-132.

Denenberg, V. H., Mobraaten, L. E., Sherman, G. F., Morrison, L., Schrott, L. M., Waters, N. S., Rosen, G. D., Behan, P. O., & Galaburda, A. M. (1991). Effects of the autoimmune uterine/maternal environment upon cortical ectopias, behavior and autoimmunity. *Brain Research*, 563(1-2), 114-122.

Denenberg, V. H., Sherman, G., Schrott, L. M., Waters, N. S., Boehm, G. W., Galaburda, A. M., & Mobraaten, L. E. (1996). Effects of embryo transfer and cortical ectopias upon the behavior of BXSB-Yaa and BXSB-Yaa plus mice. *Developmental Brain Research*, 93, 100-108.

Denenberg, V. H., Sherman, G. F., Schrott, L. M., Rosen, G. D., & Galaburda, A. M. (1991). Spatial learning, discrimination learning, paw preference and neocortical ectopias in two autoimmune strains of mice. *Brain Res*earch, 562(1), 98-104.

DeVoogd, T. J., Pyskaty, D. J., & Nottebohm, F. (1991). Lateral asymmetries and testosterone-induced changes in the gross morphology of the hypoglossal nucleus in adult canaries. *Journal of Comparative Neurology*, 307(1), 65-76.

Diamond, M. C., Johnson, R. E., & Ingham, C. A. (1975). Morphological changes in the young, adult and aging rat cerebral cortex, hippocampus, and diencephalon. *Behavioral Biology*, 14, 163-174.

Diamond, M. C., Young, D., Singh, S. S., & Johnson, R. E. (1981). Age-related morphological differences in the rat cerebral cortex and hippocampus: Male-female; right-left. *Experimental Neurology*, 81, 1-13.

Drake, W. E. (1968). Clinical and pathological findings in a child with a developmental learning disability. *Journal of Learning Disabilities*, 1, 9-25.

Dvorák, K., & Feit, J. (1977). Migration of neuroblasts through partial necrosis of the cerebral cortex in newborn rats — contribution to the problems of morphological development and developmental period of cerebral microgyria. *Acta Neuropathologica (Berlin)*, 38, 203-212.

Dvorák, K., Feit, J., & Juránková, Z. (1978). Experimentally induced focal microgyria and status verrucosus deformis in rats -- Pathogenesis and interrelation histological and autoradiographical study. *Acta Neuropathologica (Berlin)*, 44, 121-129.

Eidelberg, D., & Galaburda, A. M. (1984). Inferior parietal lobule. Divergent architectonic asymmetries in the human brain. *Archives of Neurology*, 41, 843-852.

Engbretson, G. A., Reiner, A., & Brecha, N. (1981). Habenular asymmetry and the central connections of the parietal eye of the lizard. *Journal of Comparative*

Neurology, 198, 155-165.

Finlay, B. L., Wilson, K. G., & Schneider, G. E. (1979). Anomalous ipsilateral retinotectal projections in Syrian hamsters with early lesions: topography and functional capacity. *Journal of Comparative Neurology*, 183, 721-740.

Finucci, J. M., Isaacs, S. D., Whitehouse, C. C., & Childs, B. (1983). Classification of spelling errors and their relationship to reading ability, sex, grade placement, and intelligence. *Brain and Language*, 20, 340-345.

Fitch, R. H., Brown, C. P., Tallal, P., & Rosen, G. D. (1997). Effects of sex and MK-801 on auditory-processing deficits associated with developmental microgyric lesions in rats. *Behavioral Neuroscience, 111*, 404-412.

Fitch, R. H., Brown, C. P., O'Connor, K., & Tallal, P. (1993). Functional lateralization for auditory temporal processing in male and female rats. *Behavioral Neuroscience*, *107*, 844-850.

Fitch, R. H., Tallal, P., Brown, C., Galaburda, A. M., & Rosen, G. D. (1994). Induced microgyria and auditory temporal processing in rats: A model for language impairment? *Cerebral Cortex*, 4, 260-270.

Fleming, D. E., Anderson, R. H., Rhees, R. W., Kinghorn, E., & Bakaitis, J. (1986). Effects of prenatal stress on sexually dimorphic asymmetries in the cerebral cortex of the male rat. *Brain Research Bulletin*, 16, 395-8.

Fontes, V. (1944). *Morfologia do Cortex Cerebral (Desenvolvimento)* . Lisbon: Instituto Antonio Aurelio da Costa Ferreirs.

Friede, R. L. (1975). *Developmental Neuropathology* . New York: Springer-Verlag.

Galaburda, A. M., Aboitiz, F., Rosen, G. D., & Sherman, G. F. (1986). Histological asymmetry in the primary visual cortex of the rat: Implications for mechanisms of cerebral asymmetry. *Cortex*, 22, 151-160.

Galaburda, A. M., Corsiglia, J., Rosen, G. D., & Sherman, G. F. (1987). Planum temporale asymmetry: Reappraisal since Geschwind and Levitsky.

Neuropsychologia, 25, 853-868.

Galaburda, A. M., & Eidelberg, D. (1982). Symmetry and asymmetry in the human posterior thalamus. II. Thalamic lesions in a case of developmental dyslexia. *Archives of Neurology*, 39, 333-336.

Galaburda, A. M., & Kemper, T. L. (1979). Cytoarchitectonic abnormalities in developmental dyslexia; a case study. *Annals of Neurology*, 6, 94-100.

Galaburda, A. M., Menard, M. T., & Rosen, G. D. (1994). Evidence for aberrant auditory anatomy in developmental dyslexia. *Proceedings of National Acaemy of Science (USA)*, 91, 8010-8013.

Galaburda, A. M., Sanides, F., & Geschwind, N. (1978). Human brain: Cytoarchitectonic left-right asymmetries in the temporal speech region. *Archives of Neurology*, 35, 812-817.

Galaburda, A. M., Sherman, G. F., Rosen, G. D., Aboitiz, F., & Geschwind, N. (1985). Developmental dyslexia: Four consecutive cases with cortical anomalies. *Annals of Neurology*, 18, 222-233.

Geschwind, N., & Behan, P. (1984). Laterality, hormones, and immunity. In N. Geschwind, & A. M. Galaburda (Ed.), *Cerebral Dominance: The Biological Foundations* (pp. 211-224). Cambridge, MA: Harvard University Press.

Geschwind, N., & Behan, P. O. (1982). Left-handedness: Association with immune disease, migraine, and developmental disorder. *Proceedings of National Academy of Science (USA)*, 79, 5097-5100.

Geschwind, N., & Galaburda, A. M. (1985a). Cerebral lateralization. Biological mechanisms, associations, and pathology: I. A hypothesis and a program for research. *Archives of Neurology*, 42, 428-521.

Geschwind, N., & Galaburda, A. M. (1985b). Cerebral lateralization. Biological mechanisms, associations, and pathology: II. A hypothesis and a program for research. *Archives of Neurology*, 42, 521-552.

Geschwind, N., & Galaburda, A. M. (1985c). Cerebral lateralization.

Biological mechanisms, associations, and pathology: III. A hypothesis and a program for research. *Archives of Neurology*, 42, 634-654.

Geschwind, N., & Galaburda, A. M. (1987). *Cerebral Lateralization. Biological Mechanisms, Associations, and Pathology* . Cambridge, Massachusetts: MIT Press/Bradford Books.

Geschwind, N., & Levitsky, W. (1968). Human brain: Left-right asymmetries in temporal speech region. *Science*, 161, 186-187.

Gilissen, E. (1992). The neocortical sulci of the capuchin monkey (*Cebus*): Evidence for asymmetry in the sylvian sulcus and comparison with other primates. *Comptes Rendus de Academie des Sciences [III]., 314*, 165-170.

Goldman, P. S., Crawford, H. T., Stokes, L. P., Galkin, T. W., & Rosvold, H. E. (1974). Sex-dependent behavioral effects of cerebral cortical lesions in the developing rhesus monkey. *Science*, 186, 540-2.

Gordon, H. W. (1980). Cognitive asymmetry in dyslexic families. *Neuropsychol.*, 18, 645-656.

Gordon, H. W. (1988). The effect of "right brain/left brain" cognitive profiles on school achievement. In D. L. Molfese, & S. J. Segalowitz (Ed.), *Brain Lateralization in Children* NY: The Guilford Press.

Gualtieri, T., & Hicks, R. E. (1985). An immunoreactive theory of selective male affliction. *Behavioral and. Brain Science*, 8, 427-441.

Hall, E. D., Pazara, K. E., & Linseman, K. L. (1991). Sex differences in postischemic neuronal necrosis in gerbils. *Journal of Cerebral Blood Flow and Metabolism*, 11, 292-298.

Hanson, V. L. (1991). Phonological processing without sound. In S. A. Brady, & D. P. Shankweiler (Ed.), *Phonological Processes in Literacy- A Tribute to Isabelle Y. Liberman* (pp. 153-161). Hillsdale, NJ: Lawrence Erlbaum Associates.

Harness, B. Z., Epstein, R., & Gordon, H. W. (1984). Cognitive profile of children referred to a clinic for reading disabilities. *Journal of Learning Disabilities*,

17,

Hinshelwood, J. (1917). *Congenital Word-blindness* . London: Lewis.

Ho, K. L., Chang, C. H., Yang, S. S., & Chason, J. L. (1984). Neuropathologic findings in thanatophoric dysplasia. *Acta Neuropathologica*, 63, 218-228.

Humphreys, P., Kaufmann, W. E., & Galaburda, A. M. (1990). Developmental dyslexia in women: Neuropathological findings in three cases. *Annals of Neurology*, 28, 727-738.

Humphreys, P., Rosen, G. D., Press, D. M., Sherman, G. F., & Galaburda, A. M. (1991). Freezing lesions of the newborn rat brain: A model for cerebrocortical microgyria. *Journal of Neuropathology and Experimental Neurology*, 50, 145-160.

Hyde, L., Sherman, G. F., & Denenberg, V. H. (1996). Radial arm maze learning in BXSB mice: Effects of neocortical ectopias. *Society for Neuroscience Abstracts*, 22, 485.

Innocenti, G. M., & Berbel, P. (1991a). Analysis of an experimental cortical network: i) Architectonics of visual areas 17 and 18 after neonatal injections of ibotenic acid; similarities with human microgyria. *Journal of Neural Transplantation*, 2, 1-28.

Innocenti, G. M., & Berbel, P. (1991b). Analysis of an experimental cortical network: ii) Connections of visual areas 17 and 18 after neonatal injections of ibotenic acid. *Journal of Neural Transplantation*, 2(1), 29-54.

Ivy, G. O., & Killackey, H. P. (1982). Ontogenetic changes in the projections of neocortical neurons. *Journal of Neuroscience*, 2, 735-743.

Jenner, A. R., Galaburda, A. M., & Sherman, G. F. (1995). Connectivity of cortical ectopias in autoimmune mice. *Society for Neuroscience Abstracts*, 21, 1712.

Jorm, A. F. (1983). Specific reading retardation and working memory: a review. *Br. Journal of Psychology*, 74, 311-42.

Kaufmann, W. E., & Galaburda, A. M. (1989). Cerebrocortical

microdysgenesis in neurologically normal subjects: A histopathologic study. *Neurology*, 39, 238-244.

Kemali, M. (1983). Neuroanatomical asymmetry in the telencephalic hemispheres of the frog rana esculenta. *Neuroscience Letters.*, 37, 1-5.

Kemali, M., Guglielmotti, V., & Fiorino, L. (1990). The asymmetry of the habenular nuclei of female and male frogs in spring and in winter. *Brain Research*, 517(1-2), 251-255.

Kolb, B., Sutherland, R. J., Nonneman, A. J., & Whishaw, I. Q. (1982). Asymmetry in the cerebral hemispheres of the rat, mouse, rabbit, and cat: The right hemisphere is larger. *Experimental Neurology*, 78, 348-359.

Larsen, J., Høein, T., Lundberg, I., & Ødegaard, H. (1990). MRI evaluation of the size and symmetry of the planum temporale in adolescents with developmental dyslexia. *Brain and Language*, 39(2), 289-301.

LeMay, M., & Culebras, A. (1972). Human brain: Morphologic differences in the hemispheres demonstrable by carotid arteriography. *New England Journal of Medicine,* 287, 168-170.

Levine, D. N., Fisher, M. A., & Caviness, V. S. (1974). Porencephaly with microgyria: A pathologic study. *Acta Neuropathologica*, 29, 99-113.

Liberman, A. M., & Mattingly, I. G. (1989). A specialization for speech perception. *Science, 243*, 489-494.

Liberman, I. Y., Shankweiler, D., & Liberman, A. M. (1989). The alphabetic principle and learning to read. In D. Shankweiler, & I. Y. Liberman. (Eds.) *Phonology and Reading Disability* (pp. 1-33). NY: Michigan Press.

Liederman, J., & Flannery, K. A. (1993). Male prevalence for reading disability is found in a large sample free from ascertainment bias. *Society for Neuroscience Abstracts*, 19, 1462.

Livingstone, M., Rosen, G., Drislane, F., & Galaburda, A. (1991). Physiological and anatomical evidence for a magnocellular defect in developmental dyslexia. *Proceedings of National Academy of Science*, 88, 7943-7947.

Lovegrove, W., Garzia, R., & Nicholson, S. (1990). Experimental evidence for a transient system deficit in specific reading disability. *Journal of the American Optometric Association*, 2(2), 137-146.

Lyon, G., & Robain, O. (1967). Etude comparative des encéphalopathies circulatoires prénatales et para-natales (hydranencéphalies, porencéphalies et encéphalomalacies kystiques de la substance blanche). *Acta Neuropathologica. (Berlin)*, 9(1), 79-98.

Lyon, G. R. (1995). Toward a definition of dyslexia. *Annals of Dyslexia*, 45, 3-27.

Mann, V., Liberman, I., & Shankweiler, D. (1980). Children's memory for sentences and word strings in relation to reading ability. *Memory and Cognition*, 8(8), 4.

McManus, I. C., & Bryden, M. P. (1991). Geschwind's theory of cerebral lateralization: Developing a formal, causal model. *Psychological Bulletin.*, 110(2), 237-253.

Miller, B., Nagy, D., Finlay, B. L., Chance, B., Kobayashi, A., & Nioka, S. (1993). Consequences of reduced cerebral blood flow in brain development. I. Gross Morphology, histology, and callosal connectivity. *Experimental Neurology*, 124, 326-42.

Morgan, W. P. (1896). A case of congenital word-blindness. *Speech*, 23, 357-377.

Nicolelis, M. A. L., Chapin, J. K., & Lin, R. C. S. (1991). Thalamic plasticity induced by early whisker removal in rats. *Brain Research*, 561(2), 344-349.

Norman, M. G. (1980). Bilateral encephaloclastic lesions in a 26 week gestation fetus: Effect on neuroblast migration. *Journal of Canadian Neurology*, 7, 191-194.

Nottebohm, F. (1971). Neural lateralization of vocal control in a passerine bird. I. Song. *Journal of Experimental Zoology*, 177, 229-262.

Nottebohm, F. (1972). Neural lateralization of vocal control in a passerine bird. II. Subsong, calls, and theory of vocal learning. *Journal of Experimental Zoology.*, 179, 35-50.

Nottebohm, F. (1976). Neural lateralization of vocal control in a passerine bird. *Journal of Experimental Zoology*, 177, 229-262.

Nottebohm, F., & Nottebohm, M. E. (1976). Left hypoglossal dominance in the control of canary and white-crowned sparrow song. *Journal of Comparative Physiology*, 108, 171-192.

Nowakowski, R. S., & Sekiguchi, M. (1987). Abnormalities of granule cell dendrites and axons in the dentate gyrus of the NZB/BlNJ mouse. *Society for Neuroscience Abstracts*, 13, 1117.

O'Leary, D. D. M., Stanfield, B. B., & Cowan, W. M. (1981). Evidence that the early postnatal restriction of the cells of origin of the callosal projection is due to the elimination of axonal collaterals rather than to the death of neurons. *Brain Research*, 227, 607-617.

Olson, R., Wise, B., Conners, F., Rack, J., & Fulker, D. (1989). Specific deficits in component reading and language skills: Genetic and environmental influences. *Journal of Learning Disabilities*, 22(6), 339-348.

Ortiz Alonso, T., Navarro, M., & vila Abad, E. (1990). P300 component of the auditory event-related potentials and dyslexia. *Functional Neurology*, 5(4), 333-338.

Orton, S. T. (1925). "Word-blindness" in school children. *Archives of Neurology Psychiatry*, 14, 581-615.

Petersen, M. R., Beecher, M. D., Zoloth, S., Moody, D. B., & Stebbins, W. C. (1978). Neural lateralization of species-specific vocalizations by Japanese macaques (*macaca fuscata*). *Science*, 202, 324-327.

Pieniadz, J. M., & Naeser, M. A. (1984). Computed tomographic scan cerebral asymmetries and morphological brain asymmetries: Correlation in the same cases post mortem. *Archives of Neurology*, 41, 403-409.

Rakic, P. (1988). Specification of cerebral cortical areas. *Science*, 241, 170-176.

Raz, S., Lauterbach, M. D., Hopkins, T. L., Glogowski, B. K., & Porter, C. L. (1995). A female advantage in cognitive recovery from early cerebral insult. *Developmental Psychology*, 31, 958-966.

Rosen, G. D., & Galaburda, A. M. (1995). Neocortical dysplasia, microgyria, and porencephaly: Common etiologies? *Society for Neuroscience Abstracts*, 21, 1712.

Rosen, G. D., & Galaburda, A. M. (1996). Efferent and afferent connectivity of induced neocortical microgyria. *Society for Neuroscience Abstracts*, 22, 485.

Rosen, G. D., Press, D. M., Sherman, G. F., & Galaburda, A. M. (1992). The development of induced cerebrocortical microgyria in the rat. *Journal of Neuropathology and Experimental Neurology*, 51, 601-611.

Rosen, G. D., Sherman, G. F., & Galaburda, A. M. (1989). Interhemispheric connections differ between symmetrical and asymmetrical brain regions. *Neuroscience*, 33, 525-533.

Rosen, G. D., Sherman, G. F., & Galaburda, A. M. (1991). Ontogenesis of neocortical asymmetry: A [^{3}H]thymidine study. *Neuroscience*, 41, 779-790.

Rosen, G. D., Sherman, G. F., & Galaburda, A. M. (1993). Neuronal subtypes and anatomic asymmetry: Changes in neuronal number and cell-packing density. *Neuroscience*, 56, 833-839.

Rosen, G. D., Sherman, G. F., Mehler, C., Emsbo, K., & Galaburda, A. M. (1989). The effect of developmental neuropathology on neocortical asymmetry in New Zealand Black mice. *International Journal of Neuroscience*, 45, 247-254.

Rosen, G. D., Sherman, G. F., Richman, J. M., Stone, L. V., & Galaburda, A. M. (1992). Induction of molecular layer ectopias by puncture wounds in newborn rats and mice. *Developmental Brain Research*, 67, 285-291.

Rosen, G. D., Waters, N. S., Galaburda, A. M., & Denenberg, V. H. (1995). Behavioral consequences of neonatal injury of the neocortex. *Brain Research*, 681(1-2), 177-189.

Rubens, A. B., Mahowald, M. W., & Hutton, J. T. (1976). Asymmetry of lateral (sylvian) fissures in man. *Neurology*, 26, 620-624.

Schlaug, G., Jäncke, L., Huang, Y. X., Staiger, J. F., & Steinmetz, H. (1995). Increased corpus callosum size in musicians. *Neuropsychologia*, 33(8), 1047.

Schlaug, G., Jäncke, L., Huang, Y. X., & Steinmetz, H. (1995). In vivo evidence of structural brain asymmetry in musicians. *Science*, 267, 699-701.

Schneider, G. E. (1979). Is it really better to have your brain lesion early? A revision of the “Kennard principle”. *Neuropsychologia*, 17, 557-583.

Schneider, G. E. (1981). Early lesions and abnormal neuronal connections. *Trends Neurosciences, 4,* 187-192.

Schrott, L. M., Denenberg, V. H., Sherman, G. F., Waters, N. S., Rosen, G. D., & Galaburda, A. M. (1992). Environmental enrichment, neocortical ectopias, and behavior in the autoimmune NZB mouse. *Developmental Brain Research*, 67, 85-93.

Schwartz, J., & Tallal, P. (1980). Rate of acoustic change may underlie hemispheric specialization for speech perception. *Science*, 207, 1380-1381.

Sekiguchi, M., Shimai, K., Mariya, M., & Nowakowski, R. S. (1991). Abnormalities of foliation and neuronal position in the cerebellum of NZB/BINJ mouse. *Developmental Brain Research*, 64, 189-195.

Shankweiler, D., & Crain, S. (1986). Language mechanisms and reading disorder: A modular approach. *Cognition*, 24, 139-168.

Shankweiler, D., Crain, S., Katz, L., Fowler, A. E., Liberman, A. M., Brady, S. A., Thornton, R., Lundquist, E., Dreyer, L., Fletcher, J. M., Stuebing, K. K., Shaywitz, S. E., & Shaywitz, B. A. (1995). Cognitive profiles of reading-disabled children: Comparison of language skills in phonology, morphology, and syntax.

Psychological Science, 6(3), 149-156.

Shaywitz, B., Fletcher, J., & Shaywitz, S. (1994). A conceptual framework for learning disabilities and attention-deficit/ hyperactivity disorder. *Canadian Journal of Special Education*, 9(3), 1-16.

Shaywitz, S., Shaywitz, B., Fletcher, J., & Escobar, M. (1990). Prevalence of reading disability in boys and girls. *Journal of American Medical A*ssociation, 264, 998-1002.

Sherman, G. F., Galaburda, A. M., Behan, P. O., & Rosen, G. D. (1987). Neuroanatomical anomalies in autoimmune mice. *Acta Neuropathologica (Berlin)*, 74, 239-242.

Sherman, G. F., Galaburda, A. M., & Geschwind, N. (1985). Cortical anomalies in brains of New Zealand mice: A neuropathologic model of dyslexia? *Proceedings of National Academy of Sciences (USA)*, 82, 8072-8074.

Sherman, G. F., Garbanati, J. A., Rosen, G. D., Yutzey, D. A., & Denenberg, V. H. (1980). Brain and behavioral asymmetries for spatial preference in rats. *Brain Research*, 192, 61-67.

Sherman, G. F., Morrison, L., Rosen, G. D., Behan, P. O., & Galaburda, A. M. (1990). Brain abnormalities in immune defective mice. *Brain Research*, 532, 25-33.

Sherman, G. F., Rosen, G. D., & Galaburda, A. M. (1988). Neocortical anomalies in autoimmune mice: A model for the developmental neuropathology seen in the dyslexic brain. *Drug Development and Research*, 15, 307-314.

Sherman, G. F., Rosen, G. D., Stone, L. V., Press, D. M., & Galaburda, A. M. (1992). The organization of radial glial fibers in spontaneous neocortical ectopias of newborn New-Zealand black mice. *Developmental Brain Research.*, 67, 279-283.

Sherman, G. F., Stone, J. S., Press, D. M., Rosen, G. D., & Galaburda, A. M. (1990). Abnormal architecture and connections disclosed by neurofilament staining in the cerebral cortex of autoimmune mice. *Brain Research*, 529, 202-207.

Sherman, G. F., Stone, J. S., Rosen, G. D., & Galaburda, A. M. (1990). Neocortical VIP neurons are increased in the hemisphere containing focal cerebrocortical microdysgenesis in New Zealand Black Mice. *Brain Research*, 532, 232-236.

Sherman, G. F., Stone, L. V., Denenberg, V. H., & Beier, D. R. (1994). A genetic analysis of neocortical ectopias in New Zealand Black mice. *NeuroReport*, 5, 721-724.

Sherman, G. F., Stone, L. V., Walthour, N. R., Boehm, G. W., Denenberg, V. H., Rosen, G. D., & Galaburda, A. M. (1992). Birthdates of neurons in neocortical ectopias of New Zealand Black mice. *Society for Neuroscience Abstracts*, 18, 1446A.

Siegel, L., Share, D., & Esther, G. (1995). Evidence for superior orthographic skills in dyslexia. *Psychological Science*, 6, 250-254.

Siegel, L. S., & Ryan, E. B. (1988). Development of grammatical-sensitivity, phonological, and short-term memory skills in normally achieving and learning disabled children. *Developmental Psychology*, 24, 28-37.

Siegel, L. S., & Ryan, E. B. (1989). The development of working memory in normally achieving and subtypes of learning disabled children. *Child Development*, 60, 973-80.

Slaghuis, W. L., Lovegrove, W. J., & Davidson, J. A. (1993). Visual and language processing deficits are concurrent in dyslexia. *Cortex*, 29, 601-615.

Smith, S. T., Macaruso, P., Shankweiler, D., & Crain, S. (1989). Syntactic comprehension in young poor readers. *Applied Psycholinguistics*, 10, 429-454.

Sohrabji, F., Greene, L. A., Miranda, R. C., & Toran-Allerand, C. D. (1994). Reciprocal regulation of estrogen and NGF receptors by their ligands in PC12 cells. *Journal of Neurobiology*, 25, 974-88.

Sohrabji, F., Miranda, R. C., & Toran-Allerand, C. D. (1994). Estrogen differentially regulates estrogen and nerve growth factor receptor mRNAs in adult sensory neurons. *Journal of Neuroscience*, 14, 459-71.

Springer, S. P., & Deutsch, G. (1993). *Left Brain, Right Brain* (4 ed.). New York: W.H. Freeman and Company.

Steinmetz, H., Rademacher, J., Huang, Y. X., Hefter, H., Zilles, K., Thron, A., & Freund, H. J. (1989). Cerebral asymmetry - MR planimetry of the human planum temporale. *Journal of Computer-Assisted Tomography*, 13, 996-1005.

Steinmetz, H., Volkmann, J., Jäncke, L., & Freund, H. J. (1991). Anatomical left-right asymmetry of language-related temporal cortex is different in left-handers and right-handers. *Annals of Neurology*, 29, 315-319.

Stewart, J., & Kolb, B. (1988). The effects of neonatal gonadectomy and prenatal stress on cortical thickness and asymmetry in rats. *Behavioral and Neural Biology*, 49, 344-360.

Suzuki, M., & Choi, B. H. (1991). Repair and reconstruction of the cortical plate following closed cryogenic injury to the neonatal rat cerebrum. *Acta Neuropathologica (Berlin)*, 82, 93-101.

Swanson, H. L. (1993). Working memory in learning disability subgroups. *Journal of Experimental Child Psychology*, 56, 87-114.

Swanson, H. L., Cochran, K. F., & Ewers, C. A. (1989). Working memory in skilled and less skilled readers. *Journal of Abnormal Child Psychology*, 17, 145-56.

Tallal, P., Miller, S., & Fitch, R. H. (1993). Neurobiological basis of speech: a case for the preeminence of temporal processing. In P. Tallal, A. M. Galaburda, R. Llinas, & C. von Euler (Ed.), *Temporal Information Processing in the Nervous System, with Special Reference to Dyslexia and Dysphasia* (pp. 27-47). New York: New York Academy of Sciences.

Tallal, P., & Piercy, M. (1973). Defects of non-verbal auditory perception in children with developmental aphasia. *Nature*, 241, 468-469.

Teszner, D., Tzavaras, A., Gruner, J., & Hécaen, H. (1972). L'asymmétrie droite-gauche du planum temporale: A propos de l'étude anatomique de 100 cervaeux. *Revue Neurologique (Paris)*, 126, 444-449.

Torgesen, J. K. (1991). Cross-age consistency in phonological processing. In S. A. Brady, & D. P. Shankweiler (Ed.), *Phonological Processes in Literacy- A Tribute to Isabelle Y. Liberman* (pp. 187-193). Hillsdale, NJ: Lawrence Erlbaum Associates.

Vota-Pinardi, U., & Kemali, M. (1990). Neuroelectrophysiology of the morphologically asymmetric habenulae of the frog. *Comarative Biochemistry and Physiology*, 96A(3), 421-424.

Wada, J. A., Clarke, R., & Hamm, A. (1975). Cerebral hemispheric asymmetry in humans. *Archives of Neurology*, 32, 239-246.

Walsh, C., & Cepko, C. L. (1992). Widespread dispersion of neuronal clones across functional regions of the cerebral cortex. *Science*, 255, 434-440.

Walsh, C., & Cepko, C. L. (1993). Clonal dispersion in proliferative layers of developing cerebral cortex. *Nature*, 362, 632-635.

Waters, N., Sherman, G. F., Rosen, G. D., Galaburda, A. M., & Denenberg, V. H. (In press). Effects of cortical ectopias on spatial delayed-matching-to-sample performance on BXSB mice. *Behavioral Brain Research,*

Weiskrantz, L. (1977). On the role of cerebral commissures in animals. In I. S. Russell, M. W. van Hof, & G. Berlucchi (Ed.), *Structure and Function of Cerebral Commissures* (pp. 475-478). Baltimore: University Park Press.

Williams, M. C., & Lecluyse, K. (1990). Perceptual consequences of a temporal processing deficit in reading disabled children. *Journal of American Optometry Association*, 61, 111-121.

Williams, M. C., May, J. G., Solman, R., & Zhou, H. (1995). The effects of spatial filtering and contrast reduction on visual search times in good and poor readers. *Vision Research*, 35, 285-291.

Witelson, S. F. (1985). The brain connection: The corpus callosum is larger in left handers. *Science*, 229, 665-668.

Witelson, S. F. (1989). Hand and sex differences in the isthmus and genu of the human corpus callosum. A postmortem morphological study. *Brain*, 112, 779-835.

Witelson, S. F., & Kigar, D. L. (1992). Sylvian fissure morphology and asymmetry in men and women: Bilateral differences in relation to handedness in men. *Journal of Comparative Neurology.*, 323, 326-340.

Witelson, S. F., & Nowakowski, R. S. (1991). Left out axons make men right: A hypothesis for the origin of handedness and functional asymmetry. *Neuropsychologia*, 29, 327-333.

Witelson, S. F., & Pallie, W. (1973). Left hemisphere specialization for language in the newborn: Neuroanatomical evidence of asymmetry. *Brain*, 96, 641-646.

Yeni-Komshian, G. H., & Benson, D. A. (1976). Anatomical study of cerebral asymmetry in the temporal lobe of humans, chimpanzees, and rhesus monkeys. *Science*, 192, 387-389.

The Other Side of the Error Term - N. Raz (Editor)

Chapter 3
ELECTROPHYSIOLOGICAL CORRELATES OF EARLY SPEECH PERCEPTION AND LANGUAGE DEVELOPMENT DURING INFANCY AND EARLY CHILDHOOD

Dennis L. Molfese
Southern Illinois University

ABSTRACT

It is logical to contend that early phonetic discrimination skills have direct relevance to later language development. Infants who experience difficulty in discriminating phonetic contrasts are more at risk for lower levels of later language development (Molfese & Molfese, 1985; 1997; Molfese & Searock, 1986). Moreover, this point is further supported by the fact that studies investigating some types of language related disabilities, as in the case of reading disabilities or learning disabilities, have generally indicated that these children and adults share a phonological deficit (see Lyon, 1994). The following review focuses on studies utilizing a number of paradigms conducted over the past 3 decades which indicate that event related potentials (ERPs) are sensitive to phonetic variations (Kraus, et al., 46; Molfese, 67; Molfese, et al., 72; Molfese and Molfese, 78, 79, 81, 82) and early word acquisition (Molfese, 1989, 1990; Molfese, Morse, & Peters, 1990; Molfese, Wetzel, & Gill, 1994). This review will focus on electrophysiological studies used to study phonetic discrimination abilities in young infants and children.

Infants shortly after birth, if not at birth, can discriminate many aspects of their environment, including speech sounds (Molfese, 1972; Molfese, Freeman, & Palermo, 1975; Molfese & Molfese, 1979; 1980; 1985; 1997) in a manner similar to that performed by adults (see Molfese & Betz, 1988, for a review). Both behavioral (Eimas, Sequeland, Juscyk, & Vigorito, 1971) and electrophysiological studies (Molfese, 1978; Molfese & Hess, 1978) note marked parallels in response patterns across two very different domains - behavior and brain responses. Yet, while such abilities may be present at birth, it is equally clear that these skills and the brain mechanisms which subserve them develop further over time and are modified by the environment.

Early research into infant speech perception investigated simple phonetic contrasts and generally demonstrated that even very young infants could discriminate a variety of consonant differences (Eimas et al, 1971; Moffitt, 1971; Morse, 1972, Trehub, 1973). Subsequent research expanded on this theme and noted that discrimination of speech sounds occurred independent of a variety of factors associated with the speaker's voice such as intonation and speech rate (Kuhl, 1983). While infants' ability to discriminate some speech contrasts improves with age (Kuhl, 1991), their ability to discriminate other speech contrasts that characterize non-native speech contrasts declines (Best, 1991; Werker & Tees, 1984).

It appears that such early speech perception abilities may be related to other later emerging cognitive skills including language. Infants who experience difficulty in discriminating phonetic contrasts appear more at risk for lower levels of later language development (Molfese & Molfese, 1985; 1997; Molfese & Searock, 1986).

The following review focuses on studies of infants conducted over the lpast three decades. These studies utilizing a number of paradigms indicate that event related potentials (ERPs) can be used to measure the infant's ability to discriminate phonetic variations (Molfese and Molfese, 1979, 1980, 1985) and early words (Molfese, 1989, 1990; Molfese, Morse, & Peters, 1990; Molfese, Wetzel, & Gill, 1994). Attention will be paid to similarities in cortical event related brain potentials (ERPs) elicited during speech perception and early word processing with the hope of identifying whether there are patterns of similarities in their development. First, however, we need to describe the research method used to study early phonetic and linguistic development in infants and young children.

Event Related Potentials. One procedure that has recently proven useful in studying this problem involves the recording from the scalp of an auditory

ERP. The ERP is a synchronized portion of the ongoing EEG pattern that is time-locked to the onset of some event in the subject's environment. It is usually represented as a complex waveform that reflects changes in the amplitude and frequency of electrical activity over time. Such waveforms are thought to reflect changes in brain activity via fluctuations in the amplitude or height of the wave at different points in its time course (Callaway, Tueting, & Koslow, 1978). The ERP, because of this time-locked feature, has been shown more likely to reflect both general and specific aspects of the evoking stimulus (Molfese, 1978a, 1978b) and the individual's perceptions and decisions regarding the stimulus (Molfese, 1983; Nelson & Salapatek 1986; Ruchkin, Sutton, Munson, Silver, & Macar, 1981).

The ERP technique appears to be particularly well suited for the neuropsychological study of the infant's development of speech perception and word comprehension, given its previous successes in investigations of infant speech perception (Molfese, 1972; Molfese, Freeman, & Palermo, 1975; Molfese & Molfese, 1979, 1980, 1985; see Molfese & Betz, 1988, for a review of this literature) and semantic comprehension in older children and adults (Begleiter & Platz, 1969; Brown, Marsh, & Smith, 1979; Chapman, McCrary, Bragdon, & Chapman, 1979; Molfese, 1979; Molfese, 1985; Molfese, Morris, & Romski, 1990).

Phonetic Discriminations and ERPs. Molfese and his colleagues undertook a series of studies to study the development of neuroelectrical responses to speech cues from infancy (Molfese & Molfese, 1979a, 1979b,1980) into childhood and adulthood (Molfese, 1978a, 1978b, 1980a, 1980b; Molfese & Hess, 1978; Molfese & Schmidt, 1983; Molfese, 1984). In these studies, given the association between language skills and left hemisphere activity, one additional question focused on whether such brain responses to speech sounds were in fact lateralized early in development. In addressing these questions, Molfese and his colleagues concentrated their efforts on two speech cues that had received a great deal of attention from researchers using behavioral techniques over the previous 30 years, voice onset time (VOT) and place of articulation (POA).

Voice Onset Time Studies

Previous researchers identified VOT, the temporal relationship between laryngeal pulsing and the onset of consonant release, as an important cue for the perceived distinction between voiced and voiceless forms of stop consonants such as b and p (Liberman, Cooper, Shankweiler, & Studdert-Kennedy, 1967). Adult listeners appear to discriminate a variety of speech sounds by the phonetic labels attached to them as evidenced by the fact that adults readily discriminate between consonants from different phonetic categories, such as [ba] and [pa], while they perform at only chance levels when attempting to discriminate between two different [ba] sounds that differ acoustically to the same extent as the [ba-pa] difference (Lisker & Abramson, 1970). This pattern of discrimination for *between phonetic category contrasts* while chance levels of discrimination are noted for *within-category contrasts* is referred to as "categorical perception". Studies with infants (Eimas et al., 1971; Eilers, Gavin, & Wilson, 1980), children (Streeter, 1976), and adult listeners (Lisker & Abramson, 1970) repeatedly have demonstrated that many populations exhibit categorical perception and discrimination for a wide range of contrasts such as voicing (*ba, pa; ga, ka*) and place of articulation (*ba, da, ga*).

While we already knew from Eimas et al. (1971) that young infants appeared to have categorical perception for stop consonants, little was known regarding how the brain responded to these sounds and how such responses changed across development. Molfese (1978b), in a follow-up to work by

Dorman (1974), provided the first evidence that speech cues such as VOT could elicit different ERP responses. To accomplish this, Molfese recorded ERPs from the left and right temporal regions of 16 adults during a phoneme identification task. Adults were presented with randomly ordered sequences of synthesized bilabial stop consonants with VOT values of +0 ms, +20 ms, +40 ms, and +60 ms. In the +0 ms case, the onset of consonant release and vocal fold vibration occurred simultaneously, whereas in the +60 ms condition the onset of laryngeal pulsing was delayed for 60 ms following consonant release. ERPs were recorded in response to each sound and then, after a brief delay, adults pressed a series of keys to identify the consonant sound. Two regions of the ERP (one component centered around 135 ms and the second occurring between 300 and 500 ms following stimulus onset) did change systematically as a function of the consonants phonetic category. Stop consonant sounds with VOT values of +0 and +20 ms (sounds identified as ba) were discriminated from those with VOT values of +40 and +60 ms (sounds identified as pa). However, the ERPs did not discriminate between the sounds from within the same category. Thus, there were no differences in the waveforms between the 0 and +20 ms sounds or between the +40 and +60 ms sounds.

This pattern of responding resembled what Lisker and Abramson called categorical discrimination. That is, the ERPs could discriminate between sounds from different phonetic categories but not between sounds from the same phonetic category. Electrophysiological studies employing similar stimuli with a variety of different populations have replicated this finding (Molfese & Hess, 1978; Molfese & Molfese, 1979b; Molfese, 1980a Molfese & Molfese, 1988). Surprisingly, however, in all these studies at least one region of the ERP in which this categorical discrimination effect was noted across the different age groups occurred over the RIGHT temporal region. This sense of surprise comes from the expectation that such speech sound discrimination effects would be expected to be left hemisphere in origin since the left hemisphere, not the right, is usually associated with language functions (Lenneberg, 1967).

Similar effects were noted with 4 year old children in a study involving the velar stop consonants, k and g. Molfese and Hess (1978) recorded ERPs from the left and right temporal scalp regions of 12 preschool-age children (mean age = 4 years, 5 months) in response to randomly ordered series of synthesized consonant-vowel syllables in which the initial consonant varied in VOT from +0 ms, to +20 ms, to +40 ms, to +60 ms. Analyses of the ERPs, they, like Molfese (1978b), also found a categorical discrimination effect whereby one late-occurring portion of the waveform (peak latency = 444 ms) changed systematically in response to consonants from different phonetic categories but did not respond differentially to consonants from within the same phonetic category. As in the case of Molfese (1978b), this effect occurred over the right hemisphere. Unlike the adult study by Molfese, however, they found a second portion of the auditory ERP that occurred earlier in the waveform (peak latencies = 198 and 342 ms), before this right hemisphere effect, and which was detected by electrodes placed over both hemispheres. This earlier occurring auditory ERP component also discriminated the voiced from the voiceless consonants in a categorical manner. Similar results have recently been reported by Molfese and Molfese (1988) with 3 year old children.

This work was later extended to include newborn and older infants (Molfese & Molfese, 1979a). In work with newborn infants, Molfese and Molfese presented the four consonant-vowel syllables used by Molfese (1978b) to 16 infants between 2 and 5 months of age (mean = 3 months, 25 days). ERPs were again recorded from the left and right temporal locations. Analyses revealed that one portion or component of the auditory ERP, recorded from over the right hemisphere approximately 920 ms following stimulus onset, discriminated between the different speech sounds in a categorical manner. As in the case of Molfese and Hess, they also noted a second portion of the auditory ERP that was present over both hemispheres and that also discriminated between the consonant sounds categorically. The major portion of this component occurred 528 ms following stimulus onset. These results, then, paralleled the findings of Molfese and Hess in noting two portions of the auditory ERP that discriminated between the speech sounds categorically. These included a bilateral component that occurred first in the waveform, followed by a right hemisphere lateralized component that occurred later in time and also discriminated between the sounds categorically.

A second experiment described by Molfese and Molfese (1979a) failed to note any such bilateral or right hemisphere lateralized effects with 16 newborn infants under 48 hours of age. A subsequent study by Simos and Molfese (1997) with 16 newborn infants using nonspeech auditory stimuli (TOT) which mimicked the temporal delays of the speech stop consonant voiced vs. voiceless distinction, did find categorical discrimination effects at both the N200 and N530 negative peaks over parietal electrode sites. Both effects were found with baseline-to-peak measures as well as with the PCA-ANOVA measures. Simos and Molfese interpreted these results to indicate that the "temporal voicing cue used in speech perception may have an innate basis" (p. 89). This work is summarized in Table 1.

One discrepancy between the adult study of Molfese (1978b) and the studies with children (Molfese & Hess, 1978; Molfese & Molfese, 1988) and infants (Molfese & Molfese, 1979a) concerns the absence of a bilateral effect with the adult population studied by Molfese. At first it was speculated that such a bilateral effect might drop out with further maturation and development.

However, a subsequent study with adults (Molfese, 1980a), suggests that the bilateral effect remains in adults but that the area in which this effect can be noted is more restricted. The difference, then, between the two age groups could be due to the shrinking size of the electrical fields over which the effect can be detected. As individuals mature, the scalp potentials become more and more differentiated, with more differences in electrical activity noted between even closely adjacent electrode sites.

TABLE 1.

Voice Onset Time

Study	Age	Latency	Categorical Discrimination
Infant Studies			
Molfese & Molfese, 1979	Newborn	N528, P920	None
Simos & Molfese, 1997	Newborn	N200, N530	Bilateral N200 & N530 Parietal
Molfese & Molfese, 1979	2 mo.	N528, P920	RH P920 Bilateral N528
Child Studies			
Molfese & Hess, 1978	4 yrs.	N198, N444	Bilateral N198 RH N444
Molfese & Molfese, 1988	3 yrs.	N180, N400	Bilateral N180 RH N400
Non-human Studies			
Morse et al, 1987	1 yr.	P150-N250 N340-450	RH Temporal RH N340-450
Adams, Molfese, & Betz, 1987	1 yr.	50-180, 230	RH Temporal & Parietal N50-180

RH = Right hemisphere
LH = Left hemisphere

Molfese (1980a) conducted a second study with adults to determine whether the laterality effects noted for the VOT stimuli were elicited by only speech stimuli or whether similar electrophysiological effects could be noted for both speech and nonspeech sounds. Such a comparison would allow conclusions to be reached regarding similarities in mechanisms which subserve the perception of auditory stimuli with similar temporal delays (+0-, +20-. +40-, +60-ms). If the right hemisphere and bilateral categorical effects occurred for nonspeech stimuli containing comparable temporal delays, it would be clear that such effects must be due to the temporal nature of the cues rather than to their "speech-like" quality. In this study, Molfese recorded ERPs were recorded from 16 adults to four "tone onset time" (TOT) stimuli. These TOT stimuli were obtained from Pisoni (1977). The TOT stimuli were 230 ms in duration and consisted of two simultaneously occurring tones which differed from each other in the onset of the lower frequency tone (500 Hz) relative to the higher frequency tone (1500 Hz). The lower tone began at the same time as the upper tone for the 0-ms TOT stimulus but lagged behind the upper tone by 20 ms for the +20-ms TOT stimulus. This delay increased to 40 ms and 60 ms, respectively, for the +40- and +60-ms TOT stimuli. Both tones ended simultaneously.

Analyses indicated that one region of the auditory ERP centered around 330 ms and common to electrodes placed over the temporal, central, and parietal regions of the right hemisphere categorically discriminated the +0- and +20-ms TOT sounds from the +40- and +60-ms sounds. However, no comparable changes were noted over the left hemisphere at this latency. Bilateral responses were noted earlier in time from the left and right parietal regions 145 ms following stimulus onset and over the central areas at 210 ms. Interestingly, these bilateral effects were detected by electrodes placed over regions that were not sampled in the original Molfese (1978b) study. Thus, the lack of bilateral effects in the original study appears to result from the use of a more restricted sampling of electrical activity. Consequently, as in the case of the infant and child studies, processing of the temporal cue appeared to involve both bilateral responses which occurred earlier in time, followed by later occurring right hemisphere lateralized responses. Further evidence that the TOT stimuli tap identical mechanisms engaged by the VOT sounds comes from the work by Molfese and Molfese (1988). As noted earlier, they recorded ERPs from three-year-old children to both the VOT stimuli used by Molfese and Hess and the TOT stimuli of Molfese (1980a). They found that both stimulus sets produced identical right hemisphere responses. It appears, then, that these changes noted in the ERP are indeed the result of responses to temporal delays rather than to some general "speech" quality per se.

Animal studies in which ERPs have been recorded to these types of stimuli have generally noted right hemisphere effects for rhesus monkeys (Morse, Molfese, Laughlin, Linnville, & Wetzel, 1987) as well as border collies (Adams, Molfese, & Betz, 1987). Morse et al. recorded ERPs from left and right temporal and parietal electrodes to the same four VOT stimuli employed by Molfese (1978b) from 15 Rhesus Monkeys with mean age of 1 yr. Analyses of a significant VOT × Electrodes × Hemisphere interaction indicated two RH effects. First, between 150 and 250 ms in the Control group a larger RH Positive 150 and Negative 250 peaks occurred for the 40- and 60-ms VOT sounds than for the 0- and 20-ms sounds.

Second, the RH temporal site between 340 and 450 ms also discriminated the 0- and 20-ms sounds from the 40- and 60-ms consonants but did not discriminate within either voicing category. This was reflected in the ERP as a larger negative to positive shift for 40- and 60- ms stimuli. Thus, these response resembled those reported earlier for a number of human infant, child, and adult studies. Other animal studies have also reported a right hemisphere categorical effect. Adams et al. found a VOT× Electrodes interaction for the negative peak which occurred between 50 and 180 ms. This effect reflected a right hemisphere (RH) Temporal and Parietal response which discriminated the voiced from the voiceless stop consonants but which failed to discriminate within a consonant voicing category. In contrast, the left hemisphere (LH) Temporal and Parietal sites discriminated both between as well as within each voicing category.

Although the right hemisphere discrimination of the VOT cue seems paradoxical in light of arguments that language processes are carried out primarily by the left hemisphere, two developments address this issue. First, clinical studies of VOT suggest that VOT may be discriminated, if not exclusively, then at least in part, by the right hemisphere (for a review of this literature, see Molfese, Molfese, & Parsons, 1983, or Simos, Molfese, & Brenden, 1997). For example, Miceli, Caltagirone, Gainotti, and Payer-Rigo (1978), using a nondichotic pair presentation task, noted that the left brain-damaged aphasic group made fewest errors with stimuli differing in voicing but not place of articulation. Blumstein, Baker, and Goodglass (1977) also noted fewer errors for voicing contrasts than for place contrasts with left hemisphere damaged Wernicke aphasics. Finally, Perecman and Kellar (1981), based on their own findings that left hemisphere damaged patients continue to match sounds on the basis of voicing but not place, speculated that voicing could be processed by either hemisphere but that the POA cue was more likely to be processed by only the left hemisphere. Second, the electrophysiological studies of Molfese and his colleagues point to several regions of the brain that appear responsive to voicing contrasts.

Three general findings have emerged from this series of temporal discrimination studies involving VOT and TOT studies. First, the discrimination of the temporal delay cue common to voiced and voiceless stop consonants can be detected by electrophysiological measures - specifically, the ERPs recorded from electrodes placed on the scalp over the two hemispheres. Second, from at least 2 months of age, if not before, the infant's brain appears capable of discriminating voiced from voiceless stop consonants in a categorical manner. Third, categorical discrimination across different ages appears to be carried out first by bilaterally represented mechanisms within both hemispheres and then, somewhat later in time, by right hemisphere lateralized mechanisms.

Place of Articulation (POA) Studies

In addition to studies of VOT, a number of studies with infants and adults investigated the correlates of acoustic and phonetic cues important to the perception of a second cue important for speech perception, place of articulation or POA (Molfese, 1978a, 1980b, 1984; Molfese, Buhrke, & Wang, 1985; Molfese, Linnville, Wetzel, & Leicht, 1985; Molfese & Schmidt, 1983; Molfese & Molfese, 1979b, 1980, 1985). As in the case of the VOT temporal cue, these studies of the POA cue which monitored electrical activity from multiple electrode regions, identified both lateralized and bilateral hemisphere responses that discriminated between the different consonant sounds. Furthermore, such discriminations were present from birth. There were some important differences, however, both in the development of ERP responses to the POA cue and in the character of the lateralized responses, which distinguished the perception of this cue from that for VOT. These studies are summarized in Table 2.

In the first study in this series, Molfese (1978a) attempted to isolate the neuroelectrical correlates of the second formant transition, the cue to which listeners attend in order to discriminate between different consonant sounds which are formed in different portions or places within the vocal tract. In this study, he presented a series of consonant-vowel syllables in which the stop consonants varied in POA, formant structure, and phonetic transition characteristics. Changes in the POA cue signaled either the consonants b or g. The formant structure variable referred to two sets of sounds, one set consisted of nonspeech sounds that contained formants composed of sinewaves 1 Hz in bandwidth whereas a second set of speech sounds contained formants with speech-like formant bandwidths of 60, 90, and 120 Hz for formants 1 through 3, respectively. The phonetic transition cue referred to two stimulus properties in which one stimulus set contained formant transitions that normally characterize human speech patterns while the second set contained an unusual pattern not found in the initial consonant position in human speech patterns.

TABLE 2.

Place of Articulation

Infant Studies			
Study	**Age**	**Latency**	**Place of Articulation**
Molfese & Molfese, 1980	Preterm	848	LH N848
Molfese & Molfese, 1979	Newborn	192, 630	LH N192 Bilateral N630
Molfese, Burger-Judisch, & Hans, 1991	Newborn	210	LH Females: N210 Frontal & Parietal
Molfese & Molfese, 1985	Newborn	168, 664	LH N168 Bilateral N664
Dahaene-Lambert & Dahaene, 1994	3 mo.	220, 390	ba response differed from ga LH > RH over parietal sites

RH = Right hemisphere
LH = Left hemisphere

Auditory ERP responses were recorded from the left and right temporal regions of 10 adults in response to randomly ordered series of consonant-vowel syllables that varied in consonant place of articulation, bandwidth, and phonetic transition quality. Two regions of the auditory ERP that peaked at 70 and 300 ms following stimulus onset discriminated consonant phonetic transition quality and place of articulation only over the left hemisphere temporal electrode site. As in the case of Molfese (1978b) who also used only a single left hemisphere temporal site, no bilateral place discrimination was noted. Similar left hemisphere POA discrimination effects were noted by Molfese (1980b), Molfese & Schmidt (1983), and Molfese, 1984, with the exception that, with the inclusion of auditory ERP data collected from more electrode recording sites over each hemisphere, consistent discrimination of the place cues were noted for both hemispheres (bilateral effects).

Several general findings from these adult studies can be noted. In the case of the adult studies reviewed to this point, when multiple electrode sites are employed, bilateral stimulus discrimination effects are usually found. Furthermore, these bilateral effects invariably occur early in the waveform and prior to the onset of the lateralized POA discrimination responses. This temporal relationship between bilateral and lateralized effects also can be noted in the VOT studies. Finally, in addition to stimulus related hemisphere effects, portions of the ERPs vary between hemispheres that are unrelated to stimulus, task, or subject features. Apparently, during the discrimination process both hemispheres initially discriminate between POA and VOT stimuli at the same time, somewhere approximately 100 ms following stimulus onset. Shortly afterwards, at approximately 300 ms following stimulus onset, the left hemisphere discriminates between differences in the POA cue, while the right hemisphere at approximately 400 ms discriminates the VOT or temporal offset cue. Finally, throughout this time period and afterwards there are brief periods of ERP activity during which the two hemispheres appear to be doing quite different things, which may be unrelated to the discrimination of the stimuli.

In a replication and extension of these POA findings, subsequent work with newborn and young infants, Molfese and Molfese (1979b) noted similar patterns of lateralized and bilateral responses. Unlike findings for VOT, however, POA discrimination are consistently found to be present at birth. In this study, ERPs were recorded from the left and right temporal regions (T3 and T4) referred to linked ear references of 16 full term newborn human infants within 2 days of birth. These data were recorded while the infants were presented series of consonant-vowel syllables that differed in the second formant transition (F2, which signaled the place of articulation information), and formant bandwidth. As with adults, one auditory ERP component that appeared only over the left hemisphere recording site discriminated between the two consonant sounds when they contained normal speech formant characteristics (peak latency = 192 ms). A second region of the auditory ERP varied systematically over both hemispheres and also discriminated between the two speech-like consonant sounds (peak latency = 630 ms).

In a replication and extension of this work, Molfese and Molfese (1985) presented a series of consonant-vowel syllables that varied in POA and formant structure. Two different consonant sounds, b, g, combined with three different vowel sounds were presented with speech or nonspeech formant structures. ERPs were again recorded from the left and right temporal regions (T3, T4). As in the case of Molfese and Molfese (1979b), analyses identified two regions of the auditory ERP that discriminated POA differences. One region, with a peak latency of 168 ms, was detected only over the left hemisphere site as discriminating between the two different consonant sounds; a second region with a peak latency of 664 ms, discriminated this POA difference and was detected by electrodes placed over both hemispheres.

The lateralized effect noted for infants in the Molfese series of infant studies for the POA cue occurred BEFORE that for the bilateral effect, a finding opposite to that noted for adults studied under similar circumstances. However, the reversal of the temporal relationship between the bilateral and lateralized responses appears to be a legitimate one, given that virtually identical results were found by Molfese and Molfese (1985) and Molfese and Molfese (1979b) with different populations of infants and somewhat different stimulus sets that contained the POA variable. This temporal pattern of initial lateralized responses followed by bilateral responses is opposite to that noted previously for both VOT and POA cues for adults as well as that found for infants exposed to changes in the VOT/temporal cue. Clearly, such differences in the ERP effects suggest that different mechanisms subserve the perception and discrimination of the different speech related cues. A replication and extension of this work which involved recorded ERPs from 6 scalp locations of 38 newborn infants to a somewhat different stimulus set reported comparable effects at similar latencies (Molfese, Burger-Judisch, & Hans, 1992). Unlike the VOT studies, these show a relatively stable pattern of development from infancy into adulthood (Gelfer, 1987; Molfese, 1978b, 1980b, 1984; Molfese, Buhrke, & Wang, 1985, Molfese, Linnville, Wetzel, & Leicht, 1985; Molfese & Schmidt,, 1983; Molfese & Molfese, 1979, 1980, 1985). These effects have also been replicated independently by other laboratories (Gelfer, 1987; Segalowitz & Cohen, 1989).

The relationship between lateralized and bilateral responses are not clear at this time. It does appear, however, that the bilateral response may develop after the lateralized ones, both ontogenetically as well as phylogenetically. For example, Molfese and Molfese (1980) noted only the presence of left hemisphere lateralized responses in 11 preterm infants born on average 35.9 weeks postconception. Stimuli identical to those employed in Molfese (1978a) with adults were presented to these infants while ERPs were recorded from the left- (T3) and right hemisphere (T4) temporal regions. As was found with full-term infants (Molfese & Molfese, 1979a), a portion of the auditory ERP recorded from over the left hemisphere with a peak latency at 848 ms discriminated between speech stimuli containing different consonant transition cues. An additional left hemisphere component with a peak latency of 608 ms differentiated only between the nonphonetic consonants, a finding similar to that reported by Molfese (1978a) with adults, with the exception that adults were sensitive to both phonetic and nonphonetic contrasts.

One study by Dehaene-Lambert and Dehaene (1994) also noted a POA effect in infants at 3 months of age. They tested a group of 16 infants, recording ERP activity from a series of 58 scalp electrodes to ba and ga syllables. Two conditions were used. A repeated trials condition in which a standard sound was repeated five times and a deviant trial condition in which the standard was repeated four times, followed by one instance of a different syllable. Consonant discrimination changes were noted at one peak of the ERP, at 390 ms which declined in amplitude as the standard stimulus was presented and then increased in amplitude with the presentation of the different syllable. Thus, the ERPs detected a difference in the speech sounds and recovered in amplitude in contrast to repetitions of the same stimulus which resulted in further decreases in amplitude. They also noted a moderate LH asymmetry for this peak over posterior electrode sites.

Two separate studies with one-year-old infant rhesus monkeys, one in which POA perception was studied (Molfese, Laughlin, Morse, Linnville, Wetzel, & Erwin, 1986), and one in which VOT was studied (Morse, Molfese, Laughlin, Linnville, & Wetzel, 1987), found left and right lateralized categorical discrimination responses, respectively, but no bilateral responses. A recent VOT discrimination study with two breeds of dogs, 2 month old collies and beagles, also noted a right hemisphere lateralized categorical discrimination response but no bilateral one (Adams, Molfese, & Betz, 1987). Given the absence of the bilateral response in nonhuman primates and other mammals, it may be possible that it is the bilateral response that discriminates humans from other organisms in the perception of speech cues, not, as has been usually argued, the lateralized mechanisms.

On the basis of these electrophysiological data, it appears that brain responses to speech materials from infancy into adulthood are multidimensional and that they develop in a dynamic fashion. First, it is clear that discrimination of different speech cues emerge at different times in early development. This is true from both the standpoint of behavioral research (Eimas, et al., 1971) as well as ERP research (Molfese & Molfese, 1979a, 1979b, 1985, 1997). For example, relatively stable and reliable ERP correlates of consonant POA discrimination have been noted in newborns. At the same time, however, discrimination of a different speech cue, VOT, does not appear to develop until sometime after birth, at least in the majority of the population (Molfese & Molfese, 1979b; Simos & Molfese, 1997). Second, different regions of the auditory ERP elicited by the different auditory stimuli appear to lateralize differently, depending on the evoking stimuli. The temporal cue, VOT, elicits a right hemisphere response, while the POA cue elicits a left hemisphere response. Third, the scalp distributions for ERP effects in relation to speech sound discrimination change with development. Thus, for example, Molfese & Molfese (1979a) note temporal lobe lateralized effects in newborn infants, while more pronounced frontal effects are noted in 12 - 16 month old infants (Molfese, 1989, 1990), and temporal-parietal effects in children (Molfese & Molfese, 1988) and adults (Molfese, 1978a). The fourth point is that different portions of the ERP waveform appear sensitive to phonetic contrasts at different developmental stages. Thus, shortly after birth, speech sound discriminations are noted to occur at relatively long latencies (520 - 920 ms, see Molfese & Molfese, 1979b; Simos & Molfese, 1997), while these effects shift forward in the ERP wave to 180 - 400 ms for preschoolers (Molfese & Hess, 1978; Molfese & Molfese, 1988), and from 50 to 350 ms for elementary school children and adults. Fifth, and finally, at some point during the auditory ERP to virtually all stimuli tested to date using this procedure, the two hemispheres, in both infants and adults, respond differently to all stimuli. This general hemisphere difference seems most pronounced in the preterm infants, with many different regions of the ERP varying between the two hemispheres (Molfese & Molfese, 1980). However, this difference is also present in newborn and 1 year old infants (Molfese & Searock, 1986), preschool age children (Molfese & Hess, 1978; Molfese & Molfese, 1988), and adults (Molfese, 1978a, 1978b, 1980a, 1984; Molfese & Schmidt, 1983).

Early Word Acquisition

While our knowledge of infants' speech perception has expanded rapidly over the past decade (Eimas, Siqueland, Jusczyk, & Vigorito, 1971; Kuhl, 1985; Morse, 1974; Molfese & Molfese, 1979; 1980; 1985), little is known about the infant's beginning comprehension of "names" for objects/events (Bates, 1979). While some investigations have documented and catalogued the words first comprehended by infants, beginning around 8 months of age (Benedict, 1975; Kamhi, 1986; Miller, & Chapman, 1981; Macnamara, 1982), only recently have investigations probed the nature of the older infant's early word meanings (Bloom, Lahey, Hood, Lifter, & Fiess, 1980; Clark, 1983; Snyder, Bates, & Bretherton, 1981; Retherford, Schwartz, & Chapman, 1981) and to study the very beginning stages of the infant's ability to perceive and remember the names for objects and events (Bates, Benigni, Bretherton, Camaioni, & Voltera, 1979;

Bates, Bretherton, Snyder, Shore, & Voltaire, 1980; Golinkoff, Hirsh-Pasek, Cauley, & Gordon, 1987; Hirsh-Pasek & Golinkoff, 1996; Kamhi, 1986). Moreover, virtually nothing is known about the role that the brain plays in the early acquisition of such word meanings (Molfese, 1989, 1990; Molfese, Morse, & Peters, 1990). Furthermore, while scientists have speculated that the left hemisphere plays a major role in early language acquisition (Best, 1988; Lenneberg, 1967), little actual work has been conducted to address this issue (Molfese, 1989, 1990; Molfese, et al, 1990; Molfese, 1994). Indeed, four recent papers indicate that such procedures can be successfully used to study the developmental neuropsychology of early word comprehension in infants from 12- to 16-months of age (Molfese, 1989, 1990; Molfese, Morse, & Peters, 1990; Molfese, Wetzel, & Gill, 1994).

The youngest group of infants to be studied using ERPs was a population of 12-month-old infants (Molfese, Gill, & Wetzel, 1994). This investigation represented a direct attempt to determine whether the ERPs recorded from 12-month-old infants could discriminate between words thought by infants' parents to be known to these young infants from those that parents strongly believed were not known. It was hoped that multiple electrode sites over various areas of each hemisphere would provide more information concerning the involvement of different brain regions in early word discrimination. Because the details of this study are relevant to subsequent studies which will be reviewed here, this review will be more extensive.

A group of nine infants, three females and six males, (mean age = 12.2, s.d. = .36) were tested. Initial screening indicated that each of the parents were strongly right handed as indicated by their responses to the Edinburgh Handedness Inventory (Oldfield, 1971) which yielded a mean Laterality Quotient greater than +0.7. Unique stimulus tapes were constructed for each infant, based upon the parental ratings obtained during a telephone interview during which parents were asked to identify all of the words from the original list of ten (i.e., "bottle," "book," "cookie," "key," "kitty," "ball," "dog," "baby," "duck," and "cat.") which they believed that their infant understood. Next, they were asked to rate their confidence in their identification using a five-point scale. Parents were told that a rating of "5" indicated that they were "very confident" that the infant did or did not know the word, while a rating of "1" signified that the parents were "not confident at all" about their decision. Following the interview, parent ratings were converted to a range of from "1" to "10", with "1" signifying high confidence that the infant did not know the word, and "10" signifying high confidence that the infant knew the word. The stimuli which were previously used as the "known" words in the present study had a mean rating of 9.7 (s.d. = .4). For the "unknown" words, there was a mean rating of 1.9 (s.d. = .5).

Each tape contained stimulus repetitions of two spoken words produced by an adult male speaker using flat intonation. Each word began with a voiced, stop consonant to minimize ERP variations due to acoustic factors such as voicing or rise time. One of the two words was identified by that infant's parent as known to the infant while a second word was believed to be unknown to the infant the parent. The words were arranged on the tape in a block random order, with 54 occurrences of each and a randomly varied interstimulus interval.

Six silver cup scalp electrodes were placed over the left and right sides of each infant's head. These placements included two electrodes placed respectively over the left (T3) and right (T4) temporal areas of the Ten-Twenty System (Jasper, 1958); a third electrode placed at FL, a point midway between the external meatus of the left ear and Fz; a fourth electrode placed at FR, a position midway between the right external meatus and Fz; a fifth electrode placed at PL, a point midway between the left external meatus and Pz; and a sixth electrode placed at PR, a point on the right side of the head midway between the right ear's external meatus and Pz. These electrode placements were positioned on the scalp over the left frontal (FL), temporal (T3), and parietal (PL) areas of the brain and the corresponding areas of the right hemisphere (FR, T4, and PR, respectively). Such placements, it was hoped, would provide information concerning not only left versus right hemisphere responses to the known and unknown words, but in addition, information within each hemisphere concerning general language perception areas commonly thought to be localized to the left temporal and parietal language receptive regions of the brain as well as the language production areas of the frontal lobe. The electrical activity recorded from these scalp electrodes was obtained in response to a randomly arranged series of words matched in duration and peak intensity levels. As in previous studies by Molfese and his collaborators, scalp electrodes were referred to electrodes placed on each earlobe and linked together (A1, A2). The words were presented auditorily through a speaker positioned approximately one meter over the midline of the infant's head at 80 dB SPL (A) as measured at the infant's ears and occurred while the infant was in a quiet awake state. Continuous monitoring of the infant's ongoing EEG and EMG, as well as behavioral observation, were used to determine when stimulus presentation should occur. During periods of motor activity, stimulus presentation was suspended and the infant was shown various toys and pictures until quieting. Testing was resumed when the infant's motor activity declined to an acceptable level.

Data reduction and analysis procedures first involved digitizing 70 data points over a 700 ms period beginning at stimulus onset for each electrode site, stimulus event, and infant. Next, the ERPs were subjected to artifact rejection for each electrode to eliminate from further analyses those contaminated by motor or eye movements. This resulted in rejecting less than 10% of the trials for each infant. Rejection rates were comparable across the two stimulus conditions. Following artifact rejection, the single trial data were then averaged separately for each electrode site and stimulus condition. Thus, for each infant, 12 averages were obtained. These included averages for the known and unknown words for each of the six scalp electrode sites. As in the case of the speech perception studies, the average ERPs then were submitted to a two step analysis procedure (Brown, Marsh, & Smith, 1979; Chapman, McCrary, Bragdon, & Chapman, 1979; Donchin, Teuting, Ritter, Kutas, & Heffley, 1975; Gelfer, 1987; Molfese, 1978a, 1978b; Molfese & Molfese, 1979, 1980, 1985; Ruchkin, Sutton, Munson, Silver, & Macar, 1981; Segalowitz & Cohen, 1989). This procedure first involved the use of a Principal Components Analysis (PCA) and then an Analysis of Variance. Factor scores or weights were generated by the PCA for each of the 108 averaged ERPs for each of the six rotated factors accounting for 77.84% of the total variance (Cattell, 1966). The ANOVAs were based on the design of Subjects (9) (Word Understanding (2) (Electrode Sites Within Hemispheres (3) (Hemispheres (2). These were conducted to determine if any of the regions of the ERPs identified by the six factors varied systematically as a function of the specific levels of the independent variables in this study.

Two ERP regions were noted to vary as a function of whether parents believed that the infant could recognize the meaning of a word or not. The first region which reflected variations in the initial portion of the waveform until approximately 140 ms following stimulus onset indicated that ERP activity recorded from over all left hemisphere sites discriminated the known from the unknown words. However, only electrical activity from the frontal and temporal regions of the right hemisphere made similar discriminations. The ERPs elicited by the known words were characterized by a larger negative (or downward) going peak prior to 140 ms while a markedly smaller negative peak characterized the

ERPs evoked by the unknown words. Thus, the vertical amplitude appear larger for the known words than the unknown words. A second region of the averaged ERPs between 210 and 300 ms post stimulus onset also varied systematically as a function of whether the word was thought to be understood by the infant. This effect was reflected by amplitude differences in the second major negative component of the ERP where the overall negative peak-to-peak amplitude in the region between 210 and 300 ms was generally larger for ERPs elicited by the known than by the unknown words.

These results were interpreted by Molfese and colleagues to indicate that auditory ERPs successfully discriminated between words that parents believed their 12-month-old infants knew from those that the infants were thought not to understand. Moreover, Molfese et al noted that even at this young age the process of word comprehension appeared to be dynamic in that different regions of the brain responded differently over time following the onset of the word that was known to the infant. Initially, differential electrical activity was generated early in the waveform for approximately 200 ms over the entire left hemisphere and most of the right hemisphere except the right parietal area Such early responses suggest that the infant may begin to process words as meaningful from virtually the beginning of their production. This initial response period then was followed for a 100 ms period by a spreading of the discrimination to all ERP scalp regions. Thus, the differential response of the ERPs to words appears to continue through much of the time that the infant hears the word, although it appears to be carried out by different brain regions.

In Experiment 1 of a study with older infants, Molfese (1989) recorded auditory evoked responses from frontal, temporal, and parietal scalp locations over the left and right hemispheres of 10 infants, 14 months in age, who also listened to a series of words, half of which were determined to be known to the infants (based on behavioral testing and parental report) and half of which were believed not to be known to the infant. A behavioral test was used to confirm the parents' ratings of their infant's word comprehension. As in the case of the 12-month infant study (Molfese, et al, 1994), parents rated words from a list as either words the infant would know or words they did not know. In addition, however, each infant received four behavioral trials, with two independent observers rating whether or not the infant knew the word presented. In order to assess the infant's comprehension, a specially constructed cabinet was used. The cabinet was 1 meter in height and contained four shelves, each .4 meters in length, with two shelves to the left and two shelves to the right of midline. The object representing the known or the unknown word (as appropriate) was placed in one of the four compartments of a test cabinet. Two compartments of the test box each contained distractor items randomly selected for each trial from a sack of toys while the fourth compartment remained empty. The parent then instructed the infant to look at or retrieve various toys using instructions to the infant such as, "Go get the book." or "Look at the duck." The compartments that contained the test object, the empty space, and the distracters were randomized for each trial for each infant based on a randomly generated list derived by computer prior to the test session. On each trial the raters independently determined whether they believed that the infant responded to the instructions correctly and recorded their confidence in these judgments on a 5-point scale identical to that previously used by the parents. For the children in this study, both the parents (across the two interviews) and the raters reliably rated the words they believed were known to the infant as different from those that they believed the infant did not understand.

Analyses of the ERP data isolated three regions of the evoked potential waveform that discriminated known from unknown words in this population. Initially, ERP activity across both hemispheres (with the exception of the right parietal region) between 30 and 220 ms following stimulus onset discriminated known from unknown words. This effect could be seen as a positive peak for the known words and a negative peak in this same region for the unknown words. This activity was followed shortly by a large positive to negative shift in the waveform between 270 and 380 ms across all electrode sites for both the left and right hemispheres that was larger for the known than for the unknown words. Finally, a late negative peak between 380 and 500 ms that was detected only by electrodes placed over the left and right parietal regions was larger for the known than for the unknown words.

In Experiment 2 of this study, Molfese attempted to determine whether familiarity with speech stimuli produced brain responses similar to those found for the known vs. unknown word materials. In this procedure, a different set of ten 14-month-old infants first listened to a nonsense bisyllable (CVCV) over a 2 day period. Parents encouraged their infant to play with a box on which a large orange Frisbee was mounted and connected to a series of switches. Infants played with the device for three times on each of the 2 days designated for training, with 15 minutes allowed for each of the six play sessions. Five infants heard "toto" during the familiarization process while five children heard "gigi" to decrease the likelihood that any experimental effects were due to acoustic differences between the stimuli instead of due to differences in amount of previous exposure to the different stimuli. On the third day, ERPs were recorded to this now familiar CVCV and to the novel CVCV. Electrode placements were identical to those used in Experiment 1. If the latencies and scalp distributions of the brain responses found in this study were identical to those found in the known - unknown word study, it was felt that the familiarity hypothesis could not be rejected. In fact, however, results indicated that only the brain responses recorded over both the left- and right hemisphere frontal areas discriminated between the familiar and nonfamiliar CVCVs. In addition, the major peak in the ERP that discriminated these differences occurred at 360 ms, not at the 630 ms previously found for the known - unknown word distinction. Consequently, it appears that the earlier ERP findings discussed in the first experiment did indeed reflect meaning differences and not differences in familiarity.

A subsequent study with 16-month-old infants (Molfese, 1990) modeled after Molfese, Wetzel, and Gill (1994) and Experiment 1 of Molfese (1989), found comparable differences in an older group of infants in response to known and unknown words. Molfese tested 18 infants (9 females and 9 males with a mean age of 16.57 mo. (s.d.=.6, range=15.4-17.5). As in his previous studies, parent handedness was measured and found to indicate strong right hand preferences across parents. In addition, parents were asked to rate a set of 10 words during a telephone interview and a subsequent lab visit in order to identify at least one word that parents confidently believed their infant knew and another word they believed the infant did not know. As in the case of Experiment 1 of Molfese (1989), two independent raters evaluated infants' word knowledge using the four shelf cabinet and then infants were tested whose parents and raters agreed on a set of known and unknown words. Electrodes were then applied to six electrode sites, three over each hemisphere using the same scalp locations and references used previously by Molfese in this series of studies. ERP testing then commenced with 54 repetitions of each of the two words presented auditorily in random order, separated from each other by a varied ISI random (2.5-4 Sec.).

A principal components analysis of the averaged ERPs yielded five factors (scree) accounting for 74.33% of the total variance. Two factors identified ERP regions which varied as a function of the KNOWN vs. UNKNOWN distinction. The first region, between 180 and 340 ms with a peak latency of 270 ms contained a larger N180 - P340 complex for UNKNOWN words at only the T3 site for females while the left and right frontal regions as well as T3 showed a similar effect for males. A second region, between 580 and 700, with a peak latency of 650 ms, also discriminated KNOWN vs. UNKNOWN words for females but this time at all LH sites while for males, both the LH and RH sites discriminated KNOWN vs. UNKNOWN words. In all cases, this discrimination was reflected by larger negative shifts for UNKNOWN words.

A fourth study by Molfese et al (1990) investigated aspects of the neuropsychology associated with the infant's early word comprehension and learning. Fourteen infants, seven females and seven males, at 14 month of age (mean = 14.72 months, s.d. = .63) participated in a training study in which specific CVCV nonsense syllables were systematically paired with specific objects of specific shapes and colors over a five day training period. Handedness questionnaires administered to all parents (Edinburgh Inventory, Oldfield, 1971) indicated that both parents of each infant were strongly right handed (group mean Laterality Quotient = .67, s.d. = .19). On the day before the training period, infants first were tested in a Match - Mismatch task in which on half of the trials each object was paired with its CVCV label (i.e., the label that the infant would later learn during the training period was the "name" of that object) while on the other half of the trials the objects were mispaired with the CVCV "names" of other objects. The parents and infants then returned home for 5 days of training. On the sixth day and immediately prior to the post-training session, parent were asked to indicate whether or not their infants knew the name of the object in question and then to rate their own confidence in that judgment using a 5 point scale with "1" as "completely not confident" and "5" as " very confident". The confidence ratings were then used to transform parents' ratings from a "1" of "confidently unknown" to a "unknown but completely not confident" rating of "5" to a "known but completely not confident" rating of "6" to a "confidently known" rating of "10". Using this rating system all parent rated the terms as "known" by the infant with a mean confidence rating for "bidu" at 8.71 (s.d. = .88) and for "gibu at 8.79 (s.d. = .94), indicating that the parents as a group were confident that the infants understood which terms went with which objects. Next, during the post-training test, infants again were tested in a Match - Mismatch task in which on half of the trials each object was paired with its CVCV label (Match condition) while on the other half of the trials the objects were mispaired with the CVCV "names" of other objects (Mismatch condition). The electrophysiological techniques used during this phase were identical to those employed during the pretest phase of this study.

Using artifact rejection and analysis procedures comparable to those employed in the earlier studies performed by Molfese and colleagues, the ERPs were averaged separately for the pre- and post-training tests for each of the six electrode sites and each of the two stimulus conditions. Twelve averages were obtained for each data set for each infant. Each average was based on 80 samples combining responses to "bidu" and "gibu" for the Match condition and 80 samples across "bidu" and "gibu" for the Mismatch condition.

Two regions of the ERP waveform reliably reflected Match related effects during this task - an early component of the ERP which changed bilaterally over the frontal regions of both hemispheres and a late occurring lateralized response which was restricted to only the left hemisphere electrode sites. The first, which occurred between 30 and 120 ms post stimulus onset, was characterized by a marked negativity for the Mismatch condition. A second region, which began 520 ms after stimulus onset, reached its peak at 580 ms, and then diminished by 600 ms, produced a positive going wave for the Mismatch condition over all of the left hemisphere electrode sites.

Since no such Match or Mismatch effects were noted in the pre-training

ERP session, it is clear that the ERPs detected changes which occurred as a function of training. When a correct match occurred between the auditorily presented word and the object that the infant held, both the left and right frontal regions of the brain emitted brain responses which contained an initial positive deflection or peak between 20 and 100 ms following the auditory onset of the object name. If a mismatch occurred, however, this early positive deflection inverted 180 degrees and became a negative deflection. Later in time, between 520 and 600 ms, just before the conclusion of the ERP, a large positive going wave occurred over only the three left hemisphere electrode sites when the infant listened to a stimulus which did not name the object that the infant held. Given the short latency of the initial changes in the ERP waveshape across the frontal regions, it appears that the young infant must recognize almost immediately if there is agreement between something that it hears and something that it sees and touches.

In a recent study of early infant word perception, Mills, Coffey-Corina, & Neville (1993) recorded auditory ERPs from 24 children, 16 females and 8 males (mean age = 20.5 mo.) to a series of 10 comprehended (known), unknown, and backward presented words. In order to both obtain early language measures and to identify stimuli for the ERP test, the Early Language Inventory (ELI), was administered one week before ERP testing to assess language skills. Parents rated 120 words on 1-4 scale of confidence that child did or did not comprehend word. Also a Comprehension Book with 50 object names, 9 verbs and modifiers was presented to the child who then pointed to each picture verbalized by experimenter.

To obtain ERPs, each child was seated in a parent's lap, opposite an audio speaker which was positioned behind hand puppets used to focus the child's attention. ERPs were collected to 10 known, unknown, and backward words presented 6 times each for 180 trials. An electrode cap was used with electrodes placed at F7, F8, 33% distance from T3 to C3 and from T4 to C4, 50% of distance from T3 to P3, and from T4 to P4, O1, O2, all referenced to linked mastoids. Prior to analyses the children were divided into two groups based on whether their ELI was above or below the 50th percentile. Subsequent tests then confirmed that these groups differed on vocabulary and comprehension. Overall, Mills et al reported larger temporal and parietal responses than for frontal or occipital sites for known words, while there were larger RH responses overall to unknown words.

For the N200 region (the most negative point between 125-250 ms) 90% of the children produced a larger N200 to known versus unknown words at LH temporal and parietal sites while 80% showed a larger N200 to known versus unknown words at LH frontal and RH temporal & parietal sites. When comparisons included backward speech, larger responses were noted to known and unknown words than to backward speech, with generally more positive responses over LH anterior than LH posterior sites.

At the next major peak measured (N350 - the most negative point between 275 and 450 ms), the known words elicited a faster N350 than backward speech (by 20 ms). Amplitude measures of this peak found larger responses to known than unknown words at LH temporal and parietal sites. Unknown words overall elicited larger responses over RH than LH sites. Finally, responses to known words were larger than to backward stimuli at LH sites while unknown words elicited larger responses than backward stimuli at RH sites. Measures of the negative wave in the region between 600 and 900 ms noted that all stimuli elicited larger anterior RH than LH responses.

When ERP sensitivity to language abilities was compared between the two language groups, a number of additional effects were noted. Overall, the

N200 amplitude was greater for Low language producers for both known and unknown words. N350 latency was fastest to known words for the High production group (by 28 ms). Additionally, High production group had larger N350 amplitudes at LH temporal and parietal sites.

Other later effects were also noted within the 600-900 region (mean negative amplitude between 600-900 ms). The negative amplitude was largest for known words for the High production group at RH frontal site, and the Low production group at bilateral anterior sites. Known words also produced larger responses for the Low than High producers at LH temporal & parietal sites while the unknown words produced larger responses for the Low than for the High producers at RH parietal site. Unlike Molfese (1990), who tested 16-month-olds, they did not note any sex effects. These early word acquisition studies are summarized in Table 3.

Perception of Coarticulated Cues. While the early ERP response during the first 100 ms following stimulus onset might superficially appear to have occurred before the infant could process the acoustic information of the CVCVs, such early discrimination is not without precedence. Given other behavioral and electrophysiological investigations of coarticulated speech cues (Ali, Gallagher, Goldstein, & Daniloff, 1971; Daniloff & Moll, 1968; MacNeilage & DeClerk, 1969; Molfese, 1979), it is possible that the infants used such information to discriminate between the Match and Mismatch conditions. Coarticulation refers to the finding that the shape of the vocal tract during the production of a speech sound will be altered by the place and manner of articulation for later speech sounds. Such a process clearly must involve the sequential and parallel processing of rapidly timed events (see Rosen, this volume). MacNeilage and DeClerk, in one study, made cineflurograms and electromyograms of individuals producing a series of 36 CVC syllables and found that the articulation of the initial consonant sounds changed as a function of the identify of the following sounds. Ali, et al. noted a perceptual counterpart of coarticulation. They constructed a series of CVC and CVVC syllables in which the final sound was either a nasal [m, n] or non-nasal consonant. After the final vowel-consonant and consonant transitions were removed, the resulting CV and CVV syllables were presented to a group of adults who were able to discriminate between the nasal and non-nasal sequences at well above chance levels. Ali et al. and others have argued that such coarticulated information allows the listener to perceive and process some or all of the utterance before it has been completely articulated. Molfese (1979) in a study with adults recorded ERPs to CVC words and nonsense syllables which differed from each other *only* in the final consonant sound. Adults listened to each CVC and then after a brief delay pressed one of two keys to indicate whether they had heard a word or a nonsense syllable. Three regions of the ERP, including one that peaked 60 ms following stimulus onset, changed systematically as a function of the meaningfulness of the CVC syllables. Molfese interpreted this component as well as later negative peaks at 260 and 400 ms as sensitive to the coarticulated speech cues which carried information concerning the later occurring (after 650 ms) final consonant sound.

In the Molfese et al (1990) study, given that the consonant burst and frequency transition information that discriminated one CVCV from the other occurred during approximately the first 50 ms of each stimulus (MacNeilage & DeClerk, 1969), infants could have used this coarticulated information to rapidly identify and discriminate early in time between the auditory tokens that matched or failed to match the object the infant was holding throughout a block of trials. Thus, ERP studies with young infants can be used to both successfully study early word acquisition and the processes they may use to acquire and recognize early words in their vocabularies.

TABLE 3

Early Word Discrimination.

Study	Age	Latency	Effects
Molfese, Wetzel, & Gill, 1994	12 mo.	30 -140 ms	Left hemisphere (LH) frontal, temporal, parietal Right hemisphere (RH) frontal, temporal 210-300 ms All electrode sites.
Molfese, 1989	14 mo.	30 - 220 ms	LH frontal, temporal, parietal RH frontal, temporal 270-380 ms All electrode sites. 380-500 ms. LH and RH parietal
Molfese, Morse, & Peters, 1990	14 mo.	30 - 120 ms	LH and RH frontal 530-600 ms LH frontal, temporal, parietal
Molfese, 1990	16 mo.	180-340 ms	Females: T3: known<>unknown Males: FL, T3, FR: known<>unknown 580-700 ms Females: LH frontal, temporal, parietal Males: All electrode sites.

Mills, Coffey-Corina, & Neville (1993)	20.5 mo.	N200	Known vs. unknown 90% showed larger N200 known vs. unknown words at LH temporal & parietal sites. 80% showed known > unknown words at LH frontal and RH temporal & parietal sites. Known: Temporal, parietal > frontal, occipital Unknown: RH amplitude > LH Larger to known than backward at frontal, temporal & parietal sites. Larger to unknown than backward at RH sites. Backward ERPs more positive over LH anterior than LH posterior sites.
		N350	Latency: Known < backward (by 20 ms). Amplitude: Known > unknown at LH temporal & parietal sites. Known > backward at LH sites. Unknown >backward at RH sites. Unknown larger for RH than LH sites. For all stimuli, anterior RH > LH.

Summary of early word acquisition studies. There are remarkably similarities in terms of scalp electrode effects and known - unknown word discrimination effects across studies. For example, Molfese (1989, Experiment 1) noted three regions of the ERP waveform discriminated known from unknown words. Initially, ERP activity across both hemispheres (with the exception of the right parietal region) between 30 and 220 ms following stimulus onset discriminated between known and unknown words. Thus, in two different ages of infants, 12-month-olds and 14-month-olds, similar regions of the ERP waveform distributed over the same electrode recording areas discriminated known from unknown words. A similar effect was also reported by Molfese et al (1990). Furthermore, in all three studies, this activity was follcwed shortly by a large positive to negative change in amplitude across all electrode sites for both the left and right hemispheres that was larger for the known than for the unknown words. Molfese (1989) reported that this effect occurred between 270 and 380 ms while Molfese et al (1990) identifies this area between 210 and 300 ms. These studies differ, however, in that Molfese (1989) reported a third, late negative peak between 380 and 500 ms, that was detected only by electrodes placed over the left and right parietal regions, an effect which was larger for the known than for the unknown words. No such effect was noted by Molfese et al. The absence of such a late effect in the ERP responses of 12-month-old infants could reflect differences in the developmental stages between the younger infants tested by Molfese et al (1994) and the older infants tested by Molfese (1989, 1990) .

Molfese et al (1994), as in the case of both Molfese (1989) and Molfese, Morse, & Peters (1990), observed an effect in the initial portion of the ERP that discriminated known from unknown words. Given other behavioral and electrophysiological investigations of coarticulated speech cues as noted above (Ali, Gallagher, Goldstein, & Daniloff, 1971; Daniloff & Moll, 1968; MacNeilage & DeClerk, 1969; Molfese, 1979), it is possible that the infants can use acoustic correlates of articulatory information in the initial portion of words to identify words. If so, this suggests that such perceptual strategies are available to the infant at a very early stage of the language learning process.

It is interesting to note that, although a general belief exists that language perception is carried out by mechanisms within the left hemisphere (Lenneberg, 1967), none of the known versus unknown word related effects were exclusively restricted to only the left hemisphere electrode sites. These data can be used to argue that, at least in the early stages of language acquisition, both hemispheres of the brain are dynamically involved in the process of learning to relate word sounds to word meanings. If this is indeed the case, then perhaps the reason that young infants experiencing left hemisphere brain damage during the initial stages of language acquisition are able to recover language skills more quickly than those injured later may be due to the duplicated language abilities of the right hemisphere at that stage. Consequently, the infant's language functions may continue to be served by these right hemisphere mechanisms after the loss of the left hemisphere. If, on the other hand, the child experiences left hemisphere damage later in development, the outcome could be quite different. Either due to changes in brain plasticity or further specialization of the brain with development, the ability of the non-language specialized hemisphere in the normally developing child becomes more restricted with age. Consequently, following injury to the left hemisphere at this later stage of development, there may not be a right hemisphere that is capable of performing these functions. Consequently, language performance would be impaired because the right hemisphere is unable to continue this process in the absence of a fully functioning left hemisphere. Instead, the right hemisphere would only have residual abilities that reflected its involvement at a much earlier stage of development.

Based on this review, it is clear that electrophysiological measures involving the auditory event related potential can be used successfully to discriminate between ERPs elicited by words thought to be known to an infant versus words identified as unknown. As argued elsewhere, such procedures open up a number of possibilities, both for exploring further the semantic development of the young infant and for detecting developmental problems in children who are slow in acquiring their first words. Work is now underway using these procedures to determine more accurately the size of an infant's receptive vocabulary at an earlier point in development than is now possible using conventional behavioral assessment techniques.

ACKNOWLEDGMENT

Support for this work was provided by the National Science Foundation (BNS 8210846), and the National Institutes of Health (R01-HD17860).

References

Adams, C., Molfese, D. L., & Betz, J. (1987). Electrophysiological correlates of categorical speech perception for voicing contrasts in dogs. *Developmental Neuropsychology, 3*, 175-189.

Ali, L., Gallagher, T., Goldstein, J., & Daniloff, R. (1971). Perception of coarticulated nasality. *Journal of the Acoustical Society of America, 49*, 538 - 540.

Bates, E. (1979). *Emergence of Symbols*. New York: Academic Press.

Bates, E., Benigni, L., Bretherton, I., Camaioni, L., & Volterra, V. (1979). *The emergence of symbols: Cognition and communication in infancy.* New York: Academic Press.

Bates, E., Bretherton, I., Snyder, L., Shore, C., & Volterra, V. (1980). Vocal and gestural symbols at 13 months. *Merrill-Palmer Quarterly, 26*, 407 - 423.

Begleiter, H. & Platz, A. (1969). Cortical evoked potentials to semantic stimuli. *Psychophysiology, 6*, 91 - 100.

Benedict, H. (1975, April). The role of repetition in early language comprehension. Paper presented at the meeting of the Society for Research in Child Development, Denver, April,.

Best, C. T. (1991, April). Phonetic influences on the perception of non-native speech contrasts by 6-8 and 10-12 month olds. Paper presented at the Biennial meeting of the Society for Research in Child Development, Seattle, WA.

Best, C.T. (1988). The emergence of cerebral asymmetries in early human development: A literature review and a neuroembryological model. In Molfese, D.L. & Segalowitz, S.J. (Eds.), *Brain lateralization in children: Developmental implications*. (pp. 5 - 34). New York: Guilford Press.

Bloom, L., Lahey, M., Hood, L., Lifter, K., & Fiess, K. (1980). Complex sentences: Acquisition of syntactic connectives and the semantic relations they encode. *Journal of Child Language, 7*, 235 - 261.

Blumstein, S., Baker, E., & Goodglass, H. (1977). Phonological factors in auditory comprehension in aphasia. *Neuropsychologia, 15,* 19-30.

Brown, W. S., Marsh, J. T., & Smith, J. C. (1979). Principal component analysis of ERP differences related to the meaning of an ambiguous word. *Journal of Electroencephalography and Clinical Neurophysiology, 46* , 706-714.

Callaway, E., Tueting, P., & Koslow, S. H. (1978). *Event-related brain potentials and behavior*. New York: Academic Press.

Cattell, R. B. (1966). The scree test for the number of factors. *Multivariate Behavioral Research, 1,* 245.

Chapman, R. M., McCrary, J. W., Bragdon, H. R., & Chapman, J.A. (1979). Latent components of event-related potentials functionally related to information processing. In J. E. Desmedt (Ed.), *Progress in Clinical Neuropsychology, Vol. 6: Cognitive Components in Cerebral Event-Related Potentials and Selective Attention.* Basel: Karger.

Clark, E. V. (1983). Meanings and concepts. In Paul H. Mussen (Ed.), *Handbook of Child Psychology, Vol. 3.* (4th ed.). New York: Wiley, 787 - 840.

Daniloff, R., & Moll, K. (1968). Coarticulation of lip rounding. *Journal of Speech and Hearing Research, 11*, 707 - 721.

Dehaene-Lambert, G. & Dehaene, S. (1994). Speed and cerebral correlates of syllable discrimination in infants. *Nature, 370*, 292-295.

Donchin, E., Tueting, P., Ritter, W., Kutas, M., & Heffley, E. (1975). On the independence of the CNV and the P300 components of the human averaged evoked potential. *Journal of Electroencephalography and Clinical Neurophysiology, 38*, 449 - 461.

Dorman, M. (1974). Auditory evoked potential correlates of speech sound discrimination. *Perception & Psychophysics, 15*, 215-220.

Eilers, R., Wilson, W. & Moore, J. (1979). Speech discrimination in the language-innocent and language-wise: A study in the perception of voice onset time. *Journal of Child Language, 6*, 1 - 18.

Eimas, P.D., Siqueland, E., Jusczyk, P., & Vigorito, J. (1971). Speech perception in infants. *Science, 171*, 303-306.

Gelfer, M.P. (1987). An AER study of stop-consonant discrimination. *Perception & Psychophysics, 42*, 318 - 327.

Golinkoff, R.M., Hirsh-Pasek, K., Cauley, K.M., & Gordon, L. (1987). The eyes have it: Lexical and syntactic comprehension in a new paradigm. *Journal of Child Language, 14*, 23-45.

Hirsh-Pasek, K. & Golinkoff, R.M. (1996). *The origins of grammar: Evidence from early language comprehension*. Cambridge, MA: The MIT Press.

Jasper, H. H. (1958). The ten-twenty electrode system of the International Federation of Societies for Electroencephalography: Appendix to report of the committee on methods of clinical examination in electroencephalography. *Journal of Electroencephalography and Clinical Neurophysiology, 10*, 371-375.

Kamhi, A.G. (1986). The elusive first word: the importance of the naming insight for the development of referential speech. *Journal of Child Language, 13*, 155 - 161.

Kuhl, P.K. (1985). Constancy, categorization, and perceptual organization for speech and sound in early infancy. In J. Mehler and R. Rox (Eds.), *Neonate cognition: Beyond the blooming, buzzing confusion*. Hillsdale, New Jersey: Erlbaum.

Kuhl, P. (1991). Human adults and human infants show a "perceptual magnet effect" for the prototypes of speech categories, monkeys do not. *Perception & Psychophysics, 50*, 93-107.

Kuhl, P. (1983). Perception of auditory equivalence classes for speech in early infancy. *Infant Behavior and Development, 6*, 263-285.

Lenneberg, E. (1967). *Biological Foundations of Language*. New York:

Wiley & Sons.

Liberman, A.M., Cooper, F.S., Shankweiler, D., & Studdert-Kennedy, M. (1967). Perception of the speech code. *Psychological Review, 74,* 431-461.

Lisker, L. & Abramson, A.S. (1970). The voicing dimension: Some experiments in comparative phonetics. In: *Proceedings of the 6th International Congress of Phonetic Sciences.* Prague: Academia. 563-567.

Lyon, G.R. (1994). *Frames of reference for the assessment of learning disabilities: New views on measurement issues.* Baltimore: Brookes.

Macnamara, J. (1982). *Names for things.* Cambridge, Mass.: MIT Press.

MacNeilage, P.F. & DeClerk, J.L. (1969). On the motor control of coarticulation in CVC monosyllables. *Journal of the Acoustical Society of America, 45*, 1217 - 1233.

Miceli, G., Caltagirone, C., Gianotti, G., & Payer-Rigo, P. (1978). Discrimination of voice versus place contrasts in aphasia. *Brain and Language, 6*, 47-51.

Miller, J.F. & Chapman, R.S. (1981). The relation between age and mean length of utterance in morphemes. *Journal of Speech and Hearing Research, 24*, 154 - 161.

Mills, D. L., Coffey-Corina, S. A., & Neville, H. J. (1993). Language acquisition and cerebral specialization in 20-month-old infants. *Journal of Cognitive Neuroscience, 5*, 317-334.

Moffitt, A. (1971). Consonant cue perception by twenty-to-twenty-four-week-old infants. *Child Development, 42,* 717-731.

Molfese, D. L. (1978a). Electrophysiological correlates of categorical speech perception in adults. *Brain and Language, 5*, 25-35.

Molfese, D. L. (1978b). Left and right hemispheric involvement in the speech perception: Electrophysiological correlates. *Perception and Psychophysics, 23*, 237-243.

Molfese, D. L. (1979).Cortical and subcortical involvement in the processing of coarticulated cues. *Brain and Language, 7*, 86-100.

Molfese, D. L. (1980a). Hemispheric specialization for temporal information: Implications for the processing of voicing cues during speech perception. *Brain and Language, 11*, 285-300.

Molfese, D. L. (1980b).The phoneme and the engram: Electrophysiological evidence for the acoustic invariant in stop consonants. *Brain and Language, 9*, 372-376.

Molfese, D. L. (1983). Event related potentials and language processes. In A. W. K. Gaillard & W. Ritter (Eds.), *Tutorials in ERP Research - Endogenous Components*. Amsterdam: Elsevier.

Molfese, D. L. (1984). Left hemisphere sensitivity to consonant sounds not displayed by the right hemisphere: Electrophysiological correlates. *Brain and Language, 22*, 109-127.

Molfese, D. L. (1989). Electrophysiological correlates of word meanings in 14-month-old human infants. *Developmental Neuropsychology, 5*, 79-103.

Molfese, D. L. (1990). Auditory evoked responses recorded from 16-month-old human infants to words they did and did not know. *Brain and Language, 38*, 345-363.

Molfese, D. L., & Hess, R. M. (1978). Speech perception in nursery school age children: Sex and hemispheric differences. *Journal of Experimental Child Psychology, 26*, 71-84.

Molfese, D. L., & Molfese, V. J. (1979b). Hemisphere and stimulus differences as reflected in the cortical responses of newborn infants to speech stimuli. *Developmental Psychology, 15*, 505-511.

Molfese, D. L., & Molfese, V. J. (1980). Cortical responses of preterm infants to phonetic and nonphonetic speech stimuli. *Developmental Psychology, 16*, 574- 581.

Molfese, D. L., & Molfese, V. J. (1985). Electrophysiological indices of auditory discrimination in newborn infants: The bases for predicting later language development. *Infant Behavior and Development, 8*, 197-211.

Molfese, D. L., & Molfese, V. J. (1988). Right hemisphere responses from preschool children to temporal cues contained in speech and nonspeech materials: Electrophysiological correlates. *Brain and Language, 33*, 245-259.

Molfese, D. L., & Molfese, V. J. (1979a). Infant speech perception: Learned or innate. In H. A. Whitaker and H.Whitaker (Eds.), *Advances in Neurolinguistics, Vol. 4*. New York: Academic Press.

Molfese, D. L., & Molfese, V. J. (1997). Discrimination of language skills at five years of age using event related potentials recorded at birth. *Developmental Neuropsychology, 13,* 135-156.

Molfese, D. L., & Schmidt, A.L. (1983). An auditory evoked potential study of consonant perception. *Brain and Language, 18*, 57-70.

Molfese, D.L. & Searock, K. (1986). The use of auditory evoked responses at one year of age to predict language skills at 3 years. *Australian Journal of Communication Disorders, 14,* 35-46.

Molfese, D. L., & Wetzel, W. F. (1992). Short and long term memory in 14 month old infants: Electrophysiological correlates. *Developmental Neuropsychology, 8*, 135-160.

Molfese, D. L., Buhrke, R. A., & Wang, S. L. (1985). The right hemisphere and temporal processing of consonant transition durations: Electrophysiological correlates. *Brain and Language, 26*, 289-299.

Molfese, D. L., Burger-Judisch, L. M., & Hans, L. L. (1991). Consonant discrimination by newborn infants: Electrophysiological differences. *Developmental Neuropsychology, 7*, 177-195.

Molfese, D. L., Freeman, R. B., Jr., & Palermo, D. S. (1975). The ontogeny of lateralization for speech and nonspeech stimuli. *Brain and*

Language, 2, 356- 368.

Molfese, D. L., Laughlin, N. K., Morse, P. A., Linnville, S., Wetzel, F., & Erwin, R. (1986). Neuroelectrical correlates of categorical perception for place of articulation in normal and lead-treated rhesus macaques. *Journal of Clinical and Experimental Neuropsychology, 8*, 680-696.

Molfese, D. L., Linnville, S. E., Wetzel, W. F., & Leicht, D. (1985). Electrophysiological correlates of handedness and speech perception contrasts. *Neuropsychologia, 23*, 77-86.

Molfese, D. L., Morris, R. D., & Romski, M. A. (1990). Semantic discrimination in nonspeaking youngsters with moderate or severe retardation: Electrophysiological correlates. *Brain and Language, 38*, 61-74.

Molfese, D. L., Morse, P. A., & Peters, C. J. (1990). Auditory evoked responses from infants to names for different objects: Cross modal processing as a basis for early language acquisition. *Developmental Psychology, 26*, 780-795.

Molfese, D. L., Wetzel, W. F., & Gill, L. A.(1993).Known versus unknown word discrimination in 12-month-old human infants: Electrophysiological correlates. *Developmental Neuropsychology, 3-4*, 241-258.

Molfese, V. J., Molfese, D. L., & Parsons, C. (1983). Hemispheric involvement in phonological perception. In S. Segalowitz (Ed.), *Language Functions and Brain Organization*. New York: Academic Press, 29-50.

Morse, P.A. (1974). Infant speech perception: A preliminary model and review of the literature. In R. Schiefelbusch and L. Lloyd (Eds.), *Language perspectives: Acquisition, retardation, and intervention*. Baltimore: University Park Press, 19 - 53.

Morse, P. A. (1972).The discrimination of speech and nonspeech stimuli in early infancy. *Journal of Experimental Child Psychology, 13*, 477-492.

Morse, P. A., Molfese, D. L., Laughlin, N. K., Linnville, S., & Wetzel, F. (1987). Categorical perception for voicing contrast in normal and lead-treated macaques: Electrophysiological indices. *Brain and Language, 30,* 63-80.

Nelson, C.A. & Salapatek, P. (1986). Electrophysiological correlates of infant recognition memory. *Child Development, 57*, 1483 - 1497.

Oldfield, R.L. (1971). The assessment of handedness: The Edinburgh Inventory. *Neuropsychologia, 9*, 97 - 113.

Perecman, E., & Kellar, L. (1981). The effect of voice and place among aphasic, nonaphasic right-damaged and normal subjects on a metalinguistic task. *Brain and Language, 12*, 213-223.

Pisoni, D.B. (1977). Identification and discrimination of the relative onset time of two component tones: Implications for voicing perception in stops. *Journal of the Acoustical Society of America, 61*, 1352-1361.

Retherford, K.S., Schwartz, B.C., & Chapman, R.S. (1981). Semantic roles and residual grammatical categories in mother and child speech. *Journal of Child Language, 8*, 583 - 608.

Rosen, G. D. (In press). Animal models of developmental dyslexia: lessons from developmental and cognitive neuroscience. *This volume.*

Ruchkin, D., Sutton, S., Munson, R., Silver, K., & Macar, F. (1981). P300 and feedback provided by absence of the stimulus. *Psychophysiology , 18*, 271-282.

Segalowitz, S.J. & Cohen, H. (1989).Right hemisphere EEG sensitivity to speech. *Brain and Language, 37*, 220 - 231.

Simos, P. G., & Molfese, D. L. (1997). Electrophysiological responses from a temporal order continuum in the newborn infant. *Neuropsychologia, 35*, 89-98.

Simos, P. G., Molfese, D. L., & Brenden, R. A. (1997). Behavioral and electrophysiological indices of voicing cue discrimination: Laterality patterns and development. *Brain and Cognition, 57*, 122-150.

Snyder, L., Bates, E., & Bretherton, I. (1981). Content and context in early lexical development. *Journal of Child Language, 8*, 565 - 582.

Streeter, L.A. (1976). Language perception of two-month-old infants shows effects of both innate mechanisms and experience. *Nature, 259*, 39 - 41.

Trehub, S. (1973). Infant's sensitivity to vowel and tonal contrasts. *Developmental Psychology, 9*, 91-96.

Werker, J. & Tees, R. (1984). Cross-language speech perception: Evidence for perceptual reorganization during the first year of life. *Infant Behavior and Development, 7*, 49-63.

Chapter 4
DEVELOPMENTAL AND INDIVIDUAL DIFFERENCES IN SHORT-TERM MEMORY

John Scott Saults and Nelson Cowan
University of Missouri

ABSTRACT

George Miller's (1956) seminal formulation that there are "seven plus or minus two" slots in short-term memory (STM) left plenty of room for the possibility of individual differences. Nonetheless, STM researchers since then have focused primarily on similarities among individuals, not differences. Recently, however, studies of developmental and individual differences in STM have yielded practical applications and theoretical advances. We note that the differences between individuals stem from a combination of (a) passive, automatic factors and (b) factors that depend on active, strategic processing. This chapter focuses on some of our new research on developmental and individual differences in STM for acoustic and verbal stimuli, and its relation to the work of other investigators. Our recent findings illustrate the usefulness of developmental data for a general theory of STM, and suggest that important refinements of the traditional working memory model (Baddeley, 1986) are now in order. Directions for future research are considered also.

Although there appear to be no limits to the number of memories we can accumulate during our lives, at any one moment we can think about only a small portion of this vast storage. William James (1890) noted this limitation to consciousness in what he called primary memory. More recently, this temporary storage has been referred to as short-term memory (STM), and George Miller (1956) quantified its capacity as seven plus or minus two items. Thus, seven became a magical number to cognitive psychologists seeking to define the universal characteristic of human information processing. Although Miller's qualification of "plus or minus two" allows for considerable variation among individuals, subsequent research concentrated on average capacities, often relegating individual differences to the error term.

Recent theoretical advancements have refined the idea of temporary memory, requiring a closer examination of individual and developmental differences in capacity. Although the term STM is still used to refer to the measured capacity of temporary memory, Baddeley and Hitch (1974) used the term "working memory" to refer to the structures and processes that determine this capacity.

For the past several years, we have been examining processes underlying recall and forgetting of the acoustic and phonological features of spoken words in children and adults. These processes are important in language comprehension and verbal thinking in general (see Cowan, 1994) and may be especially important in vocabulary acquisition (Gathercole & Baddeley, 1993). However, in this chapter we will explore the theoretical, rather than practical, implications of this research. Studies of developmental and individual differences in the STM for speech validate, refine, and extend theories of working memory.

Like Baddeley and Hitch (1974), we assume there are two kinds of processes contributing to working memory. Passive processes, such as the encoding and decay of acoustic and phonological information, can occur automatically. In contrast, active processes, such as mental search and rehearsal, occur only with attention and effort. This distinction has helped guide our research and will be used below to explain how our research can contribute to a more thorough model of working memory.

Baddeley's Phonological Loop Theory

According to Baddeley's (1986) model of working memory, verbal information is maintained in an phonological loop, consisting of an active process of covert rehearsal and a passive process of phonological storage. Baddeley assumed that phonological storage of verbal information occurs automatically and decays at a constant rate in all unimpaired individuals, regardless of age. However, this information can be refreshed by rehearsal since adequate representations remain in the phonological store. Consequently, the number of verbal items an individual can maintain in working memory depends on the rate of rehearsal. Faster rehearsal allows more items to be refreshed before fading from the phonological store.

Among the various findings Baddeley's theory was meant to explain, the most relevant to this discussion is the linear relationship between memory span and maximum articulation rate for a particular set of items. The maximum overt articulation rate is assumed to estimate the speed of covert rehearsal. This linear relation has been observed across means for different groups and conditions. Many studies show that the location of each mean is determined by the age of participants, with more mature children and adults capable of faster speech, and the length of words to be recalled, with length defined in terms of how long it takes to pronounce the word as rapidly as possible (e.g., Baddeley, Thomson, & Buchanan, 1975; Hulme, Thomson, Muir, & Lawrence, 1984; Naveh-Benjamin & Ayres, 1986; Schweickert & Boruff, 1986). The slope of the regression line suggests a person can recall about as many items as he or she can say in 2 s. Baddeley (1986) explained this consistency by proposing that the passive store lasts about 2 s. Rapid pronunciation rate is thought to estimate the speed of covert rehearsal (Landauer, 1962), and the rehearsal rate was assumed by Baddeley to be the factor determining how many items can be refreshed in the rehearsal loop before any are lost from the passive store.

The status and influence of Baddeley's model of working memory is based, partly, on this parsimonious account of developmental and individual differences in STM capacity. Memory span increases with development in childhood because the speed of rehearsal increases with age, increasing the amount of information that can be maintained in the phonological loop. Likewise, individual differences in speech rate, and therefore rehearsal rate, produce corresponding individual differences in memory span.

Testing and Refining the Phonological Loop Theory

Baddeley's (1986) analysis of working memory in terms of specific passive and active processes has inspired and guided much of our research on memory for speech in children and adults. The phonological loop model provides a simple, but plausible, framework for thinking about specific constraints in working memory that limit an individual's STM capacity, as measured by memory span and similar tasks. However, our analyses and subsequent investigations raise some questions about Baddeley's explanation for individual and developmental differences in memory span.

The first question concerns how this model explains STM constraints in young children. A linear relation between speech rate and memory span has been found across group means for different conditions, even in studies that include groups of children as young as 4 years (Hulme et al., 1984). An explanation of this correlation based on rehearsal speed seems inconsistent with research suggesting children who are that young probably do not rehearse (Flavell, Beach, & Chinsky, 1966; Henry, 1991a, 1991b). This problem arises again when one examines correlations between speech rate and memory span across individuals within different age groups. A roughly linear, positive relationship is found within groups of older children and adults, but not within groups of 4-year-olds (Cowan, Keller, Hulme, Roodenrys, McDougall,& Rack, 1994; Gathercole, Adams, & Hitch, 1994), suggesting the younger children are not using the phonological loop. However, the phonological loop theory explains the word length effect in terms of the increased rehearsal time required for longer words. Non-rehearsing children should not exhibit a word length effect, yet this effect is found in 4-year-olds (Hulme & Tordoff, 1989).

This first question about how the phonological loop model applies to young children has been addressed by some recent research. Information can be lost from the passive store not only while rehearsing but also while recalling the words aloud. While one word is being spoken, other words are being forgotten. When longer words are being recalled, more forgetting can occur for the remaining words on the list. This explanation has been supported by at least two studies. Cowan, Day, Saults, Keller, Johnson, & Flores (1992) presented lists that began with short or long words and, independently, ended with short or long words. Both forward and backward recall were examined. They found that only the length of words recalled first significantly affected recall, presumably because only those words delayed the recall of the remaining words. In a developmental study, Henry (1991a) found that word length can influence forgetting during both rehearsal and overt spoken recall. In one condition, children were to point to pictures to indicate each answer, rather than saying the words aloud. This condition eliminated the word length effect for 5-year-old children, though it still occurred for 7-year-old children. Presumably, the younger children engaged in little or no rehearsal, and thus the length of the words only affected their memory performance during spoken recall. It appears, therefore, that the phonological loop model applies more consistently to young children when output processes are considered along with rehearsal processes.

Another question about the standard phonological loop account is why correlations between speech rate and memory span are rather weak when examined across individuals within an age group (in the range of .3 to .5 for older children and adults) than across ages. Is the missing variance random, or does it reflect systematic individual differences? We are not satisfied to assume it is random, and prefer to consider factors other than rehearsal rate that might help account for individual differences in STM capacity. One possibility was examined by Roodenrys and Hulme (1993), who found that older children use lexical knowledge of items a little better in span tasks, slightly increasing the age difference for memory span of words as compared to nonwords. However, this effect appears to account for a relatively small amount of variance.

Our recent investigations of passive and active components of working memory have uncovered two additional factors that could account for much of the additional variance in memory span. First, passive storage may vary more than previously assumed, explaining why some individuals recall more or less than their rehearsal rate would predict. Second, an active process affecting span may have been neglected in the standard phonological loop model. Serial recall in a memory span task requires repeated searches of STM. This process appears to resemble that involved in the classic memory scanning task conceived by Sternberg (1966). In this task, the participant sees a list followed by a probe item and then must quickly decide whether the probe was in the previous list. Decision times for lists of different lengths provides an estimate of the search time per item. Search times increase by about 40 ms per additional list item in adults, but the rate of increase is larger in younger participants (Keating, Keniston, Manning, & Bobbitt, 1980). Our research suggests that search speed might be related to memory span and may help account for individual and developmental differences in memory span.

Passive Processes in Working Memory

Our approach to working memory, especially the articulation loop, is to think in terms of selective attention. (Cowan, 1988, 1993, 1995). Some information storage processes are *passive* in the sense that they go on automatically, regardless of the strategy or stance the participant adopts. Other processes undoubtedly are *active* in that they can occur only if enough attention is devoted to them and the right strategy adopted. There actually is a continuum of automaticity, in that some processes that begin as very attention-demanding can become less so with development and practice (e.g., rehearsal; see Guttentag,

1984). However, we believe that even well-practiced active processes can be distinguished from passive storage processes that require no attention at all.

Most researchers have assumed that there are no important developmental or individual differences in passive, automatic cognitive processes. Hasher and Zacks (1979) even proposed this constancy as a defining feature of an automatic process. Cognitive development textbooks have suggested that the forgetting of passively held acoustic information does not change with age (e.g., Bjorklund, 1995, p. 104; Siegler, 1991, p. 206). Indeed, although some researcher have failed to find significant age differences in presumably automatic encoding processes, others do detect age differences (for a review, see Kausler, 1990). However, our recent findings (Keller & Cowan, 1994; Saults & Cowan, 1996) suggest that there are developmental changes in some passive, automatic processes that could affect STM capacity.

How does one examine passive storage directly, independent of active processes that can renew information in the passive memory store? For acoustic memory, at least two procedures have provided evidence of totally passive storage processes. In the two-tone comparison procedure, a participant hears a sound and then, following a silent interval of variable duration, hears another and must compare the two and determine if they are the same or different (for a review, see Cowan, 1984). When the sounds are similar enough, such as tones of two slightly different pitches or vowels of slightly different quality, performance typically declines across 20 - 30 s as the interval between sounds increases, with the most severe decline in the first few seconds. Recent adult research suggests that this decline cannot be prevented (though it can be slowed somewhat) by covert rehearsal of the first sound in the pair during the intervening interval (Keller, Cowan, & Saults, 1995; Pechmann & Mohr, 1992). The acoustic memory apparently fades, for the most part, passively and automatically. In another procedure, the participant must attend selectively to one channel and ignore another channel. Some time later, the participant is asked to recall information from the ignored channel. Recall depends on acoustic qualities, phonological qualities, or whatever qualities are saved automatically, without help from attention-demanding mnemonic strategies. Although this usually has been done with attended and ignored channels presented to opposite ears (e.g., Broadbent, 1957; Glucksberg & Cowen, 1970; Norman, 1969), dichotic presentation is less than ideal for our purposes because it permits cross-channel auditory interference. When one wants to isolate and examine information in passive memory storage per se, such interference should be avoided by presenting the attended task visually, checking to make sure that attention is truly diverted away from the acoustic modality. This method has shown that there is memory representation of ignored tones (Eriksen & Johnson, 1964) and ignored syllables of speech (Cowan, Lichty, & Grove, 1990) that is lost across a period of 20 s or more during a silent, poststimulus interval.

We adapted these two kinds of procedures to look for evidence of developmental change in the passive store of auditory stimuli. The simpler technique (two-tone comparison) revealed age differences in children's memory for tonal stimuli. The other procedure (memory for ignored words) provided converging evidence of developmental change in the passive storage of speech stimuli. Together, these two approaches suggest that older children retain more auditory information than younger ones over about 10 or 15 post-stimulus seconds without assistance from active rehearsal processes.

Pitch Memory Persistence

The simplest method to study age differences in rehearsal-independent short-term storage seemed to be two-tone comparison, in which two tones separated by a variable, silent interstimulus interval (ISI) are presented and are judged to be "the same" or "not the same". This simple concept proved somewhat more complicated in practice (Keller & Cowan, 1994). Children required an elaborate training phase to ensure that they could reliably perform the task. Various computer animations built into the program that delivered the stimuli and recorded responses, presented between trials, served effectively as reinforcers to maintain children's interest in the procedure.

Additional complications stemmed from the need to match younger and older children's performance at the shortest ISI to reduce the chances of confounding forgetting rates with age differences in encoding. A basic strategy to accomplish this matching is to determine, for each participant, the frequency difference that yields the same moderate level of performance at a fixed, short ISI (2 s). In the test phase, a wider range of ISIs can be used, and differences between age groups in performance at longer ISIs can be attributed to a developmental change in the persistence of the memory representations. However, initial attempts to apply this methodology by Keller (1992) were problematic. Using several ISIs randomly intermixed in the main test phase of the experiment, many trials were needed to plot the course of forgetting. Thus, children sat through long sessions composed primarily of silent periods. This naturally led to some drifting of attention in the younger children. Though individual difficulty levels were matched initially, older participants benefitted more from practice during the long test phase and performance levels changed to defeat the matching attempts.

Keller and Cowan (1994) succeeded by reconceptualizing the problem. They realized that they could use the adjustment procedure not only initially, to pinpoint the correct level of difficulty for the participant, but also in the test phase, to pinpoint more efficiently the duration of the ISI that the participant's memory could tolerate. Both of these main phases of the experiment used the adaptive tracking procedure developed by Levitt (1971), in which incorrect responses are followed by easier stimulus values and correct responses are followed by more difficult values, until a criterion level of performance is reached with some certainty. Keller and Cowan used 200-ms-long tones and, in the initial stimulus adjustment phase, they began with pairs of tones that either were the same or differed by 20 Hz, and always were separated by 2 s of silence. If a participant got four consecutive "not-the-same" trials correct, the frequency difference between tones was cut in half. However, if a single "not-the-same" trial was answered incorrectly, the frequency difference was doubled. This adjustment process continued until the direction of change in the task difficulty reversed itself 7 times, and the geometric mean of the difficulty levels across the last 6 reversals was taken as the resulting criterion difficulty level. Levitt (1971) demonstrated that this "4-down, 1-up" protocol theoretically must result in stimulus values approximating 84% correct performance.

The criterion frequency difference obtained for each child was used throughout the critical test phase. Now, however, the ISIs varied across the trials. Trials belonging to two adaptive tracking procedures were randomly intermixed. One of them, another 4-down, 1-up procedure, was designed to determine the ISI that would produce 84% performance for these tones. Whenever four consecutive "not-the-same" trial were answered correctly, the ISI was multiplied by 1.5, and every time a "not-the-same" trial was answered incorrectly, the ISI was divided by 1.5. Barring practice or fatigue effects, the result should approximate a 2-s criterion ISI, replicating the results of the frequency-adjustment phase. However, the other adaptive track used a "2-down, 1-up" procedure, which produces a criterion level that yields approximately 71% correct performance (Levitt, 1971). An age difference in the persistence of memory for pitch would be indicated if the different age groups have the same mean criterion ISIs in the 84% track but different ones in the 71% track.

The results are shown in Figure 1, reprinted from Keller and Cowan (1994).

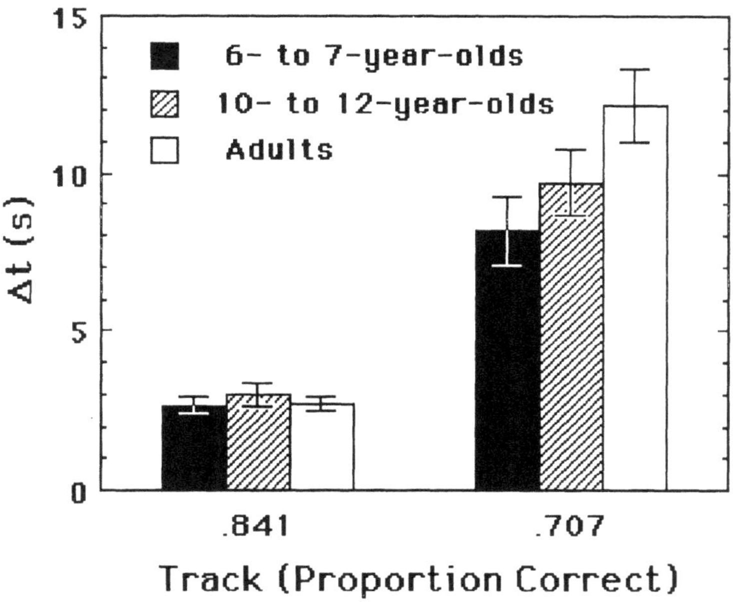

Figure 1. Tone comparison performance of participants from three age groups measured in the mean Δt, the empirically obtained time difference that allowed performance up to some criterion level. This dependent measure is shown for two different criterion levels. The absence of a group difference at the high criterion level (.841 correct) means that the group difference at the lower criterion level (.707 correct) can be interpreted as resulting from differences in memory loss over time, not from an overall performance level difference between groups. Error bars represent the standard error of the mean. Figure reprinted from Keller and Cowan (1994, p. 859, Figure 1) by permission of the American Psychological Association.

With 24 participants at each of three ages, there were clear, significant group differences in the criterion ISIs for the 71% track (right), even though the age groups were matched in the 84% track. The ISI producing that 71% performance level was about 8, 10, and 12 s for 6-7-year-olds, 10-12-year-olds, and college students, respectively. The data also revealed absolutely no differences in the "same" or catch trials that could compromise the conclusion that pitch memory persisted longer in older participants.

In a second experiment, Keller and Cowan (1994) addressed the question of whether the age differences could be attributed to rehearsal processes in the older participants. College students performed a two-tone comparison task, but rehearsal was blocked on half the trials by an interfering task. A well-known song title was presented before every trial. After the first tone in each pair, the participant saw the words "Rehearse Tone 1" or "Perform Musical Imagery Task." When the latter instructions appeared, the participant was to produce the pitch contour of the song silently, using the computer mouse to represent pitches on a visual display. Detailed coding of the musical imagery showed that it was carried out diligently, and should have blocked attempts to rehearse the tones. Nevertheless, performance levels on the pitch comparison task were the same for the two conditions. Neither accuracy nor rate of responding in the musical imagery task were correlated with pitch memory performance in the presence of that task (r = -.07 and .13, respectively), ruling out tradeoffs between the two tasks. In contrast, pitch memory performance in the rehearsal and imagery conditions were correlated with one another (r = .63, p < .02, 2-tailed), as they should if they rely on common processes.

Keller and Cowan's (1994) conclusion that the age differences they observed were due to memory rather than attention is strengthened by an electrophysiological study of mismatch negativity (MMN) (Gomes, Sussman, Ritter, Kurtzberg, Cowan & Vaughn, 1966). MMN is a negative-going component of the auditory event related potential that is thought to reflect the underlying transient memory upon which auditory discrimination depends (Näätänen, 1992; Ritter, Deacon, Gomes, Javitt, & Vaughan, 1995). It occurs when a repeated sound changes discriminably, whether or not the subject actively listened to the sounds. Therefore, the MMN is considered to be basically preattentive and automatic. It is thought to reflect a process in which the deviant tone's characteristics are compared to the memory of the prior standard tone and found to differ from it. Of course, this can occur only if the memory of the standard has remained active long enough for the comparison to be carried out. Gomes et al. presented trains of eight 100-ms-long tones separated by silent periods of 250 ms within à train. The trains of tones were separated by silent inter-train intervals (ITIs) of 1 or 8 s. All tones were standards (1000 Hz) except for the first tone of each train, which was deviant (1200 Hz) for half of the trains. The participants, 12 adults and 20 children from three age groups, 6 to 7 years, 8 to 10 years, and 11 to 12 years, sat quietly and ignored the stimuli by either reading a book or watching a video without sound. MMN was derived by subtracting the responses to the standard tones in the initial position within a train from the responses to the deviant tone in that same position. In the 1-s ITI condition, MMNs were observed for all age groups. However, in the 8-s ITI condition, MMNs were only detected for the adults and the 11-12 year old children. Presumably, the reason the MMN was not obtained with an 8-s ITI in the younger children is that the memory representation of the standard tones did not survive the ITI. Therefore, Gomes et al. argued that these age differences were due to longer-lasting preattentive auditory memory representations in the older participants.

Although Keller and Cowan (1994) and Gomes et al. (1996) provide important evidence for age differences in the passive storage of simple tones, a similar demonstration with speech stimuli would be more clearly related to the phonological loop. Unfortunately, it seems inappropriate to extend this technique to speech sounds because they occur along a continuum that is divided into phonemic categories. The tone comparison difficulty had to be individually adjusted, and it would be impossible to make comparable adjustments of speech sounds without crossing category boundaries for some participants. Thus, we turned to a different procedure to look for converging evidence of development change in the passive storage of speech.

Persistence of Memory for Ignored Speech

Unlike the exact pitches of slightly different pure tones, speech stimuli are easily recoded and rehearsed, at least in sufficiently advanced participants (Gathercole & Baddeley, 1993). To examine the rate of loss of memory for the automatically encoded features of speech, we selected a procedure that would minimize recoding and rehearsal. Saults and Cowan (1996) used procedures in which participants were to ignore speech sounds when presented, engaging instead in a silent visual task until a visual cue interrupted the visual task and prompted the participant to identify the most recent speech sound. Eriksen and Johnson (1964) had used a similar procedure to demonstrate that adults' memory for tones is lost gradually with increases in the silent test delay between the last sound and the tone recall period. Cowan et al. (1990) modified their procedure to examine loss of memory for speech sounds in adults. We subsequently adopted this strategy for our developmental research.

In Saults and Cowan (1996), the acoustic stimuli to be ignored were digitally stored and reproduced tokens of the four words bee, tea, bow, and toe in a male voice (with three different recordings of each word to create more variety in the acoustic representation). They were presented in random order with randomly arranged ISIs of 1, 5, or 10 s between words. In the Experiment 1, the silent visual task was one in which four designs were presented in the quadrants of the computer screen and a fifth design, presented in the center of the screen, was identical to one of the four surrounding ones. The matching design was to be selected using a computer joystick.

In the test phase of this experiment, the visual matching task was occasionally replaced by pictures representing a bee, tea, a bow, and a toe. Then the participant was to select the picture depicting the most recently heard word, and after that the matching task resumed. This test phase was preceded by practice on the auditory identification task alone, and on the visual matching task alone. Additional sessions of the visual matching task alone were conducted immediately before and after the test phase, allowing us to check the allocation of attention in the main test phase. Colorful computer animations within the program that presented stimuli and recorded responses helped maintain participants' interest level.

This first experiment included children from two age groups (5-7-year-olds and 8-10-year-olds). We found that attention was allocated as expected. The accuracy on the visual matching task was very high for both age groups (though the older participants carried it out more quickly), and both the accuracies and the speeds of this task were nearly identical when the visual task was performed alone as when it was punctuated by speech recall trials. This strongly suggests that participants, as a rule, did not withdraw attention from the visual matching task in order to listen to the sounds that they were instructed to ignore.

Performance on the speech recall task presented alone was nearly perfect at all age groups, but performance was somewhat lower when the spoken stimuli were to be ignored at the time of their presentation, during the visual matching task. In this situation, averaged across test delays, the younger and older groups of children identified the correct word on 87% and 95% of the trials, respectively, a difference that is significant at $p < .001$. However, the interaction of age with test delay was not significant in this experiment. Therefore, it was possible that encoding processes, rather than memory loss over time, could account for the age differences. We also worried that memory performance was too high to be maximally sensitive to age differences. We refined our methods in a second experiment and obtained less ambiguous results.

For Experiment 2 of Saults and Cowan (1996), we introduced two changes to increase the sensitivity to age differences. First, we switched to a different visual task in which matches between various pictures had to be made on the basis of which ones rhymed. We hoped that this new task would not only engage participants' attention but also would tie up phonemic encoding processes and further reduce the chances for rehearsal. The visual task was formally the same as before, but different in content. Children initially learned the names of various pictures. Then, in the matching task, four peripheral pictures and a central picture were presented, as before; but in this task, the one that was to be selected had a name that rhymed with the name of the central picture. A second change was to increased the range of ages in order to examine a broader range of developmental change. In Experiment 2, there were 24 participants at each of three age ranges: 6-7 years, 8-9 years, and college students.

Unlike Experiment 1, Experiment 2 of Saults and Cowan (1996) did yield a significant interaction of Age x Test Delay, $p < .005$. The results of both experiments are shown in Figure 2, reprinted from Saults and Cowan (1996). The interaction in Experiment 2, shown in the right-hand panel of the figure, was not caused solely by the addition of the adult group. Even when only the two child groups were analyzed, the interaction remained significant, $p < .05$. This is important because the child groups performed similarly at the 1-s delay, as the figure shows, yet the loss of information across 10 s differed markedly between the two age groups. As in the first experiment, the levels of performance on the visual matching task were the same no matter whether it was carried out alone or punctuated by occasional speech recall trials.

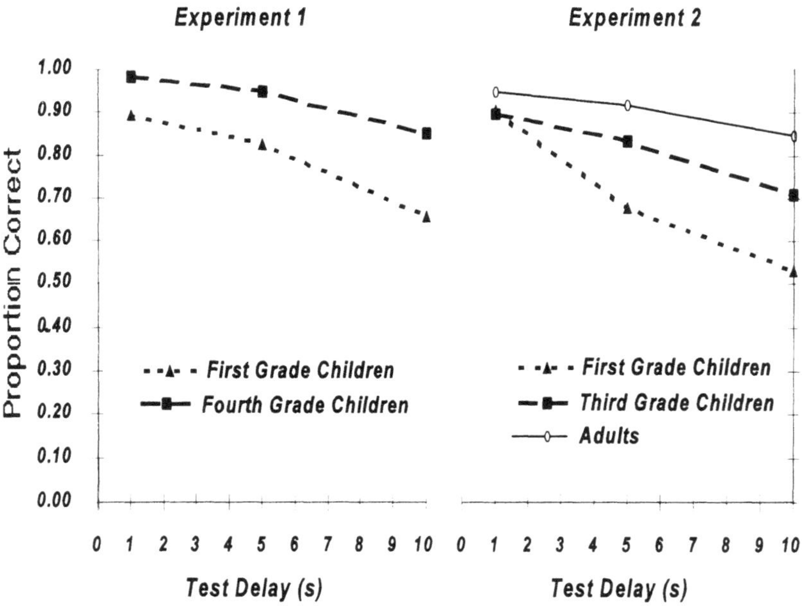

Figure 2. Memory for ignored speech in two different experiments, for participants of several age groups. Experiment 1 (left panel) involved a nonverbal primary task and did not produce an age difference in memory loss across test delays, whereas Experiment 2 (right panel) involved a silent, picture-rhyming task and did result in age differences in memory loss across delays. Figure redrawn from Saults and Cowan (1996).

Summary

Our tone and speech research converge to suggest that there are developmental differences in at least some automatic, passive memory processes, contrary to conventional wisdom. This has important implications for theories of working memory. Baddeley (1986) assumed that the rate of passive memory loss or decay stays fixed across ages and that developmental increases in STM capacity reflect improvements in the rate of covert rehearsal. That assumption now seems less certain. If the form of passive memory for ignored speech seen here turns out to be the same as the form termed the "phonological store" in

Baddeley's (1986) model, or at least turns out to operate in the same way (a question that has not yet been addressed empirically), then age differences in passive as well as active components may contribute to developmental differences in STM capacity.

Active Processes in Working Memory

Although the active processes of working memory clearly have been assumed to change with age, the situation seems more complex than is generally believed. Earlier, we mentioned that Cowan et al. (1992) and Henry (1991a) demonstrated that memory decay during recall can affect short-term serial recall performance and contribute to the word length effect. We have done additional studies regarding how recall occurs and how it may change across ages in childhood.

Cowan (1992) and Cowan et al. (1994) examined children's recall by using a computer equipped with an acoustic waveform editor to measure, rather tediously and precisely, the durations of words and inter-word pauses in the tape-recorded responses within individual trials in a word span task. Only the responses to correctly recalled lists were used. Results were inconsistent with a simple hypothesis that information decays in a monotonic fashion during the recall period. Using 4-year-old participants, Cowan (1992) showed that there was no fixed duration of recall within an individual. Instead, longer lists not only led to longer times for recall (e.g., up to about 5 s or longer in some children) but also to slower rates of recall. The list length did not affect the actual duration of words in the response, but did affect the duration of silent pauses between words.

Figure 3, based on the data from Cowan (1992), shows this pattern. Each bar in the figure represents the mean timing of recall for a particular group of 4-year-old children on a particular type of word. The first two bars are for children with a memory span of 3 items, when these children are to repeat lists of two items (one below their span, top bar) or three items (equal to their span, second bar). The third and fourth bars show the same thing for children with a span of 4 items, when repeating lists of two or three items.

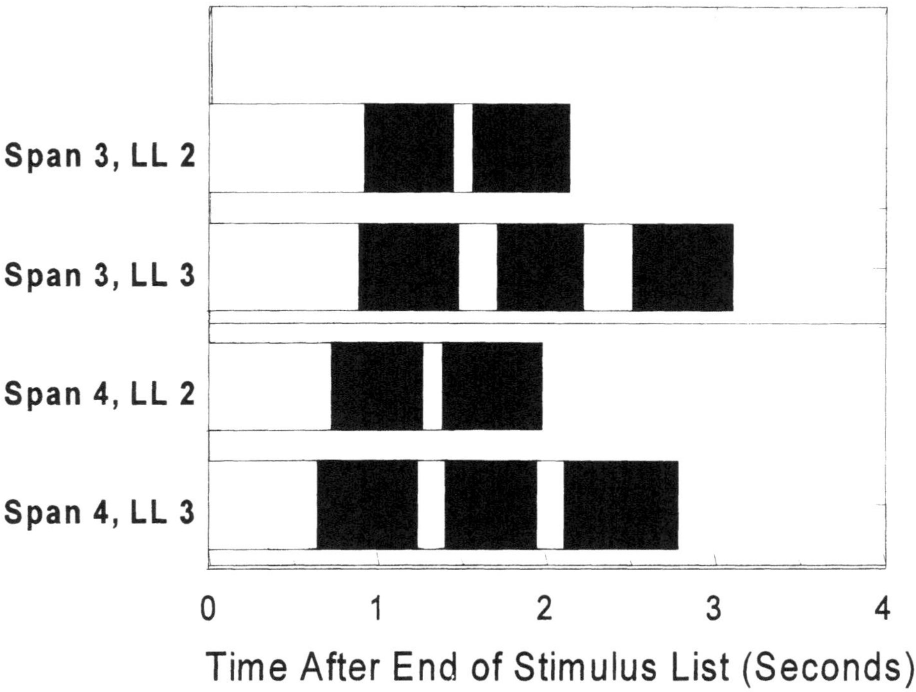

Figure 3. The mean timing of words within 4-year-olds' spoken responses to word lists of different list lengths (LL). Dark segments are words and light ones are silent intervals; see text for further explanation. The data are from Cowan (1992).

Within each data bar in Figure 3, the first white segment represents the mean duration of the preparatory interval between the last stimulus and the first response word; the dark segments represent the mean durations of words in each serial position in the response; and the intervening white segments represent the mean durations of inter-word pauses. In this study, no significant effects of list length occurred for the preparatory intervals or word durations, but the list length effect was significant for the inter-word pauses. Specifically, for a group of children with a particular span, longer list lengths resulted in longer inter-word pauses. This effect can be seen in the figure (compare Bars 1&2; 3&4). Notice also that, for a particular length of lists, children with a higher span produced shorter inter-word pauses (compare Bars 1&3; 2&4), an effect that was significant. There was no such difference between these groups in the word durations.

Though we still have little more than an educated guess about what processes take place during the silent inter-word pauses, the data do seem to suggest one reasonable possibility. The results are generally consistent with previous theories (Sternberg, Monsell, Knoll, & Wright, 1978; Sternberg, Wright, Knoll, & Monsell, 1980) emphasizing how serial recall requires repeated searches through the entire STM representation to determine which word to say next. This search presumably takes more time for longer lists, slowing the rate of recall.

Cowan et al. (1994) compared the timing of responses in a span task of children 4 and 8 years of age. They found age differences in the inter-word pauses. For a particular list length, the older children produced shorter inter-word silent pauses in their responses. In this study, younger children's correct repetitions of span-length lists (M = 3.00 items) were compared to older children's correct repetitions of lists one below span (M = 3.51 items). Despite the slightly longer list length for the older children in this comparison, the inter-word pauses in the younger children (M = .38 s) were longer than in the older children (M = .23 s). There was no such age difference in the duration of words in the response; even though older children were capable of speaking faster than younger ones, they did not do so in the span task, which was not speeded. Thus, combining the studies of Cowan (1992) and Cowan et al. (1994), the results suggest that the retrieval of items from STM during inter-word pauses may occur more efficiently in more capable or older children.

There was, it should be noted, a potentially important discrepancy between the individual difference results of Cowan (1992) and the developmental results of Cowan et al. (1994). Preparatory intervals produced a large age effect, with shorter preparatory intervals in older children than in younger ones (Cowan et al., 1994), even though the preparatory intervals did not seem to be related to individual differences in span among 4-year-olds (Cowan, 1992). Mechanisms of individual and developmental differences thus do not appear to be identical. The processing occurring in preparatory intervals may be quite complex, perhaps including a mixture of rehearsal, memory search, and motor preparation processes, some of which may vary among individuals of a particular age more than others.

According to Baddeley (1986), the participant's age and the length of words to be recalled both affect recall for the same reason; both affect the rate at which the items can be rehearsed. However, Cowan et al. (1994) found that these variables have different effects on the timing of spoken recall. Age affects the duration of silent pauses, whereas word length affects the duration of recalled items but not the pauses between items. Given the absence of word length effects in these pauses, the STM retrieval processes occurring during the pauses are not likely to involve covert articulation. Instead, they may include a search through lexical nodes that are the same for words of any length. Other research provides converging evidence that the rate of memory search does not depend on the length of words in the search set (Clifton & Tash, 1973; Chase, 1977). What these results imply for models of working memory is that the processes contributing to memory span must be more complex than Baddeley (1986) assumed. They must include a process during inter-word pauses that is not the same as covert rehearsal.

Cowan et al. (1994) also included a rapid speech task. While most other investigators have examined the relation between speech rate and memory span only in terms of group means across different conditions, Cowan et al. examined the relation within each age group. The expected positive correlation was obtained within 8-year-olds, but not within 4-year-olds (who showed a slight negative correlation). Gathercole et al. (1994) reported a similar finding, a significant speech rate / span correlation in adults but not in 4-year-olds. These results further argue that rehearsal rate cannot provide a complete account of individual and group differences in memory span. Our research suggests that the rate of memory search might account for some additional variation in span.

Recently researchers in this laboratory have tried a slightly different approach to help our understanding of how various factors contribute to memory span. Cowan, N. Wood, P. Wood, T. Keller, Nugent, & C. Keller (in press) found that the inter-word pause durations and rapid speech durations had a fairly high level of internal intercorrelation, and that both correlated with memory span (with correlations in the range of -.3 to -.5); but these two types of timing measures nevertheless did not correlate with one another (with most correlations below .1). Instead, they appeared to explain independent portions of the variance in memory span. We combined measures of each type to form a latent variable model of performance, which accounted for about 60% of the variance in span and about 87% of the age-related variance.

The latent variable model presented by Cowan et al (in press) does not seem entirely consistent with recent theories on memory development, which hypothesize that time affects cognitive performance based on a single, global speed of processing (e.g., Hale & Jansen, 1994; Kail & Park, 1994; Salthouse &

Coon, 1993). Given that speech rate and interword pauses are unrelated to one another, both cannot be attributed to a single, truly global speed of processing.

It might be worth speculating as to how two active processes, memory search and covert rehearsal, could contribute to span. Minimal modification of Baddeley's (1986) model would involve the added assumption that various active processes affect span for similar reasons. Specifically, the longer an active process takes, the greater the time that elapses, during which the decay of information in phonological storage can continue.

In summary, our research suggests additional factors involving active process that might have to be incorporated in processing models of working memory, though more work will be needed to determine the exact nature of these processes. A modification of Baddeley's (1986) model that accommodates our recent results would include the idea that measures of STM capacity depend on the efficiency of various active mnemonic operations because information can be lost from the passive, short-term representation while those active operations are ongoing. Rehearsal and memory search are examples of these active operations. The duration of passive storage may differ among individuals and change with age as well, as the evidence from Keller and Cowan (1994) and Saults and Cowan (1996) suggests.

Passive and Active Processes in STM: Where Do We Go From Here?

Our recent developmental research discussed above (Cowan, 1992; Cowan et al., 1994; Cowan et al., in press; Keller & Cowan, 1994; Saults & Cowan, 1996) was designed to look at very basic processes that may change with development and may differ among individuals. Some of our future research will be devoted to seeking further evidence for the developmental and individual differences we have observed, and some will be devoted to obtaining further clarification of the nature of the underlying processes. Additionally, though, it will be important to put these processes in a broader context. How do the processes we have examined relate to intellectual functioning in general? More reflection upon methodology will be helpful here, and various research from other laboratories can also provide insights.

What is the Pattern of Intercorrelations between Tests of Active and Passive STM Processes?

Where multiple processes are involved, one important initial question is what is related to what. The number of underlying domains of individual and developmental difference may be smaller than the number of processes that we have measured. For example, we have not yet determined the relationships between the duration of auditory memory (as examined by Keller & Cowan, 1994; Saults & Cowan, 1996) and the speed of the active processes (as examined, for example, by Cowan, 1992; Cowan et al., 1994; Hulme & Tordoff, 1989). Cowan et al. (in press) found no correlation between two active processes, maximal pronunciation rate and STM search rate. However, it is possible that other skills we have examined correlate with one another. One way in which this could work is that several domains of processing could exist that are subserved by different neural subsystems, each with its own internal integrity. For example, there could be an auditory/verbal processing domain (probably most dependent on the temporal lobes) that is relatively independent of another, executive processing domain (probably most dependent on the frontal lobes). If this speculation is correct, one might expect a correlation between passive memory decay rates and verbal rehearsal rates, on one hand, and a correlation between STM search and other tasks that have been taken as indices of a "global" processing speed (e.g., Hale & Jansen, 1994; Kail & Salthouse, 1994), on the other hand. Yet, the auditory/verbal and central processing domains could be relatively independent, with low or no correlations between tasks reflecting different domains. We are not proposing that this is necessarily true, but we wish to illustrate the point that comprehensive correlational findings could be important and exciting in this research area.

Is There Other Evidence of Developmental and Individual Differences in Passive STM Processes We Have Examined?

Research that has been conducted in other laboratories may be tapping into some of the same processes that we have been investigating, though in many cases it is too soon to tell. For example, Gathercole and Baddeley (1989, 1990) have examined performance on a nonword repetition task and have found that it is related to vocabulary acquisition in children. The same task has been shown to be related to language comprehension (Montgomery, 1995) and language production (Adams & Gathercole, 1995). However, we do not understand the essential difference between children who do better or worse on this nonword repetition task. According to the model of Baddeley (1986) and of Gathercole and Baddeley (1993), nonword repetition ability might depend on the persistence of memory in the passive phonological store. If so, it could be closely akin to the kinds of memory found to change with development by Keller and Cowan (1994) and/or by Saults and Cowan (1996). Alternatively, it is possible that some more active process accounts for individual and developmental differences in nonword repetition ability.

A candidate that seems even more likely to be related to the passive storage we have examined is auditory memory as studied with the suffix effect (Crowder & Morton, 1969; Morton, Crowder, & Prussin, 1971). In this effect, a list of spoken items to be recalled is followed by one final item that is not to be recalled. (It typically is a particular nonsense word or a signal such as the word "go," which is not easily confused with a list item to be recalled.) When the suffix item is acoustically similar to the list items and is interpreted perceptually as coming from a similar source (Ayres, Jonides, Reitman, Egan, & Howard, 1979), there is considerable interference with memory for the last few items in the list.

At least for the final serial position, this effect can be attributed to interference with the automatically held auditory memory for the last few items, inasmuch the effect in that position is not influenced by strategic factors in processing (Balota & Engle, 1981; Greenberg & Engle, 1983). Sipe and Engle (1986) found that the suffix effect was larger in children who were poorer readers, and Gillam, Cowan, and Day (1995) found the same thing for language-impaired children, in comparison with other children matched to the impaired group for reading level.

Sipe and Engle (1986) also carried out a selective listening task in which children had to recall items in the channel that had been ignored. As a function of time and the amount of intervening material (which were confounded), memory dropped off more quickly in poorer readers. Like the suffix effects, these results could tap a process similar to the memory for ignored speech, which Saults and Cowan (1995) found to change with normal development.

Is There Other Evidence of Developmental and Individual Differences in the Active STM Processes We Have Considered?

Rehearsal. It is worth noting that the speed at which a person can pronounce words has been shown to predict not only developmental differences in memory span within childhood (e.g., Hulme et al., 1984), but also individual differences in span (e.g., Baddeley et al., 1975; Gathercole et al., 1994), language differences (e.g., Naveh-Benjamin & Ayres, 1986; Nicolson, 1981; Stigler, Lee, & Stevenson, 1986) and differences due to aging in adulthood (Kynette, Kemper, Norman, & Cheung, 1990; Multhaup, Balota, & Cowan, 1996). However, it appears as if the individual differences within a group are not accounted for as closely as are the differences between group means, which typically fall nicely into a linear relationship between speech rate and memory span. For example, in adult participants, Gathercole et al. (1994, Experiment 3) found a speech rate / memory span correlation of .43 between speech rate and memory span for digits, and a similar correlation of .45 for word stimuli. These findings underscore the point that much of the variance in span is not accounted for by speech rate.

Memory search. Cowan (1992) and Cowan et al. (1994) proposed that the duration of silent, inter-word pauses in children's recall may reflect the duration of memory search processes taking place during those silent periods. This is a key point in need of further investigation. Currently, the point rests on the absence of correlation between these pauses and the rate of rapid pronunciation (Cowan et al., in press) and on the absence of word length effects both in the inter-word pauses (Cowan et al., 1994, in preparation) and in memory search tasks (Chase, 1977; Clifton & Tash, 1973).

There are, however, some additional findings tying memory search tasks directly to developmental changes and individual differences. There is a marked developmental improvement in the rate of memory search (Keating et al., 1980), and search rates are slower than normal in children with language impairment (Sininger, Klatzky, & Kirchner, 1989), who also show a deficit in STM (e.g., Gillam et al., 1995).

It seems reasonable, then, that memory search could account for some of the variance in memory span. Here, we in fact may find a pattern similar to that found for rehearsal speed. Specifically, Cavanagh (1972) found a strong linear relation between memory search rate and memory span when the means for various types of stimulus material, accumulated across various published studies, were plotted. However, the relation between search rate and memory span is apparently much weaker when examined on an individual subject basis (Puckett & Kausler, 1984), although there is still not enough evidence on that point.

The reason that the within-subject relations between span and other processing variables are weak may be that no one of them alone accounts for memory span well, whereas several of these variables together might do a much better job. Recall that Cowan et al. (in press) found little relation between rapid speech rate and the inter-word pauses in a span task, though both correlated with span. In a second experiment, using adult participants, a similar pattern was obtained with a paper-and-pencil task that was modeled loosely after Sternberg's (1966) memory search procedure. In this task, adult participants had a fixed period to find and circle as many of the target items as they could within a large array. The number circled could be converted in to a search rate (which was much slower than in Sternberg's procedure). The search rate in this procedure correlated moderately well (and significantly) with memory span, as did the speed of rapid covert rehearsal; but the search and rehearsal rates nevertheless did not correlate with each other. This is further preliminary evidence that memory search is important in span for a reason that is not the same as covert rehearsal, though evidence with more conventional search tasks is needed.

Are Other Active Processes That We Have Not Discussed Important for STM?

Certainly they are. We have focused on one type of verbal STM, the type that is important when a short list of items drawn from a small set is to be recalled in the correct serial order. In other tasks, it is clear that somewhat different faculties of the mind are used. For example, the system of effects described by Baddeley (1986) does not operate in the same way if the circumstances are different. In one important interaction, the word length effect (advantage in recall for words that can be pronounced more quickly) disappears when rehearsal is blocked by articulatory suppression, a repetitive articulatory task. However, LaPointe and Engle (1990) found that when stimuli were drawn from a much larger set, the word length effect was no longer eliminated by articulatory suppression. Perhaps the remaining word length effect in that condition is only the part related to output delays (Cowan et al., 1992), and not the part related to rehearsal.

It also has been shown that memory span depends critically on participants' knowledge of the items; memory span for nonsense words is much worse than for real words (e.g., Case, Kurland, & Goldberg, 1982). The knowledge component appears separate from the phonological loop component. Thus, Hulme, Maughan, and Brown (1991) found that the slope of the relation between speech rate and memory span was the same for words and nonwords, but at a higher level for words, suggesting that word knowledge and rehearsal rate affected span through unrelated mechanisms. (For discrepant results challenging the supposed separateness of the mechanisms, however, see Multhaup et al., 1996).

Considering cognition more broadly still, the correlation between memory span tasks and more complex problem-solving tasks, such as language comprehension, is not very large. Daneman and Carpenter (1980) obtained a larger correlation using what is termed a "working memory span" task, in which information must be processed and held in storage at the same time. They had subjects read sentences for comprehension and also remember the last word in each sentence, with the requirement that they recall the words after a set of sentences had been presented. The number of words successfully repeated in this task was taken as the working memory span. Other extensions of this "operation span" type of task also have been used; for example, a mathematics processing task can be combined with word or digit recall (Engle & Oransky, in press; Turner & Engle, 1989). A recent meta-analysis of operation span tasks (Daneman and Merikle, 1996) suggests that the correlation between working memory span and comprehension and problem-solving tasks is in the order of .3 to .5, whereas correlations of ordinary span with comprehension are typically weaker. The fact that working memory span tasks correlate with comprehension and problem-solving tasks more strongly than do ordinary memory span tasks suggests that the mechanisms entering into ordinary, verbal STM tasks comprise only some of the working memory mechanisms used in everyday cognition. The difference is that the more complex working memory tasks stress the control of attention. Kyllonen and Christal (1990) even proposed, on the basis of a great deal of testing with practical reasoning tasks and working memory tasks in the same individuals, that the main component of reasoning is working memory capacity. In such a view, working memory capacity is conceived as the ability to use attentional processes to retain and manipulate information in the service of a problem-solving goal. This makes sense because the solution of a problem often requires that several key facts be held in mind at the same time so that they can be combined.

At least two studies have suggested that a key feature of the working memory span task is the ability to inhibit irrelevant stimuli. First, Conway and Engle (1994) found that participants with a relatively high working memory span could search memory at a more rapid rate than those with a lower working memory span. This forms a bridge between working memory span and the processes that we have suggested for ordinary memory span. However, this relation of working memory span and memory search rate was obtained by Conway and Engle only when the memory search task involved searching for sets of items that each occurred within two different sets in the experiment. This introduced a potential confusion between sets, which presumably had to be inhibited or suppressed mentally for accurate performance to take place. Second, May, Kane, Hasher, and Valenti (1996) compared young and elderly adults and found that the advantage for the young in working memory span tasks was eliminated when the lists were presented in descending order instead of the usual ascending order. They reasoned that the most difficult, longest lists ordinarily are tested only after many other, shorter lists have been presented, in which case proactive interference from earlier lists has built up. (After many trials, the participant may begin to experience confusion as to whether an item was presented in the current trial or in a previous trial). The information from earlier trials must be inhibited for successful performance, and therefore the difficulty of the longest lists is reduced when the order of lists is descending rather than ascending.

At present, it is unclear how inhibition might or might not apply to ordinary STM measures. It is quite possible that much of the difference between individuals in memory span is the result of differences in the ability to inhibit irrelevant information so as to avoid proactive inhibition from previous trials. If this is the case, however, it does not necessarily invalidate traditional conceptions of the mechanisms entering into memory span (e.g., phonological loop mechanisms). It may be that when there is not much proactive inhibition, long-term memory can be used to save the items in a trial adequately for recall. Further, it may be that the role of proactive inhibition and its impairment of long-term memory retrieval is to make the phonological loop mechanisms necessary for the adequate recall of items in a list, on many or most trials.

In sum, in this section we have discussed a number of active processing mechanisms that have not been explicitly emphasized within a simple account of the phonological loop theory (Baddeley, 1986). However, these could be considered long-term memory and central executive processes. It would not be surprising to Baddeley or almost anyone else if new central executive processes were discovered, given the relatively complex and uncharted nature of that component of the working memory model. In contrast, our findings regarding new aspects of the phonological loop (Cowan, 1992; Cowan et al., 1992, 1994, in press; Keller & Cowan, 1994; Saults & Cowan, 1996) might be viewed as a bit more unforseen, though not incompatible with Baddeley's theory.

Concluding Observations

After the prolonged reliance upon the working memory model in the theoretical and applied cognitive fields (Baddeley, 1986) the time has come for a careful refinement of the theory, without throwing out its still-valid aspects. The present chapter has argued for an analytic approach toward refining the model, with special reliance on individual and developmental differences and what they may tell us.

We have relied largely on developmental data from children in these studies. One can make a case that these participants have something to offer theoretically that adults do not. In adults, individual differences emerge largely because an extensive repertoire of strategies exists. These strategies modulate performance to a striking extent even in the simplest tasks. In the case of the phonological loop, Logie, Sala, Laiacona, Chalmers, and Wynn (1996) showed how strategies can influence the word length and phonological similarity effects. Although phonological similarity and word length affected the group means robustly as expected, Logie et al. found that 43% of their subjects failed to show at least one of these effects. When some of their participants were retested, the presence of a word length or phonological similarity effect on the first test was a poor predictor of the presence of that effect on the retest. Participants' reports suggested that this variability could be partly accounted for by variations in strategies. Subjects who consistently chose a strategy of subvocal rehearsal were more likely to exhibit phonological similarity or word length effects. Subjects who reported other strategies or mixed strategies showed smaller effects.

In children, in contrast, the repertoire of strategies of use in STM is smaller (e.g., Flavell et al., 1966; Henry, 1991a, 1991b). Illustrating this point, Cowan,

Cartwright, Winterowd, and Sherk (1987) found that articulatory suppression serving to block rehearsal strategies in adult participants reduced their level of serial recall and their phonological similarity effect to magnitudes comparable to what is ordinarily obtained in 5-year-old children without rehearsal.

At this point in the research program, unfortunately, we cannot provide satisfactory answers to some haunting questions: what people place in their minds, how much they can place there, how long they can retain it and by what method. We do provide some intriguing clues about developmental and individual differences and their implications for the processing system used in STM, suggesting that some of the variance can be taken out of the error term (quantitatively speaking) and that some of the missing pieces in the intricate puzzle that is STM can be put in place (qualitatively speaking).

ACKNOWLEDGMENT

This project was supported by NIH Grant R01 HD21338 to NC.

REFERENCES

Adams, A.-M., & Gathercole, S.E. (1995). Phonological working memory and speech production in preschool children. *Journal of Speech and Hearing Research, 38,* 403-414.

Ayres, T.J., Jonides, J., Reitman, J.S., Egan, J.C., & Howard, D.A. (1979). Differing suffix effects for the same physical suffix. *Journal of Experimental Psychology: Human Learning & Memory, 5*, 315-321.

Baddeley, A.D. (1986). *Working memory.* Oxford, England: Clarendon Press.

Baddeley, A., & Hitch, G.J. (1974). Working memory. In G. Bower (ed.), *Recent advances in learning and motivation, Vol. VIII.* New York: Academic Press.

Baddeley, A.D., Thomson, N., & Buchanan, M. (1975). Word length and the structure of short-term memory. *Journal of Verbal Learning and Verbal Behavior, 14,* 575-589.

Balota, D. A., & Engle, R. W. (1981). Structural and strategic factors in the stimulus suffix *effect. Journal of Verbal Learning and Verbal Behavior, 20,* 346-357.

Bjorklund, D.F. (1995). *Children's thinking: Developmental function and individual differences.* Pacific Grove, CA: Brooks/Cole.

Broadbent, D.E. (1957). Immediate memory and simultaneous stimuli. *Quarterly Journal of Experimental Psychology, 9*, 1-11.

Brown, H.L., & Kirsner, K. (1980). A within-subjects analysis of the relationship between memory span and processing rate in short-term memory. *Cognitive Psychology, 12*, 177-187.

Case, R., Kurland, D.M., & Goldberg, J. (1982). Operational efficiency and the growth of short-term memory span. *Journal of Experimental Child*

Psychology, 33, 386-404.

Cavanagh, J.P. (1972).Relation between the immediate memory span and the memory search rate. *Psychological Review, 79*, 525-530.

Chase, W.G. (1977). Does memory scanning involve implicit speech? In S. Dornic (ed.), *Attention and performance VI.* Hillsdale, NJ: Erlbaum. (pp. 607-628)

Clifton, C., & Tash, J. (1973). Effect of syllabic word length on memory-search rate. *Journal of Experimental Psychology, 99*, 231-235.

Conway, R.A., & Engle, R.W.(1994). Working memory and retrieval: A resource-dependent inhibition model. *Journal of Experimental Psychology: General, 123*, 354-373.

Cowan, N. (1984). On short and long auditory stores. *Psychological Bulletin, 96*, 341-370.

Cowan, N. (1988). Evolving conceptions of memory storage, selective attention, and their mutual constraints within the human information processing system. *Psychological Bulletin, 104*, 163-191.

Cowan, N. (1992). Verbal memory span and the timing of spoken recall. *Journal of Memory & Language, 31*, 668-684

Cowan, N. (1993). Activation, attention, and short-term memory. *Memory & Cognition, 21*, 162-167.

Cowan, N. (1994). Mechanisms of verbal short-term memory. *Current Directions in Psychological Science, 3*, 185-189.

Cowan, N. (1995). *Attention and memory: An integrated framework.* New York: Oxford University Press.

Cowan, N., Cartwright, C., Winterowd, C., & Sherk, M. (1987). An adult model of preschool children's speech memory. *Memory & Cognition, 15*, 511-517.

Cowan, N., Day, L., Saults, J.S., Keller, T.A., Johnson, T., & Flores, L. (1992). The role of verbal output time in the effects of word length on immediate memory. *Journal of Memory & Language, 31*, 1-17.

Cowan, N., Keller, T., Hulme, C., Roodenrys, S., McDougall, S., & Rack, J. (1994). Verbal memory span in children: Speech timing clues to the mechanisms underlying age and word length effects. *Journal of Memory & Language, 33*, 234-250.

Cowan, N., Lichty, W., & Grove, T.R. (1990). Properties of memory for unattended spoken syllables. *Journal of Experimental Psychology: Learning, Memory, & Cognition, 16*, 258-269.

Cowan, N., Wood, N.L., Wood, P.K., Keller, T.A., Nugent, L.D., & Keller, C.V. (in press). Two separate verbal processing rates contributing to short-term memory span. *Journal of Experimental Psychology: General.*

Crowder, R. G., & Morton, J. (1969). Precategorical acoustic storage. *Perception & Psychophysics, 5*, 365-373.

Daneman, M., & Carpenter, P.A. (1980). Individual differences in working memory and reading. *Journal of Verbal Learning & Verbal Behavior, 19*, 450-466.

Daneman, M., & Merikle, P.M. (1996). Working memory and language comprehension: A Meta-Analysis. *Psychonomic Bulletin & Review, 3*, 422-433.

Engle, R.W., & Oransky, N. (in press). The evolution from short term to working memory: Multi-store to dynamic models of temporary storage. In R. Sternberg (ed.), *The concept of cognition.* Hillsdale, NJ: Erlbaum.

Eriksen, C.W., & Johnson, H.J. (1964). Storage and decay characteristics of nonattended auditory stimuli. *Journal of Experimental Psychology, 68*, 28-36.

Flavell, J.H., Beach, D.H., & Chinsky, J.M. (1966). Spontaneous verbal rehearsal in a memory task as a function of age. *Child Development, 37*, 283-

299.

Gathercole, S.E., Adams, A.M., & Hitch, G.J. (1994). Do young children rehearse? An individual-differences analysis. *Memory & Cognition, 22*, 201-207.

Gathercole, S. E., & Baddeley, A. D. (1989). Evaluation fo the role of phonological STM in the development of vocabulary in chidlren: A longitudinal study. *Journal of Memory and Language, 28*, 200-213.

Gathercole, S. E., & Baddeley, A. D. (1990). Phonological memory deficits in language disordered children: Is there a causal connection? *Journal of Memory and Language, 29*, 336-360.

Gathercole, S.E., & Baddeley, A.D. (1993). *Working memory and language.* Hove, U.K.: Erlbaum.

Gillam, R.B., Cowan, N., & Day, L.S. (1995). Sequential memory in children with and without language impairment. *Journal of Speech and Hearing Research, 38,* 393-402.

Glucksberg, S., & Cowen, G.N., Jr. (1970). Memory for nonattended auditory material. *Cognitive Psychology, 1*, 149-156.

Gomes, H., Sussman, E., Ritter, W., Kurtzberg, D., Cowan, N., & Vaughan, H.G., Jr. (1996, November). Developmental changes in an electrophysiological measure of short term memory. Paper presented to the Society for Neuroscience, Washington, D.C..

Greenberg, S.N., & Engle, R.W. (1983). Voice changes in the stimulus suffix effect: Are the effects structural or strategic? *Memory and Cognition, 11*, 551-556.

Guttentag, R. E. (1984). The mental effort requirement of cumulative rehearsal: A developmental study. *Journal of Experimental Child Psychology, 37,* 92-106.

Hale, S., & Jansen, J. (1994). Global processing-time coefficients characterize individual and group differences in cognitive speed. *Psychological Science, 5,* 384-389.

Hasher, L., & Zacks, R.T. (1979). Automatic and effortful processes in memory. *Journal of Experimental Psychology: General, 108*, 356-388.

Henry, L.A. (1991a). Development of auditory memory span: The role of rehearsal. *British Journal of Developmental Psychology, 9*, 493-511.

Henry, L.A. (1991b). Development of auditory memory span: The role of rehearsal. *British Journal of Developmental Psychology, 9*, 493-511.

Hulme, C., Maughan,S., & Brown, G.D.A. (1991). Memory for familiar and unfamiliar words: Evidence for a long-term memory contribution to short-term memory span. *Journal of Memory & Language, 30,* 685-701.

Hulme, C., Thomson, N., Muir, C., & Lawrence, A. (1984). Speech rate and the development of short-term memory span. *Journal of Experimental Child Psychology, 38*, 241-253.

Hulme, C., & Tordoff, V. (1989). Working memory development: The effects of speech rate, word length, and acoustic similarity on serial recall. *Journal of Experimental Child Psychology, 47*, 72-87.

James, W. (1890). The principles of psychology. NY: Henry Holt.

Kail, R., & Park, Y.S. (1994). Processing time, articulation time, and memory span. *Journal of Experimental Child Psychology, 57*, 281-291.

Kail, R., & Salthouse, T. A. (1994). Processing speed as a mental capacity. *Acta Psychologica, 86*, 199-255.

Kausler, D. (1990). Automaticity of encoding and episodic memory processes. In E. A. Lovelace (Ed.), *Aging and cognition: Mental processes, self-awareness, and interventions.* Amsterdam: North-Holland.

Keating, D.P., Keniston, A.H., Manis, F.R., & Bobbitt, B.L. (1980).

Development of the search-processing parameter. *Child Development, 51*, 39-44.

Keller, T.A. (1992). A developmental study of auditory sensory memory. Masters Thesis, University of Missouri, Columbia, MO.

Keller, T.A., & Cowan, N. (1994). Developmental increase in the duration of memory for tone pitch. *Developmental Psychology, 30*, 855-863.

Keller, T.A., Cowan, N., & Saults, J.S. (1995). Can auditory memory for tone pitch be rehearsed? *Journal of Experimental Psychology: Learning, Memory, & Cognition, 21*, 635-645.

Kyllonen, P.C., & Christal, R.E. (1990). Reasoning ability is (little more than) working-memory capacity?! *Intelligence, 14*, 389-433.

Kynette, D., Kemper, S., Norman, S., & Cheung, H. (1990). Adults' word recall and word repetition. *Experimental Aging Research, 16,* 117-121.

Landauer, T.K. (1962). Rate of implicit speech. *Perceptual & Motor Skills, 15*, 646.

LaPointe, L.B., & Engle, R.W. (1990). Simple and complex word spans as measures of working memory capacity. *Journal of Experimental Psychology: Learning, Memory, & Cognition, 16*, 1118-1133.

Levitt, H. (1971). Transformed up-down methods in psychoacoustics. *Journal of the Acoustical Society of America, 49,* 467-477.

Logie, R.H., Sala, S.D., Laiacona, M., Chalmers, P., & Wynn, V. (1996). Group aggregates and individual reliability: The case of verbal short-term memory, *Memory & Cognition, 24*, 305-321.

May, C.P. Kane, M.J., Hasher, L., & Valenti, M. (1996, November). Proactive interference and working memory span. Paper presented at the annual meeting of the Psychonomic Society, Chicago, IL.

Miller, G.A. (1956). The magical number seven, plus or minus two: Some limits on our capacity for processing information. *Psychological Review, 63,* 81-

97.

Morton, J., Crowder, R.G., & Prussin, H.A. (1971). Experiments with the stimulus suffix effect. *Journal of Experimental Psychology, 91*, 169-190.

Multhaup, K.S., Balota, D.A., & Cowan, N. (1996). Implications of aging, lexicality, and item length for the mechanisms underlying memory span. *Psychonomic Bulletin & Review, 3*, 112-120.

Näätänen, R. (1992). *Attention and brain function*. Hillsdale, N.J.: Erlbaum

Naveh-Benjamin, M., & Ayres, T.J. (1986). Digit span, reading rate, and linguistic relativity. *Quarterly Journal of Experimental Psychology, 38A*, 739-751.

Nicolson, R. (1981). The relationship between memory span and processing speed. In M. Friedman, J.P. Das, & N. O'Connor (eds.), *Intelligence and learning*. Plenum Press. (pp. 179-184)

Norman, D.A. (1969). Memory while shadowing. *Quarterly Journal of Experimental Psychology, 21*, 85-93.

Pechmann, T., & Mohr, G. (1992). Interference in memory for tonal pitch: Implications for a working-memory model. *Memory & Cognition, 20*, 314-320.

Puckett, J.M., & Kausler, D.H. (1984). Individual differences and models of memory span: A role for memory search rate? *Journal of Experimental Psychology: Learning, Memory, & Cognition, 10*, 72-82.

Ritter, W., Deacon, D., Gomes, H., Javitt, D.C., & Vaughan, H.G., Jr. (1995). The mismatch negativity of event-related potentials as a probe of transient auditory memory:A review. *Ear & Hearing, 16*, 52-67.

Roodenrys, S., Hulme, C., & Brown, G. (1993). The development of short-term memory span: Separable effects of speech rate and long-term memory. *Journal of Experimental Child Psychology, 56*, 431-442.

Salthouse, T.A., & Coon, V.E. (1993). Influence of task-specific processing speed on age differences in memory. *Journal of Gerontology: Psychological Sciences, 48,* 245-255.

Saults, J.S., & Cowan, N. (1996). The development of memory for ignored speech. *Journal of Experimental Child Psychology, 63*, 239-261.

Schweickert, R., & Boruff, B. (1986). Short-term memory capacity: Magic number or magic spell? *Journal of Experimental Psychology: Learning, Memory, and Cognition, 12,* 419-425.

Siegler, R.S. (1991). *Children's thinking.* Englewood Cliffs, NJ: Prentice-Hall.

Sininger, Y.S., Klatzky, R.L., & Kirchner, D.M. (1989). Memory scanning speed in language-disordered children. *Journal of Speech and Hearing Research, 32,* 289-297.

Sipe, S., Engle, R. W. (1986). Echoic memory processes in good and poor readers. *Journal of Experimental Psychology: Learning, Memory, and Cognition, 12*, 402-412.

Sternberg, S. (1966). High-speed scanning in human memory. *Science,* 153, 652-654.

Sternberg, S., Monsell, S., Knoll, R.L., & Wright, C.E. (1978). The latency and duration of rapid movement sequences: comparisons of speech and typewriting. In G.E. Stelmach (ed.), *Information processing in motor control and learning.* NY: Academic Press.

Sternberg, S., Wright, C.E., Knoll, R.L., & Monsell, S. (1980). Motor programs in rapid speech: Additional evidence. In R.A. Cole (ed.), *Perception and production of fluent speech.* Hillsdale, NJ: Erlbaum.

Stigler, J.W., Lee, S.-Y., & Stevenson, H.W. (1986). Digit memory in Chinese and English: Evidence for a temporally limited store. *Cognition, 23*, 1-20.

Turner, M.L., & Engle, R.W. (1989). Is working memory capacity task dependent? *Journal of Memory and Language, 28*, 127-154.

The Other Side of the Error Term - N. Raz (Editor)

Chapter 5

LIFESPAN STUDIES OF MENTAL CHRONOMETRY: INSIGHTS DERIVED FROM CHRONOPSYCHOPHYSIOLOGY

Theodore R. Bashore

University of Northern Colorado

K. Richard Ridderinkhof

University of Amsterdam

Maurits W. van der Molen

University of Amsterdam

ABSTRACT

The maturation and decline of the structure and timing of mental processing (i.e., mental chronometry) is explored from the perspective of chronopsychophysiology; that is, the methodology in which conjoint measures of reaction time and the latencies of components of the event-related brain potential are used to fractionate human information processing. Our discussion centers on the extent to which the structures mediating mental processing speed change from childhood to late adulthood in a generalized, task- and process-independent or in a local, task- and process-specific manner. A large body of reaction time studies supports the conclusion that the changes are generalized. We demonstrate that, in contrast, (1) chronopsychophysiological studies reveal that the pattern of development and decline is varied across the lifespan, but that (2) there is convergence on stimulus-response translation processes as being the most sensitive to developmental influences and the most vulnerable to the aging process which (3) suggests that the growth and decay of brain structure/function relationships has a certain symmetrical nature.

There is a heated debate among research scientists in cognitive development and aging over the extent to which the speed of information processing develops and declines across the lifespan in a generalized, task-independent or in a process-specific, task-dependent manner (see review in Bashore, 1994). This debate originates from work pioneered by Brinley (1965) that was elaborated and refined by Cerella and colleagues (Cerella, 1985; Cerella, Poon, & Williams, D.M., 1980). Brinley first suggested that age-related differences in processing speed could be characterized by regressing the reaction times (RTs) of older subjects on those of young subjects across levels of several tasks of varying difficulty. His analysis yielded a linear function with a slope exceeding 1.0 (1.67) and an intercept approximating zero. The shape of this function encouraged him to conclude that "...response times for both groups and for each type of task variation may be conceived as varying along a single dimension which might be termed 'task difficulty'." (Brinley, 1965, p. 131).

Brinley's original observation did not stir the imaginations of his contemporaries, however. Interest in this analytic technique and the conclusions it supports did not begin to emerge until Cerella et al. (1980) published the results of a meta-analysis in which the mean RT's of older subjects, taken from a wide variety of tasks in a large number of different studies, were regressed on those of matched young subjects. Like Brinley before them, Cerella et al. found that the points in the coordinate space were described by a linear function with a slope exceeding 1.0 (1.36) and an intercept approximating zero. On the basis of the form of this function, along with the results of a series of other regression analyses, Cerella et al. concluded that the effects of advancing age on response speed could be characterized by a single slowing parameter, the slope of the regression line. That is, age-induced slowing was generalized and task-independent. Cerella (1985) followed with a series of analyses on both actual and simulated data that extended his earlier work and provided seemingly strong support for the position taken in his first paper. It also led to a theoretical refinement of that work: age-induced slowing was evident in both sensorimotor and central processing, as revealed in the intercept and the slope of the regression line, respectively, with central slowing accounting for the lion's share of the age effect (see also Salthouse, 1985a,b). Thus, age-related slowing in response speed could be explained by recourse to two parameters, the intercept and slope of the regression function.

In these analyses, both verbal and nonverbal tasks were grouped together. Shortly after the Cerella (1985) paper appeared, Hale, Myerson, and Wagstaff (1987) demonstrated in a meta-analysis that age-induced slowing in the processing of nonverbal material was characterized by a nonlinear (exponential) function. This observation laid the foundation for the extant distinction between age-induced generalized slowing in the lexical and nonlexical domains, the first systematic demonstration of which was by Lima, Hale, and Myerson (1991). According to this view, slowing is generalized in both processing domains, although it is more dramatic in the nonlexical domain. The shape of slowing functions associated with age-effects differs between the two domain: It is exponential for nonlexical and linear for lexical information processing.

Regression analysis has also been applied to aggregated RT data from studies of the development of cognitive processing speed in children. In a series of papers, Kail and colleagues (1986; 1991a, b,c; 1992; 1993; Kail & Park, 1992; Kail & Salthouse, 1994) have argued eloquently for a global mechanism underlying developmental changes in mental processing speed. Like his predecessors in cognitive aging, Kail (1991a) completed a series of regression analyses in which the RTs of children of various ages were regressed on those of young adults. He found that the points generated for children at each yearly age from 4 to 14 were described by linear functions with slopes that diminished systematically (from around 3.0 to 1.19). Hale (1990) evaluated the relation between the RT's of children 10, 12, and 15 and young adults on four RT tasks and, like Kail, found linear functions with slopes that decreased from 1.82 to 1.56 to 1.0 for the three respective age groups (see also Hale, Fry, & Jessie, 1993).

This pattern of results suggests that a global mechanism mediates developmental changes in response speed.

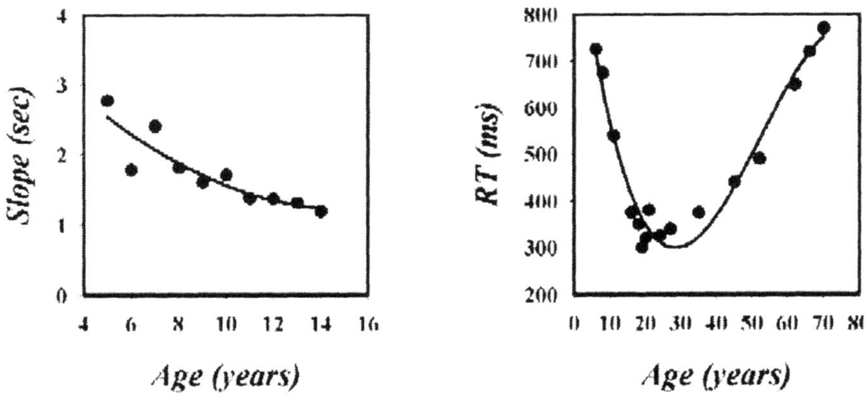

Figure 1. (left) Growth function from Kail (1991a) for tasks with RTs less than 2 seconds. The values are in Table 2 in the Kail article. From "Developmental change in speed of processing during childhood and adolescence", *Psychological Bulletin, 109*, 490-501 (p. 497). Copyright 1991 by the American Psychological Association. Adapted by permission. (right) Growth and decay function, adapted from Cerella and Hale (1994). The data points in each plot are estimates from Figure 8 in their article and represent only a subset of the data points they used. Adapted from *Acta Psychologica, 66*, 109-198 (p. 150), J. Cerella and S. Hale, "The rise and fall of information-processing rates over the life span", 1994, with kind permission of Elsevier Science - NL, Sara Burgerhartstraat 25, 1055 KV Amsterdam, The Netherlands.

To infer the dynamics of developmental changes in response speed, Kail (1991a) derived growth functions in which the slopes of the regression functions for each age group were regressed on chronological age. These functions revealed an exponential decline in the slope of the regression line from childhood to adolescence corresponding to substantial changes in early and middle childhood and slower change thereafter (see Figure 1, left). More recent work by Cerella and Hale (1994) has applied growth function analysis to the entire lifespan. They derived 'growth and decay' functions to describe how rapidly response speed increases through childhood and diminishes through adulthood.

Their analyses yielded roughly U-shaped functions with exponential growth and decay rate parameters (see Figure 1, right). Since the rate parameters in both types of functions were shown to characterize lifespan changes in response speed across a wide range of tasks, they reinforce the conclusion from the regression analyses that lifespan changes in response speed are controlled by a single global factor.

On the basis of the aforementioned body of work and related work, Kail and Salthouse (1994) have argued that changes in the speed of central information processing contribute significantly to the development and decline of all neurocognitive functions, speeded and unspeeded alike. They have characterized processing speed as a "cognitive primitive" (p. 221), arguing that it may be a "...fundamental component of the architecture of human cognition" (p. 221). Indeed, Salthouse (1991) has conceptualized processing speed as a basic cognitive resource, along with attention and working memory. In their characterization, Kail and Salthouse have likened the mechanism mediating the rate of human information processing to the clock speed of a microcomputer. They asserted that individuals who differ in 'clock speed' do not differ from one another in the structural components of their processing architectures, but only in the speed with which processing takes place in those structures. That is, individuals with slow clock speeds process information at slower rates than do individuals with rapid clock speeds, but the identical structures are engaged in qualitatively the same ways in fast or slow processors. Thus, according to this reasoning, as children grow older their clock speed increases, and this increase is accompanied by equivalent increases in the speeds of processing in all cognitive processes until adult rates are attained. Conversely, as the clock speed of older adults decreases, mental processing takes place at slower rates in each structural component.

If the Global Hypothesis of cognitive development and aging is true, then the search for the neural substrates that mediate the changes is simplified greatly. In its most elemental form this conceptualization implies the existence of a single timing center in the brain whose maturation and aging produces the speed changes evident across the lifespan. That is, one structure controls the speed of information transmission in the brain (the metaphoric clock of Kail & Salthouse?) and the development and decline of this structure produces the global and undifferentiated transformation of processing speed that humans experience over the lifespan. The clock metaphor aside, when neurocognitive processing speed is assumed to develop and decline in a global, undifferentiated manner an equally straightforward interpretation is that both the development and decline reflect diffuse, widespread changes in neural structures. These changes may be controlled, in turn, by a single neural mechanism. Alternatively, the Global Hypothesis can be construed as suggesting the existence of a specific neural circuit that mediates processing speed, the individual components of which develop and later decline at the same rate in a task-indifferent manner. A global perspective could also support the interpretation that there are domain-specific circuits, perhaps with some overlapping structural components, that develop and decline in a component-independent manner.

Thus, the results of the meta-analyses on reaction time suggest the intriguing possibility that both the development and decline of neurocognitive processing speed may be mediated by a common mechanism and/or a limited set of neural circuits. However, the conclusion that the transformation of response speed from childhood to senescence is global and undifferentiated depends on a critical assumption: age-related differences in processing speed are entirely quantitative in nature. In other words, the basic components of processing engaged by a given task are qualitatively identical at all ages and, consequently, differences in response speed among various age groups are produced solely by changes in the speed with which these processing components are executed--Cerella's (1990) *Correspondence Axiom*. We present data that challenge the validity of this assumption.

In addition, critics of the between-experiment regression approach argue that it obscures task-dependent and process-specific effects of development and aging that are exposed by within-experiment analysis of variance (ANOVA) (e.g., Fisk, Fisher, & Rogers, 1992; Fisher, Fisk, & Duffy, 1995). This criticism has engendered the sometimes acrimonious debate among proponents and opponents of the meta-analytic regression technique (e.g., Cerella, 1991, 1994; Fisk & Fisher, 1994; Fisk et al., 1992; Myerson, Wagstaff, & Hale, 1994; Perfect, 1994). In this debate, however, both advocates and critics of the regression approach draw inferential support for their positions from analyses that have utilized one dependent measure, RT. In our view, exclusive reliance on this measure is insufficient to resolve issues pertinent to the current methodological debate, to the nature of changes in neurocognitive processing speed over the lifespan, and to the fundamental role of processing speed in human cognition. In this chapter, we review research in which behavioral measures have been taken conjointly with measures of changes in brain electrical activity to assess influences of development and aging on neurocognitive processing speed. Our review supports the conclusion that this combined methodology (chronopsychophysiology) yields insights that are not accessible to behavioral measures alone. In addition, we demonstrate that, even with multiple dependent measures, regression analysis may obfuscate task- and process-specific effects that are revealed in the analysis of variance. Finally, we conclude with speculations on the neurocognitive mechanisms that may mediate processing speed in young adults, on those mechanisms that may be especially vulnerable to the aging process, and then offer some brief speculations on what we believe to be an essential symmetry in the development and decline of neural structure and function.

Brinley Analyses of Cognitive Aging

Cerella et al. (1980) used a meta-analytic version of the regression analysis introduced by Brinley (1965) because they thought it would provide the most stringent test of Birren's (1965) Complexity Hypothesis of age-related cognitive slowing. Birren's hypothesis asserts that peripheral (i.e., sensorimotor) processing speed is spared with advancing age, while all components of central processing speed are slowed in a task-independent manner that becomes increasingly pronounced as processing complexity is increased. With publication of the regression analysis by Cerella et al. (known today as a Brinley analysis), the seeds were sown for the current debate. Recall that the points generated by this analysis were described by a linear function with an intercept around zero and a slope exceeding 1.0. Cerella et al. (as well as Cerella, 1985) reasoned that the intercept of the regression function expresses peripheral, sensorimotor processing speed that is invariant across levels of cognitive complexity. Hence, an elevation in the intercept was thought to reveal a fixed contribution of sensorimotor slowing to the overall slowing of response speed. In contrast, the slope of the regression line was assumed to express slowing in central, computational information processing speed. Hence, a slope exceeding 1.0 was presumed to expose declines in central information processing speed that increase with increases in cognitive demands. Thus, identification of a multiplicative function was offered by Cerella et al. as convincing support for the conclusion that all elements of cognitive processing are slowed equivalently by advancing age. Later, Cerella, Poon, and Fozard (1981) referred to the concept of equivalent slowing as the strong version of the Complexity Hypothesis, in contrast to the weak version which asserts that all components are slowed, but the magnitude of the slowing varies from one component to another.

This conclusion was derived, however, from the assumption that the properties of the regression function provide indices of particular elements of nervous system processing. That assumption was formulated exclusively on the basis of analyses in which RT was the sole measure of processing speed. These analyses, almost without exception, yield functions that are linear with intercepts near zero and slopes around 1.40 to 1.50, both within and across tasks. This set of results, taken in isolation, provides overwhelming support for global cognitive slowing among the elderly (see reviews in Allen, Madden, & Slane, 1995; Bashore, 1993, 1994; Bashore & Smulders, 1995; Cerella & Hale, 1994; Fisher et al., 1995; Myerson & Hale, 1993; Kail & Salthouse, 1994). We have been troubled, however, by the fact that the inferences drawn from the results of these analyses concern the transmission of information between registration of a stimulus and execution of a response when only an aggregate measure of processing speed, reflective of the final output of this complicated series of information processing transactions, was used. This concern encouraged Bashore, Osman, and Heffley (1989) to perform a series of Brinley analyses that included two measures of processing speed, RT and the latency of the P300 component of the event-related brain potential (ERP). The results of this meta-analysis offered a challenge to the interpretation by Cerella et al. of the functional significance of the properties of the regression function for RT.

This dissent may be rooted in the very nature of the ERP. The ERP comprises a series of positive and negative deflections in the polarity of brain electrical activity, measured at the human scalp, as stimulus and response decisions are being made. These deflections, called components of the ERP, represent the engagement of different elements of the decision-making process as they emerge (see Coles & Rugg, 1995; Polich, 1993; Ridderinkhof & Bashore,

1995). Bashore et al. used P300 latency in their analysis because it (1) increases systematically across the adult lifespan; (2) varies with increases in stimulus processing demands while being relatively invariant as response processing demands change; (3) is unchanged, unlike RT, by variations in speed/accuracy trade-offs; and (4) increases, as memory load increases in a Sternberg (1969) memory scanning task, at comparable rates among older and young adults, while RT increases at a greater rate among the elderly than the young (for reviews, see Bashore, 1990, 1993; Bashore & Smulders, 1995; Coles, Smid, Scheffers, & Otten, 1995; Donchin, Karis, Bashore, Coles, & Gratton, 1986; Polich, 1996).

The ERP-RT analyses conducted by Bashore and colleagues were inspired by the widely reported observations that factor effects on RT and P300 latency were experimentally dissociable (i.e., not all experimental manipulations produce the same effect on the two measures). Particularly elegant illustrations of this dissociation were provided in the seminal studies of McCarthy and Donchin (1981) and Ford, Roth, Mohs, Hopkins, and Kopell (1979). McCarthy and Donchin demonstrated that P300 latency was prolonged when discrimination of a target stimulus from its surround, but not selection of a response, was made difficult. Ford et al. showed that increases in memory set size (in a Sternberg memory scanning task) produced increases in P300 latency among older and young subjects that were comparable, but increases in RT that were much greater among older than young subjects. Examples of these and other dissociations are are reviewed elsewhere (e.g., see Bashore, 1990; Bashore & Smulders, 1995; Coles & Rugg, 1995; Verleger, 1997).

On the basis of these observed dissociations, Bashore et al. (1989) reasoned that a meta-analysis on P300 latency, like Cerella et al.'s meta-analysis of the RT experiments, might reveal differential effects of aging on stimulus and response processing. If the meta-analysis uncovered similar patterns of slowing for both P300 latency and RT, very strong evidence would be offered for generalized slowing. If the patterns differed for the two measures (i.e., there was a dissociation), support would be offered for differential slowing. The analysis on the RT data yielded a regression function resembling that reported by Cerella et al. (1980): linear, with a slope greater than 1.0 and an intercept that did not differ from zero. However, the functions for the P300 latency data departed from that pattern. Separate analyses, one including data from tasks that required an overt response (i.e., RT tasks)and another that included data from both RT tasks and tasks in which only covert responses were required (i.e., the P300 is elicited when either an overt response, such as a button press, or a covert response, such as mental counting, is made to a critical stimulus), yielded functions with elevated intercepts and slopes approximating 1.0.

The logical framework within which the properties of the regression analysis on RT are interpreted supports the conclusion that the function for P300 latency uncovers only peripheral (i.e., sensorimotor) slowing. We know, however, that the P300 is generated from multiple cerebral, subcortical and cortical, sources (e.g., Johnson, 1993; Knight, 1990). Thus, the relationship between the properties of the regression function and nervous system transmission may be more complicated than advocates of the Brinley analysis on RT have assumed. Further, the results for RT and P300 latency suggest that advancing age produces a pattern of changes in information processing that may not, or cannot, be revealed using RT measures alone. These results indicate that declines in the rate of information processing evident among the elderly may be more dramatic at the response end of processing than they are at the stimulus end (implied by the slope of the RT function exceeding 1.0). Moreover, the influence of age on the various aspects of stimulus processing may not be uniform: The early elements of stimulus processing (e.g., stimulus encoding) may be slowed with age (implied by the elevated intercept for the P300 latency function), while some later elements (e.g., stimulus identification) may be spared (implied by the slope of the P300 latency function approximating 1.0). The results from several recent behavioral studies support this conclusion as well (e.g., Allen, Ashcraft, & Weber, 1992; Amrhein, 1995; Ellis, Goldberg, & Detweiler, 1996; Greenwood & Parasurman, 1991; Madden, 1992; Madden, Pierce, & Allen, 1993; Swearer & Kane, 1996). The suggestion is that aging induces selective, process-specific, effects on processing speed in which the degree of slowing varies among those elements that are slowed, while some elements are not slowed at all.

The preceding demonstrates that the precision with which the temporal dynamics of age-related changes in mental chronometry is articulated can be enhanced using combined behavioral and ERP measures. Later we discuss research from our laboratories that offers support for this conclusion (see also Bashore & Smulders, 1995). In summary, although meta-analyses of RT data have generated impressive support for global slowing among the elderly, the addition of chronopsychophysiological data to the analysis casts doubt on both the interpretation offered originally of the properties of the regression function for RT that guides advocates of the Brinley analysis, and on the assertion that aging induces a global, undifferentiated slowing of cognitive processing speed. Now we turn to developmental studies that raise similar doubts.

Growth Functions: Characterizing the Dynamics of Cognitive Development

A challenge to Kail's (1991a) conclusion that the development of processing speed is global and undifferentiated has been offered by Ridderinkhof and van der Molen (1995). They investigated developmental differences in visual selective attention using a task in which young adults (mean age 23.2) and children in three age groups (mean ages 6.4, 8.7, 11.2) responded in the direction indicated by an arrow that was flanked by two arrows on each side that pointed in either the same or the opposite direction (constituting congruent and incongruent arrays, respectively). In addition to RT, the onset latency of the lateralized readiness potential (LRP) and P300 latency were measured. The LRP is a component of the ERP that is thought to originate from motor cortex and to provide an index of response system activation (Coles, 1989; Miller, Riehle, & Requin, 1992), the onset latency of which has proven to be quite sensitive to variations in response system activation (e.g., Band & Miller, 1997; DeJong, Liang, & Lauber, 1994; Gratton, Coles, Sirevaag, Eriksen, & Donchin, 1992; Hackley & Miller, 1989; Miller, Coles, & Chakraborty, 1996; Miller & Hackley, 1992; Osman, Bashore, Coles, Donchin, & Meyer, 1992; Smid, Mulder, Mulder, & Brands, 1992). Ridderinkhof and van der Molen found that RT, the onset latency of the LRP, and P300 latency were all longer to an incongruent than to a congruent array. However, they observed a dissociation of factor effects on the dependent measures: the detrimental effect of incongruent flankers decreased with increasing age for RT and LRP onset, but not for P300 latency. These results suggest a differential pattern of maturation in processing speed that is inconsistent with the Global Hypothesis.

To evaluate these data further, Ridderinkhof and van der Molen (1997) fit separate growth functions to these measures, finding that no less than 94% of the variance could be explained. According to the Global Hypothesis, maturation of the latencies of the P300, LRP onset, and the overt response should be described accurately by one growth function. However, the growth rate parameters were not equivalent, thus indicating process-specific maturation. As can be seen in Figure 2 (left), the rate parameter was substantially larger for P300 latency than for LRP onset latency and RT, and for LRP onset it was marginally larger than for RT. The P300 latency index approached asymptote more rapidly and earlier in development than did the onset latency of the LRP and RT. In their entirety, these results provide strong evidence for the conclusion that stimulus-related processing, indexed by P300 latency, matures at a faster rate than does response-related processing, indexed by LRP onset latency. Thus, they challenge the basic assumption of the Global Hypothesis that developmental changes in processing speed are equivalent across all elements of processing.

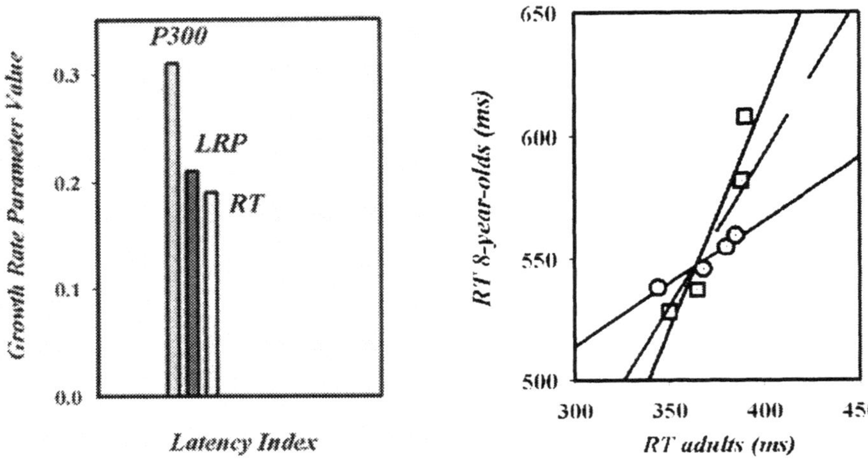

Figure 2. (left) Growth rate parameters derived from Ridderinkhof & van der Molen (1997) for children of three age groups (6.4, 8.7, 11.2 years old) and young adults (23.2 years old) for P300 latency, the onset latency of the LRP, and RT. (right) Brinley plot for data from Shepp and Barrett (1991) used in regression analyses by Ridderinkhof et al. (submitted). The dashed line represents the regression function for the entire data set. Data points from the task in which redundancy gain was not induced are shown as unfilled squares; data points from the task with correlated dimensions are shown as unfilled circles. The solid lines in close proximity to each set of data points represents the linear function for each respective set of points.

The Correspondence Axiom

At the conceptual heart of the Global Hypothesis is Cerella's (1990) Correspondence Axiom. He reasoned that if the rank ordering of response times does not change with age, then the Correspondence Axiom is satisfied and differences between age groups may be considered quantitative rather than qualitative (see also Cerella & Hale, 1994). However, Ridderinkhof, Bashore, van der Molen, and Band (submitted) provide an example of data from the developmental literature that satisfies this axiom, while at the same time violates fundamental assumptions of the Global Hypothesis, including the presumed quantitative nature of age-related changes in processing speed.

If a subject's task is to classify stimuli on one of two physically integrated dimensions, such as hue and brightness, then response speed is usually facilitated when the values on relevant and irrelevant dimensions covary as compared to when the irrelevant dimension is held constant (a phenomenon called *redundancy gain*; Garner, 1974). By contrast, if multidimensional stimuli are composed of physically separable dimensions that are perceived as separate aggregates of distinct dimensions, then the degree to which correlated dimensions elicit redundancy gain is much weaker, as the irrelevant dimension is excluded from analysis.

Perception in young children has been hypothesized to be biased toward holistic properties of multidimensional stimuli and that of older children and adults to be biased toward featural properties (e.g., Gibson, 1969). Thus, from a developmental perspective, the most interesting stimuli have integrated dimensions, such as size and shape, that can be perceived either as integrated wholes or as separate aggregates. Young children typically perceive these stimuli holistically, experiencing redundancy gain when dimensions are correlated; whereas older children and adults perceive the constituent dimensions separately and show no redundancy gain (see review by Shepp, 1989). An example of this developmental difference in perception is found in a study by Shepp and Barrett (1991). In one of the experiments in this study, 8-year-olds and young adults were required to respond to multidimensional stimuli that were either physically separable or integral. Both groups were observed to produce slower responses when stimulus dimensions were physically integrated as compared to separated.

With integrated stimuli, however, children responded faster when relevant and irrelevant dimensions covaried as opposed to when the irrelevant dimension was held constant, while adults did not show this redundancy gain. Redundancy gain was not observed in either age group with separated dimensions.

The observation of redundancy gain in children, but not in adults, indicates that the same multidimensional stimuli were perceived as composed of separate dimensions by adults but of integrated dimensions by children. However, the rank ordering of response times across conditions remained invariant from 8-year-olds to adults. Thus, even though the Correspondence Axiom was satisfied, a qualitative age change in perceived structure occurred, violating the assumption of the Global Hypothesis that age-related changes in response speed are merely quantitative in nature. Further, RT's were slower to integrated than to separated stimuli, but the size of this effect was smaller for children than for adults. The Global Hypothesis assumes that effect sizes will always be larger for children than for adults. Ridderinkhof et al. performed a Brinley analysis on the data reported by Shepp and Barrett. As shown in Figure 2 (right), the function is linear with a slope exceeding 1.0, as would be predicted by the Global Hypothesis. However, inspection of the Brinley plot suggests that two functions exist, not one. A two-task indicator-variable linear regression analysis demonstrated just that. It revealed that only those conditions that failed to induce redundancy gain yielded a function with a slope greater than 1.0. The spread of points from conditions with the irrelevant dimension held constant was described by a linear function with a slope appreciably greater than 1.0. Data from conditions with correlated dimensions were described by a separate linear function with a slope much less than 1.0. Thus, the pattern observed by Shepp and Barrett produced a Brinley function with a slope less than 1.0 when the Global Hypothesis predicts a slope greater than 1.0. Moreover, the Brinley analysis on the overall data obscured this inconsistency (for a similar analysis and outcome of the slowing of counting speed among older persons, see Sliwinski, 1997).

These results make three critical points. First, when rank orderings of response times from different age groups correspond it does not necessarily imply that age-related changes in response speed are only quantitative. Second, age-related changes in response speed originating from qualitative differences in information processing may be concealed in a Brinley analysis. Third, in direct contradiction to a fundamental assumption of the Global Hypothesis, an increase in task complexity is not always associated with an increase in the size of the age effect.

Chronopsychophysiological Exploration of Age-induced Changes in Neurocognitive Processing Speed: An Illustrative Case

In the foregoing review we have presented evidence that contradicts the Global Hypothesis of lifespan changes in neurocognitive processing speed and challenges the Brinley analysis from which it emanates. In particular, we have highlighted the utility of using multiple dependent measures in the analysis of changes in processing speed over the lifespan and, in so doing, described a set of findings that converges on the conclusion that the response end of processing is the slowest to develop and the most vulnerable to the effects of advancing age. We have also illustrated how Brinley analyses may obfuscate this pattern of effects and, in so doing, provide apparent support for the Global Hypothesis. Moreover, we have summarized an empirical demonstration of qualitative age-related differences in cognitive processing that falsifies the critical assumption of the Global Hypothesis that age changes in response speed are always quantitative in nature. Together, these findings raise serious challenges to the conceptual and analytical bases of the Global Hypothesis. We now present data from our experiments aimed at critical examination of the differential growth and decline of neurocognitive functions induced by aging and comparison of the analytic outputs of the regression and ANOVA techniques.

A Direct Test of Differential Decline

To evaluate the relative effects of older age on stimulus and response processing across tasks of varying complexity, Bashore, Martinerie, Ridderinkhof, van der Molen, and Heffley (in preparation) obtained multiple measures of processing speed from 34 young (mean age=27) and 34 older (mean age=70) men, matched on IQ and screened medically, in three RT tasks (simple, disjunctive, choice). The tasks were variants of the task developed by McCarthy and Donchin (1981) and elaborated by Magliero, Bashore, Coles, and Donchin (1984). Stimulus discriminability was varied in the choice reaction by presenting the word LEFT or RIGHT in a 4 row by 6 column matrix of number signs (#) or of letters chosen randomly from the set A-G or A-Z; and S-R compatibility was manipulated by having subjects make either a compatible or an incompatible response to the target word (e.g., compatible--LEFT signals a response with the left thumb; incompatible--LEFT signals a response with the right thumb). The target word appeared randomly in any one of the four rows of the matrix, thus subjects had to search the matrix to locate the target. They were forewarned of the compatibility of the impending response by presentation of a cue word, SAME or OPPOSITE, 1000 ms before onset of the matrix, thereby being provided an opportunity to prepare the type of response, compatible or incompatible, in advance of the matrix presentation. In the disjunctive reaction, stimulus discriminability was varied, as it was in the choice reaction, but subjects only made compatible responses to one of the words while withholding responses to the other word. The simple reaction required subjects to make a unimanual response to the matrix, ignoring its contents by treating it as a flash of light.

ERP activity was measured from midline scalp sites (Fz, Cz, Pz, Oz) in conjunction with RT. Each task elicited a series of positive and negative components in the ERP, shown in Figure 3, that was similar in the two age groups. These similarities suggest that a comparable set of processing structures was engaged in both age groups. The components in each task are labeled on the basis of their polarity and representative peak latency. These labels and the midline scalp orientation of each component are presented in Table 1.

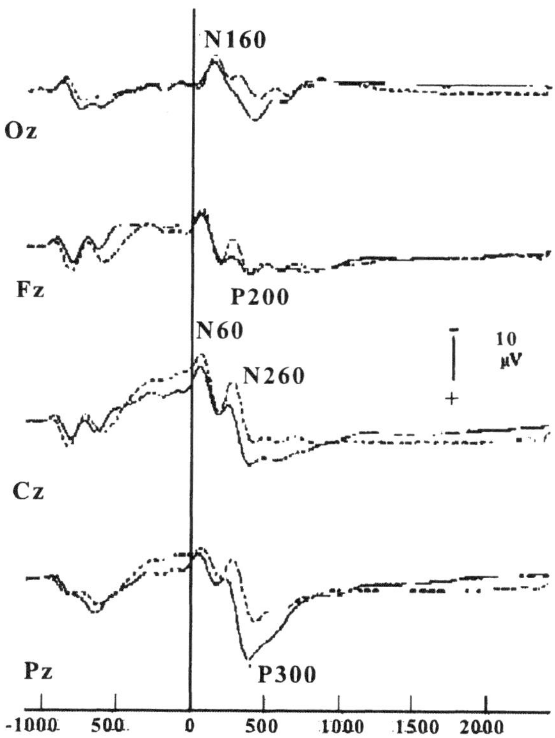

Figure 3. Examples of ERPs from Bashore et al. (in preparation) that show the different components of interest (N60, N160, P200, N260, and P300) in one experimental condition (compatible response, # signs). The components are shown for the midline scalp site (Fz, Cz, Pz, Oz) where they typically were largest in amplitude. Dashed lines represent the ERPs for older subjects, and solid lines represent the ERPs for young subjects. The dashed vertical line indicates the time at which the cue word was presented, and the solid vertical line indicates the time at which the matrix appeared.

Performance accuracy

As would be expected, there were no differences in accuracy among the two age groups in the simple reaction. There were, however, differences in performance accuracy associated with age in the disjunctive reaction which suggested that the disjunctive reaction was more difficult for older than for young subjects, particularly when the target and nontarget words were difficult to identify in the matrix. Under these circumstances, older subjects were more likely to withhold a response to thetarget (i.e., miss its occurrence) or to make a response to the nontarget (i.e., produce a false alarm). Overall performance accuracy did not differ among the two age groups (93% young, 92% older) in the choice reaction. However, the pattern of performance accuracy in this reaction indicated that the introduction of letters to the target surround had a more debilitating effect on older subjects than it did on younger subjects, as was the case in the disjunctive reaction. Performance accuracy was higher among older subjects when the target stimulus was easy to discriminate (i.e., number signs surrounded the target), particularly when an incompatible response was required, suggesting that young, but not older, subjects may havetraded some accuracy for speed when they were able to identify the target quickly but had to execute the more difficult response.

Brinley Analyses

We entered the mean RT data from all three tasks into a regression analysis that yielded what is now considered a classic Brinley function, linear with an intercept approximating zero and a slope exceeding 1.0. A regression analysis on the P300 latency data from the disjunctive and choice reactions revealed a linear function with a positive intercept and a slope approximating 1.0, like that reported by Bashore et al. (1989).

Separate regression analyses on all of the component latencies and RT exposed task-dependent variations in the forms of the regression functions, however. The points from the simple reaction were described by a linear function with an intercept at the origin and a slope equivalent to 1.0; the points from the disjunctive reaction were fit by a linear function with a slight, nonsignificant negative intercept and a slope somewhat larger than 1.0; and the points from the choice reaction were described by a linear function with a nonsignificant negative intercept and a slope exceeding 1.0, the values of both the intercept and slope being larger than for the disjunctive reaction. As would be expected, the distribution of points for the entire set of tasks was fit by a linear function with a nonsignificant negative intercept and a slope greater than 1.0.

In this series of regression analyses we have an illustration, then, of how the indiscriminant aggregation of data points can yield a regression function that supports the conclusion that advancing age produces task- and process-independent slowing. By merely segregating the data by task and doing separate analyses on each task we uncovered task-specific patterns of slowing within a processing domain suggestive of a well-ordered increase in generalized slowing that becomes greater in magnitude as processing demands are increased. This pattern replicates the pattern reported by Cerella (1985) when he demonstrated that systematic changes in the slope of the regression function are tied very closely to variations in central processing complexity (see also Cerella et al., 1980; Salthouse, 1985a,b).

Had we completed no other analyses on these data, the task-related ordering of regression functions we found would have been interpreted within the context of the Global Hypothesis: as central processing complexity increases across tasks, the slopes of the regression lines for those tasks steepen.

TABLE 1

ERP Components--Scalp Orientations

Task/Response	*ERP Component*	*Scalp Orientation-Y*	*Scalp Orientation-O*
Simple	*N60*	Frontocentral*	Frontocentral
	N130	Occipital	Occipital
	P150	Central	*Centrofrontal*
	N260	Frontal	Frontal
Disjunctive	*N60*	Centrofrontal	Centrofrontal
	N130	Occipital	Occipital
	P150	Centrofrontal	*Frontal*
	N260	Centroparietal	Centroparietal
	P300	Parietocentral	*Centroparietal*
Choice	*N60*	Central	Central
	N160	Occipital	Occipital
	P200	Centrofrontal	Centrofrontal
	N260	Centrofrontal	*Centroparietal*
	P300	Parietocentral	*Centroparietal*

* Scalp orientations were determined by interpolating points across the midline from Fz to Oz that totaled 100. A value of 0 identified a component with a strong frontal focus, 33 a strong central focus, 66 a strong parietal focus, and 100 a strong occipital focus. Values approximating these are labeled accordingly. However, intermediate values are labeled in a way to reflect the interpolated location of the electrical activity. For example, centrofrontal would be a value of around 20, but frontocentral might be a value of 10. Distinctions were made when the values for the two age groups were found to differ statistically. Italics indicate a difference in orientation. Y indicates young subjects; O indicates older subjects.

This function is shown in Figure 4.

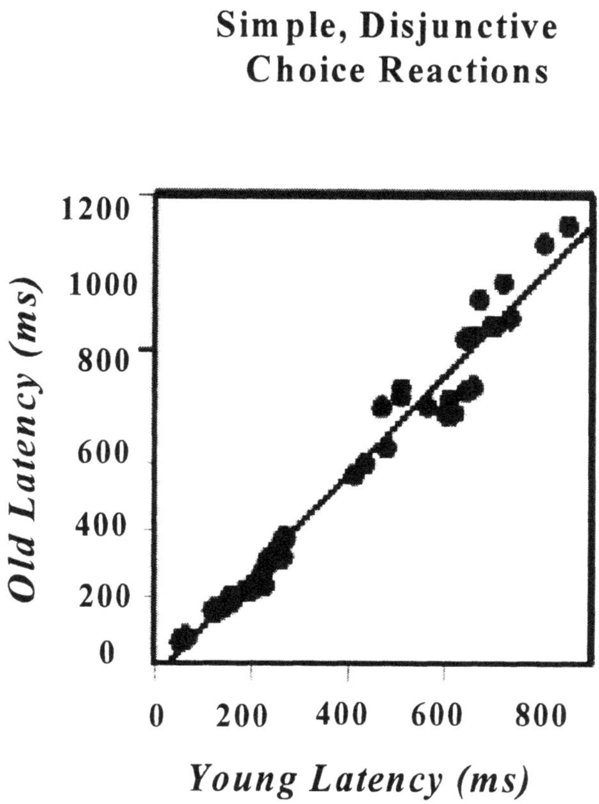

Figure 4. The Brinley plot for the entire set of mean component and response latencies from Bashore et al. (in preparation).

In turn, this would then have been offered as evidence for task-specific generalized slowing (i.e., all elements of processing are slowed equivalently within a task) in a manner analogous to the distinctions made of domain-specific generalized slowing in the lexical and nonlexical domains (Lima et al., 1991; Hale, Myerson, Faust, & Fristoe, 1995). Under these conditions, the Global Hypothesis is both supported and refined in that process-independent slowing has been revealed once again, while task-specific differences in the magnitude of this slowing have been characterized. However, the results of a series of MANOVA's on these data undermine the former conclusion. These analyses uncovered a complex pattern of process-specific effects of age on neurocognitive processing speed that were not evident in the regression analyses. The MANOVA's, like the regression analyses, indicated that processing speed did not differ among the two age groups in the simple reaction and that age-related differences first emerged in the disjunctive reaction.

The MANOVA's

Tables 2 and 3 summarize the results for the disjunctive and choice reactions, respectively. It is apparent that the pattern of age effects differed in the two reactions. In the disjunctive reaction, the latencies of the N60 and P150 components did not vary with age, where the latencies of the N130, N260, and P300 components were prolonged in older subjects, as was RT. In addition, a number of age-related dissociations of factor effects were observed. First, the decision to withhold a response was associated with an increase in N260 latency among young, but not older, subjects. Second, the addition of letters to the target surround induced (i) a decrease in N60 latency among young, but not older, subjects; (ii) a decrease in N130 latency that was larger in young, than in older, subjects; (iii) increases in N260 and P300 latencies that were larger among young than older subjects; and (iv) an increase in RT that tended to be larger in older compared to young subjects. Here, then, in the disjunctive reaction we see a varied pattern of age effects, not the pattern of indiscriminant general slowing predicted by the Global Hypothesis.

A complex pattern of age effects was also observed in the choice reaction. There were, in addition, some differences in the factor effects seen in this reaction as compared to the disjunctive reaction. First, unlike the disjunctive reaction, the rate of processing in the choice reaction was comparable among the two age groups for approximately 160 ms following presentation of the stimulus.

A difference in processing rate between the two age groups did not become manifest for another 30 or 40 milliseconds, at the level of the P200. However, the latency of this component was *shorter* among older than young subjects. The pattern seen for P200 reversed at the latency of the N260 component, however. It was during this time period that slowing first emerged among the older subjects; N260 latency was longer among older than young subjects. This slowing persisted through to the overt response, with P300 latency and RT being longer in older than in young subjects. As was the case for the disjunctive reaction, there were a number of age-related dissociations of factor effects. (1) When the target was embedded in a matrix of letters (a) N60 latency decreased among young, but not older, subjects; (b) N160 latency decreased among older, but not young, subjects; and (c) P200 latency decreased among older subjects only when they made a compatible response. (2) When an incompatible response was made (a) an increase in N260 latency was evident among older subjects only when the target was surrounded by number signs; and (b) P300 latency increased more among young than older subjects.

Reaction time was lengthened in both age groups either when an incompatible response was executed or when letters surrounded the target word. An interesting double dissociation was observed for RT, however. First, RT was slowed by a larger magnitude among the elderly than the young when letters surrounded the target. Second, the cost of making an incompatible response did not change among young subjects with increases in the difficulty of discriminating the target, replicating earlier findings by McCarthy and Donchin (1981) and Magliero et al. (1984), but it was greater among older subjects when letters, as opposed to number signs, surrounded the target (see Table 4). It is important to note that this difference between the two age groups in the combined effects of variations in S-R compatibility and noise was observed despite the fact that the rank orders of the RT's were identical in both age groups, as compelled by the Correspondence Axiom to infer structural identity (see Table 5).

It important to note that this difference between the two age groups in the combined effects of variations in S-R compatibility and noise was observed despite the fact that the rank orders of the RTs were identical in both age groups, as compelled by the Correspondence Axiom to infer structural identity (see Table 5). Moreover, the combined effects of these two factors on the different latency measures varied among the two age groups, as can be seen in Table 4. Whereas the effects of adding letters to the target surround and of requiring an incompatible response to the target induced additive effects on the latencies of the P200, N260, and P300 components and RT for young adults, for older adults they produced underadditive effects on N260 latency and overadditive effects on RT.

TABLE 2

Summary of MANOVA's: Age Effects on Component Latencies and Reaction Time--Disjunctive Reaction

Factor	*N60*	*N130*	*P150*	*N260*	*P300*	*RT*
			Young Ss			
Withhold R				Increase	Increase	
Letters	Decrease	Decrease	Decrease	Increase	Increase	Increase
			Older Ss			
Withhold R				*	Increase	
Letters	*	Decrease	Decrease	Increase	Increase	Increase
			Y v O			
Older Age		Increase		Increase	Increase	Increase
Withhold R				Increase in Y not O		
Letters	Decrease in Y not O	Decrease larger in Y		Increase larger in Y	Increase larger in Y	+Increase larger in O

* Identifies a departure between the age groups; +: Trend at $p=.07$; Y indicates young subjects; O indicates older subjects

TABLE 3

Summary of MANOVA's: Age Effects on Component Latencies and Reaction Time--Choice Reaction

Factor	*N60*	*N160*	*P200*	*N260*	*P300*	*RT*
			Young Ss			
Incomp R		Increase	Decrease	Increase	Increase	Increase
Letters	Decrease		Decrease	Increase	Increase	Increase
			Older Ss			
Incomp R	1	Increase	*2	Increase	Increase	Increase
Letters	*	Decrease*	Decrease	Increase	Increase	Increase
			Y v O			
Older Age	3		Decrease	Increase	Increase	Increase
Incomp R	Decrease in Y not O		Decrease in Y not O		Increase larger in Y	
Letters		Decrease in O not Y	Decrease larger in Y	Increase larger in O		Increase larger in O
Incomp R x Letters				Increase by Ip larger in O when numbers in surround		Increase by Ip larger in O when letters in surround

* = a departure between the age groups; Ip=incompatible response; R=response; Y=young Ss; O=older Ss. 1: Tendency to be prolonged by Ip response ($p = .08$); 2: tendency to be reduced by Ip response ($p = .07$); 3: tendency to be reduced in young but not older Ss when noise added to matrix.

TABLE 4

Factor Effects: Absolute Magnitudes--Choice Reaction

	N60	*N160*	*P200*	*N260*	*P300*	*RT*
Young Ss						
Ip	NS	+4	-12	+6	+40	+132
AG	-2	NS	-21	+17	+192	+161
AZ	-1	NS	-5	+2	+34	+49
Ip + Le	NI	NI	A	A	A	A
Older Ss						
Ip	NS	+3	NS	+6	+22	+141
AG	NS	-12	-6	+34	+186	+237
AZ	NS	+1	-3	+2	+21	+46
Ip + Le	NI	A	NI	Ip# +9	A	Ip# +127
				IpAG +7		IpAG +146
				IpAZ +2		IpAZ +148

Ip=incompatible response; AG=letters in surround selected from A-G; AZ=letters in surround selected from A-Z; Le=letters in surround; #=number signs; NS=statistically nonsignificant; values are given in milliseconds; the values for AG represent the change from a # matrix and for AZ the change from an A-G matrix to an A-Z matrix; NI indicates that there was an absence of a main effect for at least one of the factors and the combined effect did not produce an interaction; A indicates that the main effects were additive.

TABLE 5

Rank Ordering of Reaction Times: Choice Reaction

	CNN	*CAG*	*CAZ*	*INN*	*IAG*	*IAZ*
Young Ss	507	668	717	639	801	849
Older Ss	703	930	975	830	1076	1123
Rank Y/O	*1/1*	*3/3*	*4/4*	*2/2*	*5/5*	*6/6*

It is readily apparent that the pattern of results yielded by our experiment does not fit neatly into the conceptual framework of the Global Hypothesis.

Rather, it reveals a complicated mosaic in which both age effects and the absence of such are evident. In order for the Global Hypothesis to be supported, three fundamental assumptions about the effects of older age on mental processing speed must be satisfied: (1) the slowing associated with increases in processing demands is task-independent within a processing domain; (2) all components of processing slow equivalently within a processing domain; and (3) the structure of processing remains constant across the lifespan (Correspondence Axiom). If these three assumptions are satisfied, then the slowing induced by advancing age can be conceptualized as global and task-independent. Each of these assumptions was violated in the data from our study.

Violation of the first assumption was evident in the results of both the Brinley analyses and the MANOVAs. A systematically graded task-dependent slowing within a processing domain was revealed in the Brinley analysis and confirmed in the MANOVA's. The second assumption was violated in the outcomes of the MANOVA's for both the disjunctive and choice reactions. These analyses revealed a complex pattern in which there was evidence for equivalent processing rates at some levels of processing among the two age groups, slower processing rates among the elderly at other levels, a faster processing rate among older subjects at one level of processing, and a variety of differential influences of factor effects on component and response latencies in the two age groups. The third assumption was not satisfied when the MANOVA on the choice reaction revealed that the additive effect of stimulus discriminability and S-R compatibility on RT observed in this and other studies for young adults was transformed into an overadditive interaction among the elderly, despite the fact that the RT's for each factor level shared the same rank order for the two age groups. This interaction suggests that the output of the S-R translation process depends on the input it receives from the stimulus identification process, which may be compromised in older individuals by prolonged processing. If so, transmission of the identity of the stimulus to the appropriate response output channel (i.e., S-R translation) takes place in a qualitatively different way in the older information processor than it does in the young information processor. Thus, processing correspondence does not obtain between the two age groups in the choice reaction we studied. Next we turn to behavioral data we have collected with children that raise similar challenges to the Global Hypothesis.

A Direct Test of Differential Growth

We completed a study of selective attention in which children in three age groups (mean ages 6.4, 8.8. and 10.9 years) and young adults (mean age 21.0) performed an arrow task like the one used by Ridderinkhof and van der Molen (1995) that we discussed earlier (Ridderinkhof, van der Molen, Band, & Bashore, 1997). Subjects were instructed to respond to the direction of a central target arrow and to ignore arrows on the flanks (two on each side) that pointed either in the same direction as the target (a congruent array) or in the opposite direction (an incongruent array). Typically, the delay in RT to incongruent as compared to congruent arrays decreases in children with age, which is taken to reflect an age-related improvement in the ability to resist interference from irrelevant information (for reviews, see Lane & Pearson, 1982; Plude, Enns, & Brodeur, 1994).

We manipulated three experimental factors in addition to age group and congruence: relative target size, thought to influence the speed of target identification; S-R compatibility, thought to influence the speed of S-R translation processes; and foreperiod mixture (foreperiods were varied in mixed versus pure blocks), thought to influence response activation processes. Because we were interested in the extent to which age-related changes in the effects of incongruent flankers on processing speed involved each of these processes, we examined the interactions of congruence with relative target size, with S-R compatibility, and with foreperiod mixture to determine which of these interactions decreased as a function of age.

Variations in congruence and S-R compatibility produced an underadditive interaction on RT; that is, the cost of making an incompatible response was reduced when the target was flanked by arrows pointing in the opposite (i.e., correct) direction. This finding replicates previous findings from our laboratories (see Bashore & Osman, 1987; Ridderinkhof, van der Molen, & Bashore, 1995). We have interpreted this interaction in terms of a dual-process model in which the target arrow is assumed to engage an attentive S-R translation process while the flankers are assumed to by-pass this translation process and concurrently activate the corresponding response channel directly, regardless of the S-R rule (Ridderinkhof, 1997; Ridderinkhof et al., 1995). The most important observation in our experiment was that the magnitude of the interaction between congruence and S-R compatibility decreased gradually with age, whereas the interactions of congruence with relative target size and foreperiod mixture were not influenced substantially by age. The overall pattern of results led us to conclude that developmental differences in flanker effects on processing speed are determined by improvements in the speed and efficiency of processing in S-R translation processes, rather than in target identification or response activation processes.

Such process-specific developmental differences in processing speed are in disagreement with the notion of general, process-independent age-related changes in processing speed. However, these conclusions were based strictly on the results of an ANOVA, whereas evidence for the Global Hypothesis derives primarily from regression analyses. Analysis of variance can be used for a direct test of the predictions of the Global Hypothesis, however, through the application of appropriate transformations on the data prior to the ANOVA. In such a procedure, RT's for the young adults are transformed by multiplying them with the parameters of the best-fitting regression function (Madden, Pierce, & Allen, 1992); the transformed RT's are then submitted to ANOVAs. The rationale for these transformations on RT is as follows: If RT's from subjects in any age group can be predicted accurately from the RT's of young adults through a global regression function, these transformations will align RT[AGE] and RT[adults] such that age group by task interactions should be absent. The occurrence of any such interaction after transformation would indicate the presence of task-specific age effects not attributable to a global age-related change in processing speed.

In the case of multiple age groups, Ridderinkhof and van der Molen (1997) proposed doing ANOVAs on RT's transformed according to the regression parameters of the best-fitting growth or decay function, as these functions capture best the developmental dynamics of global age-related change in processing speed. They demonstrated that transformation of a hypothetical data set (mean RTs for 5-, 8-, 11-, and 21-year-olds in three experimental conditions), which contained a significant age group by condition interaction, by the best-fitting growth function for the average RTs for each age group (which accounted for 99.7% of the variance) eliminated the interaction. Thus, transformation of the RT's provides a means by which general and task-specific age changes can be distinguished.

The transformation is most powerful in a multifactorial design that offers the possibility of demonstrating both global and local effects, or more than one separate local effect, within a single study (Mayr & Kliegl, 1993; Ridderinkhof & van der Molen, 1997). The merits of this approach will be illustrated using the results of a re-analysis of the RT data from the developmental study by

Ridderinkhof et al. (1997). Ridderinkhof and van der Molen (1997) re-analyzed these data using the transformation procedures described above. They first computed a growth function on group mean RTs of each of sixteen experimental conditions, and found that the best-fitting regression explained the variance almost perfectly (r^2=.982). This finding indicates that a single global factor was responsible for the age-related changes in RT in this study. Next, the growth function regression parameters were used to transform individual mean RTs and the transformed scores were submitted to ANOVA. If the ANOVAs had shown that age-by-task interactions changed into additive relations after the transformation procedure described above, the notion of global age changes would be supported and extended; by contrast, if age-by-task interactions remained this position would have to be abandoned in favor of the notion of local, task-dependent age differences.

As expected, the effect of age group disappeared, indicating that the growth function accurately predicted overall age differences in processing speed. Most important, however, the size of the congruence by S-R compatibility relation decreased monotonically and significantly as a function of age, as shown in Figure 5, whereas, according to the Global Hypothesis, the size of the interaction should have displayed developmental stability. This result supports the existence of local, process-specific age-related changes in processing speed. In particular, developmental differences in the speed and efficiency of S-R translation processes were larger than predicted by the Global Hypothesis. Moreover, this analysis provides a demonstration of the potential of ANOVAs on transformed RTs to unveil process-specific developmental differences that can be obscured in growth function analyses.

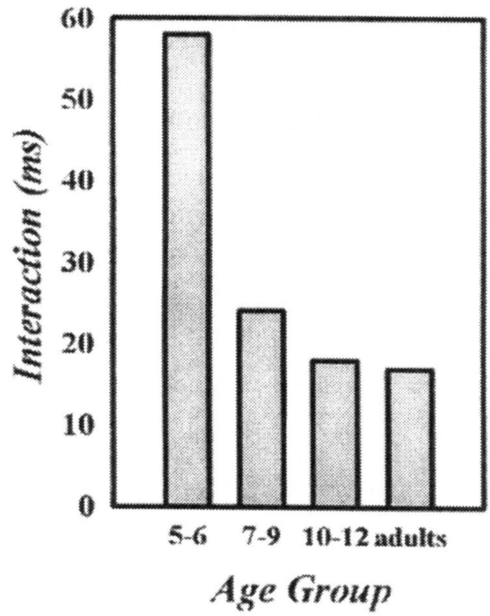

Figure 5. The diminishing interaction between congruence and S-R compatibility that remained after transformation of the mean RTs for three groups of children and one group of young adults using the best-fitting growth function. Adapted from *Biological Psychology*, *45*, 241-261 (p. 253), K.R. Ridderinkhof and M.W. van der Molen, "Mental resources, processing speed, and inhibitory control: A developmental perspective", 1997, with kind permission of Elsevier Science - NL, Sara Burgerhartstraat 25, 1055 KV Amsterdam, The Netherlands.

Summary and Speculations

The results from our developmental and aging studies offer a significant challenge to the very foundations of the Global Hypothesis (see Table 6 for a summary of the developmental findings). Clear violations of the fundamental assumptions of this hypothesis have been revealed in each of our analyses. Our results converge on the conclusion that process-specific changes in neurocognitive processing speed vary as a function of task demands. They suggest, in particular, that the most dramatic changes in neurocognitive processing speed, both early and late in life, occur near the response end of processing at the level of S-R translation. A particularly interesting example of the varied effects of aging on mental chronometry is provided, in our view, in the results from the choice reaction investigated by Bashore et al. (in preparation). Two findings from this study that relate to the influence of advancing age on neurocognitive processing speed are especially intriguing: (1) the observation that the latency of the P200 component of the ERP was shorter among older than young subjects; and (2) the emergence of an overadditive interaction on RT among older, but not young, subjects when levels of stimulus discriminability and S-R compatibility were varied. To our knowledge, these observations are unique. Indeed, the findings that P200 latency was shorter among the elderly, when the target was difficult to discriminate, and when an incompatible response was executed (by young subjects) may even be considered counterintuitive. We have no satisfactory explanation for this set of observations. The interpretive process is complicated further by the fact that little is known about the relations to cognitive processing of most of the components we have evaluated. Thus, it is premature to speculate on the full complement of processes that may be differentially influenced by aging in this reaction. Nonetheless, with a spirit of adventure, we shall offer an admittedly highly speculative interpretation of a subset of these findings.

The Choice Reaction in Young Adults

First, we offer some thoughts about which elements of processing are manifest in the various ERP components evident in young adults as they performed the choice reaction. Then, we speculate on which elements of this processing may be influenced by the aging process. The model of processing offered for young adults is shown in Figure 6. Table 4 should be referred to during the following discussion.

When the target was embedded in a matrix of letters, as opposed to # signs, the latency of the N60 component was decreased by 2 (A-G letters) to 3 (A-Z letters) ms. These decreases were statistically significant, but it is difficult to determine if they are neurocognitively significant until the effect is replicated and explored in more depth. Hence, we shall discuss it no further. The reader should not assume, however, that this implies the conclusion that a small absolute effect is meaningless. (We know, for example, that interhemispheric transmission rates on the order of 1 to 2 ms have important implications for the efficient transfer of information between the two cerebral hemispheres over the corpus callosum [see review in Bashore, 1981]). The latency of the N160 was unaffected by changes in the content of the matrix surround (but see the discussion below of older adults), but it was increased when an incompatible response was made. Here, again, the absolute magnitude was small (4 ms), rendering any interpretation dangerously speculative until there is converging evidence supportive of the consistency of this effect.

We have found what may be a very interesting effect at the level of the P200 component. The common observation, without exception to our knowledge, is that when it is more difficult to discriminate a critical stimulus or to select a response to the critical stimulus, RT increases as do the latencies of the components of the ERP that have been measured (e.g., the onset latency of the LRP, the peak latencies of the N200 or the P300). That was not the case, however, for the P200. The latency of this component decreased when an incompatible response was made (by 12 ms) and when letters surrounded the target (by 21 ms for A-G and 26 ms for A-Z). How can we account for this decrease in latency? This dual (reductive) influence suggests the possibility that the appearance of the P200 may reflect the activation of a mechanism associated with changes in the effort required to do the processing, if a decrease in latency can be equated with effort. It certainly requires more effort to extract feature information from the letter-filled than from the #-filled matrices and to make an incompatible, as opposed to a compatible, response. Thus, rather than reflecting the engagement of any particular stage of processing, the appearance of the P200 may reveal the activation of a mechanism that influences the transmission of information between certain stages of processing.

The time between elicitation of the N160 and of the N260 may represent an important period of transition in which increased effort, a stage-independent process manifest by the P200, initiates the process of narrowing the search of the matrix to the target location, identifying the target, and activating the response it signals. In other words, changes in P200 latency may reflect the engagement of a mechanism, resembling the mechanism postulated by Sanders (1983), that coordinates the transfer of stimulus information to the response system. The mutual, but additive, influences of variations in stimulus discriminability and S-R compatibility on the latencies of the N260 and P300 components (in both instances, prolongation when the target was difficult to locate and when an incompatible response was made; see Table 4) may reveal the engagement of different elements of stimulus and response processing. We have labeled these stages as target location, response activation, target identification, S-R translation, and response output. That these stages may be discrete subprocesses is suggested, according to additive factors reasoning, by the additive effects of variations in stimulus discriminability and S-R compatibility on the latencies of the N260 and P300.

Although we have no direct evidence to support this inference, engagement of processing manifest in the N260 may be associated with locating the target and transmitting this information to the response system to initiate its activation, whereas elicitation of the P300 may represent activation of the target identification process and transfer of this information, the identity of the word associated with a compatible response, to the response output stage via the S-R translation stage (see Verleger, 1997, for a related interpretation of P300 latency).

The substantially larger influence of making an incompatible response on RT than on P300 latency may result from the need to inhibit the prepotent compatible response, which is activated initially, so that the correct, but incompatible, response can be executed. That the increase in RT produced by the addition of letters to the matrix surround was similar to that evident for P300 latency, perhaps even a bit shorter, whereas the cost of incompatibility grew appreciably, suggests that convergence on the specific response output decision dominated processing as it neared its completion. The additivity of factor effects on RT may, therefore, reflect a dissociation of stimulus and response processes as the response output command was executed.[1]

Speculations about the Effects of Older Age on the Choice Reaction

Recall that the overall latencies of the N60 (older, 64 ms; young, 66 ms) and N160 (older, 159 ms; young, 156 ms) components were comparable among the age groups. However, whereas N60 latency decreased in young adults when letters filled the matrix, there was no change in N60 latency among older subjects. In contrast, whereas the young did not manifest any change in latency of the N160 with variations in the content of the matrix, the elderly evinced decreases of 11 and 12 ms when the target was surrounded by A-G and A-Z letters, respectively, as compared to when it was surrounded by # signs. Sanders (1983) has postulated that presentation of a stimulus automatically engages an arousal mechanism. It may be that presentation of the target/letter-filled, as opposed to a target/# sign-filled, matrix differentially arouses the elderly, but not the young, as they initiate the process of extracting critical features from the stimulus array, and this differential arousal is expressed in the latency of the N160 component.

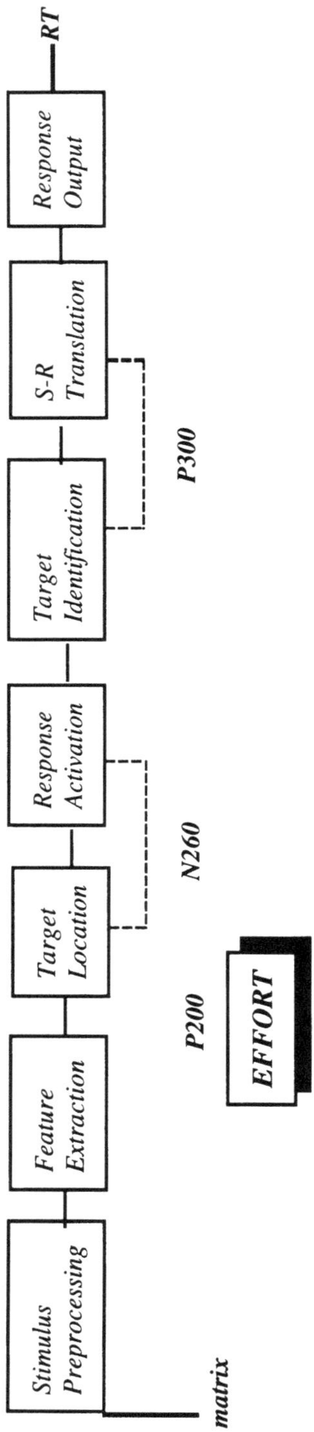

Figure 6. Hypothetical structure of processing in the choice reaction studied by Bashore et al. (in preparation).

TABLE 6
Summary of Developmental Findings

Study	*Pattern of Results*
Ridderinkhof & van der Molen (1995)	Central target arrow flanked by incongruent flanking arrows -- the onset latency of the LRP, P300 latency and RT are increased; the magnitude of increases declines from 6 to 23 years for the LRP and RT, but not for P300.
Ridderinkhof & van der Molen (1997)	Growth functions were larger for P300 latency than for the onset latency of the LRP and RT Transformation of the RT's of children using growth function parameters eliminated main effect of age, but the size of the underadditive interaction between stimulus congruence and S-R compatibility still decreased monotonically with maturation (from 6 to 21)
Ridderinkhof, van der Molen, Band, & Bashore (1997)	Processing of central target arrow flanked by incongruent flanking arrows influenced by variations in foreperiod duration, stimulus congruence, S-R compatibility, and relative target size Underadditive effect of the stimulus congruence by S-R compatibility interaction decreased from 6 to 21 years old; other interactions were not influenced
Ridderinkhof, Bashore, van der Molen, & Band (submitted)	Correspondence axiom violated in Shepp & Barrett (1991): the rank ordering of RT's was identical among children and adults for the multidimensional stimuli composed of either physically integrated or separated dimensions, but theintegrated stimuli were processed in a qualitatively different way by children; the Global hypothesis violated by the finding that the difference in RT between physically integrated and separated stimuli was smaller in children Regression analysis on the entire dataset yielded a linear function with slope exceeding 1.0; regression analysis on stimuli with separable dimensions produced a linear function with a slope exceeding 1.0; however, regression analysis on stimuli with integrated dimensions yielded a linear function with a slope less than 1.0

If the P200 reflects engagement of an effort mechanism that coordinates the transition between stimulus and response processing, then the presentation of the letter-filled matrix and the requirement to make an incompatible response may engage this mechanism in a compensatory manner among older, but not young, individuals. Namely, older subjects may have to invest greater effort in very early stimulus processing and response preparation, the investment of which is expressed in an overall latency for the P200 that is shorter for them than it is for young subjects (older, 189 ms; young, 204 ms). That the latency of this component decreased among the elderly when letters surrounded the target, as it did among the young, but did not decrease among them when an incompatible response was being prepared, as it did among the young, presents an interpretive conundrum. Some insight may be provided by examination of the ERP activity in the foreperiod. We have not completed analyses on these data, so the ideas presented here are categorically speculative. Inspection of Figure 7 suggests that the CNV (at site Cz) is larger for older than for young subjects across all levels of the choice reaction. This difference is statistically reliable, thereby suggesting that older subjects invested more effort than young subjects activating the response system prior to the onset of the matrix. If so, this investment may have produced a level of activation for the response system that was maximal, thereby eliminating any further influence on it by a post-matrix effort mechanism. Young subjects may have expended less effort than older subjects activating the response system during the foreperiod and were thus able to invest additional effort subsequent to stimulus presentation in activating an incompatible response. In contrast, since the contents of the matrix were not available until the matrix was presented, there could be no anticipatory preparation for it. Hence, the component of the effort mechanism associated with processing of the matrix was not engaged maximally in older subjects, allowing further activation of this aspect of effort.

However, if there is an increase in effort in the older information processor, it may not be sufficient to compensate for an age-induced decline in visual search (i.e., target location); the insufficiency of which is expressed in a longer latency N260 (older, 301 ms; young, 261 ms) and a larger increase in the latency of this component when letters surrounded the target (34 ms vs 17 ms). This increase, considered in conjunction with a comparable increase induced among the two age groups (6 ms) by production of an incompatible response, suggests that the early aspects of target location are slowed among the elderly but that the early elements of response activation are not.

This interpretation is consistent with the observation that the cost of incompatibility on N260 latency was largest among the elderly when # signs surrounded the target, therefore rendering it easiest to locate, and reduced systematically with the addition of letters to the surround (# 9 ms; A-G 7 ms, A-Z 2 ms). Here, then, we are proposing that a *serial* sequence of processing in young adults is transformed into an *overlapping* sequence among the elderly which, as we suggest next, continues through to the response output. A similar interpretation applies to the P300 latency findings. The addition of letters to the surround produced comparable slowing of P300 latency among the two age groups (192 ms young vs 186 ms old), while the cost of incompatibility on P300 latency was smaller among the older subjects (22 ms vs 40 ms). This suggests that the time required to identify the target is comparable among the two age groups. However, since these processes are embedded in a processing system that is slowed among the elderly at this level (as revealed in the overall P300 latency [older, 797 ms; young, 626 ms]), the influence of incompatibility may have been obscured as it was at the level of the N260.

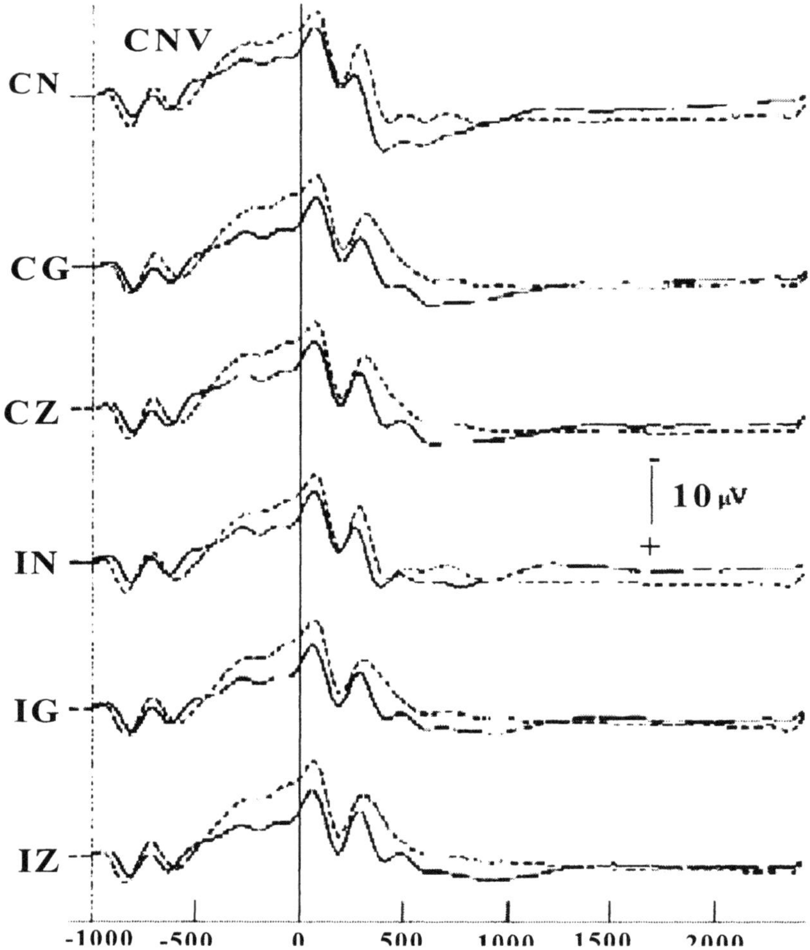

Figure 7. Examples of ERPs recorded from young (solid lines) and older (dashed lines) subjects at electrode site Cz in each of the six levels of the choice reaction (Bashore et al., in preparation). These ERPs reveal the difference in amplitude between the two age groups for the CNV in the foreperiod between the warning and imperative stimuli. Note that the CNV during this time period is larger among older than young subjects across all levels of the task. CN--compatible response, # signs; CG--compatible response, A-G noise; CZ--compatible response, A-Z noise; IN--incompatible response, # signs; IG--incompatible response, A-G noise; IZ--incompatible response, A-Z noise. The dashed and solid vertical lines indicate, respectively, the times at which the cue word and matrix were presented.

Recall, the relationship between stimulus and response processing changed, however, in the elderly when the reaction approached its end, as revealed in factor effects on RT (overall RT: older, 940 ms; young, 697 ms). The increase in RT produced by the addition of letters to the matrix surround was appreciably larger among the elderly than the young (237 ms vs 161 ms), and the cost of incompatibility increased with the addition of letters (# 127 ms, A-G 146 ms, A-Z 148 ms), while it was unchanged among the young. Thus, the dissociation in stimulus and response processing that characterized the young adult information processor near the end of processing, did not characterize the older information processor. Where the complexity of the stimulus input had no differential influence on the S-R translation process in the young adult, it did in the older adult. It appears that with age comes not only quantitative changes in the rate of processing, but also qualitative changes in the relationship between stimulus and response processing over the later portions of a complicated choice reaction. When the older adult was obliged to make an effortful stimulus-response transformation (i.e., execute an incompatible response) the need to search the matrix for the target may have delayed the onset of target identification sufficiently to cause the compatible response to be activated as the S-R translation mechanism was being engaged. In turn, the compatible response, once activated, had to be inhibited prior to activation and execution of the incompatible response, a process that may take longer in older subjects (Salthouse's, 1996, model of cognitive slowing includes a simultaneity mechanism which may share a kinship with our proposal.).

Theoretical Speculations on the Neural Basis of Lifespan Changes in Neurocognitive Processing Speed

The convergence of our empirical findings on stimulus-response translation processes as the most sensitive to developmental influences and the most vulnerable to the effects of advancing age fits nicely with the theoretical perspective that has guided our work for the past few years (see Bashore, 1993; van der Molen & Ridderinkhof, in press). This view is that the neurocognitive changes evident in development and aging are mediated primarily by structural changes that take place in the frontal lobes. In particular, we view development and decline as having a certain symmetry; that is, those structures, and the functions they subserve, that are the last to develop are the first to decline. Similar views can be traced to the work of J. Hughlings Jackson (1884/1958) and Theodore Ribot (1883), and have been suggested by contemporary investigators (e.g., Plude et al., 1994; Raz, Gunning, Head et al., 1997). A large literature has documented the fact that frontal lobe structures and functions develop at the slowest rates (van der Molen & Ridderinkhof, in press) and a growing literature is documenting the fact the they decline at the fastest rate (Bashore, 1993; van der Molen & Ridderinkhof, in press; West, 1996; but see Hall, 1922).

Indeed, the pattern of preferential decline in cell morphology, blood flow, and metabolic activity in the neostriatum and frontal lobes of the aged brain provide a strong neurobiological underpinning for the importance of the frontal lobes, working in tandem with the neostriatum, in mediating integrative actions (see reviews in Bashore, 1993; van der Molen & Ridderinkhof, in press). Among the age-related changes observed are: (1) the density of dopamine (DA) D2 receptors varies directly with reaction time; (2) the loss of DA receptors in the neostriatum may be the most consistent change in DA in the aged brain; (3) the loss of DA receptors is coincidental with a significant loss of cholinergic activity in neostriatal neurons that receive dense projections from motor and somatosensory cortex, which may compromise thalamic relay centers and, in so doing, impair speeded motor performance; (4) small to medium sized neurons that constitute about 85% of neostriatal cells and on which almost all afferents from frontal motor areas (arcuate premotor, supplementary motor), thalamus, and midbrain converge undergo substantial loss of their dendritic surface later in life, urging Scheibel (1982) to write that "...aging...may result in profound changes in information transfer and the readiness with which action can be begun and terminated" (p. 582); (5) synapse loss that is not evident in postcentral cortical structures occurs in premotor cortex and among the most vulnerable cells to aging are the giant Betz cells in primary motor cortex, prompting Jones (1988) to write "...motor performance in particular may be impaired in healthy elderly individuals" (p. 31); (6) reduction of brain volume may be largest in the frontal lobes, thalamus and basal ganglia, with perhaps the greatest reductions occurring in premotor (Haug, Barmwater, Eggers, Fischer, Kuhl, & Sass, 1983) and prefrontal cortex (Raz et al., 1997); and (7) reductions in blood flow and glucose utilization may be greatest in frontal cortex (Waldemar, 1995).

In addition, neuropsychological evidence suggests that the important functional distinction between young and older adults is in the anterior-posterior, not the left-right, plane of the brain, with the pattern of results suggesting that frontal lobe functions are compromised more by age than are functions subserved by other parts of cortex (reviewed in Bashore, 1993). The frontal lobes subserve a wide range of neurocognitive functions, known generically as 'executive' functions (Kimberg & Farah, 1993; West, 1996). An important historical characterization of these functions is that they represent the final common pathway for human action, a fundamentally important component of which is motor action. Indeed, the vital role of the frontal lobes in the control of movement has been appreciated for more than a century, prompting Stuss and Benson (1984) to write: "Of all frontal lobe functions, the control of motor responses is most obvious. It has long been recognized that the frontal portion of the brain subsumed motor actions, in contrast to the sensory activities of the parietal, temporal, and occipital lobes (Meynert, 1872). Bianchi (1895) posited that the frontal lobe not only initiated the "final common pathway" for brain responses but served to integrate information from other parts of the brain and thus to modulate the final response." (p. 6) Like Bianchi, a contemporary theorist, Fuster (1989), has speculated that the frontal lobes control the organization, timing, and inhibition of responses, as well as the translation of stimulus input that calls for action into an appropriate response output. More recently, West (1996) has argued that prefrontal cortex controls the temporal integration of action.

Thus, we view the neostriatal-frontal lobe circuitry as the crucial mediator of the age-related changes we have observed in neurocognitive processing speed. In an elegant review of the neurocognitive aging literature, West (1996) argued that an important decline in frontal lobe function evident among the aged is a decrement in their ability to inhibit a prepotent response. This decline may have been expressed, in part, in the particular difficulty older subjects were found by Bashore et al. (in preparation) to have in making an incompatible response when stimulus processing demands were high. It may reflect a compromised stimulus-response translation process that is secondary to the inability of older adults to efficiently integrate complicated stimulus information with an appropriate response choice when an overlearned response must be inhibited. That is, the effort required to perform this reaction may overtax the limited capacity of the older information processing system.

Closing Thoughts

The focus of our chapter has been on the development and decline of neurocognitive processing speed early and late in life. Our discussion of young adults has been primarily as the referent group for determining if differential patterns of growth and loss of processing speed can be isolated among children and older adults. It should not be concluded by the reader, however, that our interests do not encompass young and middle adulthood. They do. Indeed, from our perspective neurocognitive processes are best conceptualized as evolving dynamically over the entire lifespan, a lifespan that includes periods of more or less processing stability. As such, each period in the lifespan is characterized in the context of the periods that have preceded it and those that are to follow it (save at the near-end of life). For example, to our knowledge, there is no work in mental chronometry that has attempted to characterize the relative sensitivity of the young adult information processor to variations in stimulus and response processing demands, or in the differential ability of young adults to learn the variety of stimulus and response components of a neurocognitive skill. Differential processing sensitivity and/or skill acquisition may link very closely to the differential development of stimulus and response processing described in this chapter. If so, a reasonably cogent account of the pattern in young adulthood could be offered in the context of a well-understood developmental process. Similarly, the sensitivity to and recovery of function from neurological damage in young adults may be articulated with greater precision and understood in more depth when framed within the context of a developmental history. For example, the work in the last century of Jackson (1884/1958) and Ribot (1883) suggested that those functions that were the last to develop were the most susceptible to significant compromise following brain damage. Work like that described in this chapter can help establish the veracity of this view.

The study of mental chronometry has a long and glorious history in psychology (see review in van der Molen et al., 1991). However, since the inception of work in this area, efforts have been directed almost exclusively toward characterizing the information processing apparatus of one age group, young adults. The assumption underlying this work is that the structure of information processing in young adults is typical of all humankind. That may not be the case. Moreover, research in mental chronometry has typically emphasized the quantitative aspects of information processing (i.e., rate of processing) to the exclusion of the qualitative aspects of processing. As is evident from the work with children and older adults we have presented in this chapter, the qualitative properties of information processing deserve our attention in young adults. Hence, research at the beginning and end of life and the conceptualizations derived from it may suggest both new possibilities for research and new theoretical perspectives for the investigation of information processing in young adults, the result of which may be a synergism that yields insights that are not possible when the population is restricted to one or another age group. This possibility is not new. It was recognized in the latter part of the 19th century by Preyer but was lost in criticisms of his views by Wundt (see van der Molen, 1990). It should not be lost on contemporary investigators.

ACKNOWLEDGEMENT

Preparation of this chapter was supported in part by grants to the first author from the National Institute on Aging (AG04581, AG12263) and from the Research Corporation at the University of Northern Colorado, a fellowship awarded by the Royal Netherlands Academy of Sciences to the second author, and a grant to the third author from the Dutch government (NWO 575-63-093). We would like to thank Slidemakers, Inc., of Landsdowne, Pennsylvania, for preparation of Figures 3 and 7. We would also like to thank Dr. Robert Kail for providing the data used from Kail (1991a) in Figure 2. The first author would also like to express his appreciation to the Moss Rehabilitation Research Institute (Director, Dr. John Whyte) for its support, during his sabbatical at the Institute, in the final stages of preparation of this chapter. In addition, we would like to commend Dr. Naftali Raz on the wisdom of the editorial insights he conveyed to us during preparation of this chapter.

Note

1. We have portrayed target location, response activation, target identification, and S-R translation as separate stages of processing, our justification for this deriving from the logic of the additive method (Sternberg, 1969; van der Molen et al., 1991); factors that have additive effects are presumed to influence different stages of processing, whereas factors that have interactive effects are presumed to influence a common stage. The additive effects of variations in stimulus discriminability and S-R compatibility on the latencies of the N260 and P300 components suggest, according to this reasoning, that the effects of these two experimental factors on the respective component latencies indicate the engagement of different stages of processing. However, reasonable alternative interpretations are suggested by the work of Miller (1988) and McClelland (1979). The former, embodied in the Asynchronous Discrete Coding model, could argue that a stimulus evaluation stage exists which is responsible for locating and identifying the target, and the output of each of these subprocesses is represented by a discrete code. When the target is located, the code represented by it is passed to a later stage, say, stimulus-response translation, as the stimulus evaluation process continues, and so on. Similarly, McClelland's (1979) Cascade Model supports the observation that additive factor effects may be produced by variations in subprocesses within a single stage.

References

Allen, P.A., Ashcraft, M.H., & Weber, T.A. (1992). On mental multiplication and age. *Psychology and Aging*, *7*, 536-545.

Allen, P.A., Madden, D.J., & Slane, S. (1995). Visual word encoding and the effect of adult age and word frequency. In P.A. Allen & T.R. Bashore (Eds.), *Age differences in word and language processing* (pp. 30-71). Amsterdam: North-Holland.

Amrhein, P.C. (1995). Evidence for task specificity in age-related slowing: A review of speeded picture-word processing studies. In P.A. Allen & T.R. Bashore (Eds.), *Age differences in word and language processing* (pp. 143-170). Amsterdam: North-Holland.

Band, G.P.H. & Miller, J. (1997). Mental rotation interferes with response preparation. *Journal of Experimental Psychology: Human Perception and Performance*, *23*, 319-338.

Bashore, T.R. (1981). Vocal and manual reaction time estimates of interhemispheric transmission time. *Psychological Bulletin*, *89*, 352-368.

Bashore, T.R. (1990). Age-related changes in mental processing revealed by analyses of event-related brain potentials. In J. Rohrbaugh, R. Parasuraman, & R. Johnson, Jr. (Eds.), *Event-related brain potentials: Basic issues and applications* (pp. 242-275). New York: Oxford University Press.

Bashore, T.R. (1993). Differential effects of aging on the neurocognitive functions subserving speeded mental processing. In J. Cerella, J. Rybash, W. Hoyer, & M.L. Commons (Eds.), *Adult information processing: Limits on loss* (pp. 37-76). New York: Academic Press.

Bashore, T.R. (1994). Some thoughts on neurocognitive slowing. *Acta Psychologica*, *86*, 295-325.

Bashore, T.R., & Osman, A. (1987). "On the temporal relation between perceptual analysis and response selection: A psychophysiological investigation of stimulus congruency and S-R compatibility effects on human information processing". Poster presented at the Fourth International Conference on Cognitive Neurosciences, Dourdan-Paris, France, June.

Bashore, T.R., Osman, A., & Heffley, E.F. (1989). Mental slowing in elderly persons: A cognitive psychophysiological analysis. *Psychology and Aging*, *4*, 235-244.

Bashore, T.R., & Smulders, F. (1995). Do general slowing functions mask local slowing effects? A chronopsychophysiological perspective. In P.A. Allen & T.R. Bashore (Eds.), *Age differences in word and language processing* (pp. 390-425). Amsterdam: North-Holland.

Bashore, T.R., Martinerie, J.M., Ridderinkhof, K.R., van der Molen, M.W., & Heffley, E.F. (in preparation). Task- and process-specific neurocognitive slowing among the elderly revealed using chronopsychophysiological measures.

Birren, J.E. (1965). Age changes in speed of behavior: Its central nature and physiological correlates. In A.T. Welford & J.E. Birren (Eds.), *Behavior, aging and the nervous system* (pp. 191-216). Sprinfield, IL: Charles C. Thomas.

Brinley, J.F. (1965). Cognitive sets, speed and accuracy of performance in the elderly. In A.T. Welford & J.E. Birren (Eds.), *Behavior, aging and the nervous system* (pp. 114-149). Springfield, Ill: C.C. Thomas.

Cerella, J. (1985). Information processing rates in the elderly. *Psychological Bulletin*, *98*, 67-83.

Cerella, J. (1990). Aging and information processing rate. In J.E. Birren & K.W. Schaie (Eds.), *Handbook of the psychology of aging* (pp. 201-221). New York: Academic Press.

Cerella, J. (1991). Age effects may be global, not local: Comment on

Fisk and Rogers. *Journal of Experimental Psychology: General, 120*, 215-223.

Cerella, J. (1994). Generalized slowing in Brinley plots. *Journal of Gerontology: Psychological Sciences, 49*, P65-P71.

Cerella, J., & Hale, S. (1994). The rise and fall in information-processing rates over the life span. *Acta Psychologica, 86*, 109-197.

Cerella, J., Poon, L.W., & Fozard, J.L. (1981). Mental rotation and age reconsidered. *Journal of Gerontology, 36*, 620-624.

Cerella, J., Poon, L.W., & Williams, D.M. (1980). Age and the complexity hypothesis. In L. Poon (Ed.), *Aging in the 1980s: Psychological issues* (pp. 332-340). Washington, DC: American Psychological Association.

Coles, M.G.H. (1989). Modern mind-brain reading: Psychophysiology, physiology, and cognition. *Psychophysiology, 26*, 251-269.

Coles, M.G.H., & Rugg, M.D. (1995). Event-related brain potentials: An introduction. In M.D. Rugg & M.G.H. Coles (Eds.), *Electrophysiology of mind* (pp. 1-26). Oxford: Oxford University Press.

Coles, M.G.H., Smid, H.G.O.M., Scheffers, M.K, & Otten, L. (1995). Mental chronometry and the study of human information processing. In M.D. Rugg & M.G.H. Coles (Eds.), *Electrophysiology of mind* (pp. 86-131). Oxford: Oxford University Press.

DeJong, R., Liang, C.C., & Lauber, E. (1994). Conditional and unconditional automaticity: A dual-process model of effects of spatial stimulus-response correspondence. *Journal of Experimental Psychology: Human Perception and Performance, 20*, 731-750.

DeJong, R., Wierda, M., Mulder, G., & Mulder, L.J.M. (1988). Use of partial stimulus information in response processing. *Journal of Experimental Psychology: Human Perception and Performance, 14*, 682-692.

Donchin, E., Karis, D., Bashore, T.R., Coles, M.G.H., & Gratton, G.

(1986). Cognitive psychophysiology and human information processing. In M.G.H. Coles, E. Donchin, & S.W. Porges (Eds.), *Psychophysiology: Systems, processes, and applications* (pp. 244-267). New York: The Guilford Press.

Ellis, R.D., Goldberg, J.H., & Detweiler, M.C. (1996). Predicting age-related differences in visual information processing using a two-stage queuing model. *Journal of Gerontology: Psychological Sciences*, *51B*, P155-P165.

Fisher, D.L., Fisk, A.D., & Duffy, S.A. (1995). Why latent models are needed to test hypotheses about slowing of word and language processes in older adults. In P.A. Allen & T.R. Bashore (Eds.), *Age differences in word and language processing* (pp. 1-29). Amsterdam: North-Holland.

Fisk, A.D., & Fisher, D.L. (1994). Brinley plots and theories of aging: The explicit, muddled, and implicit debates. *Journal of Gerontology: Psychological Sciences*, *49*, P81-P89.

Fisk, A.D., Fisher, D.L., & Rogers, W.A. (1992). General slowing alone cannot explain age-related search effects: Reply to Cerella (1991). *Journal of Experimental Psychology: General*, *121*, 73-78.

Ford, J.M., Roth, W.T., Mohs, R.C., Hopkins, W.F., & Kopell, B.S. (1979). Event-related potentials recorded from young and old adults during a memory retrieval task. *Electroencephalography and Clinical Neurophysiology*, *47*, 450-459.

Fuster, J.M. (1989). *The prefrontal cortex* (second edition). New York: Raven Press.

Garner, W. R. (1974). *The processing of information and structure*. Potomac, MD: Erlbaum. Gibson, E.J. (1969). *Principles of perceptual learning and development*. New York: Academic Press.

Gratton, G., Coles, M.G.H., Sirevaag, E., Eriksen, C.W., & Donchin, E. (1988). Pre-and poststimulus activation of response channels: A psychophysiological analysis. *Journal of Experimental Psychology: Human Perception and Performance*, *14*, 331-344.

Greenwood, P., & Parasuraman, R. (1991). Effects of aging on the speed and attentional cost of cognitive operations. *Developmental Neuropsychology*, *7*, 421-434.

Hackley, S.A., & Miller, J.O. (1989). Lateralized readiness potentials preceding simple and complex finger movements. *Psychophysiology*, *26* (Supplement), S30.

Hale, S. (1990). A global developmental trend in cognitive processing speed in children. *Child Development*, *61*, 653-663.

Hale, S., Fry, A.F., & Jessie, K.A. (1993). Effects of practice on speed of information processing in children and adults: Age sensitivity and age invariance. *Developmental Psychology*, *29*, 880-892.

Hale, S., Myerson, J., Faust, M., & Fristoe, N. (1995). Converging evidence for domain-specific slowing from multiple nonlexical tasks, and multiple analytic methods. *Journal of Gerontology: Psychological Sciences*, *50B*, P202-P211.

Hale, S., Myerson, J., and Wagstaff, D. (1987). General slowing of nonverbal information processing: Evidence for a power law. *Journal of Gerontology*, *42*, 131-136.

Hall, G.S. (1922). *Senescence: The last half of life.* New York: Appleton.

Haug, H., Barmwater, U., Eggers, R., Fischer, D., Kuhl, S., & Sass, N.-L. (1983). Anatomical changes in aging brain: Morphometric analysis of the human prosencephalon. In J. Cervos-Navarro & H.-I Sarkander (Eds.), *Brain aging: Neuropathology and neuropharmacology* (Volume 21: Aging, pp. 1-12). New York: Raven Press.

Jackson, J.H. (1884). Evolution and dissolution of the nervous system. In *Selected writings of John Hughlings Jackson* (volume 2, pp. 45-91), J. Taylor (Ed.). New York: Basic Books.

Johnson, R. (1993). On the neural generators of the P300 component of the event-related brain potential. *Psychophysiology, 30*, 90-97.

Jones, D.G. (1988). Synaptic trends and synaptic remodelling in the developing and mature neocortex. In T.L. Petit & G.O. Ivy (Eds.), *Neural plasticity: A lifespan approach* (pp. 21-42). New York: Liss.

Kail, R. (1986). Sources of age differences in speed of processing. *Child Development, 57*, 969-987.

Kail, R. (1991a). Developmental change in speed of processing during childhood and adolescence. *Psychological Bulletin, 109*, 490-501.

Kail, R. (1991b). Development of processing speed in childhood and adolescence. *Advances in child development, 23*, 151-185.

Kail, R. (1991c). Processing time declines exponentially during childhood and adolescence. *Developmental Psychology, 27*, 259-266.

Kail, R. (1992). Processing speed, speech rate, and memory. *Developmental Psychology, 28*, 899-904.

Kail, R. (1993). Processing time decreases globally at an exponential rate during childhood and adolescence. *Journal of Experimental Child Psychology, 56*, 254-265.

Kail, R., & Park, Y.-S. (1992). Global developmental change in processing time. *Merrill-Palmer Quarterly, 38*, 525-541.

Kail, R., & Salthouse, T.A. (1994). Processing speed as a mental capacity. *Acta Psychologica, 86*, 199-226.

Kimberg, D.Y., & Farah, M.J. (1993). A unified account of cognitive impairments following frontal lobe damage: The role of working memory in complex, organized behavior. *Journal of Experimental Psychology: General, 122*, 411-428.

Knight, R.T. (1990). Neural mechanisms of event-related potentials: Evidence from human lesion studies. In J. Rohrbaugh, R. Parasuraman, & R. Johnson, Jr. (Eds.), *Event-related potentials: Basic issues and applications* (pp. 3-18). New York: Oxford University Press.

Lane, D.M., & Pearson, D.A. (1982). The development of selective attention. *Merrill-Palmer Quarterly*, *28*, 317-337.

Lima, S.D., Hale, S., & Myerson, J. (1991). How general is general slowing? Evidence from the lexical domain. *Psychology and Aging*, *6*, 416-425.

Madden, D. (1992). Four to ten milliseconds per year: Age-related slowing of visual word identification. *Journal of Gerontology: Psychological Sciences*, *47*, P59-P68.

Madden, D.J., Pierce, T.W., & Allen, P.A. (1993). Adult age differences in attentional allocation during memory search. *Psychology and Aging*, *7*, 594-601.

Madden, D.J., Pierce, T.W., & Allen, P.A. (1993). Age-related slowing and the time course of semantic priming in visual word identification. *Psychology and Aging*, *8*, 490-507.

Magliero, A., Bashore, T.R., Coles, M.G.H., & Donchin, E. (1984). On the dependence of P300 latency on stimulus evaluation processes. *Psychophysiology*, *21*, 171-186.

Mayr, U., & Kliegl, R. (1993). Sequential and coordinative complexity: Age-based processing limitations in figural transformations. *Journal of Experimental Psychology: Learning, Memory, and Cognition*, *19*, 1297-1320.

McCarthy, G., & Donchin, E. (1981). A metric for thought: A comparison of P300 latency and reaction time. *Science*, *211*, 77-80.

McClelland, J.L. (1979). On the time relations of mental processes: An examination of processes in cascade. *Psychological Review*, *86*, 287-330.

Miller, J.O. (1988). Discrete and continuous models of human information processing: Theoretical distinctions and empirical results. *Acta Psychologica*, *67*, 191-257.

Miller, J., & Hackley, S.A. (1992). Electrophysiological evidence for temporal overlap among contingent mental processes. *Journal of Experimental Psychology: General*, *121*, 195-209.

Miller, J.O, Coles, M.G.H., & Chakraborty, S. (1996). Dissociation between behavioral and psychophysiological measures of response preparation. *Acta Psychologica*, *94*, 189-208.

Miller, J., Riehle, A., & Requin, J. (1992). Effects of preliminary perceptual output on neuronal activity of the primary motor cortex. *Journal of Experimental Psychology: Human Perception and Performance*, *18*, 1121-1138.

Myerson, J., & Hale, S. (1993). General slowing and age invariance in cognitive processing: The other side of the coin. In J. Cerella, J. Rybash, W. Hoyer, & M.L. Commons (Eds.), *Adult information processing: Limits on loss* (pp. 115-141). Academic Press: New York.

Myerson, J., Wagstaff, D., & Hale, S. (1994). Brinley plots, explained variance, and the analysis of age differences in response latencies. *Journal of Gerontology: Psychological Sciences*, *49*, P72-P80.

Osman, A., Bashore, T.R., Coles, M.G.H., Donchin, E., and Meyer, D.E. (1992). On the transmission of partial information: Inferences from movement-related brain potentials. *Journal of Experimental Psychology: Human Perception and Performance*, *18*, 217-232.

Perfect, T.J. (1994). What can Brinley plots tell us about cognitive aging? *Journal of Gerontology: Psychological Sciences*, *49*, P60-P64.

Plude, D.J., Enns, J.T., & Brodeur, D. (1994). The development of selective attention: A life-span overview. *Acta Psychologica, 86*, 227-272.

Polich, J. (1993). Cognitive brain potentials. *Current Directions in Psychological Science*, *2*, 175-179.

Polich, J. (1996). Meta-analysis of P300 normative aging studies. *Psychophysiology*, *33*, 334-353.

Raz, N., Gunning, F.M., Head, D., Dupuis, J.H., McQuain, J., Briggs, S.D., Loken, W.J., Thornton, A.E., & Acker, J.D. (1997). Selective aging of the human cerebral cortex observed *in vivo*: Differential vulnerability of the prefrontal gray matter. *Cerebral Cortex*, *7*, 268-282.

Ribot, T. (1883). The diseases of memory. *Popular Science Literature*.

Ridderinkhof, K.R. (1997). A dual route processing architecture for stimulus-response correspondence effects. In B. Hommel & W. Prinz (Eds.), *Theoretical issues in stimulus-response compatibility* (pp. 119-131). Amsterdam: Elsevier Science.

Ridderinkhof, K.R., & Bashore, T.R.. Using event-related brain potentials to draw inferences about human information processing. In *Age differences in word and language processing*, P.A. Allen & T.R. Bashore (Eds.), Amsterdam: North-Holland, 1995, pp. 295-314.

Ridderinkhof, K.R., Bashore, T.R., van der Molen, M.W., & Band, G.P.H. (submitted). Qualitative versus quantitative age-related changes in processing speed.

Ridderinkhof, K. R., & van der Molen, M. W. (1995). A psychophysiological analysis of developmental differences in the ability to resist interference. *Child Development*, *66*, 1040-1056.

Ridderinkhof, K. R., & van der Molen, M. W. (1997). Mental resources, processing speed, and inhibitory control: A developmental perspective.

Biological Psychology, *45*, 241-261.

Ridderinkhof, K.R., van der Molen, M.W., & Bashore, T.R. (1995). Limits on the application of additive factors logic: Violations of stage robustness suggest a dual-process architecture to explain flanker effects on target processing. *Acta Psychologica*, *90*, 29-48.

Ridderinkhof, K.R., van der Molen, M.W., Band, G.P.H. & Bashore, T.R. (1997). Sources of interference from irrelevant information: A developmental study. *Journal of Experimental Child Psychology*, *65*, 315-341.

Salthouse, T.A. (1985a). *A theory of cognitive aging*. Amsterdam: North-Holland.

Salthouse, T.A. (1985b). Speed of behavior and its implications for cognition. In J.E. Birren & K.W. Schaie (Eds.), *Handbook of the psychology of aging* (2nd edition) (pp. 400-426). New York: Van Nostrand Reinhold Co..

Salthouse, T.A. (1991). *Theoretical perspectives on cognitive aging*. Hillsdale, NJ: Lawrence Erlbaum.

Salthouse, T.A. (1996). The processing speed theory of adult age differences in cognition. *Psychological Review*, *103*, 403-428.

Sanders, A.F. (1983). Towards a model of stress and human performance. *Acta Psychologica*, *53*, 61-97.

Schiebel, A. (1982). Age-related changes in human forebrain. *Neurosciences Research Program Bulletin*, *20*, 577-585.

Shepp, B.E. (1989). On perceived objects: Holistic versus featural properties. In B.E. Shepp and S. Ballesteros (Eds.), *Object perception: Structure and process* (pp. 203-233). Hillsdale, NJ: Erlbaum.

Shepp, B.E., & Barrett, S.E. (1991). The development of perceived structure and attention: Evidence from divided and selective attention tasks. *Journal of Experimental Child Psychology*, *51*, 434-458.

Sliwinski, M. (1997). Aging and counting speed: Evidence for process-specific slowing. *Psychology and Aging*, *12*, 38-49.

Smid, H.G.O.M., Mulder, G., Mulder, L.J.M., & Brands, G.J. (1992). A psychophysiological study of the use of partial information in stimulus-response translation. *Journal of Experimental Psychology: Human Perception and Performance*, *18*, 1101-1119.

Sternberg, S. (1969). The discovery of processing stages: Extensions of Donders' method. In W.G. Koster (Ed.), *Attention and Performance* (Volume II, pp. 276-315). Amsterdam: North-Holland.

Stuss, D.T., & Benson, D.F. (1984). Neuropsychological studies of the frontal lobes. *Psychological Bulletin*, *95*, 3-28.

Swearer, J.M., & Kane, K. (1996). Behavioral slowing with age: Boundary conditions of the generalized slowing model. *Journal of Gerontology: Psychological Sciences*, *51B*, P189-P201.

van der Molen, M.W. (1990). Energetics of cognitive development. In W. Koops, H.J.G. Soppe, G.L. van der Linver, P.C.M. Molenaar, & J.J.F. Schroots (Eds.), *Developmental psychology behind the dikes. An outline of developmental psychological research in the Netherlands* (pp. 123-139). Delft, The Netherlands: Eburon.

van der Molen, M.W., & Ridderinkhof, K.R. (in press). The growing and aging brain: Life-span changes in brain development and human performance. In A. Demetriou, W. Doise, & C.F.M. van Liesshout (Eds.), *Lifespan developmental psychology: A European perspective*. London: J. Wiley.

van der Molen M.W., Bashore, T.R., Halliday, R.F., & Callaway, E. (1991). Chronopsychophysiology: Mental chronometry augmented by psychophysiological time markers. In: J.R. Jennings & M.G.H. Coles (Eds.). *Handbook of Cognitive Psychophysiology* (pp. 9-178), New York: J. Wiley &

Sons.

Verleger, R. (1997). On the utility of P3 latency as an index of mental chronometry, *Psychophysiology*, *34*, 131-156.

Waldemar, G. (1995). Functional brain imaging with SPECT in normal aging and dementia: Methodological, pathophysiological, and diagnostic aspect. *Cerebrovascular and Brain Metabolism Review*, *7*, 89-130.

West, R.L. (1996). An application of prefrontal cortex function theory to cognitive aging. *Psychological Bulletin*, *120*, 272-292.

Chapter 6

DIFFERENTIAL CONTRIBUTION OF FRONTAL AND MEDIAL TEMPORAL LOBES TO MEMORY: EVIDENCE FROM FOCAL LESIONS AND NORMAL AGING

Elizabeth L. Glisky

University of Arizona

ABSTRACT

In recent years, the study of memory has become very much an interdisciplinary enterprise in which cognitive psychology and neuropsychology have been the principal participants. This collaboration has yielded a wealth of information concerning the brain-behavior relations involved in normal human memory. This chapter provides an overview of the empirical and theoretical developments that have emerged from the study of focal lesion patients and the normal elderly. The chapter focuses on the roles played in memory by two broad areas of brain--the medial temporal lobe regions and prefrontal cortex--and attempts to show how these areas make distinct but complementary contributions to human memory.

When Warrington and Weiskrantz (1968; 1970; 1974) made their initial discovery that amnesic patients, although unable to recall or recognize recently-presented words or pictures, were nevertheless able to produce those items to partial cues, they could not have foreseen the impact that these observations would have on the future course of psychology. At that time, although information processing models from the emerging field of cognitive psychology were beginning to be used to explain memory deficits, the reverse influence was not at all evident. Cognitive psychologists had shown little interest in the descriptions of memory-impaired patients that were being reported in the neuropsychological literature. They were interested in establishing broad general principles of normal memory function and saw little reason to try to explain exceptions before a more basic understanding of normative behavior was achieved (e.g., Murdock, 1974).

Not until the early 1980s was the significance of Warrington and Weiskrantz's work for theories of normal memory recognized. In 1982, Tulving, Schacter & Stark published a seminal paper demonstrating that normal young college students, like amnesic patients, responded to fragment cues with previously studied words, even when they did not consciously remember the prior occurrence of the word. Normal subjects, of course, could also explicitly remember many of the prior presentations, but their ability to complete fragments with recently-experienced words was independent of their ability to retrieve those words consciously. This demonstration--inspired by Warrington and Weiskrantz's findings with a small group of amnesic patients--and the many related observations that followed led ultimately to a new understanding of the nature of human memory. It suggested that human memory was not a unitary entity subject to a single set of laws or principles and dependent on a single underlying brain structure or system, but rather a set of systems and processes that relied on different neural substrates, governed by different rules of operation, responsive to different variables, and able to function independently. Just as importantly, it signaled a new era in memory research--one that involved a close collaboration between neuropsychologists and cognitive psychologists--which took as its data the performance of both brain-damaged patients and normal individuals and took as its primary goal, the understanding of normal, human memory processes. Whereas the two separate disciplines had focused on group studies and the similarities among individuals, the new cognitive neuropsychology included an emphasis on single-case as well as group studies and considered more closely the differences among individuals.

From these studies has emerged a multi-faceted picture of memory dependent on multiple brain structures. This chapter is concerned with the function of two broadly-defined regions of brain that have been implicated in memory--the medial temporal/diencephalic area and the prefrontal cortex. Although in this chapter, I will refer in global terms to these two regions, it is becoming increasingly evident that structures within these areas contribute differently to memory performance (Aggleton, & Saunders, 1997; Zola-Morgan, & Squire, 1993), although the exact function of individual structures remains controversial. Despite the differences observed among patients with lesions to different parts of the medial temporal/diencephalic memory system, however, the commonalities are more striking. At the same time, the contribution of prefrontal cortex to memory appears to be substantively different, although perhaps closely interrelated. My task here is to contrast, in broad terms, the functions of these two regions. The chapter will focus primarily on episodic memory--memory for specific events experienced in a particular spatiotemporal context--and will touch only briefly on other related forms of memory. In particular, I will not discuss working memory--a temporary, short-term form of memory that has been associated with prefrontal cortex (e.g., Goldman-Rakic, 1995) but is typically not impaired in amnesic patients.

Although focal lesion patients have provided the bulk of the evidence concerning the role of different brain regions in memory, studies of the normal elderly may also be informative. Because changes in memory that occur in normal aging mimic changes observed in brain-damaged patients, albeit to a lesser degree, studies of older adults can provide additional or converging evidence about the processes necessary for normal memory function. Further, because memory performance in the elderly is much more variable than in the young (Weintraub, Powell, & Whitla, 1994), the range of normal processes that can be observed is much greater and more easily identifiable among the elderly. The mapping of these processes onto neural structures, however, has until recently, been less than straightforward. Developments in structural and functional neuroimaging techniques, however, have begun to enable researchers to develop a much clearer picture of how different parts of the brain are involved in various aspects of memory.

This chapter reviews a select group of studies of memory-impaired patients and the normal elderly that have provided insights into the functioning of normal human memory and have suggested particular roles for the medial temporal and prefrontal regions of the brain. The chapter will focus first on the role of the medial temporal lobes, then on the role of the frontal lobes, and finally suggest how the functions of these two regions may be complementary though distinct.

Role of The Medial Temporal Lobes

Historically, memory has been associated with the brain structures situated in either the medial temporal lobes, including the hippocampus and adjacent cortical regions, or the midline diencephalon, including the mammillary bodies and dorsomedial and/or anterior nuclei of the thalamus (Zola-Morgan & Squire, 1993). Although there has been debate over the possibly different contributions of these two closely connected regions to memory impairment (e.g., Hunkin, Parkin, & Longmore, 1994; Squire, 1981), behavioral support for such a differentiation has been difficult to obtain. I will not make such a distinction here, but instead will consider these regions to be part of the same functional memory system. Evidence supporting the role of these midline brain structures in memory comes largely from studies of patients with focal lesions who, as a result of damage to medial temporal or diencephalic brain regions, develop serious memory impairments.

Evidence from Focal Lesion Patients

The amnesic syndrome. Earliest evidence implicating the medial temporal lobes in memory was provided in reports of patient H.M. who, following bilateral excision of the hippocampus and surrounding structures to relieve his intractable epilepsy, was found to be globally amnesic (Milner, 1966; Scoville, & Milner, 1957). Although the surgery reduced his seizures, it became immediately apparent that H.M. was left with a much more serious deficit: he had a profound anterograde amnesia (AA) for both verbal and non-verbal materials and was unable to acquire or remember any new information. H.M. also had a limited retrograde amnesia (RA)--an inability to retrieve events that occurred prior to surgery--that initially appeared to cover a period of about 3 years but later was found to extend back approximately 11 years (Corkin, 1984). H.M.'s intelligence was intact, as was his general knowledge of the world. He also had what appeared to be, at the time, a sparing of the ability to acquire new motor skills (Corkin, 1968). His short-term memory was normal.

The characteristics that H.M. displayed were similar in most respects to those previously documented in cases of Korsakoff's syndrome, a neurological disorder associated with chronic alcohol abuse and thiamine insufficiency (Talland, 1965; Victor, & Yakovlev, 1955), which results in damage to diencephalic brain structures. The same general pattern of deficits, which constitutes what is now referred to as the amnesic syndrome, has since been observed in a range of patients with either diencephalic lesions caused by infarct or tumor, for example, or medial temporal lobe damage stemming from neurological disorders such as herpes simplex encephalitis, posterior cerebral artery strokes or other ischemic episodes, anoxia as a result of cardiac arrest, carbon monoxide poisoning, or near-drowning, and traumatic brain injury (for reviews, see Parkin, & Leng, 1993; Shimamura, 1989). All of these conditions share the memory impairments exhibited by H.M. to varying degrees, the principal feature in common being an inability to acquire new memories.

At the same time, old memories that were acquired some time prior to the onset of the amnesia remain largely intact, although there is usually a period of RA that is variable across patient groups. So, for example, many Korsakoff patients experience an extensive loss of their autobiographical past that may extend back 30-40 years sparing only the most remote memories (Butters, & Cermak, 1986; Cohen, & Squire, 1981). Other patients, like H.M. have a milder retrograde impairment (Corkin, 1984; Marslen-Wilson, & Teuber, 1975), and still others like R. B. with bilateral damage confined to the CA1 region of the hippocampus (Zola-Morgan, Squire, & Amaral, 1986) and N.A. with diencephalic damage (Shimamura, 1989; Teuber, Milner, & Vaughan, 1968) have almost no retrograde loss. In most cases, the RA has a temporal gradient, with recent memories more affected than remote memories, although there are exceptions to this pattern (e.g., Cermak, & O'Connor, 1983). Several reasons for the variability observed in RA across patients have been suggested, but none of them are able to account for all of the findings. The severity and extent of RA may be related to the severity of AA, to the extent of medial temporal/diencephalic damage, or to the involvement of brain structures outside the hippocampal memory system (Squire, 1992). Whatever the explanation, the finding that amnesic patients often retain memories that were acquired earlier in life suggests that the medial temporal/ diencephalic region, although essential for the formation of new memories, is unlikely to be the place where memories are permanently stored.

As studies of amnesic patients accumulated, it became evident that although patients were unable to acquire new episodic memories they were nevertheless able to retain some aspects of recent experiences. So, as noted previously, H.M. was able to learn some motor tasks in a relatively normal fashion (Corkin, 1968), and Warrington and Weiskrantz's patients appeared able to produce previously-presented words and pictures in response to partial cues (Warrington & Weiskrantz, 1974). Many more examples of such preserved memory abilities in amnesia have now been documented, and they have led to important theoretical advances in the understanding of memory. It now appears that amnesic patients retain some record of previous experience, which they are able to express in their behavior, even though they have no conscious or explicit awareness of that prior experience. This "implicit" expression of memory in the absence of explicit knowledge of the prior episode--what is called priming--has now been demonstrated in various tasks (for reviews, see Schacter, Chiu, & Ochsner, 1993; Squire, 1992) including word-stem and word-fragment completion, tachistoscopic identification, lexical decision, object decision, and auditory identification in noise (Schacter, Church, & Treadwell, 1994). In all cases, patients show an enhanced ability to perform these tasks as a result of prior exposure to the relevant material, but they cannot recollect the previous occurrence. Amnesic patients also show normal learning of various skills including rotary pursuit, the reading of mirror-reversed text, the solving of puzzles and the learning of spatiotemporal sequences (for review, see Cohen, & Eichenbaum, 1993).

These demonstrations of preserved implicit memory performance in amnesic patients in the absence of explicit memory suggest that the medial temporal lobe memory system is essential for normal recollective processes such as those demonstrated on tests of recall and recognition but not for the retention of information needed to support priming and skill learning. These findings of two kinds of memory, which appear able to operate independently, led ultimately to the formulation of a new and radically different view of memory--one that probably could not have been developed from studies of normal memory alone: that human beings possess more than one memory system, each operating under a different set of rules, relying on a different neural substrate, and serving a different function (Schacter, & Tulving, 1994b).

The findings raised further questions concerning the exact role of the medial temporal lobes in memory, and suggested that their contribution was likely much more specific than had previously been assumed. Debate concerning how to characterize the kind of memory that was spared in amnesic patients and the kind of memory that was impaired centered initially on the issue of whether differences necessarily required the postulation of separate memory systems or whether they could be accounted for within a single undifferentiated memory system in terms of different processing demands. Although this debate has never been entirely resolved (see Blaxton, 1995; Gabrieli, 1995 for reviews of the major issues), the dominant view among neuropsychologists appears to be one that recognizes the existence of multiple memory systems, although exactly on what basis these systems should be distinguished remains controversial (Schacter, & Tulving, 1994a).

As further evidence has accumulated concerning the kinds of memory tasks that amnesic patients can and cannot accomplish, there has emerged some consensus concerning the functional role of the medial temporal lobe system, but many theoretical differences still exist. At the very least, it is agreed that the medial temporal lobes perform some function that enables the explicit or conscious recollection of specific facts or events. Different theorists, however, have focused on different aspects of this claim as being essential: for example, the type of information processed--episodic as opposed to semantic (Tulving, 1983), declarative as opposed to procedural or non-declarative (Squire, 1994)--or whether retrieval of prior experience is conscious or proceeds without awareness (Jacoby, 1984; Schacter, 1987). Although these theoretical differences are interesting and important, a thorough discussion of them is beyond the scope of this chapter (see Schacter & Tulving, 1994a). Instead, in the balance of this section, I will focus on the information processing roles of the medial temporal region and consider the extent to which evidence from focal lesion patients implicates this part of the brain in encoding, storage, consolidation or retrieval. This summary will be selective, sampling only a few theories of the amnesic deficit, and highlighting some of the more recent empirical findings..

Encoding. One of the earliest explanations of the amnesic syndrome was that it represented a semantic encoding deficit (Cermak, 1979). It was argued that amnesic patients failed to analyze incoming information at a semantic level and therefore did not lay down memory records that were well-elaborated and easily retrievable. Although general semantic information was thought to be encoded, more precise semantic analysis that could make memory traces readily distinguishable from one another was thought to be beyond the capability of amnesic patients (Cermak, 1982). Evidence supporting this position came from studies showing that Korsakoff patients did not benefit from category cues in a cued recall task (Cermak, & Butters, 1972) and did not show normal release from proactive interference (PI) following semantic category shifts (Cermak, Butters, & Moreines, 1974). It was proposed that these failures came from inadequate encoding of semantic features. Later studies, however, particularly those with the encephalitic patient S.S., showing, for example, normal release from PI (Cermak, 1976) suggested a modification of this position: that some patients could perform the semantic analysis (as S.S. could) but could not profit from it (Cermak, 1989). Exactly what was responsible for this failure to benefit from the initial semantic analysis has never been adequately articulated although Cermak has suggested that the problem lies in some further extension of conceptual or organizational processing that is essential for adequate storage (Cermak, 1989; Cermak, 1994). Cermak's point seems to be that whether the problem is construed as an encoding or a storage deficit, the basic difficulty lies at the input end of the information processing sequence. What patients fail to do is encode or store information in an elaborate semantic form that later can be readily retrieved.

We have similarly argued, on the basis of studies of new semantic learning in amnesia, that patients with damage to medial temporal lobe regions fail to encode or store adequate semantic information (Glisky, 1997; Glisky, Schacter, & Butters, 1994). In particular, we hypothesized that patients often do not link new information to existing semantic knowledge, so that even if they did store the information, it would remain isolated from related semantic structures and impossible to retrieve (cf., Tulving, 1983). Several studies have demonstrated that memory-impaired patients have great difficulty learning arbitrary associations such as unrelated paired associates (Shimamura, & Squire, 1984) or name-face associations (Wilson, 1987). Yet they can learn related paired associates or novel associations that are meaningful. So, for example, Hayman, Macdonald and Tulving (1993) found that the severely amnesic patient K.C. could learn novel pairs such as "a talkative featherbrain -- parakeet" and the final word for unique phrases such as "Medicine cures *hiccups*" (Tulving, Hayman, & Macdonald, 1991). These findings suggest that amnesic patients can learn new information if it fits readily into existing knowledge structures. In these cases, little semantic analysis has to be initiated and carried out by the patient because the stimuli themselves drive the semantic processing. When the materials are less meaningful, however, such as with unrelated paired associates, links to prior knowledge have to be intentionally established by the patient. These more difficult semantic processes, which seem to be absent in amnesic patients, may require the medial temporal lobes. However, in a recent study (Thoene, & Glisky, 1995), we found that amnesic patients could learn arbitrary name-face associations using a mnemonic strategy that specifically related the name to information in the semantic system and formed an interactive link between the name and the face through visual imagery. These findings suggest that although the hippocampal memory system may normally be involved in integrating new information with existing knowledge, other brain structures may be able to perform that function under some conditions.

If the amnesic deficit is attributable to ineffective conceptual analysis, then memory-impaired patients should show deficits on implicit memory tasks that are dependent on conceptual processing and should show normal patterns of performance on explicit memory tasks that are not conceptually-driven. Consistent with this prediction, Blaxton (1992) reported that patients with temporal lobe epilepsy were impaired on an implicit test of general knowledge and showed relative sparing of performance on an explicit test of graphemic cued recall. She argued, like Cermak, that the memory deficit in these patients could be accounted for in terms of impaired conceptual processing.

There are a number of other findings that argue against an encoding deficits view, however. First, there is ample evidence that at least some amnesic patients do analyze incoming information conceptually (Cermak, 1976; Mayes et al., 1993). Second, recent evidence indicates that most amnesic patients perform normally on conceptual priming tasks, such as free association (Cermak, Verfaellie, & Chase, 1995; Vaidya, Gabrieli, Keane, & Monti, 1995) and category exemplar generation (Keane et al., 1997). For example, they are as likely as normal subjects to produce previously studied words on a category-cued production task, suggesting that such words must have been initially encoded at a semantic level (Keane et al., 1997). Other evidence suggests, however, that this may differ across patients. Cermak (1994) reported that the extent to which patients showed conceptual priming in a lexical decision task with homonyms was dependent on the extent to which they processed the biased semantic relation during encoding. If such processing was engaged spontaneously (as it was in a sub-group of patients) then normal conceptual priming occurred. If the initial semantic relation was not processed (as in another sub-group of patients), conceptual priming was not observed. This finding provided further evidence that some amnesic patients may have an encoding deficit whereas others appear to be normal with respect to their conceptual processing abilities.

A related finding was reported by Keane et al (1997). Although they found normal conceptual implicit memory among amnesic patients in a category exemplar production task following incidental learning, they found impaired implicit memory when the same task was intentional. They suggested that, under intentional learning conditions, amnesic patients engage in less elaborative processing than control subjects, and so are impaired on implicit memory tasks that are sensitive to prior semantic processing. This finding seems consistent with a deficit in self-initiated semantic processing, although these authors did not think that such an explanation could account for the range of explicit memory deficits seen in amnesia.

Cermak (1997) has recently offered a similar argument with respect to conceptual priming. He suggests that conceptual priming may not be impaired in amnesic patients if it relies on an automatic form of conceptual processing involving preexisting semantic representations. If, however, strategic processing is required (such as under intentional learning conditions, for example) then amnesic patients will show deficits. This view then is similar to the one that we suggested earlier to account for findings in the domain of new semantic learning--that learning can be achieved when the stimuli themselves drive the semantic processing but is extremely difficult if the patients have to establish links to prior knowledge on their own.

The encoding deficit theory in recent years has not been the most popular among neuropsychologists. Although many agree that encoding deficits are observed under some conditions, most believe that the encoding problem is not a consequence of medial temporal damage, but instead reflects incidental frontal damage common in some amnesic patients, particularly those with Korsakoff's syndrome who were the focus of many of the early studies of amnesia (Mayes, 1988). Some of the disagreement stems from definitional ambiguity, however, and in the difficulty in distinguishing between the processes of encoding and storage. So, for some theorists encoding implies storage, whereas for others encoding refers to the formation of representations that may or may not be stored in memory (e.g., Mayes & Downes, 1997). Although most people refer to Cermak's view as an encoding theory, he himself states that it was originally intended as a storage view in which poor encoding processes resulted in ineffective storage (Cermak, 1997). Although he pointedly does not attempt to localize memory encoding or storage processes or to claim that lesions to specific areas of the brain will have particular consequences, his theory appears to implicate the medial temporal/diencephalic brain regions in semantic encoding processes. Whether an encoding deficit constitutes the main problem in the amnesic syndrome or not, it cannot provide the sole explanation, because it is unable to account for RA.

Retrieval. An alternative account of the amnesic deficit is that it represents a retrieval problem. A retrieval deficit could account for memory failures in both the anterograde and retrograde domains. Patients with medial temporal damage such as H.M., however, often have only a limited RA despite an extensive AA, indicating that retrieval processes are at least partly intact and that the medial temporal lobes are not essential for retrieval of previously stored events. Nevertheless, it is possible that the retrieval of old, well-rehearsed memories can be accomplished rather automatically, requiring fewer or qualitatively different processes than retrieval of recent events and that only the latter requires the medial temporal lobes.

A related view hypothesizes that the medial temporal lobes are needed for the retrieval (or storage) of context (Mayes, Meudell, & Pickering, 1985), particularly spatiotemporal context, which enables people to recollect that an event took place in a particular time and place. Note, however, that encoding variants of the context deficit view have also been proposed (e.g., Winocur, Moscovitch, & Witherspoon, 1987). Consistent with this view, numerous studies have shown that amnesic patients, although able to acquire new information, are unable to remember the time and place of learning. A context retrieval deficit would be expected to affect memory for recent events, but have much less effect on tests of remote memory that tend often to tap knowledge that is largely context-free such as the identity of famous people. Thus, this hypothesis could account for the reports of less severe RA than AA in medial temporal lobe amnesia.

Other evidence that has favored a retrieval deficit comes from studies showing greater memory impairments in recall than in recognition (Hirst et al., 1986; Hirst, Johnson, Phelps, & Volpe, 1988). This finding, however, has not been replicated consistently, and other investigators (Haist, Shimamura, & Squire, 1992) have suggested that it might depend on the locus of the brain damage. In particular, recognition appears to be less affected than recall in Korsakoff patients and in patients with ruptured aneurysms of the anterior communicating artery (ACoA) both of whom frequently have frontal damage in addition to their other brain pathology (Parkin & Leng, 1993). On the other hand, patients with damage confined to medial temporal lobe regions appear to have a recognition deficit that is as severe as their recall deficit. Thus, it is possible that disproportionate deficits in recall compared to recognition, reflect impaired search or retrieval processes that arise as a consequence of frontal rather than medial temporal lobe damage. The same argument might apply to the context deficit view: this hypothesis also predicts greater deficits in free recall than in recognition because free recall relies more on retrieval of episodic context. But retrieval of context may depend on frontal lobe functioning rather than on processes associated with the medial temporal lobes. I will consider this possibility again when addressing the role of the frontal lobes.

The finding that memories can be retrieved to partial cues, as in word-stem or word-fragment completion priming, has also been interpreted as support for a retrieval deficit in amnesic patients (Warrington & Weiskrantz, 1970). It has been argued that information must have been encoded and stored if it was subsequently accessible to partial cues, and that failure to recollect prior experience in the absence of cues therefore necessarily constitutes a retrieval problem. Again, however, it is possible that the encoding and storage may be sufficient to support cue-dependent priming but insufficient to support explicit recall.

Another retrieval explanation (sometimes expressed as part of a general processing deficit view in which similar impairments are postulated to occur at both encoding and retrieval) proposes that retrieval is impaired to the extent that it requires controlled rather than automatic processing (Cermak, & Verfaellie, 1992; Jacoby, 1991). This account may be able to explain the inconsistent findings with respect to recognition in amnesic patients and also account for the findings of intact priming. Jennings and Jacoby (1993) suggested that all memory tasks involve both automatic and controlled processes but differ in the degree to which each kind of process is necessary for successful performance. So, for example, free recall relies almost exclusively on controlled recollective processes whereas various priming tasks, such as word-stem completion or perceptual identification, are largely stimulus-driven and can usually be performed well on the basis of automatic processes. Processing requirements for successful recognition, however, may vary depending on the task. Some easy recognition tasks may be accomplished primarily on the basis of familiarity judgments--an automatic process--whereas other more difficult recognition decisions may require retrieval of context, a controlled process (see also, Mandler, 1980). If amnesic patients are impaired at controlled recollective processing, then they should perform poorly on free recall tasks and well on priming tasks, but may be variable in recognition performance depending on whether the task can be performed automatically on the basis of perceptual fluency (Jacoby & Dallas, 1981) or requires the retrieval of episodic context.

Cermak and his colleagues have conducted a number of experiments to test this hypothesis and assess the differential contribution of automatic and controlled processes to different kinds of task performance in amnesic patients (Cermak, Verfaellie, Sweeney, & Jacoby, 1992; Verfaellie & Treadwell, 1993). Using the process dissociation procedure developed by Jacoby (1991), Cermak and colleagues have shown that amnesic patients appear to rely largely on perceptual fluency, an automatic process, when performing various memory tasks whether they are implicit or explicit, and appear unable to override the effects of fluency even when it leads to incorrect performance. For example, in one experiment they (Cermak et al., 1992) tested word-stem completion performance under one of two conditions: exclusion, in which patients were instructed to complete stems with a word not on a previously studied list, and inclusion, in which patients were instructed to complete stems with the first word that came to mind. In both cases, amnesic patients completed stems with words from the study list. They were unable to oppose the automatic influence of the prior presentation to withhold the list words in the exclusion condition. Control subjects, on the other hand, produced many fewer list words in the exclusion condition, presumably using recollection of the prior presentation--a controlled process--to meet the task demands and optimize their performance. In a later experiment using a similar procedure (Verfaellie & Treadwell, 1993), it was found that whereas normal control subjects used both automatic and controlled processes to make their recognition decisions, patients relied almost exclusively on familiarity judgments, using automatic processes to the same degree as normal subjects, but showing significantly less use of controlled recollective processes.

There are as yet only a few studies testing amnesic patients in the process dissociation paradigm, and the extent to which controlled recollective processes rely on structures in the medial temporal lobe regions has not been directly examined. In all of the studies, the patient groups were of mixed etiologies including Korsakoff patients as well as others with lesions to different brain structures. So localization of the recollective processes has not been possible. Nevertheless, the inference from the studies to date would seem to be that the medial temporal/diencephalic structures are necessary for controlled recollective processes, which are impaired in amnesic patients, but not for the automatic familiarity processes, which are intact.

Storage/Consolidation. Currently, among neuropsychologists, the prevailing view of medial temporal lobe amnesia is that it represents a storage or consolidation deficit--that is, an inability to store or retain any long-term or permanent representation of recent events. The consolidation hypothesis has taken a number of different forms over the years. It was suggested by Milner (1966) to account for the fact that H.M. could hold information in short-term memory (STM)but could not transfer it to long-term memory (LTM). At the time, this position was consistent with information processing models of memory (Atkinson & Shiffrin, 1968) that proposed two separate memory stores, one for maintenance of information in the short-term and the other for more permanent, long-term representations. Although later findings demonstrated that the strictly sequential aspect of the model was incorrect (i.e., information does not have to pass through STM to reach LTM), the notion of a consolidation deficit to explain the long-term memory problems of medial temporal lobe amnesic patients has nevertheless retained its appeal, particularly among neuropsychologists.

One challenge for consolidation theory has been to try to account for the extensive RA that accompanies some amnesic deficits. Squire, Cohen and Nadel (1984) proposed that consolidation may occur over a period of months or even years. Thus, remote memories may have been consolidated prior to trauma, but more recent pre-morbid memories may have experienced incomplete consolidation and therefore be relatively inaccessible. Moscovitch (1994) has suggested that there may be two kinds of consolidation processes: one, which he calls cohesion, occurs within seconds or minutes and involves the rapid binding of elements into a memory trace; the other process, which is long-term consolidation per se, is slower, continuing perhaps for years and resulting in a permanent memory trace. Failure of cohesion would prevent any new memories from being formed--the hallmark characteristic of the amnesic syndrome. Failure of consolidation would be expressed as RA. Although it seems clear that a short-term or even intermediate-term consolidation process must be involved in the establishment of new memories, a lengthy consolidation period seems much less likely. Because RA is variable across patients and is associated with damage to areas other than the medial temporal lobes both in the amnesic syndrome and in cases of focal RA (Kapur, 1993), it is likely that multiple brain structures are involved. The exact role of the medial temporal lobes in the process, however, is still uncertain.

Although the medial temporal lobes may be necessary for consolidation of new memories, it is reasonably certain that this brain region--at least the hippocampus per se--is not the permanent storage site for these memories. Zola-

Morgan et al. (1986) described a patient R.B., with damage limited to the CA1 region of the hippocampus bilaterally, who despite a moderately severe AA had virtually no loss of memories acquired pre-morbidly (see also patient G.D. in (Rempel-Clower, Zola, Squire, & Amaral, 1996). And as noted previously, even severely amnesic patients retain remote memories. What is more commonly assumed is that the hippocampus and related structures are required for some limited time period, possibly storing some simple form of a memory for a brief time, until some more permanent storage site can be established in neocortex (Eichenbaum, Otto, & Cohen, 1994; Squire, 1992). When the consolidation process is complete, the memories, now stored in neocortex can be retrieved without the assistance of the hippocampus.

A number of different, but related views of the role of the hippocampus in consolidation have been formulated. Squire (1992) has suggested that the hippocampal memory system is involved in the formation of new associations between previously unrelated events or features of an event, which are initially processed and represented in different parts of the neocortex. The hippocampus binds the various aspects of an event together and links them with their unique spatiotemporal context and with related semantic information already in the knowledge system. According to Squire, associations acquired with the assistance of the hippocampus are flexible and readily accessible via multiple response systems, unlike the associative memories that are acquired without the aid of the hippocampus. This view is consistent with findings showing that amnesic patients, with lesions to medial temporal regions, can acquire new associative bonds that are highly specific and do not generalize to new contexts. So, for example, we found in a series of studies that, with repetition, amnesic patients could learn new computer vocabulary (Glisky, Schacter, & Tulving, 1986) and various computer tasks (Glisky, 1995; Glisky, & Schacter, 1989), but their learning was hyperspecific and inflexible and could not be accessed to changed cues. However, we also found that transfer increased if several overlearning trials were given (Butters, Glisky, & Schacter, 1993) suggesting that the medial temporal lobe system was not the only way to confer flexibility on new semantic representations.

A similar view of the consolidation process has been proposed by Cohen & Eichenbaum (Cohen & Eichenbaum, 1993; Cohen, Poldrack, & Eichenbaum, 1997). They have suggested that the binding of the components of an event depends on an interaction between the hippocampal system and neocortical processing networks that encode and store the individual components of an experience. This interaction results in an integrated or compositional representation of an entire event, while at the same time preserving the individual components and the relations among them. In the absence of the medial temporal lobe system, only highly specific, situation-dependent representations of an experience can be formed and retained; these cannot be placed into a global associative framework or context, nor can they be related to pre-existing knowledge structures. The constituents in these representations become fused rather than associated and cannot be accessed independently.

The failure to find implicit memory for new associations despite normal priming of individual words or preexisting conceptual relations is consistent with this view. If the essential function of the medial temporal lobe structures is to support the formation of new associations and such associations cannot be formed without this brain region, then there should be no evidence for the acquisition of new associations whether the retention test is explicit or implicit. As described earlier, priming of new associations has been very difficult to demonstrate consistently in amnesic patients and may be related to the extent of medial temporal lobe damage.

Curran & Schacter (1997) have also proposed a distinction between storage and binding, and have suggested that amnesic patients may lack the ability to bind attributes of a single event together in an integrated trace although they may retain the ability to store the individual components. Evidence comes from a series of studies in voice-specific auditory priming. In one experiment, Schacter, Church & Bolton (1995) found that although normal subjects were able to identify degraded words more accurately when they were repeated in the same voice than in a different voice, a mixed group of amnesic patients failed to show this voice-specific effect. Different voices, in this study, were all previously presented during study but were re-paired with different words at test. In follow-up experiments, however, Schacter & Church (1995) reported that voice-specific priming could be demonstrated in amnesic patients if novel, rather than re-paired voices, constituted the different voice condition. They argued that the amnesic patients could not bind the specific perceptual features of an event together interactively and so could not distinguish between same and re-paired voices. They were able, however, to distinguish between previously heard and entirely new voices indicating that the individual voice information had been stored.

A related finding was reported by Kroll and colleagues (Kroll et al., 1996) in a recognition memory study. In this study, subjects studied bi-syllabic words, whose syllables could be re-paired to produce new words (e.g., barter and valley, re-paired to produce barley). On a later recognition test, people showed an increased tendency to identify the re-paired syllables (e.g., barley) as study words, relative to new words that included only one previously studied syllable (e.g., bargain), suggesting a binding failure. Of particular interest for our purposes was the finding that these conjunction errors were much more frequent in amnesic patients with left or bilateral medial temporal lobe damage than in normal individuals, consistent with the view that these structures are involved in binding (see also, Reinitz, Verfaellie, & Milberg, 1996).

These studies of amnesic patients seem to indicate that the medial temporal lobes are essential for memory of new associative information. Because the processes of encoding, storage and retrieval are so completely intertwined, it has been impossible to say with any certainty whether one is more dependent on this brain region than the others. What seems reasonably clear is that the medial temporal lobe structures are necessary for the creation of memory representations that link multiple aspects of an experience together. The exact role played by this region in retrieval remains uncertain.

Evidence from Normal Aging

Most studies of normal aging are not able to provide direct evidence concerning the brain regions involved in different memory processes but instead provide indirect evidence that, along with information gained from studies of focal lesion patients, converge on a particular conclusion. Although we know quite a bit about changes in memory that occur with advanced age, and have gathered considerable information concerning brain changes that accompany normal aging, the mapping between the two has only recently begun, aided substantially by advances in functional neuroimaging techniques.

As people age, their ability to remember recent events declines, although they often report no problem remembering events from the remote past. In general, age decrements tend to be largest in tasks that require free recall of unrelated pieces of information and least in tasks that require only recognition. Older adults also seem to experience more difficulty remembering contextual information, and are particularly disadvantaged relative to young adults when material is novel and not well-organized conceptually. Although episodic memory declines, however, other kinds of memory--in particular, semantic and implicit memory--hold up reasonably well with age (for reviews, see Craik,

Anderson, Kerr, & Li, 1995; Craik & Jennings, 1992; Howard, 1996). Because this pattern of age-related changes in memory in many ways resembles that observed in focal lesion patients, although to a lesser degree, it has been assumed that the changes are attributable to declines in the same neural structures that have been most commonly implicated in the amnesic syndrome, namely the medial temporal/diencephalic structures.

Structural imaging studies, however, have yielded inconsistent evidence concerning the brain structures affected by normal aging. Most have agreed that the frontal lobes show the most significant age-related declines in brain volume, but have disagreed about the extent of hippocampal or medial temporal lobe atrophy. So, for example, Golomb et al. (1993) reported that 1/3 of their sample of 154 people over the age of 55 showed signs of hippocampal atrophy, the likelihood of which increased with age. The affected individuals were also more likely to perform poorly on tests of verbal recall than were subjects who did not show hippocampal decline. A number of other studies have similarly reported reductions in medial temporal lobe volume (e.g., Coffey et al., 1992; Jernigan et al., 1991; Raz et al., 1997), but in all cases, where such comparisons were possible, the volumetric declines in medial temporal structures were less than in frontal lobe regions. In one study (Sullivan et al., 1995), no age-related changes were observed in hippocampal volume although reductions in overall temporal lobe gray matter were found. Functional imaging studies have tended to corroborate the structural neuroimaging findings showing preferential reductions in blood flow to prefrontal cortex with increasing age and smaller decreases in more posterior brain regions (Martin, Friston, Colebatch, & Frackowiak, 1991).

Given this pattern of age-related changes in brain structures, it is not surprising that the majority of memory deficits observed in normal aging have been attributed to frontal system decline rather than to hippocampal or medial temporal decline. Nevertheless, there are a few recent findings using positron emission tomography (PET) with older adults that suggest a role for the medial temporal lobes. One of the advantages of neuroimaging studies over studies of patients with brain lesions is that encoding and retrieval processes can be separated and investigated independently so that the contributions of different brain regions to each of these kinds of processes may be determined.

Grady et al. (1995) compared young and elderly subjects in a recognition memory task in which people encoded unfamiliar faces under intentional learning instructions and later were asked to recognize them in a two-alternative forced-choice task. Regional cerebral blood flow (rCBF) was measured using PET both during encoding and during recognition. Behavioral results indicated that the older adults were significantly impaired in recognition memory relative to younger adults and that they showed different patterns of brain activation. Specifically, during encoding the older adults failed to show the left inferior pre-frontal activation or the activation of right medial temporal regions that was observed in young adults. Alternatively, during recognition, older adults showed similar activation of right prefrontal cortex, but neither group showed any increased activation of the hippocampus. The lack of prefrontal and medial temporal activation in older adults during encoding and the relatively normal patterns of activation during retrieval suggest that, in this face recognition task, impaired performance was caused, at least in part, by an encoding or storage failure (see also, Cabeza et al., 1997). These findings also implicate the hippocampus in encoding/storage (see also, Kapur et al., 1996; Stern et al., 1996), along with left prefrontal cortex, while providing no evidence for hippocampal involvement in retrieval.

Contrary to Grady et al.'s findings, Schacter et al. (1996b) recently reported in a PET study that older and younger adults showed equivalent hippocampal activation during the cued recall of recently studied words, implicating the hippocampus in some aspect of retrieval (cf., Kapur et al., 1995a). Because such activation was associated with successful recall (see also Nyberg et al., 1996) and was similar in old and young people, Schacter et al. attributed it to a cue/trace matching process that might be preserved in older adults. This notion is similar to one proposed by Moscovitch & Winocur (1992) who suggested that the hippocampus automatically delivers stored information to consciousness at time of retrieval in response to an appropriate cue. When trace and cue information are both good (as in the "high recall" condition of the Schacter et al. experiment), recall is successful. This relatively automatic function of the hippocampal memory system appears to be intact in older adults. Contrary to this normal activation of the hippocampal region, however, older adults showed reduced activation of anterior prefrontal cortex compared to young subjects, particularly on the right, when trying to retrieve "low recall" (i.e., difficult to retrieve) items. Schacter et al. suggested that this might reflect deficits in initiating appropriate retrieval processes, which may be required when the more automatic hippocampal matching processes are not successful.

Although these neuroimaging studies suggest that the medial temporal lobes are involved in both encoding and retrieval, they shed little light on the exact nature of that involvement. They seem somewhat more informative, however, concerning the role of prefrontal cortex, and suggest that the deficits observed among the normal elderly may stem more from declining frontal lobe function than from reduced medial temporal lobe efficiency. The next section considers the possible role of the frontal lobes in memory.

Role of the Frontal Lobes

The frontal lobes have traditionally been associated not with memory but with executive function. Patients with lesions to prefrontal cortex have exhibited a range of impairments including planning deficits, difficulty in initiating and organizing goal-directed behaviors, deficits in sustained and selective attention, problems in monitoring their own actions and evaluating outcomes, and impaired reasoning and decision making. They often appear underaroused, tend to perform in stereotypic ways, routinely repeat or perseverate on old responses, and are often distracted by irrelevant environmental stimuli (for reviews, see Damasio & Anderson, 1993; Levin, Eisenber, & Benton, 1991; Stuss, Eskes, & Foster, 1994). Because of the range of deficits associated with damage to prefrontal cortex, it is often thought of as a control center--a place where plans and strategies are formulated to deal with novel and non-routine events (Shallice, 1982)--or as a working memory space (Goldman-Rakic, 1995), where information of various sorts can be organized and manipulated pending action or response. Although one can imagine how such control or strategic processes might impact normal memory functioning, early studies of patients with focal frontal lesions revealed little in the way of general memory deficits such as had been found in patients with medial temporal/diencephalic brain damage. Instead what was observed were highly specific memory deficits, affecting a limited range of content domains, usually associated with contextual or non-focal aspects of an experience.

Other evidence concerning the role of the frontal lobes in memory has been derived from studies of patients who have a global amnesia, but also have frontal involvement. For example, patients suffering from Korsakoff's syndrome often have frontal lobe damage in addition to their diencephalic lesions. Also, patients whose amnesia stems from damage to the basal forebrain, usually caused by rupture of anterior cerebral or anterior communicating arteries, often have damage to the ventromedial aspects of the frontal lobes. Comparison of these patients to those whose amnesia is confined to medial temporal/diencephalic regions provides further indications of the role of the frontal lobes in memory.

Evidence from Focal Lesion Patients

Recall and recognition. Patients with focal frontal lesions, although not globally amnesic, nevertheless show mild to moderate memory impairments particularly on tests of free recall and to a lesser degree on cued recall, (for review, see Wheeler, Stuss, & Tulving, 1995). Generally only small and non-significant differences are found between frontal patients and normal control subjects on tests of recognition memory (for exception, see Stuss et al., 1994). For example, Janowsky and colleagues (Janowsky, Shimamura, Kritchevsky, & Squire, 1989) showed that on a multitrial free-recall test for 15 unrelated words, patients with frontal lesions were impaired across all trials, although they were normal on a comparable test of recognition memory. Jetter, Poser, Freeman, & Markowitsch (1986) reported similar results after a single exposure of a list of unrelated words, and Incisa della Rocchetta (1986) reported that frontal patients were impaired in free recall of a group of categorizable pictures. In addition, amnesic patients with frontal lobe pathology (i.e., Korsakoff and ACoA patients) often have deficits in recall that are more severe than in recognition (Parkin & Leng, 1993). This pattern of findings suggests that the frontal lobes are involved in aspects of remembering that are strategic. Strategies may be used at encoding to organize incoming material into conceptual categories or other subjective groupings, or at retrieval to develop and initiate appropriate search processes. Strategic processing will be more important when material is unorganized (e.g., lists of unrelated words) and cues have to be self-generated (e.g., free recall) than when the information to be learned is already semantically organized at input (e.g., textual material) or when good cues are available at time of test (e.g., cued recall and recognition). In the latter case, the frontal lobes may play a more limited role and memory processes may run off relatively automatically (cf.,

Moscovitch, 1994; Moscovitch & Winocur, 1992).

Source or context memory. Studies of patients with frontal lobe pathology have also reported deficits in what has been termed source memory--memory for the origin or source of acquired knowledge, including who conveyed the information and when and where it was learned. For example, Janowsky, Shimamura and Squire (1989) tested recall and recognition of recently presented factual information, as well as recall for the place and time that the facts were acquired. Patients with lesions confined to the frontal lobes made more source errors than normal control subjects--ascribing their knowledge to extra-experimental sources--but did not differ in memory for the facts. Similarly, studies of source memory in amnesic patients have shown that, although patients may show similar and substantial deficits in memory for episodically presented facts, they show variable memory for source, which tends to be correlated with their performance on tests of frontal lobe function (Schacter, Harbluk, & McLachlan, 1984; Shimamura, & Squire, 1987). Amnesic patients without frontal dysfunction can generally remember when and where they learned a piece of information (to the extent that they remember the information at all), whereas those with frontal damage cannot.

Related findings have been reported in studies investigating temporal order memory. Patients with frontal lobe lesions, although relatively unimpaired at recognizing words or objects that were presented in a study list, were significantly impaired in their ability to judge accurately which of two items had been seen more recently (Butters et al., 1994; McAndrews, & Milner, 1991; Milner, Corsi, & Leonard, 1991) or to re-create the order in which items occurred (Mangels, 1997; Shimamura, Janowsky, & Squire, 1990). Contrary findings, however, have also been reported. For example, Kopelman (1989) found that the extent to which Korsakoff patients showed impairments in a list discrimination task was unrelated to the presence or degree of frontal lobe atrophy or to performance on tests of frontal lobe function, but was associated with performance on standard tests of memory (see also, Hunkin et al., 1994). And Mangels (1997) reported that a temporal order memory impairment (i.e., in reconstructing list order) was not present in frontal lobe patients when encoding was incidental as opposed to intentional, suggesting a deficit in strategic processing rather than in the formation of temporal codes per se.

On the other hand, memory for spatial location--another type of context memory--has tended to be associated with medial temporal rather than frontal lobe function. Smith & Milner (1984) reported that patients with extensive right hippocampal damage were impaired on location recall whereas frontal-lesion patients performed normally. Shoqeirat & Mayes (1991; also Mayes, Meudell, & MacDonald, 1991), in a mixed group of amnesic patients, found no correlation between memory for the spatial location of an item and performance on two tests of frontal lobe function (FAS and WCST), but instead found associations between spatial location memory and recall and recognition. Pigott and Milner (1993) reported data suggesting that recognition of the relative location of objects in space depended specifically on the right hippocampus. Patients with frontal lesions showed no deficits in memory for the location of objects. These findings then are consistent with theories that ascribe a specific deficit in spatial memory to the hippocampus (Nadel, 1994), and suggest that, although the frontal lobes may be involved in some aspects of source or context memory they appear not to be involved in others.

False memories. An area of considerable recent interest, in which the frontal lobes have been implicated, concerns the construction and report of false memories. It has been known for some time that some amnesic patients, particularly those that have damage to frontal lobe structures in addition to basal forebrain or diencephalic damage, tend to produce confabulations, which may consist of misplacements of events in space and time, which are produced in response to direct questioning, or spontaneous bizarre fabrications that are clearly false and may be triggered by environmental stimuli (Dalla Barba, 1993; Fischer, Alexander, D'Esposito, & Otto, 1995; Kopelman, 1987). These confabulations represent what Moscovitch (1995) has called "honest lying", because there seems to be no intention on the part of patients to deceive, and they appear to be completely unaware of the falsity or absurdity of their responses. Moscovitch (1995) has suggested that confabulation may be related partly to a source memory deficit--an inability to place an event in its appropriate spatiotemporal context--and partly to a failure to monitor or inhibit output from the hippocampal system, which occurs automatically in response to environmental cues (see also, Schacter, & Curran, 1995). Thus, when the hippocampus is relatively intact as in patients with aneurysms of the ACoA, memories may be triggered automatically; but without the frontal lobes their veracity or plausibility cannot be evaluated.

Patients with frontal lobe damage also have an exaggerated tendency towards false recognition, which may occur with or without spontaneous confabulation. A number of recent studies have revealed that on standard laboratory tests of recognition memory frontal patients, although as accurate as normal subjects at identifying old items, show increased numbers of false alarms to new items. Schacter and colleagues (Schacter et al., 1996a) reported a case study of a patient, B.G., who had sustained damage to the right frontal lobe. B.G. not only showed pathologically high false alarm rates across a range of stimulus materials but was extremely confident in his responses. Parkin (1997; Parkin, Bindschaedler, Harsent, & Metzler, 1996) reported similar findings in patient J.B., who had damage to left frontal cortex as the result of an ACoA aneurysm. In both studies, the patients appeared able to distinguish between targets and distractors only at the broadest categorical level. Although the two groups of investigators have disagreed concerning whether the deficit likely occurs at encoding (Parkin et al.) or retrieval (Schacter et al.), both have proposed that the problem stems from an overly general or fuzzy event description, which lacks the specific contextual information required to discriminate targets from lures (Brainerd, Reyna, & Kneer, 1995). J.B., who has left frontal damage, may be capable of forming only poorly elaborated, very general memory representations during encoding, whereas B.G., the patient with right frontal damage may fail to form appropriately specific search strategies at retrieval. This interpretation is consistent with findings from PET studies that have found structures in the left frontal lobe to be particularly important for episodic encoding whereas structures in the right frontal lobe have been implicated in retrieval (for reviews, see Nyberg, Cabeza, & Tulving, 1996; Tulving et al., 1994).

A patient recently studied in our laboratory (Rapcsak et al., submitted), who had bilateral medial frontal lobe damage extending further on the right side (as a result of an ACoA aneurysm), showed similar tendencies toward false recognition in the retrograde domain, consistent with a retrieval deficit. Patient J.S., although unimpaired in his ability to identify famous faces from the past, incorrectly labeled almost 70% of unfamiliar faces as familiar. Rapcsak et al. argued that the false recognition responses resulted from a breakdown of the strategic retrieval and monitoring functions normally carried out by the frontal lobes, leading the patient to rely only on general stimulus familiarity for his recognition decisions rather than on the retrieval of specific contextual information.

In general, the findings from patients with frontal damage suggest that the frontal lobes are critically involved in several aspects of encoding and retrieval including strategic planning, the integration of an event with its context, controlled and effortful search, and the monitoring of output from posterior brain structures. It may be that different aspects of encoding and retrieval depend on different parts of the frontal lobes, but so far, such fine discriminations have been difficult to identify because of the scarcity of patients with small discrete lesions. Improved neuroimaging techniques, however, should help to achieve more precise localization of functions in the future. At the same time, a clearer understanding of the cognitive processes required by different kinds of memory tasks is also important for establishing specific brain-behavior relations. Studies of the normal elderly may help in this regard. A review of some of this work is presented in the next section.

Evidence from Normal Aging

Studies of memory in older adults have generally focused on age-related changes in strategic processing that occur at both encoding and retrieval. These changes, which are consistent with the MRI and PET findings of reduced frontal volume and blood flow in aging, suggest that older adults should show many of the same deficits as frontal patients, although in a reduced form.

Recall and recognition. Older adults, like frontal patients, tend to be more impaired in free recall than in cued recall or recognition (Craik & McDowd, 1987). Craik (1986) has interpreted this pattern of age-related memory decline in terms of a deficiency in self-initiated retrieval processes. In recognition and to a lesser extent in cued recall, search processes are guided by externally provided cues, whereas in free recall, individuals have to generate and implement their own retrieval strategies. Because of reduced processing resources, according to Craik, older adults have difficulty initiating effortful retrieval strategies and so their free recall performance suffers. Similarly, elderly people may fail to engage in effortful, semantic encoding processes, resulting in poorly elaborated memory representations that are difficult to retrieve. When such elaborations are provided, however (West & Boatwright, 1983), or when the stimulus materials themselves are especially complex and so automatically engage elaborative processing (Park, Puglisi, & Smith, 1986), age deficits are reduced. If environmental support is provided (in the form of semantic cues) at both encoding and retrieval (Craik, Byrd, & Swanson, 1987), age differences are essentially eliminated.

As noted earlier, PET studies with older adults have found reduced activation in left prefrontal cortex during encoding (Cabeza et al., 1997; Grady et al., 1995), consistent with a failure to engage in semantic encoding processes, and in right prefrontal cortex during retrieval (Cabeza et al., 1997; Schacter et al., 1996b), consistent with a failure to initiate appropriate retrieval processes. The right prefrontal activations only occurred in young adults when retrieval was difficult (Schacter et al., 1996b) their absence in older adults is consistent with Craik's view that the elderly fail to initiate search processes in difficult retrieval situations.

Source and context memory. Older adults also show disproportionate deficits in source or context memory compared to item memory, a finding that has been attributed to declining frontal lobe function, although a direct link between source memory and brain function in older adults has yet to be demonstrated (for reviews, see Johnson, Hashtroudi, & Lindsay, 1993; Spencer, & Raz, 1995). A study by Craik, Morris, Morris and Loewen (1990) found that source memory performance in older adults was correlated with performance on tests of frontal lobe function--verbal fluency and the Wisconsin Card Sorting Test (WCST)--and was uncorrelated with fact recall. Schacter and colleagues (1991) also reported a weak correlation between source errors and perseverative errors on the WCST in older adults. Spencer and Raz (1994), however, failed to find such a correlation, but reported instead that source memory was correlated with fact recall.

In an attempt to sort out these issues and to investigate further the exact role of the frontal lobes in source memory, we have begun a series of studies with older adults that attempt to capitalize on the cognitive variability of healthy older individuals. Specifically, we have characterized our normal elderly population as high or low in frontal function and high or low in medial temporal lobe function according to their performance on a group of neuropsychological tests (Glisky, Polster, & Routhieaux, 1995). Using selected sub-groups from this population in a variety of source memory studies, we have determined that performance on item and source memory tasks is significantly affected not by age per se, but by neuropsychological status. For instance , in one study (Glisky et al., 1995) older adults listened to sentences spoken in one of two voices and were then given tests of both sentence memory and voice memory (i.e., source memory). The results indicated that the low frontal elderly were impaired relative to high frontal elderly on memory for source but not on memory for the sentence. Conversely, the low medial temporal lobe subjects were impaired relative to high medial temporals on memory for the sentence but not on memory for the voice. This double dissociation provided strong evidence that the two kinds of memory rely on different neural mechanisms--item memory on the medial temporal lobe memory system, and source memory on some aspect of frontal lobe function.

Providing further support for this conclusion, Senkfor & Van Petten (in press), using a similar source memory paradigm in an event-related potential (ERP) study with young adults, found a late prefrontal positivity during the source memory task that was not evident during item memory. They interpreted this prefrontal effect as a "voice search effect" because it was observed during both correct and incorrect source judgments. Successful retrieval of both item and source was marked by positive ERPs that were distinct from the prefrontal effect both in scalp distribution and latency. The search for voice information occurred after retrieval of item information, suggesting that the linking of content and context was not automatic but was under the control of the frontal lobes. These findings were thus consistent with those from recent PET studies, which have implicated the frontal lobes in retrieval attempts or retrieval effort but not in retrieval success (Kapur et al., 1995b; Schacter et al., 1996b). Whether the frontal lobes are involved in all difficult retrievals or search processes or whether they play a specific role in the retrieval of source or context information will have to be determined in future studies.

Evidence with respect to other aspects of source or context memory in the elderly is sparse. Although age differences are generally observed in memory for temporal order and spatial location, few studies have linked these age differences to brain function. In one such study, Parkin, Walter & Hunkin (1995) required subjects to recognize previously heard sentences and to assign them accurately to one of two presentation lists. Results indicated that older adults were as accurate as young adults in recognizing the sentences, but were significantly impaired in assigning sentences to lists. In addition, list discrimination but not recognition correlated with some measures of frontal lobe performance but not others. This finding is consistent with a role for the frontal lobes in temporal order memory, but provides little information about the nature of that role. Additional studies are needed to explore further the processes involved in context memory in the elderly.

False memories. Schacter (1995) has suggested that failures of source memory may contribute to memory distortions or false memories, and since older adults are impaired in source memory, they may also be more susceptible to memory illusions. In support of this hypothesis, Dywan and Jacoby (1990) found that older adults were more susceptible than young adults to the false fame effect. In their study, old and young people were presented with a list of nonfamous names. Subsequently, they were given a fame judgment task that included truly famous as well as nonfamous names. Nonfamous names had either been recently studied or were new. The results indicated that older adults were much more likely than young adults to call previously studied nonfamous names 'famous'. Dywan and Jacoby argued that young adults were able to remember the recent occurrence of the nonfamous names from the previous study list and were thus able to reject them. Older adults, on the other hand, found the names familiar, but were unable to identify the source of that familiarity. They therefore mistakenly attributed it to fame. (See Cermak, Verfaellie, Butler, & Jacoby, 1993, for a similar result with amnesic patients).

Over-reliance on automatic familiarity processes and reduced use of effortful retrieval processes has been demonstrated in a number of recognition memory studies in the elderly (e .g., Jacoby, Jennings, & Hay, 1996; Jennings & Jacoby, 1993). To the extent that automatic processing is sufficient for making accurate recognition judgments, older adults perform normally. If controlled, recollective processing is necessary, however, as in the fame judgment task for instance, older adults are prone to error, and their performance is impaired relative to young subjects. One interpretation of these findings is that controlled, recollective processing depends on the integrity of the frontal lobes, which are compromised in normal aging, whereas familiarity judgments rely more on posterior brain regions that are less affected by age. To my knowledge, this hypothesis has not been tested directly. Dywan, Segalowitz, and Williamson (1994) reported, however, that source errors in the fame judgment task were not correlated with a standard neuropsychological measure of frontal function--perseverative errors on the WCST; they were, however, associated with an electrophysiological index of frontal function. This finding is consistent with the idea that the frontal lobes involve multiple processes, only some of which may be required for conscious recollection. Studies with amnesic patients have found a similar reliance on automatic rather than controlled processes for recognition decisions (e.g., Verfaellie & Treadwell, 1993), suggesting that medial temporal/diencephalic structures are also important for conscious recollection. These studies, however, tested patients of mixed etiology, some of whom also had frontal lesions, and so conclusions concerning the specific brain regions involved in conscious recollection cannot be made with any confidence.

Older adults have also been shown to be more susceptible to false recognition effects in the Deese (1959) paradigm. In a study by Norman & Schacter (in press), younger and older adults were presented with lists of words that were associates of a non-presented theme word. In a subsequent recognition test, older adults were significantly more likely than young adults to falsely identify the non-presented theme word (i.e., the critical lure) as a target item. This tendency towards increased false recognition in the elderly may be attributable to reduced control or monitoring by the frontal lobes. In the absence of such control, subjects may respond on the basis of general familiarity rather than on the basis of specific, retrieved contextual information.

The findings from the studies of normal elderly agree substantially with those obtained from focal frontal lesion patients. The frontal lobes seem to be involved in controlled strategic processes both during encoding of an event and during its retrieval. They may help to integrate an event with its context during study or to search for contextual information at test. They seem not to be particularly important in assigning a familiarity value to a memory, but seem to be needed to evaluate or retrieve the source of that familiarity. It is likely that they interact with medial temporal lobe structures, contributing to the construction of trace information and participating in its retrieval.

Summary

Studies of focal lesion patients and the normal elderly have provided a wealth of empirical data concerning the possible roles of the medial temporal lobes and the prefrontal cortex in normal memory processes. At the same time, numerous theories have been advanced to explain various aspects of the data. Although some common themes can be identified across theories, many theoretical disagreements and inconsistencies persist, and no theory can account for all of the data. Although much has yet to be learned about the brain-behavior interactions involved in memory, considerable progress has been made in the past few years, largely because of the cooperation between cognitive psychology and neuropsychology with each discipline contributing aspects of their particular methodologies to the joint enterprise.

What seems reasonably clear from the evidence presented in this chapter is that a good memory depends on an interaction between medial temporal and frontal lobe structures. The frontal lobes appear to be involved primarily in the construction and implementation of strategic processes both at encoding and retrieval. This might include the encoding of elaborate semantic information at encoding and the construction of a detailed event description to guide retrieval. The medial temporal lobes, although possibly involved in these strategic processes as well, are primarily responsible for binding together multiple, unrelated aspects of an experience and integrating them with related information already present in the knowledge system. The frontal lobes appear to assist in this process, perhaps by helping to encode non-focal, contextual or source information at input or by initiating and controlling search processes at retrieval. The frontal lobes also evaluate the output of the medial temporal lobe system, which may respond to environmental cues in a relatively automatic fashion through a cue/trace matching process. Although this automatic process may produce correct memory responses some of the time, it is also prone to error. The frontal lobes may be able to prevent or reduce errors that might otherwise occur if memory decisions were based largely on automatic familiarity processes. Finally, the medial temporal memory system also interacts with other neocortical processors that ultimately store the permanent records of experience.

This theoretical account, which is consistent with much of the data presented in this chapter, is similar in many respects to the global memory model proposed by Moscovitch (1994; Moscovitch & Winocur, 1992). Moscovitch characterizes the frontal component in his model as a "working with memory" system that contributes to the effective operation of the actual memory system--the medial temporal lobe system--through the application of encoding and retrieval strategies. The hippocampus, in his view, is modular; it binds all consciously apprehended information together at input, and automatically delivers it back to consciousness at output when presented with an appropriate, matching retrieval cue. Interpretation of the output, however, has to be accomplished by the frontal lobes, which are also responsible for placing retrieved information into proper spatiotemporal context.

Because the medial temporal and frontal lobes interact to produce memory performance, it is difficult to separate and assess their independent contributions. Both sets of structures have been implicated in encoding and retrieval processes, and both have appeared as activated regions in PET studies during encoding and retrieval. Similarly, the medial temporal lobes have been characterized as essential for binding together aspects of an experience that occur in close temporal contiguity. At the same time, the frontal lobes have been considered essential for source memory, which requires the integration of an item with its context. The difference between these two integrative operations has yet to be determined.

There are now available multiple ways of addressing these complex issues--cognitive paradigms and models, neuropsychological assessment techniques, electrophysiological measures, and structural and functional neuroimaging procedures. A complete understanding of memory will almost certainly require all of these and others that have yet to be identified or fully exploited. The study of focal lesion patients and the normal elderly has helped to identify aspects and components of memory function that might otherwise have remained invisible, and at the same time has introduced a complexity that had not previously been appreciated. The challenge for theory is to account for the diversity that exists in memory capabilities across all of these groups of individuals including those whose performance is considered normal as well as those in whom memory is compromised. The merging of cognitive psychology and neuropsychology has provided a rich and ever-expanding database on which theories of normal memory can be built. The ultimate understanding of those data will require an even broader interdisciplinary effort.

References

Aggleton, J. P., & Saunders, R. C. (1997). The relationships between temporal lobe and diencephalic structures implicated in anterograde amnesia. *Memory, 5*, 49-71.

Atkinson, R. C., & Shiffrin, R. (1968). Human memory: A proposed system and its control processes. In K. W. Spence & J. T. Spence (Eds.), *The psychology of learning and motivation* (Vol. 2, pp. 89-195). New York: Academic Press.

Blaxton, T. A. (1992). Dissociations among memory measures in memory-impaired subjects: Evidence for a processing account of memory. *Memory & Cognition, 20*, 549-562.

Blaxton, T. A. (1995). A process-based view of memory. *Journal of the International Neuropsychological Society, 1*, 112-114.

Brainerd, C. J., Reyna, V. F., & Kneer, R. (1995). False-recognition reversal: When similarity is distinctive. *Journal of Memory and Language, 34*, 157-185.

Butters, M. A., Glisky, E. L., & Schacter, D. L. (1993). Transfer of new learning in memory-impaired patients. *Journal of Clinical and Experimental Neuropsychology, 15*, 219-230.

Butters, M. A., Kaszniak, A. W., Glisky, E. L., Eslinger, D. L., & Schacter, D. L. (1994). Recency discrimination deficits in frontal lobe patients. *Neuropsychology, 8*, 343-353.

Butters, N., & Cermak, L. S. (1986). A case study of the forgetting of autobiographical knowledge: implications for the study of retrograde amnesia. In D. C. Rubin (Ed.), *Autobiographical memory* (pp. 253-289). Cambridge, MA: Cambridge University Press.

Cabeza, R., Grady, C. L., Nyberg, L., McIntosh, A. R., Tulving, E., Kapur,

S., Jennings, J. M., Houle, S., & Craik, F. I. M. (1997). Age-related differences in neural activity during memory encoding and retrieval: A positron emission tomography study. *Journal of Neuroscience, 17*, 391-400.

Cermak, L. S. (1976). The encoding capacity of a patient with amnesia due to encephalitis. *Neuropsychologia, 14*, 311-322.

Cermak, L. S. (1979). Amnesic patients' level of processing. In L. S. Cermak & F. I. M. Craik (Eds.), *Levels of processing in human memory* (pp. 119-139). Hillsdale, NJ: Erlbaum.

Cermak, L. S. (1982). The long and short of it in amnesia. In L. S. Cermak (Ed.), *Human memory and amnesia* (pp. 43-59). Hillsdale, NJ: Erlbaum.

Cermak, L. S. (1989). Synergistic ecphory and the amnesic patient. In I. H. L. Roediger & F. I. M. Craik (Eds.), *Varieties of memory and consciousness: Essays in honour of Endel Tulving* (pp. 121-131). Hillsdale, NJ: Erlbaum.

Cermak, L. S. (1994). Processing deficits of amnesic patients: Nearly full cycle? In L. S. Cermak (Ed.), *Neuropsychological explorations of memory and cognition: Essays in honor of Nelson Butters* (pp. 31-43). New York: Plenum.

Cermak, L. S. (1997). A positive approach to viewing processing deficit theories of amnesia. *Memory, 5*, 89-98.

Cermak, L. S., & Butters, N. (1972). The role of interference and encoding in the short-term memory deficits of Korsakoff patients. *Neuropsychologia, 10*, 89-96.

Cermak, L. S., Butters, N., & Moreines, J. (1974). Some analyses of the verbal encoding deficit of alcoholic Korsakoff patients. *Brain and Language, 1*, 141-150.

Cermak, L. S., & O'Connor, M. (1983). The anterograde and retrograde retrieval ability of a patient with amnesia due to encephalitis. *Neuropsychologia, 21*, 213-234.

Cermak, L. S., & Verfaellie, M. (1992). The role of fluency in the implicit and explicit task performance of amnesic patients. In L. R. Squire & N. Butters (Eds.), *Neuropsychology of memory* (pp. 36-45). New York: Guilford Press.

Cermak, L. S., Verfaellie, M., Butler, T., & Jacoby, L. L. (1993). Attributions of familiarity in amnesia: Evidence from a fame judgment task. *Neuropsychology, 7*, 510-518.

Cermak, L. S., Verfaellie, M., & Chase, K. A. (1995). Implicit and explicit memory in amnesia: An analysis of data-driven and conceptually driven processes. *Neuropsychology, 9*, 281-290.

Cermak, L. S., Verfaellie, M., Sweeney, M., & Jacoby, L. L. (1992). Fluency versus conscious recollection in the word completion performance of amnesic patients. *Brain and Cognition, 20*, 367-377.

Coffey, C. E., Wilkinson, W. E., Parashos, I. A., Soady, S. A. R., Sullivan, R. J., Patterson, L. J., Figiel, G. S., Webb, M. C., Spritzer, C. E., & Djang, W. T. (1992). Quantitative cerebral anatomy of the aging human brain: A cross-sectional study using magnetic resonance imaging. *Neurology, 42*, 527-536.

Cohen, N. J., & Eichenbaum, H. (1993). *Memory, amnesia, and the hippocampal system*. Cambridge, MA: MIT Press.

Cohen, N. J., Poldrack, R. A., & Eichenbaum, H. (1997). Memory for items and memory for relations in the procedural/declarative memory framework. *Memory, 5*, 131-178.

Cohen, N. J., & Squire, L. R. (1981). Retrograde amnesia and remote memory impairment. *Neuropsychologia, 19*, 337-356.

Corkin, S. (1968). Acquisition of motor skill after bilateral medial temporal-lobe excision. *Neuropsychologia, 6*, 255-265.

Corkin, S. (1984). Lasting consequences of bilateral medial temporal lobectomy: Clinical course and experimental findings in H.M. *Seminars in*

Neurology, 4, 249-259.

Craik, F. I. M. (1986). A functional account of age differences in memory. In F. Klix & H. Hagendorf (Eds.), *Human memory and cognitive capabilities, mechanisms and performances* (pp. 409-422). Amsterdam: Elsevier.

Craik, F. I. M., Anderson, N. D., Kerr, S. A., & Li, K. Z. H. (1995). Memory changes in normal ageing. In A. D. Baddeley, B. A. Wilson, & F. N. Watts (Eds.), *Handbook of memory disorders* (pp. 211-241). Chichester: John Wiley & Sons.

Craik, F. I. M., Byrd, M., & Swanson, J. M. (1987). Patterns of memory loss in three elderly samples. *Psychology and Aging, 2*, 79-86.

Craik, F. I. M., & Jennings, J. M. (1992). Human memory. In F. I. M. Craik & T. A. Salthouse (Eds.), *The handbook of aging and cognition* (pp. 51-110). Hillsdale, NJ: Erlbaum.

Craik, F. I. M., & McDowd, J. M. (1987). Age differences in recall and recognition. *Journal of Experimental Psychology: Learning, Memory, and Cognition, 13*, 474-479.

Craik, F. I. M., Morris, L. W., Morris, R. G., & Loewen, E. R. (1990). Relations between source amnesia and frontal lobe functioning in older adults. *Psychology and Aging, 5*, 148-151.

Curran, T., & Schacter, D. L. (1997). Implicit memory: What must theoreies of amnesia explain? *Memory, 5*, 37-47.

Dalla Barba, G. (1993). Different patterns of confabulation. *Cortex, 29*, 567-581.

Damasio, A. R., & Anderson, S. W. (1993). The frontal lobes. In K. M. Heilman & E. Valenstein (Eds.), *Clinical neuropsychology* (3rd ed., pp. 409-460). New York: Oxford University Press.

Deese, J. (1959). On the prediction of occurrence of particular verbal instrusions in immediate recall. *Journal of Experimental Psychology, 58*, 17-22.

Dywan, J., & Jacoby, L. (1990). Effects of aging on source monitoring: Differences in susceptibility to false fame. *Psychology and Aging, 5*, 379-387.

Dywan, J., Segalowitz, S. J., & Williamson, L. (1994). Source monitoring during name recognition in older adults: Psychometric and electrophysiological correlates. *Psychology and Aging, 9*, 568-577.

Eichenbaum, H., Otto, T., & Cohen, N. J. (1994). Two component functions of the hippocampal memory system. *Behavioural and Brain Sciences, 17*, 449-517.

Fischer, R. S., Alexander, M. P., D'Esposito, M., & Otto, R. (1995). Neuropsychological and neuroanatomical correlates of confabulation. *Journal of Clinical and Experimental Neuropsychology, 17*, 20-28.

Gabrieli, J. D. E. (1995). A systematic view of human memory processes. *Journal of the International Neuropsychological Society, 1*, 115-118.

Glisky, E. L. (1995). Acquisition and transfer of word processing skill by an amnesic patient. *Neuropsychological Rehabilitation, 5*, 299-318.

Glisky, E. L. (1997, March). *Rehabilitation of memory disorders: Tapping into preserved mechanisms.* Paper presented at the 7th Annual Rotman Research Institute Conference, Toronto.

Glisky, E. L., Polster, M. R., & Routhieaux, B. C. (1995). Double association between item and source memory. *Neuropsychology, 9*, 229-235.

Glisky, E. L., & Schacter, D. L. (1989). Extending the limits of complex learning in organic amnesia: Computer training in a vocational domain. *Neuropsychologia, 27*, 107-120.

Glisky, E. L., Schacter, D. L., & Butters, M. A. (1994). Domain-specific learning and remediation of memory disorders. In M. J. Riddoch & G. W. Humphreys (Eds.), *Cognitive neuropsychology and cognitive rehabilitation* (pp.

527-548). Hove, UK: Erlbaum.

Glisky, E. L., Schacter, D. L., & Tulving, E. (1986). Learning and retention of computer related vocabulary in memory-impaired patients: Method of vanishing cues. *Journal of Clinical and Experimental Neuropsychology, 8*, 292-312.

Goldman-Rakic, P. S. (1995). Architecture of the prefrontal cortex and the central executive. *Annals of the New York Academy of Sciences, 769*, 71-83.

Golomb, J., deLeon, M. J., Kluger, A., George, A. E., Tarshish, C., & Ferris, S. H. (1993). Hippocampal atrophy in normal aging. *Archives of Neurology, 50*, 967-973.

Grady, C. L., McIntosh, A. R., Horwitz, B., Maisog, J. M., Ungerleider, L. G., Mentis, M. J., Pietrini, P., Schapiro, M. B., & Haxby, J. V. (1995). Age-related reductions in human recognition memory due to impaired encoding. *Science, 269*, 218-221.

Haist, F., Shimamura, A. P., & Squire, L. R. (1992). On the relationship between recall and recognition memory. *Journal of Experimental Psychology: Learning, Memory, and Cognition, 18*, 691-702.

Hayman, C. A. G., Macdonald, C. A., & Tulving, E. (1993). The role of repetition and associative interference in new semantic learning in amnesia: A case experiment. *Journal of Cognitive Neuroscience, 5*, 375-389.

Hirst, W., Johnson, M. K., Phelps, E. A., Risse, G., & Volpe, B. T. (1986). Recognition and recall in amnesics. *Journal of Experimental Psychology: Learning, Memory, and Cognition, 12*, 445-451.

Hirst, W., Johnson, M. K., Phelps, E. A., & Volpe, B. T. (1988). More on recognition and recall in amnesics. *Journal of Experimental Psychology: Learning, Memory, and Cognition, 14*, 758-762.

Howard, D. V. (1996). The aging of implicit and explicit memory. In F.

Blanchard-Fields & T. M. Hess (Eds.), *Perspectives on cognitive change in adulthood and aging* (pp. 221-254). New York: McGraw-Hill.

Hunkin, N. M., Parkin, A. J., & Longmore, B. E. (1994). Aetiological variation in the amnesic syndrome. *Neuropsychologia, 32*, 819-825.

Jacoby, L. L. (1984). Incidental versus intentional retrieval: Remembering and awareness as sepatate issues. In L. R. Squire & N. Butters (Eds.), *Neuropsychology of memory* (2nd ed., pp. 145-156). New York: Guilford Press.

Jacoby, L. L. (1991). A process dissociation framework: Separating automatic from intentional uses of memory. *Journal of Memory and Language, 30*, 513-541.

Jacoby, L. L., & Dallas, M. (1981). On the relationship between autobiographical memory and perceptual learning. *Journal of Experimental Psychology: General, 110*, 306-340.

Jacoby, L. L., Jennings, J. M., & Hay, J. F. (1996). Dissociating automatic and consciously controlled processes: Implications for diagnosis and rehabilitation of memory deficits. In D. Hermann, C. McEvoy, C. Hertzog, P. Hertel, & M. K. Johnson (Eds.), *Basic and applied memory research: Theory in context* (Vol. 1, pp. 161-193). Mahwah, NJ: Erlbaum.

Janowsky, J. S., Shimamura, A. P., Kritchevsky, M., & Squire, L. R. (1989). Cognitive impairment following frontal lobe damage and its relevance to human amnesia. *Behavioral Neuroscience, 103*, 548-560.

Janowsky, J. S., Shimamura, A. P., & Squire, L. R. (1989). Source memory impairment in patients with frontal lobe lesions. *Neuropsychologia, 27*, 1043-1056.

Jennings, J. M., & Jacoby, L. L. (1993). Automatic versus intentional uses of memory: Aging, attention, and control. *Psychology and Aging, 8*, 283-293.

Jernigan, T. L., Archibald, S. L., Berhow, M. T., Sowell, E. R., Foster, D.

S., & Hesselink, J. R. (1991). Cerebral structure on MRI, Part I: Localization of age-related changes. *Biological Psychiatry, 29*, 55-67.

Johnson, M. K., Hashtroudi, S., & Lindsay, D. S. (1993). Source monitoring. *Psychological Bulletin, 114*, 3-28.

Kapur, N. (1993). Focal retrograde amnesia in neurological disease: A critical review. *Cortex, 29*, 217-234.

Kapur, N., Friston, K. J., Young, A., Frith, C. D., & Frackowiak, R. S. J. (1995a). Activation of human hippocampal formation during memory for faces: A PET study. *Cortex, 31*, 99-108.

Kapur, S., Craik, F. I. M., Jones, C., Brown, G. M., Houle, S., & Tulving, E. (1995b). Functional role of the prefrontal cortex in retrieval of memories: a PET study. *NeuroReport, 6*, 1880-1884.

Kapur, S., Tulving, E., Cabeza, R., McIntosh, A. R., Houle, S., & Craik, F. I. M. (1996). The neural correlates of intentional learning of verbal materials: a PET study in humans. *Cognitive Brain Research, 4*, 243-249.

Keane, M. M., Gabrieli, J. D. E., Monti, L. A., Fleischman, D. A., Cantor, J. M., & Noland, J. S. (1997). Intact and impaired conceptual memory processes in amnesia. *Neuropsychology, 11*, 59-69.

Kopelman, M. D. (1987). Two types of confabulation. *Journal of Neurology, Neurosurgery and Psychiatry, 50*, 1482-1487.

Kopelman, M. D. (1989). Remote and autobiographical memory, temporal context memory, and frontal atrophy in Korsakoff and Alzheimer patients. *Neuropsychologia, 27*, 437-460.

Kroll, N. E. A., Knight, R. T., Metcalfe, J., Wolf, E. S., & Tulving, E. (1996). Cohesion failure as a source of memory illusions. *Journal of Memory and Language, 35*, 176-196.

Levin, H. S., Eisenberg, H. M., & Benton, A. L. (Eds.) (1991). *Frontal lobe function and dysfunction.* New York: Oxford University Press.

Mandler, G. (1980). Recognizing: The judgment of previous occurrence. *Psychological Review, 87*, 252-271.

Mangels, J. A. (1997). Strategic processing and memory for temporal order in patients with frontal lobe lesions. *Neuropsychology, 11*, 207-221.

Marslen-Wilson, W. D., & Teuber, H.-L. (1975). Memory for remote events in anterograde amnesia: recognition of public figures from news photographs. *Neuropsychologia, 13*, 353-364.

Martin, A. J., Friston, K. J., Colebatch, J. G., & Frackowiak, R. S. J. (1991). Decreases in regional cerebral blood flow with normal aging. *Journal of Cerebral Blood Flow and Metabolism, 11*, 684-689.

Mayes, A. R. (1988). *Human organic memory disorders*. Cambridge: Cambridge University Press.

Mayes, A. R., & Downes, J. J. (1997). What do theories of the functional deficit(s) underlying amnesia have to explain? *Memory, 5*, 3-36.

Mayes, A. R., Downes, J. J., Shoqeirat, M., Hall, C., & Sagar, H. J. (1993). Encoding ability is preserved in amnesics: Evidence from a direct test of encoding. *Neuropsychologia, 31*, 745-759.

Mayes, A. R., Meudell, P. R., & MacDonald, C. (1991). Disproportionate intentional spatial-memory impairments in amnesia. *Neuropsychologia, 29*, 771-784.

Mayes, A. R., Meudell, P. R., & Pickering, A. (1985). Is organic amnesia caused by a selective deficit in remembering contextual information? *Cortex, 21*, 167-202.

McAndrews, M. P., & Milner, B. (1991). The frontal cortex and memory for temporal order. *Neuropsychologia, 29*, 849-859.

Milner, B. (1966). Amnesia following operation on the temporal lobes. In

C. W. M. Whitty & O. L. Zangwill (Eds.), *Amnesia* (pp. 109-133). London: Butterworths.

Milner, B., Corsi, P., & Leonard, G. (1991). Frontal-lobe contribution to recency judgements. *Neuropsychologia, 29*, 601-618.

Moscovitch, M. (1994). Memory and working with memory: Evaluation of a component process model and comparisons with other models. In D. L. Schacter & E. Tulving (Eds.), *Memory systems 1994* (pp. 269-310). Cambridge, MA: MIT Press.

Moscovitch, M. (1995). Confabulation. In D. L. Schacter (Ed.), *Memory distortion* (pp. 226-251). Cambridge, MA: Harvard University Press.

Moscovitch, M., & Winocur, G. (1992). The neuropsychology of memory and aging. In F. I. M. Craik & T. A. Salthouse (Eds.), *The handbook of aging and cognition* (pp. 315-372). Hillsdale, NJ: Erlbaum.

Murdock, B. B., Jr. (1974). *Human memory: Theory and data.* Potomac, MD: Erlbaum.

Nadel, L. (1994). Multiple memory systems: What and why, an update. In D. L. Schacter & E. Tulving (Eds.), *Memory systems 1994* (pp. 39-63). Cambridge, MA: MIT Press.

Norman, K. A., & Schacter, D. L. (in press). False recognition in younger and older adults: Exploring the characteristics of illusory memories. *Memory & Cognition.*

Nyberg, L., Cabeza, R., & Tulving, E. (1996). PET studies of encoding and retrieval: The HERA model. *Psychonomic Bulletin & Review, 3*, 135-148.

Nyberg, L., McIntosh, A. R., Houle, S., Nillson, L.-G., & Tulving, E. (1996). Activation of medial temporal structures during episodic memory retrieval. *Nature, 380*, 715-717.

Park, D. D., Puglisi, J. T., & Smith, A. D. (1986). Memory for pictures:

Does an age-related decline exist? *Psychology and Aging, 1*, 11-17.

Parkin, A. J. (1997). The long and winding road: Twelve years of frontal amnesia. In A. J. Parkin (Ed.), *Case studies in the neuropsychology of memory* . Hove, UK: Erlbaum.

Parkin, A. J., Bindschaedler, C., Harsent, L., & Metzler, C. (1996). Pathological flase alarm rates following damage to the left frontal cortex. *Brain and Cognition, 32*, 14-27.

Parkin, A. J., & Leng, N. R. C. (1993). *Neuropsychology of the amnesic syndrome*. Hove, UK: Erlbaum.

Parkin, A. J., Walter, B. M., & Hunkin, N. M. (1995). Relationships between normal aging, frontal lobe function, and memory for temporal and spatial information. *Neuropsychology, 9*, 304-312.

Pigott, S., & Milner, B. (1993). Memory for different aspects of complex visual scenes after unilateral temporal- or frontal-lobe resection. *Neuropsychologia, 31*, 1-15.

Rapcsak, S. Z., Kaszniak, A. W., Reminger, S. L., Glisky, M. L., Glisky, E. L., & Comer, J. F. (submitted). Dissociation between overt and covert measures of memory in a patient with false recognition following frontal lobe damage. .

Raz, N., Gunning, F. M., Head, D., Dupuis, J. H., McQuain, J., Briggs, S. D., Loken, W. J., Thornton, A. E., & Acker, J. D. (1997). Selective aging of the human cerebral cortex observed in vivo: Differential vulnerability of the prefrontal gray matter. *Cerebral Cortex, 7*, 268-282.

Reinitz, M. T., Verfaellie, M., & Milberg, W. P. (1996). Memory conjunction errors in normal and amnesic subjects. *Journal of Memory and Language, 35*, 286-299.

Rempel-Clower, N. L., Zola, S. M., Squire, L. R., & Amaral, D. G. (1996). Three cases of enduring memory impairment after bilateral damage limited to the hippocampal formation. *The Journal of Neuroscience, 16*, 5233-5255.

Schacter, D. L. (1987). Implicit memory: History and current status. *Journal of Experimental Psychology: Learning, Memory and Cognition, 13*, 501-508.

Schacter, D. L. (1995). Memory distortion: History and current status. In D. L. Schacter (Ed.), *Memory distortion: How minds, brains, and societies reconstruct the past* (pp. 1-43). Cambridge, MA: Harvard University Press.

Schacter, D. L., Chiu, C. Y. P., & Ochsner, K. N. (1993). Implicit memory: A selective review. *Annual Review of Neuroscience, 16*, 159-182.

Schacter, D. L., & Church, B. (1995). Implicit memory in amnesic patients: When is auditory priming spared? *Journal of the International Neuropsychological Society, 1*, 434-442.

Schacter, D. L., Church, B., & Bolton, E. (1995). Implicit memory in amnesic patients: Impairment of voice-specific priming. *Psychological Science, 6*, 20-25.

Schacter, D. L., Church, B., & Treadwell, J. (1994). Implicit memory in amnesic patients: Evidence for spared auditory priming. *Psychological Science, 5*, 20-25.

Schacter, D. L., & Curran, T. (1995). The cognitive neuroscience of false memories. *Psychiatric Annals, 25*, 726-730.

Schacter, D. L., Curran, T., Galluccio, L., Milberg, W. P., & Bates, J. F. (1996a). False recognition and the right frontal lobe: A case study. *Neuropsychologia, 34*, 793-808.

Schacter, D. L., Harbluk, J. L., & McLachlan, D. R. (1984). Retrieval without recollection: An experimental analysis of source amnesia. *Journal of Verbal Learning and Verbal Behavior, 23*, 593-611.

Schacter, D. L., Kaszniak, A. W., Kihlstrom, J. F., & Valdiserri, M. (1991).

The relation between source memory and aging. *Psychology and Aging, 6*, 559-568.

Schacter, D. L., Savage, C. R., Alpert, N. M., Rauch, S. L., & Albert, M. S. (1996b). The role of hippocampus and frontal cortex in age-related memory changes: a PET study. *NeuroReport, 7*, 1165-1169.

Schacter, D. L., & Tulving, E. (Eds.) (1994a). *Memory systems 1994*. Cambridge, MA: MIT Press.

Schacter, D. L., & Tulving, E. (1994b). What are the memory systems of 1994? In D. L. Schacter & E. Tulving (Eds.), *Memory systems 1994* (pp. 1-38). Cambridge, MA: The MIT press.

Scoville, W. B., & Milner, B. (1957). Loss of recent memory after bilateral hippocampal lesions. *Journal of Neurology, Neurosurgery and Psychiatry, 20*, 11-21.

Senkfor, A. J., & Van Petten, C. (in press). Who said what: An event-related potential investigation of source and item memory. *Journal of Experimental Psychology: Learning, Memory, and Cognition.*

Shallice, T. (1982). Specific impairments of planning. *Philosophical Transactions of the Royal Society of London, B, 298*, 199-209.

Shimamura, A. P. (1989). Disorders of memory: the cognitive science perspective. In F. Boller & J. Grafman (Eds.), *Handbook of neuropsychology* (Vol. 3, pp. 35-73). Amsterdam: Elsevier.

Shimamura, A. P., Janowsky, J. S., & Squire, L. R. (1990). Memory for the temporal order of events in patients with frontal lobe lesions and amnesic patients. *Neuropsychologia, 28*, 803-813.

Shimamura, A. P., & Squire, L. R. (1984). Paired-associate learning and priming effects in amnesia: A neuropsychological study. *Journal of Experimental Psychology: General, 11*, 556-570.

Shimamura, A. P., & Squire, L. R. (1987). A neuropsychological study of fact memory and source amnesia. *Journal of Experimental Psychology: Learning, Memory, and Cognition, 13*, 464-473.

Shoqeirat, M. A., & Mayes, A. R. (1991). Disproportionate incidental spatial-memory and recall deficits in amnesia. *Neuropsychologia, 29*, 749-769.

Smith, M. L., & Milner, B. (1984). Differential effects of frontal lobe lesions on cognitive estimation and spatial memory. *Neuropsychologia, 22*, 697-705.

Spencer, W. D., & Raz, N. (1994). Memory for facts, source and context: Can frontal lobe dysfunction explain age-related differences? *Psychology and Aging, 9*, 149-159.

Spencer, W. D., & Raz, N. (1995). Differential effects of aging on memory for content and context: A meta-analysis. *Psychology and Aging, 10*, 527-539.

Squire, L. R. (1981). Two forms of human amnesia: an analysis of forgetting. *The Journal of Neuroscience, 1*, 635-640.

Squire, L. R. (1992). Memory and the hippocampus: A synthesis from findings with rats, monkeys, and humans. *Psychological Review, 99*, 195-231.

Squire, L. R. (1994). Declarative and nondeclarative memory: Multiple brain systems supporting learning and memory. In D. L. Schacter & E. Tulving (Eds.), *Memory systems 1994* (pp. 203-231). Cambridge, MA: MIT Press.

Squire, L. R., Cohen, N. J., & Nadel, L. (1984). The medial temporal region and memory consolidation: A new hypothesis. In H. Weingartner & E. S. Parker (Eds.), *Memory consolidation* (pp. 185-210). Hillsdale, NJ: Erlbaum.

Stern, C. E., Corkin, S., Gonzalez, R. G., Guimaraes, A. R., Baker, J. R., Jennings, P. J., Carr, C. A., Sugiura, R. M., Vedantham, V., & Rosen, B. R. (1996). The hippocampal formation participates in novel picture encoding: Evidence from functional magnetic resonance imaging. *Proceedings of the*

National Academy of Sciences USA, 93, 8660-8665.

Stuss, D. T., Eskes, G. A., & Foster, J. K. (1994). Experimental neuropsychological studies of frontal lobe functions. In F. Boller & J. Grafman (Eds.), *Handbook of neuropsychology* (Vol. 9, pp. 149-185). Amsterdam: Elsevier.

Stuss, D. T., Alexander, M. P., Palumbo, C. L., Buckle, L., Sayer, L., & Pogue, J. (1994). Organizational strategies of patients with unilateral or bilateral frontal lobe injury in word list learning tasks. *Neuropsychology, 8*, 355-373.

Sullivan, E. V., Marsh, L., Mathalon, D. H., Lim, K. O., & Pfefferbaum, A. (1995). Age-related decline in MRI volumes of temporal lobe gray matter but not hippocampus. *Neurobiology of Aging, 16*, 591-606.

Talland, G. A. (1965). *Deranged memory*. New York, NY: Academic Press.

Teuber, H.-L., Milner, B., & Vaughan, H. G. J. (1968). Persistent anterograde amnesia after stab wound of the basal brain. *Neuropsychologia, 6*, 267-282.

Thoene, A. I. T., & Glisky, E. L. (1995). Learning of name-face associations in memory impaired patients: A comparison of different training procedures. *Journal of the International Neuropsychological Society, 1*, 29-38.

Tulving, E. (1983). *Elements of episodic memory*. Oxford: Clarendon Press.

Tulving, E., Hayman, C. A. G., & Macdonald, C. A. (1991). Long-lasting perceptual priming and semnatic learning in amnesia: A case experiment. *Journal of Experimental Psychology: Learning, Memory, and Cognition, 17*, 595-617.

Tulving, E., Kapur, S., Craik, F. I. M., Moscovitch, M., & Houle, S. (1994). Hemispheric encoding/retrieval asymmetry in episodic memory: Positron emission tomography findings. *Proceedings of the National Academy of Sciences, 91*, 2016-2020.

Tulving, E., Schacter, D. L., & Stark, H. A. (1982). Priming effects in word-fragment completion are independent of recognition memory. *Journal of Experimental Psychology: Learning, Memory and Cognition, 8*, 336-342.

Vaidya, C. J., Gabrieli, J. D. E., Keane, M. M., & Monti, L. A. (1995). Perceptual and conceptual memory processes in global amnesia. *Neuropsychology, 9*, 580-591.

Verfaellie, M., & Treadwell, J. R. (1993). Status of recognition memory in amnesia. *Neuropsychology, 7*, 5-13.

Victor, M., & Yakovlev, P. I. (1955). S. S. Korsakoff's psychic disorder in conjunction with peripheral neuritis. *Neurology, 5*, 394-406.

Warrington, E. K., & Weiskrantz, L. (1968). New method of testing long-term retention with special reference to amnesic patients. *Nature, 217*, 972-974.

Warrington, E. K., & Weiskrantz, L. (1970). Amnesic syndrome: Consolidation or retrieval? *Nature, 228*, 628-630.

Warrington, E. K., & Weiskrantz, L. (1974). The effect of prior learning on subsequent retention in amnesic patients. *Neuropsychologia, 12*, 419-428.

Weintraub, S., Powell, D. H., & Whitla, D. K. (1994). Successful cognitive aging: Individual differences among physicians on a computerized test of mental state. *Journal of Geriatric Psychiatry, 27*, 15-34.

West, R. L., & Boatwright, L. K. (1983). Age differences in cued recall and recognition under varying encoding and retrieval conditions. *Experimental Aging Research, 9*, 185-189.

Wheeler, M. A., Stuss, D. T., & Tulving, E. (1995). Frontal lobe damage produces episodic memory impairment. *Journal of the International Neuropsychological Society, 1*, 525-536.

Wilson, B. (1987). *Rehabilitation of memory*. New York: Guilford.

Winocur, G., Moscovitch, M., & Witherspoon, D. (1987). Contextual cuing and memory performance in brain-damaged amnesics and old people. *Brain and Cognition, 6*, 129-141.

Zola-Morgan, S., & Squire, L. R. (1993). The neuroanatomy of memory. *Annual Review of Neuroscience, 16*, 547-563.

Zola-Morgan, S., Squire, L. R., & Amaral, D. G. (1986). Human amnesia and the medial temporal region: Enduring memory impairment following a bilateral lesion limited to field CA1 of the hippocampus. *Journal of Neuroscience, 6*, 2950-2967.

The Other Side of the Error Term - N. Raz (Editor)

Chapter 7

DOES WORKING MEMORY WORK IN LANGUAGE COMPREHENSION? EVIDENCE FROM BEHAVIORAL NEUROSCIENCE

Arthur Wingfield,
Brandeis University
Gloria S. Waters,
McGill University
& Patricia A. Tun,
Brandeis University

ABSTRACT

Models of language comprehension have traditionally included a role for short-term or working memory to serve as a storage or computational platform to allow needed time and "computational space" for syntactic and interpretive analyses and to allow second-pass operations to repair errors in initial interpretation. In this chapter we present data from elderly adults and from individuals with neurological impairment who show good language comprehension in the face of significant reductions in memory capacity as measured by traditional span tests. We discuss current conceptions of working memory and traditional span measures in terms of language comprehension and the need for briefly sustained traces of the sensory input and the products of ongoing syntactic and semantic computations in the comprehension process.

In recent years behavioral neuroscience has gained considerable insight into a range of cognitive functions through the study of special populations such as the elderly and brain injured adults. In this chapter we review research that focuses on memory constraints in language processing using data from these populations. We show how this research has shed critical light on our understanding of the structure of working memory and its role in language comprehension.

The notion of a short-term "buffer" memory for temporary storage of verbal material was established in the 1950s with the demonstration that materials such as three letter trigrams could be retained for less than 18 seconds without active rehearsal (Brown, 1958; Peterson & Peterson, 1959). Because of this memory's short duration, a more permanent store of verbal materials would have to rely on its transfer (or consolidation) from the short-term store to a long-term store.

Over the years, short-term memory became reified in a number of models as a stage in a linear sequence of information flow running from short- to long-term memory (Waugh & Norman, 1965). The appearance of acoustic confusions in recall of visually presented letters supported the view that short-term memory held verbal input in the form of a phonological or articulatory code (Conrad, 1963; Wickelgren, 1965). By contrast, semantic confusions in long-term recall (Baddeley & Dale, 1966; Kintsch & Buschke, 1969) suggested that transfer from short-to long-term retention reflected not simply the strengthening of a single trace, but the transformation of the trace from an acoustic or phonological representation in short-term memory to a semantic representation in long-term memory. These demonstrations led to the so-called "modal model" of memory of the 1960s that now grew to include sensory registers, feed-back loops, and control processes (e.g., Atkinson & Shiffrin, 1968).

Twenty-plus years after the heyday of the modal model, Shiffrin reports being taken aback when a colleague asked him, "What ever happened to short-term memory? Didn't people used to study that?" (Shiffrin, 1993, pg. 193). The existence of a short duration phonologically based memory system was not denied. What occurred, according to Shiffrin, was an absorption of short-term memory into even more broadly defined cognitive theory. This shift is most notably found in the concept of *working memory:* a memory system consisting of an articulatory loop for rehearsing verbal materials, a visuo-spatial scratchpad for temporary storage of non-linguistic visual input, and a limited capacity central executive for the general control of these two subsystems (Baddeley, 1986).

The contrast between traditional notions of short-term memory and working memory is reflected in the way the two spans are typically measured. Short-term memory was commonly tested by the forward digit span of the WAIS-R (1981) or recall of word lists following a single presentation. Common tests of working memory span are the WAIS-R backward digit span or the Daneman and Carpenter (1980) working memory span task. In the Daneman and Carpenter task the subject reads or listens to a series of sentences, in some cases giving true-false judgments to insure the sentences are being comprehended. After a certain number of sentences have been presented the subjects must then give from memory the final word in each of the sentences presented in that set. These tests capture the essence of working memory because of the way they emphasize the manipulation of information, rather than emphasizing simple storage capacity.

The Role of Short-Term Memory in Language Comprehension.

The existence of a short-term phonological trace, perhaps kept alive by recycling through an articulatory loop that can hold a veridical trace of verbal sequences, has become a part of established memory theory. Studies with normal speakers demonstrated that although verbatim memory for connected speech has a longer span than for unrelated word-lists, the unrehearsed surface forms of sentences fade rapidly while the meanings of the sentences do not (Sachs, 1967). Given the demonstration that subjects can produce verbatim the last clause heard in a spoken sentence (Jarvella, 1970, 1971), it was perhaps natural to presume that the phonological short-term store as described in the traditional memory literature served language comprehension by holding clauses in verbatim form long enough to allow syntactic analysis and integration of meaning across clauses and sentences (Fodor, Bever & Garrett, 1974).

In language processing models that assume that listeners (and readers) ordinarily conduct syntactic and semantic processing on-line, as the linguistic input is arriving (e.g., Frazier & Rayner, 1982; Just & Carpenter, 1987; Marslen-Wilson, 1984; Moss & Marslen-Wilson, 1993), the role of a short-term phonological store tends to be relegated to a back-up system to be used whenever processing lags behind the input. One can easily enumerate such instances.

(1) *Recovery of poorly articulated phonological forms*. It is well-known in the speech perception literature that words in connected speech are often poorly articulated. This can be demonstrated by splicing single words out of spoken sentences and presenting them in isolation. The same words that are difficult to identify in isolation sound very clear when they are spliced back into their original linguistic surround (Lieberman, 1963; Pollack & Pickett, 1963; Wingfield, Alexander & Cavigelli, 1994). That is, at all levels, from the effect of *coarticulation* on phoneme identification, to the level of sentence context on the perception of words, speech perception is known to be heavily context dependent (Cole & Jakimik, 1980; Cole & Scott, 1974; Liberman, Cooper, Shankweiler & Studdert-Kennedy, 1967).

In order to use context, whether at the acoustic-phonetic level (e.g., perceptual information supplied by coarticulation) or at the level of linguistic context (syntactic, semantic and pragmatic information), there must exist some brief memory trace of the acoustic signal representing both the target and its immediate acoustic surround. This need for a brief memory trace becomes especially apparent when an initially unintelligible word becomes clarified by linguistic context that *follows* the acoustically ambiguous region (Connine, Blasko & Hall, 1991; Grosjean, 1985; Wingfield et al., 1994).

(2) *Second pass repair of parsing errors*. Local ambiguities can lead to

an initial parsing error that requires the listener or reader to "back up" for a second pass analysis of a sentence when a parsing error has been discovered. Extreme cases are so-called "garden path sentences," such as "The old man the boats". The confusion lies in the tendency to hear the word *man* as a modified noun, instead of the verb it is intended to be. Current processing models give considerable attention to the balance between the likelihood of initial parsing errors at points of local ambiguity against a more conservative "wait and see" strategy that would tax a limited capacity memory system needed to hold the original input for a second pass reanalysis (Abney & Johnson, 1991).

(3) *Assembly of phrases, clauses and sentences for a comprehension structure*. The development of coherence at the sentence and discourse level implies the necessity for holding the output of earlier linguistic analyses for integration with syntactic and semantic elements that follow. In processing models, especially at the discourse level, working memory plays a critical role (Kintsch, 1988).

This listing does not exhaust all claims for the need of a short-term verbal store for effective language processing. These would include handling a sentence with complex syntax, such as those with embedded clauses or sentences with extended left-branching structure (King & Just, 1991) and recovering antecedents in dealing with anaphoric reference.

Interestingly, retention of verbatim forms of utterances is apparently quite good for very long periods for socially interactive utterances such as jokes and insults (Murphy & Shapiro, 1994). Such long-term retention of surface forms, however, is probably the exception rather than the rule. We take the position here that the verbatim surface form of sentences are lost rather quickly. (It is also difficult to calculate the extent to which apparent word-for-word reproduction may actually reflect in whole or in part the successful outcome of reconstructive processes.)

What Kind of Memory?

There are several important points to be made in regard to the examples given above. The first is that the short-term acoustic trace of the syllabic surround of a phoneme necessary to allow its recognition need not be the same kind of memory representation needed to carry language comprehension at the sentence or discourse level. For example, analysis at the syllable level might be identified with a precategorical auditory memory image with a duration in the order of 100 to 250 milliseconds (Huggins, 1974; Massaro, 1972). One approach to modeling the memory system for language comprehension might thus include the postulate of a sequence of increasingly larger and more abstract processing units (syllables, words, clauses, sentences and discourse units), each with its own memory store of a size and nature necessary to hold that unit long enough for perceptual analysis and integration.

Models of human memory have been increasing in their complexity over the years, partly in the expression of the number of memory systems postulated (e.g., Monsell, 1984). There has also been a shift from the easily visualizable boxes-and-arrows of sequential stage models (Atkinson & Shiffrin, 1968; Broadbent, 1971; Waugh & Norman, 1965) to models based on a connectionist architecture (Schneider & Detweiler, 1987; Schneider, 1993). We would argue that our attempts to understand mechanisms of language processing should be guided, and constrained, by the changing views of the memory systems that would presumably be needed for their support. We would also argue that language processing may serve as a useful vehicle for our developing models of memory.

A second important point is that the presumed roles for short-term memory in language comprehension have been based as much on perceived reasonableness, as they have been on experimental evidence. Thus, as theories of language processing become less sequentially based, and more interactive in nature, the emphasis on memory support for language comprehension has tended to undergo a corresponding change. At the experimental level, the distinction between recall based on a transient veridical trace, and equally accurate recall derived from reconstructive processes, is surprisingly difficult to distinguish (Potter, 1993; Potter & Lombardi, 1990; Schweickert, 1993; Wingfield, Tun & Rosen, 1995). For example, if an experimental subject recalls a sentence exactly as it was presented, one might assume that the subject was relying on a verbatim trace. However, it might equally be true that the subject reconstructed the material from an abstraction. The point is that, without errors, one would not be able to distinguish between these two types of recall.

Generally speaking, however, in the area of language processing there has been relatively little challenge to the presumption that the memory spans *du jour*, whether the short-term memory of the modal memory model of the 1960s, or the contemporary construct of working memory (Just & Carpenter, 1992), represent *the* memory systems that subserve language comprehension. It may be fair to say that models of language comprehension have devoted more effort to showing the logical necessity for the temporary maintenance of recent linguistic input than in looking deeply into the kind of memory store, or stores, that might be operating.

In the following sections we will draw evidence from two populations, elderly subjects with small but significant limitations in working memory capacity, and brain injured patients with significantly reduced spans of phonological and working memory. We will use these data to show that current conceptions of the role of memory in language comprehension do not fare well under close scrutiny.

Working Memory and Language Processing: Evidence from aging

In Stine's (1995) important analysis of the role of working memory in language processing, she contrasts between the term "short-term memory" (STM) to refer to an acoustically or phonologically based storage buffer that is needed to conduct a preliminary analysis of language, and the term "working memory" that refers to the processing component that manipulates information (Stine, 1995, pg. 173). This distinction follows Baddeley's claim for (at least) two buffer stores (an articulatory loop for verbal materials and a visuo-spatial scratchpad for holding non-verbal materials), and a limited capacity central executive that controls the allocation of limited resources that must be shared by the processes needed for maintenance and manipulation of information in memory (Baddeley, 1981).

The way people rehearse a series of unrelated words or numbers to keep them alive in memory represents the sort of subvocal rehearsal epitomized by the "articulatory loop" of the working memory system. Analysis of regional cerebral blood flow using positron emission tomography (PET) has been taken to support two components of the articulatory loop: the subvocal rehearsal system, associated with increased blood flow activity in Broca's area, and a phonological store, associated with activity in the left supramarginal gyrus (Paulesu, Frith, & Frackowiak, 1993; but see also Poeppel, 1996). The notion of central resources that must be allocated among various mental processes has a very long history in the literature on attention, whether these resources are referred to as psychic energy (Titchener, 1910) or attentional resources (Kahneman, 1973). The trend toward fractionation evident in cognitive theory appeared in later postulates of multiple processing systems that do not share resources (McLeod, 1977). Because of arguments that verbal and non-verbal processing seem to have different resource characteristics (e.g. Daneman & Tardif, 1987), we will restrict our discussion of working memory and aging to the domain of language processing.

It is generally accepted that normal aging is accompanied by significant losses in the capacity of working memory (Salthouse, 1991). That is, when the same young and elderly subjects are tested on simple digit or word span, age differences are absent or minimal. However, when tested on a "loaded" listening span task patterned after the Daneman and Carpenter task (1980), in which subjects must listen to and comprehend a series of sentences and then recall the last word in each sentence, age differences become marked (Wingfield, Stine, Lahar & Aberdeen, 1988). At the same time, it is also known that, barring neuropathology, linguistic knowledge and its utilization remain well-preserved in normal aging (Light, 1990; Wingfield & Stine, 1992; Kempler & Zelinski, 1994).

As evidence for the resistance of linguistic knowledge to the aging process one can cite the way in which healthy elderly adults can use linguistic context to recognize artificially degraded written words (Madden, 1988), artificially degraded spoken words (Cohen & Faulkner, 1983; Wingfield, Aberdeen & Stine, 1991; Perry & Wingfield, 1994) and normally underarticulated spoken words (Wingfield, et al., 1994). In such cases, the elderly can be shown to use linguistic context as well as, or better, than young adults.

In spite of these factors, there are age-related differences in language performance, albeit subtle ones. For example, elderly adults can have more difficulty than the young in handling sentences with especially complex syntax, such as those with left-branching constructions (Norman, Kemper, Kynette, Cheung, & Anagnopulos, 1991), or drawing linguistic inferences (Cohen, 1981). However, when these differences occur, they are invariably attributed to processing limitations imposed by an age-related reduction in working memory (Light, 1990; Norman, et al, 1991).

Within this context, Stine (1995) points out that if (a) one were to divide working memory into the storage capacity of the phonological store, and the operational capacity of a "central executive" or "computational space", and if (b) the operational capacity of working memory declines systematically with age, as seems to be the case (Salthouse & Babcock, 1991; Wingfield, et al., 1988), then (c) one would expect to see reliable age by complexity-of-materials interactions in a range of studies. As Stine points out, however, a sample of the literature shows only about a 50% hit rate in obtaining such results.

The evidence for age-related declines in working memory capacity seems persuasive, supported as it is by numerous studies comparing span scores for young adults (typically college students) and older adults (over the age of 60) on standard tests of working memory (Dobbs & Rule, 1989; Gick, Craik, & Morris, 1988; Kemper, 1986; Light & Anderson, 1985, Exp. 1; Marmurek, 1990; Pratt & Robins, 1991; Stine & Wingfield, 1987, 1990; Tun, Wingfield, & Stine, 1991; Wingfield et al., 1988). Although not all studies have shown such differences (Hartley, 1986, 1988; Light & Anderson, 1985, Exp. 2), the consensus in the field of aging is that working memory capacity does decline with age (see reviews by Carpenter, Miyake & Just, 1994, and Daneman & Merikle, 1996).

The thorniest problem for the concept of working memory, however, is that even when significant age-group differences in working memory span have been demonstrated, span has proven inconsistent as a predictor of other types of cognitive performance. In the following section we focus on this question in terms of comprehension and memory for language.

Working memory span as a predictor of age differences in language processing.

In some cases, aging research has found working memory span to be useful in predicting performance on language processing tasks. For example, Kemper (1988) concluded that working memory plays a key role in the ability of older adults to produce complex syntactic constructions. In a dual-task study Tun et al. (1991) found expected age differences in subjects' ability to listen to spoken passages while carrying out a speeded reaction time task. When performance was compared for a subset of older adults who were matched with young adults on working memory span, however, the performance patterns for the two groups were strikingly similar to each other. Others have shown that statistically controlling for differences in working memory scores can attenuate age differences in performance (e.g. Pratt, Boyes, Robins, & Manchester, 1989; Stine & Wingfield, 1987). Age-related differences in working memory capacity were also used to account for the finding that older adults are less likely than young adults to establish the referent of a pronoun across a long distance in text (Light & Capps, 1986; see also Zurif, Swinney, Prather, Wingfield & Brownell, 1995), as well as Light, Zelinski, and Moore's (1982) finding of age-related difficulties in reasoning from new information, and Cohen's (1981) report that elderly adults are less likely than young adults to infer a causal connection between sentences.

Although the above studies are frequently cited as support for working memory limitations restricting language processing performance in elderly adults, as we have indicated, working memory span has not always proven to be a reliable predictor of text-processing performance. There are, for example, several text processing studies in which working memory spans have not correlated consistently with outcome measures of prose recall (Cohen & Faulkner, 1981; Hartley, 1986; 1988; Light & Anderson, 1985; Pratt et al., 1989). Sometimes correlations between memory span measures and language performance appear, but with a correlational pattern that is puzzling. Returning to spoken input, for example, Stine and Wingfield (1990) found that working memory spans accounted for individual differences in processing spoken passages that were relatively simple, but not for materials that were more difficult. This, as we shall see, is the exact opposite of what limited-capacity theory would predict.

In the course of carrying out research on memory and language processing in our laboratory we have been collecting working memory span scores of young and elderly subjects for a number of years. When one is conducting aging research, it is important to insure that elderly subjects are cognitively intact, and therefore we routinely screen our elderly participants by giving them a variety of cognitive tests, including reading and listening span tests following the Daneman and Carpenter (1980) method. It is of some interest, then, to look at the results of an internal, mini-meta-analysis on the findings from working memory span scores and other performance measures from a number of our previous studies.

Figure 1 shows the correlations between memory performance in seven experimental studies completed in our laboratory and six memory span measures. In all of these studies the young subjects were college students in their twenties and the elderly subjects were healthy community-dwelling volunteers with good levels of education and verbal ability that were at least equal to those of the young subjects.

The three panels on the left show the correlation between performance in the studies and three simple span tests that require only storage (forward digit span, listening word span, and reading word span). The three panels on the right show the correlation between memory performance in these same seven studies, and working memory spans that involve both storage and reorganization (backward digit span and both the listening and reading working memory spans patterned after Daneman and Carpenter, 1980). For each study, correlations are shown separately for young and elderly adults. (Not all measures were available for all studies.)

The outcome measures for the studies consisted of free recall of verbal materials, including spoken short passages (Study 1: Tun & Wingfield, 1994;

Study 2: Tun et al., 1991; Study 3: Tun, Tun, & Wingfield, 1997; Study 4: Wingfield, Tun, & Rosen, 1995), spoken sentences (Study 5: Tun & Wingfield, unpublished data; Study 6: Tun, Wingfield, Stine, & Mecsas, 1992), and recall of word lists (Study 7: Tun, Wingfield, Rosen & Blanchard, unpublished data).

The most outstanding impression one receives from scanning the various panels of Figure 1 is the erratic, unsystematic pattern of the correlations. As can be seen, sometimes the correlations between text recall for a given study and the simple spans depicted in the three panels on the left are smaller than the correlations of that recall measure with the working memory spans shown on the right, and sometimes they are larger. In some cases correlations are present but very weak, and in several cases the correlations appear to be negative. Similarly, although the correlations between memory performance and working memory spans tend to be higher for older adults than for young adults, we can also see that this is not always the case.

In short, these findings do not show any systematic advantage for working memory spans in predicting text recall in the type of studies of natural language that we have carried out in our laboratory. (We should note that our examination of the range of working memory and other span scores in these studies did not suggest that the sizes of these correlations were artifactually constrained by a restriction in the range of scores obtained.)

Failure to obtain predicted Age by Complexity interactions

If old age is associated with a reduced working memory capacity, then one might predict that a manipulation that increases the processing burden on working memory should be especially detrimental to the performance of elderly adults relative to young adults. The processing load might be increased, for example, by increasing the syntactic complexity, the propositional density, or the average inter-word predictability of the materials. These various methods of manipulating processing complexity should thus lead to reliable findings of Age by Complexity interactions in language processing studies. However, this predicted Age by Complexity interaction has proven to be elusive.

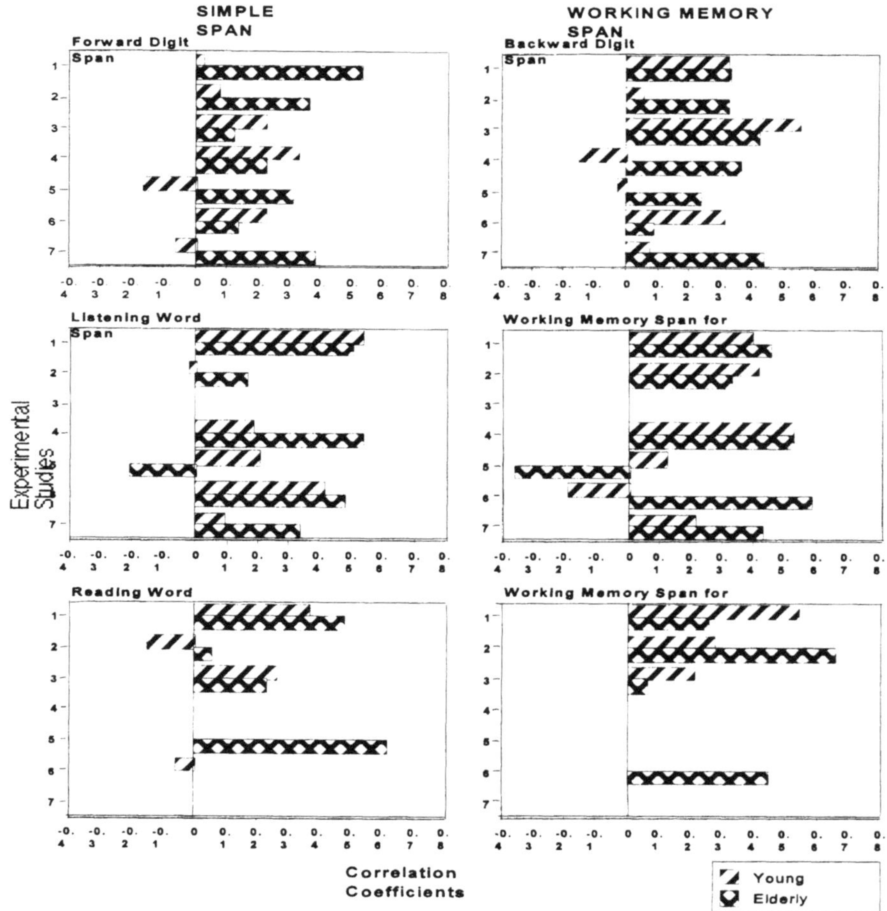

Figure 1. Correlations between span measures and memory performance on seven experimental studies with young and elderly adults. Spans that measure simple storage are shown on the left (forward digit span, listening word span, and reading word span) and working memory spans are shown on the right (backward digit span, working memory listening span, and working memory reading span). (Not all measures were available in all studies.)

Some investigators who have manipulated the syntactic complexity of text materials have found that complex syntax is differentially harder for older adults to process than for young adults (Emery, 1985, 1986; Kemper, 1986; Obler, Fein, Nicholas, & Albert, 1991). On the other hand, one group (Morris, Craik, & Gick, 1990) found that sentence complexity had a greater detrimental effect on young subjects than on elderly subjects in carrying out a working memory task involving sentence verification with a memory preload. This finding is difficult to reconcile with an argument that age-related reductions in working memory capacity should constrain task performance.

In our own laboratory we have frequently found no differential decrement in the performance of elderly adults when we have increased the difficulty of to-be-remembered text materials in various ways. The fact that all subjects, young and old, recall less in the more difficult conditions confirms the effectiveness of these manipulations. Nevertheless, even though our elderly subjects typically perform at a lower level on various span tests than the young, and produce overall lower levels of performance on our language recall tasks, they are not differentially impaired by the more difficult conditions. It is difficult to account for the absence of an Age by Complexity interaction within the current conception of working memory. Let us examine these studies in greater detail.

In several studies we have manipulated the informational density of text materials by varying the number of idea units (propositions) that are contained in sentences or passages of a given length. According to the model of text processing proposed by Kintsch (e.g. van Dijk & Kintsch, 1983), each additional idea unit or proposition should represent an additional processing load on working memory, and it has been shown that processing time is a function of the number of propositions contained within a text (Kintsch & Keenan, 1973). In a study based on this principle, Stine, Wingfield and Poon (1986) had subjects listen to 16- to 18-word sentences that varied in the number of propositions each contained. Further, the sentences were presented at normal or very fast speech rates. Although propositionally dense sentences were remembered less well than sentences that contained relatively less new information, older adults were not affected differentially more by propositional density, as would be predicted if performance were being constrained by an age-related limitation in working memory capacity. Elderly subjects' recall suffered more than that of the young from increased speech rates, but we interpret this as due to central slowing of processing rate rather than a limitation in working memory capacity per se.

We found a similar pattern in another study that tested recall of spoken prose passages varying in propositional density that subjects heard as they carried out a secondary speeded judgment task (Tun, et al., 1991). Again, although both young and older subjects recalled less as the informational density of the passages was increased, the effect was not greater for the elderly than for the young. This was so even though the young group had significantly higher working memory span scores than did the older group.

One can also manipulate the difficulty of text materials by using the average inter-word predictability of passages as determined by a cloze procedure, such as those made available by Miller and Coleman (1967). In one study making use of these materials, young and elderly adults listened to a series of to-be-remembered passages that ranged from low to high in inter-word predictability, while also performing a concurrent secondary reaction time task (Tun et al., 1994). For both young and older adults, passages that were low in predictability were remembered less well than those that were higher in predictability. However, even though the elderly group had lower average working memory scores than the young adults, the overall effect of predictability was not magnified for the elderly relative to the young. Age differences for low predictability text were greater at the level of detail, but there was no Age by Predictability interaction as would be expected based on the working memory differences.

A similar pattern was observed in a second study that also used passages ranging from low to high in inter-word predictability. In this case the passages were also presented at varying speech rates (Riggs, Wingfield, & Tun, 1993). Again, an effect of passage predictability was obtained on passage recall, but this effect was not magnified for the elderly adults relative to young adults. Similarly, although the elderly's memory was differentially impaired by very fast speech presentation rates, there was no three-way interaction between age, passage predictability and presentation rate.

These are not the only studies that fail to show the Age by Complexity interactions that would be predicted by a limited-capacity working memory that constrained task performance. For example, in a reading study, Tun (1989) examined the effects of text genre by testing comprehension and recall for narrative and expository passages. Narratives proved to be read faster and remembered better than expository passages by both young and old subjects, presumably because of the supportive structure offered by the narratives. This genre effect, however, was not differentially greater for the elderly compared to the young adults.

In summary, then, a series of studies from our laboratory has shown that even when older adults score lower on working memory span tests than young adults, the elderly's memory performance is not *differentially* impaired relative to the young by manipulations that increase the difficulty of text processing, and presumably, the burden on working memory.

Failure to obtain differential effects of divided attention in the elderly

When we turn to the area of divided attention research, we encounter yet another apparent paradox. This is the frequent finding that, at least with tasks involving natural language, dividing attention does not necessarily impair the performance of elderly adults to a greater degree than that of young adults. Divided attention is commonly believed to mimic the effect of reduced processing capacity (e.g. Carpenter et al., 1994). Indeed, age-related declines in the ability to divide attention between two tasks have often been considered to be a hallmark of the aging process (Craik, 1977; Welford, 1958). If dividing attention has the functional result of reducing processing capacity for any given task, and if older adults already suffer from age-related declines in working memory capacity, then it would be logical to expect that low-span individuals such as the elderly should be especially impaired by the requirement to divide their attention between two tasks.

However, this has not proven to be the case in a substantial number of studies involving language processing. In a review that surveyed a large number of dual-task studies that involved verbal processing (Tun & Wingfield, 1993), it appeared that elderly adults suffered differentially more than young adults from the requirement to divide attention on some tasks but not others. Specifically, interactions between adult age and divided attention appeared primarily when the to-be-remembered materials were digits (e.g. Barr & Giambra, 1990) or unrelated words (e.g. Craik & McDowd, 1987), with age differences appearing primarily in latency measures, rather than in recall accuracy. By contrast, Age by Divided attention interactions were seldom found for dual-task studies that used meaningful sentences (e.g. Gick et al., 1988; Tun et al., 1992) or prose materials (Tun, 1989; Tun et al., 1991; Tun & Wingfield, 1994). The resolution to this apparent paradox lies, we believe, in the unique status of speech processing among the cognitive abilities.

We can illustrate this point by describing a dual-task study in which subjects listened to 150-word prose passages for immediate recall while carrying out concurrent speeded tasks (Tun & Wingfield, 1994). The secondary tasks involved making speeded judgments about pairs of letters, based on either a simple criterion (physical match, e.g., E-E), or more demanding criteria (name match, e.g., E-e, or vowel-consonant category match, e.g., E-A or E-O). The prose passages also differed in difficulty, ranging from easy to difficult materials based on inter-word cloze predictability. Neither of these tasks were trivial: the passages were well beyond adults' recall span, and the secondary task often required a relatively complex judgment. In fact, both young and older adults recalled significantly less from the passages when they were required to divide attention between listening to the passages and making concurrent letter-judgments. Importantly, however, although elderly adults recalled less overall than young adults, especially when the passages were less predictable, the cost of dividing attention was not differentially greater for the older adults.

Findings such as these are difficult to resolve within the framework of working memory constraints associated with adult aging. Indeed, the modest conclusion one can draw from these and other dual-task studies is that processing meaningful prose seems not to depend on, or necessarily be constrained by, the memory system that is measured by traditional working memory span tests.

Age, Inhibition, and Working Memory Capacity

One line of research that has been used to support the role of working memory in language processing involves individual differences in the ability to hold in mind alternative interpretations of ambiguous material. Carpenter et al. (1994) have argued that such a requirement places a burden on working memory, as evidenced by studies in which low span subjects show less ability than high span subjects to maintain alternative interpretations. For example, Miyake, Just, & Carpenter (in press) studied word-by-word reading times in sentences that involved cases of linguistic ambiguity, such as when the word "boxer" could refer to either a pugilist or a short-haired dog. They reported that low span subjects' reading times were differentially slowed, relative to high span subjects, when sentences were disambiguated in a way that derived from the less preferred interpretation. Similar findings were reported in a study of syntactic ambiguity in which low span subjects were less likely than high span subjects to maintain a less preferred interpretation (MacDonald, Just, & Carpenter, 1992). Kemtes and Kemper (1996) extended this work by studying both young and older adults who ranged from low to high span. These findings have been taken as evidence for the role of working memory in text processing, whereby individuals with greater working memory capacity are able to maintain alternative interpretations of ambiguous material longer than low span subjects.

However, such a conclusion is directly contradicted by a series of studies carried out by Hasher and Zacks and colleagues, who suggest that because elderly adults have a reduced ability to inhibit irrelevant material, they are *more* likely than young adults to keep a broader range of material active, including alternative interpretations (e.g., Connelly, Hasher, & Zacks, 1991; Stoltzfus, Hasher, & Zacks, 1996). For example, in one study subjects were primed with incomplete sentences that were missing a final word, with the sustained activation of alternative sentence endings tested by response speed on a lexical decision task (Stoltzfus et al, 1996). Subjects made speeded judgments about words that were either highly expected based on the sentence context, relatively unexpected, or neutral. Findings showed that although younger adults showed priming only for the highly expected words, older adults also showed priming for the less expected words, indicating that a broader range of endings had been activated for the elderly. If the elderly had reduced working memory capacity relative to the younger adults, as would be expected for these populations, according to the argument advanced by Carpenter et al. (1994) one would have predicted a reduced range of priming for the elderly rather than a broader range.

In summary, the first line of reasoning advanced here would suggest that elderly adults have reduced working memory capacity, and therefore maintain less material in an active state. The second line of research suggests that elderly adults suffer inhibition deficits, which produces increased breadth and/or persistence of activation of material in working memory. At this point it is not clear how these two views can be reconciled within the traditional notions of working memory capacity.

Effects of Age, Speech Rate, and Content Complexity on Spontaneous Segmentation of Recorded Speech

Elderly subjects do show declines in memory capacity. Our question, however, is whether the traditionally measured short-term or working memory spans are relevant to language processing. Let us assume, for a moment, the existence of a working memory system that contains as one element a content-free articulatory or phonological store that serves as a precursor to linguistic processing. Evidence for such an articulatory loop is abundant in the cognitive literature. The question remains whether this articulatory/phonological loop serves syntactic processing and conceptual encoding of natural speech input. We recently attempted to test this hypothesis using the simple expedient of varying speech rate and content complexity of spoken prose and examining the effects of these variables on subjects' spontaneous segmentations of the speech input for immediate recall (Wingfield & Lindfield, 1995). Let us describe this experiment and its rationale.

One way to consider how memory might be involved in spoken language comprehension is to consider a technique we have referred to as "spontaneous segmentation." In this task, subjects hear a prerecorded passage of spoken prose, and are told that the passage is too long for accurate verbatim recall. Rather, they are given control of a pause button on a tape-recorder containing the recorded passage, with the instructions to interrupt the tape whenever they wished to recall a segment they have selected. In this way they are to work through the passage on a segment-by-segment basis, stopping the tape at points of their choosing, recalling that segment, restarting the tape, and so forth, until the passage is finished (Wingfield & Butterworth, 1984; Wingfield & Nolan, 1980).

One might consider several alternative predictions based on how one imagined that incoming discourse is processed. It might be that subjects would process the speech input by segmenting the speech stream into identifiable morphemes (words), and listening until the capacity of the phonological store was reached. If this capacity were represented by an articulatory loop, the lengths of the words in syllables would be a factor: the shorter the words, the faster each could be articulated, and hence the more words that could be held. Alternatively, the size of the segment might be determined by an upper-limit on the number of words that could be held, or an upper-limit on the time duration of a segment. What should have *no effect*, however, would be the linguistic content of the speech input. At least that would be the case if the phonological/articulatory store serves the function of holding temporarily the just-arrived input for a syntactic or propositional analysis. That is, if the role of the working memory system is to allow time and space for the conduct of a linguistic analysis of the speech input, how could the linguistic structure of the speech input be used to determine how much information will be selected for temporary holding in working memory?

Our studies using the spontaneous segmentation technique showed that subjects do not interrupt the speech at regular intervals, as determined by either the passage of time or by the number of words contained in a segment. Rather, subjects reliably segment the input at naturally occurring linguistic boundaries such as at the ends of sentences and clauses. Further, regardless of the segment sizes selected, recall is typically excellent. That is, in selecting segment sizes as they are hearing the speech, subjects rarely bite off more than they can chew (Wingfield & Butterworth, 1984). We have shown this to be true for elderly subjects as well as for young adults (Wingfield, Lahar & Stine, 1989; Wingfield & Stine, 1986).

It might be argued that subjects were selecting points for interruption of the speech input on the basis of the prosodic marking of these syntactic boundaries, holding these segments in a phonological short-term store as yet unanalyzed for content. Both young and elderly subjects are certainly sensitive to prosodic information in the detection of syntactic structure of sentences (Wingfield & Klein, 1971; Wingfield, Wayland & Stine, 1992). Or perhaps there exists some modular system that detects surface boundaries independent of an analysis of the message content of the speech.

The fundamental question we wish to ask, however, is whether the content of the speech input is taken into account when subjects segment the input for recall. This question is critical for testing the putative role of working memory as a holding store or work space for the analysis of linguistic content of the rapidly arriving speech stream. We examined this question in the following experiment in which we varied three factors that would be expected to bear on this issue (Wingfield & Lindfield, 1995).

First, we varied the content complexity of the speech input. The way we chose to do this was again to use speech passages that varied in their cloze predictability. The passages we used were taken from Miller and Coleman (1967), who gave subjects speech passages with words periodically deleted from those passages. They calculated the average cloze value of a passage based on the number of subjects who could correctly guess the identity of the missing words. The cloze procedure thus yields the average predictability of words in a passage.

The cloze procedure has a long history in psycholinguistic research, with passages containing low inter-word predictability known to be judged as more difficult to comprehend, and to be more difficult to recall (Acquino, 1969). If speech input is held temporarily in a phonological buffer to allow analysis of speech content, then speech content could *not* serve as the defining element of what subjects would chose to hold in this putative buffer store.

Second, we used two groups of subjects: a group of young adult university students and a group of healthy elderly adults, both selected to have good levels of education and general verbal ability. These two subject groups, however, differed significantly in test scores of working memory capacity. Hence, to the extent that working memory plays a major part in processing informational content of the speech input we would expect large age differences in the nature of the segments selected by the young and elderly adults. For example, the elderly subjects' selections of segments might be less principled than those of the young subjects if a limitation in working memory capacity made them less efficient in input processing.

Our final variable was speech rate. Slowing is considered by many investigators to be a common accompaniment of normal aging (Cerella, 1990; Salthouse, 1991), and it is certainly the case that elderly subjects are poorer at handling rapid speech input than young adults (Wingfield, Poon, Lombardi & Lowe, 1985). This special vulnerability to artificially accelerated (time-compressed) speech appears independently of age-related changes in auditory sensory acuity (Gordon-Salant & Fitzgibbons, 1993; Konkle, Beasley, & Bess, 1977; Luterman, Wesh, & Melrose, 1966; Sticht & Gray, 1969)

Although rapid speech input might make the processing task especially difficult for the elderly, it is a different kind of difficulty than adding content complexity to the speech material. Thus, in a test of recall of the selected segments, one would expect speech rate to have a differential effect on elderly subjects' recall, but one might or might not expect to see speech rate interact in a multiplicative way with passage predictability.

In terms of our focus on the size and nature of the segments subjects select for recall, two alternative hypotheses could be entertained. If a transient verbatim store was needed to support a higher-level content analysis, then one would not expect to see an effect of content complexity on the sizes of the segments selected. Specifically, one should not expect to see an effect of passage predictability, or a passage predictability by speech rate interaction, on the size or nature of the segments selected. Alternatively, a finding that passage predictability (our estimate of content complexity) does affect the sizes of the segments selected would be expected, on the other hand, if an on-line analysis of the linguistic content of the speech is being conducted *prior to* selection of a segment for storage and recall.

The stimuli were eighteen 150-word prose passages taken from Miller and Coleman (1967). Six were High predictability passages (mean predictability level = .41), six were Medium predictability (mean predictability level = .34), and six were Low predictability passages (mean predictability level = .24). The passages were recorded by a female speaker of American English at an average speech rate of 180 words per minute (wpm), a rate falling at the upper end of average speech rates in ordinary conversation. We refer to this as the Normal speech rate. Each of the passages was then time-compressed using the sampling method of compression so as to be reproduced in 78% and 60% of the original playing time. (These compression ratios corresponded to average speaking rates of 230 and 300 wpm). The sampling method of time-compression reduces both speech and silent durations to equal amounts, thus maintaining the relative temporal pattern and pitch of the original speech. The effect is thus to present the speech at an accelerated rate without disturbing the prosodic contour of the speech samples (Foulke, 1971; Wingfield, 1975).

In the course of the experiment each subject heard all eighteen passages, six at each of the above speech rates (Normal, and compression to 78% and 60% of original playing time). The particular passages heard at each speech rate were of course varied between subjects in a counter-balanced design such that, by the end of the experiment, each passage had been heard an equal number of times at each speech rate.

The subjects in this experiment were 36 healthy adults, including 18 university undergraduates ranging in age from 18 to 21 years ($M = 19.1$ years), and 18 community-dwelling elderly volunteers ranging in age from 61 to 85 ($M = 70.1$). Both groups were well educated and had good scores on the WAIS-R vocabulary test. The subjects in this experiment fit a classic pattern in normal aging: the young and elderly subjects were comparable on forward digit spans (7.8 versus 8.3, $t(34) = 1.37$, *n.s.*), and simple memory span for spoken words (5.7 versus 5.6, $t < 1$). They did, however, differ in their working memory spans, which were tested using an auditory version of the Daneman and Carpenter (1980) span test. The spans for the young and elderly subjects were 3.8 and 2.7 words respectively, $t(34) = 3.38$, $p < .01$.

The results of the experiment showed that there was an effect of passage predictability on the sizes of the segments selected for recall, with both young and elderly subjects tending to reduce the sizes of the segments they selected as passage predictability decreased. This in itself need not necessarily counter the traditional view of working memory. That is, it might simply be that low cloze passages tend on average to have longer words, thus reducing the number of words that could be maintained via an articulatory loop (Baddeley, 1981). This would be consistent with segments being held in the articulatory store while being processed for speech content, with the segment-sizes selected for this store being constrained by the capacity of the articulatory loop.

As it happens, however, the sizes of the segments selected are a reflection of the place of segmentation in terms of the linguistic content of the speech input. In order to conduct this analysis we classified subjects' places of interruption of the speech input in terms of whether they segmented the speech at (a) sentence boundaries, (b) major clause boundaries, (c) ends of substantial syntactic constituents that were not major clauses, such as noun or prepositional phrases, or (d) after constituent components such as nouns, verbs, prepositions, or other elements that could signal the nature of an upcoming constituent. As we have previously found, the frequency with which each of the constituent boundaries attracted an interruption followed their linguistic importance: ends of sentences attracting the most interruptions, then major clause boundaries, then at the ends of substantial syntactic components, and finally, at smaller constituent boundaries (Wingfield & Butterworth, 1984). The present study (Wingfield and Lindfield, 1995) confirmed that this same pattern holds for elderly subjects as well as for young adults. Segmentations of the speech input at points that did not coincide with any of these boundaries accounted for 10% or less of the interruptions regardless of age of the subjects or stimulus condition.

Figure 2 presents a general summary of the findings with respect to the effects of age, speech rate and passage predictability on subjects' segmentations of the input. The figure shows the mean percentage of interruptions that occurred at either sentence or major clause boundaries (categories *a* and *b* above) for the High, Medium and Low predictability passages presented at each of the three speech rates tested. The young subjects' data are shown in the left panel and the elderly subjects' data are shown in the right panel.

As we can see from Figure 2, as passage predictability decreased, the percentage of interruptions occurring at sentence or clause boundaries decreased relative to interruptions at minor constituent boundaries.

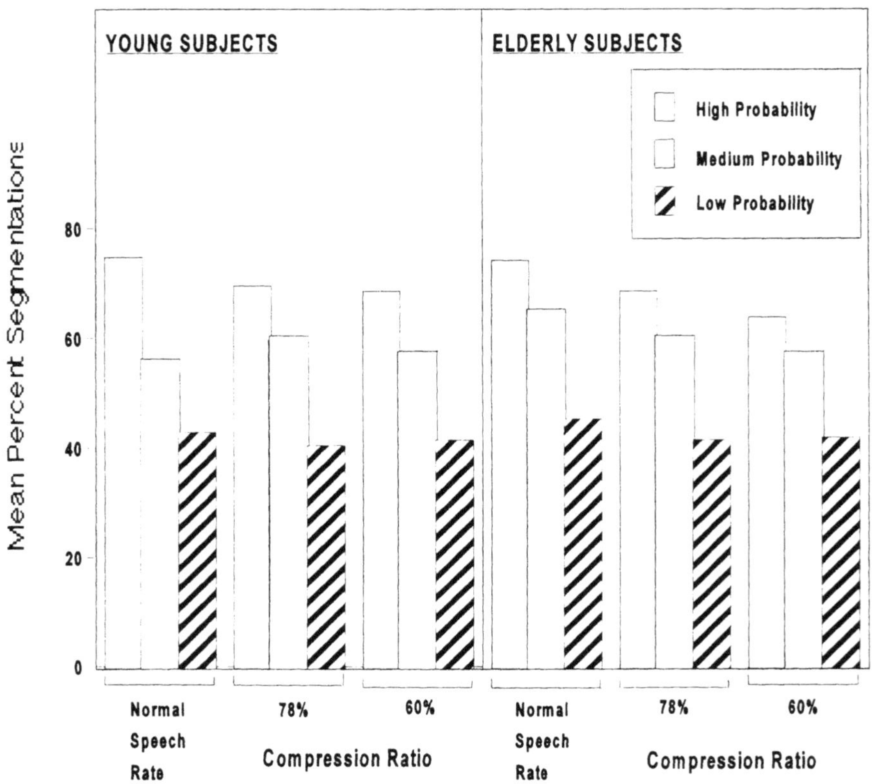

Figure 2. Mean percentage of segmentations occurring at sentence and major clause boundaries for high, medium, and low predictability passages heard at three speech rates (normal speech rate and speech time-compressed to be heard in 78% and 60% of the original speaking time). Data for young subjects are shown in the left panel and data for elderly subjects are shown in the right panel.

That is, subjects to stop more frequently at minor linguistic boundaries to keep the segment sizes short. A three-way mixed design ANOVA showed the reduction in percentage of interruptions at sentence and major clause boundaries to decrease significantly with decreasing Passage predictability (p <.001). Increasing speech rate also led to a relative decrease in interruptions at major boundaries in favor of interruption at more minor boundaries (p <.05). Most important, however, there was no effect of Age on place of segmentation (F <1), nor were any of the interactions involving Age, Passage predictability, or Speech rate, significant.

The above analyses relate to the sizes of the segments selected by the subjects. At recall, a slightly different picture occurs that is consistent with an age-related reduction in memory capacity. When one examines the percentage of words recalled correctly for the segments once selected, there were significant effects of Age, Passage predictability, and Speech rate, as well as significant Age by Speech Rate, Age by Passage predictability, and Passage predictability by Speech rate interactions.

The results of this study showed that both young and elderly subjects were sensitive to the content complexity of the speech input, with subjects reacting to this difficulty by selecting smaller segments as the passage difficulty (as manipulated by cloze predictability) increased. This is especially striking when one considers that there must be a minimum reaction time necessary in deciding to stop the tape-recorder, and in actually operating the pause button itself. Thus, in order to stop the input at a sentence or clause boundary without inadvertently stopping the tape in the middle of a following word, the decision as to when to stop the tape would have to have been made in advance of that point being reached. Neither subject group showed an appreciable number of such split words. We can thus infer that they were forming hypotheses as to appropriate boundary endings as the speech was being heard, and prior to the arrival of these boundaries themselves.

As we argued when we first obtained these data (Wingfield & Lindfield,

1995), the findings run counter to any notion of a content-free articulatory or phonological store for temporary holding of speech input to allow time for an analysis of linguistic content. The sensitivity of the subjects' input segmentations to linguistic content makes it unlikely that this is so.

The contribution of the elderly subjects' data to this issue is an important one. That is, in spite of the elderly subjects' significantly lower working memory scores, their patterns of segment selection were affected by the same factors as the young adults. Working memory limitations may have constrained the elderly subjects' recall of what they had heard, but their treatment of the speech input as it was being heard was essentially equivalent to that of the young.

A part of the problem in analyzing the role of working memory in language processing lies in the definition of working memory and its components. The limited capacity "central executive" and "computational space" have proven especially difficult to define independent of the tests developed to measure their capacity. In the following section we look more specifically at the working memory subsystems of the "articulatory loop" and the "phonological store". Probably the most striking tests of the role of these components of working memory in language processing comes from the study of neurologically impaired subjects with dramatically limited short-term or working memory spans.

Working Memory and Language Processing: Evidence from Focal Brain Lesions and Neuropathology

More than 30 years ago, neuropsychologists made the striking discovery that subsequent to brain damage, some patients showed a normal digit span but a severe impairment of long-term retention of new information (e.g., patient H.M. studied by Milner, 1966), while other patients show the opposite pattern (e.g., patient K.F. studied by Warrington & Shallice, 1969). These patients were claimed to provide support for the modal model of memory, outlined at the beginning of the chapter, which postulated separate short-term and long-term memory stores. However, the finding that some patients had normal long-term retention despite limited short-term memory spans contradicted the assumption of the modal model that information had to be retained in short-term memory (STM) in order to be entered into long-term memory. This difficulty was accommodated by the working memory model originally postulated by Baddeley (Baddeley & Hitch, 1974) by assuming that serial recall of lists of items, as is required in digit span, is primarily supported by a special buffer, the articulatory loop, and that patients such as K.F. have an impairment in this but not other components of working memory.

Since the discovery of patients such as K.F., numerous additional patients have been identified who have impairments in one or more components of the working memory system. The performance of these patients on a variety of language tasks has provided important data relevant to contemporary models of language processing. In particular, patients with impairments to the articulatory rehearsal and phonological storage buffers of working memory have been studied to provide a window on the question of whether the ability to rehearse and to hold information in a phonological form is necessary for normal language comprehension. Patients who have intact functioning of these buffer systems, but who nonetheless have significantly reduced working memory capacity, have been studied to provide data relevant to the question of the amount of working memory capacity required to perform various language operations, such as structuring a sentence syntactically. The following sections provide an overview of existing data from these and other patients with neurological impairment.

Studies of Patients with Articulatory Rehearsal/Phonological Storage Impairments

In their original formulation, Baddeley and Hitch (1974) claimed that the working memory system is responsible for the processing and storage of information in most cognitive tasks. However, some of the earliest studied cases of patients with STM deficits called into question the role that the articulatory loop and other components of the working memory system play in various aspects of cognition. For example, patient K.F. studied by Warrington and Shallice (1969), showed fairly good language comprehension and general cognitive abilities, despite the fact that he had a STM span of only one item as measured on a digit span test.

However, studies of several additional STM cases in the 1970's and early 1980's led to the claim that there was a connection between reduced phonological storage capacity and some aspects of language processing; in particular, the ability to structure sentences syntactically. For example, Saffran and Martin (1975) reported that the STM patient they had studied had difficulty with more complex syntactic structures on a repetition task. Caramazza, Basili, Koller and Berndt (1981) reported a similar finding for their STM patient using a sentence-picture matching task. (The expression, "STM patient," is a common short-hand for a brain-injured patient with a poor STM span as measured by standard tests such as digit or word spans.)

Subsequent to the original claims by Saffran and Marin (1975), and Caramazza et al.(1981), several researchers used the co-occurrence of deficits in STM with claimed deficits in syntactic parsing to argue for a role of STM in structuring a sentence syntactically. Such co-occurrences of deficits might be compatible with their being related, but they do not necessarily prove that this is so (Caplan, 1987; Bub & Bub, 1988). On the other hand, the absence of parsing deficits in patients with STM or working memory limitations would show that STM is not involved in parsing.

In order to evaluate the claims concerning the relationship between phonological STM and sentence comprehension, we can examine the results of a review of the sentence comprehension abilities of almost 20 published cases of patients with a dramatically limited STM capability (Caplan & Waters, 1990). That review argued that in order to document the existence of a deficit in syntactic parsing, a patient must demonstrate either a complexity effect in syntactic comprehension (i.e., more complex structures must be especially difficult for the patient), or a deficit specific to particular syntactic structures or parsing operations. Furthermore, in order to make the case that the parsing deficit is related to the STM deficit, it should be demonstrated that the parsing deficit is related to the STM demands of the task. Two ways of doing this that have been suggested in the literature are to show that the syntactic comprehension deficit is worse with longer sentences (Saffran, 1985; Baddeley, Vallar & Wilson, 1987), or that the syntactic deficit lessens or disappears under conditions of unlimited viewing (Martin, 1987).

Using these criteria, the Caplan and Waters (1990) review of the neuropsychological literature suggested that significant reductions in STM functions have very limited effects on language processing. There appeared no instances of clear effects of STM limitations on any sort of on-line automatic language processes, even when these processes make use of phonological representations, except in cases in which an STM impairment is itself secondary to a low-level acoustic phonetic processing disturbance. The literature since 1990 also bears out this pattern: although both articulatory rehearsal and phonological storage impairments can affect certain aspects of comprehension, such as second-pass or interpretive operations, storage and rehearsal have not been related to syntactically-based sentence comprehension difficulties.

On the other hand, the Caplan and Waters review also showed that language processing is not entirely normal in STM patients. It was argued that the sentence and discourse comprehension impairments that have been documented in STM cases can all be attributed to an impairment in processes that occur *after* the initial interpretation of the sentence. These include the ability to check semantic readings against the presented sentence, or to operate on selected items (such as proper nouns and possibly nouns in the focus of discourse) in propositional and discourse representations. The STM system appears to be involved in a number of processes that involve checking or manipulation of representations derived by automatic first-pass processing but not on the first-pass processing itself. That is, the data do not support the view that STM is used in first-pass sentence and discourse processing, but rather suggests that STM can be used optionally to review input when such processing fails to produce a coherent propositional or contextual representation.

Dramatic support for this position comes from a study of the sentence comprehension abilities of B.O., a stroke patient with a STM deficit attributable to a combination of a major impairment of articulatory rehearsal processes and a minor impairment of the phonological store (Waters, Caplan, & Hildebrandt, 1991). Patient B.O. had suffered a left anterior cortical-subcortical stroke in the territory of the middle cerebral artery. She had a memory span of only 2 to 3 items when tested both on recall and probe recognition tasks. When tested on the Daneman and Carpenter task she had a working memory span of only one item, despite the fact that she had no difficulty understanding the sentences used in this task when they were presented in isolation. This patient demonstrated excellent comprehension of a wide range of syntactic structures with auditory, written, and speeded written presentations. Moreover, she showed no effect of syntactic structural complexity on comprehension functions.

Figure 3 shows B.O.'s performance on a sentence enactment task in which she was required to use small toys to enact the meaning of eleven different types of sentences ranging from sentences with simple syntactic structures, such as active sentences (e.g., "The bear kissed the donkey."), to sentences with more complex syntactic structures, such as sentences with subject-object relative clauses (e.g., "The bear that the donkey kissed patted the goat."). As can be seen in the figure, B.O.'s performance is virtually indistinguishable from that of age-matched normal control subjects with no history of brain-damage, and substantially better than a group of patients who were aphasic subsequent to a left hemisphere stroke. (The eleven sentence types are arranged along the abscissa in the empirical order of difficulty as observed for the aphasic subjects.)

B.O.'s performance is incompatible with a theory that maintains that items are held in phonological form in phrase markers, because performance should be poor if this function is required for all syntactic comprehension. It is also incompatible with a variant of this theory which holds that lexical items are held in phrase markers in phonological form when the demands of syntactic processing increase. If this were the case it would lead to complexity effects in syntactic comprehension tasks, not seen in B.O. In contrast, Waters et al. (1991) argued that these preserved abilities in patient B.O. indicate that the STM system was not needed for the assignment of syntactic structure and its utilization to establish aspects of propositional semantics (thematic roles and co-indexation of noun phrases).

It was the case that B.O. had difficulty understanding sentences that contained three or four noun phrases, and that she made errors referable to the maintenance of particular items in propositional memory systems. These features of her performance were interpreted as being consistent with the view that the role of articulatory rehearsal mechanisms in sentence comprehension involves maintenance of items in an interpreted (semantic) structure after initial syntactic processing has been conducted.

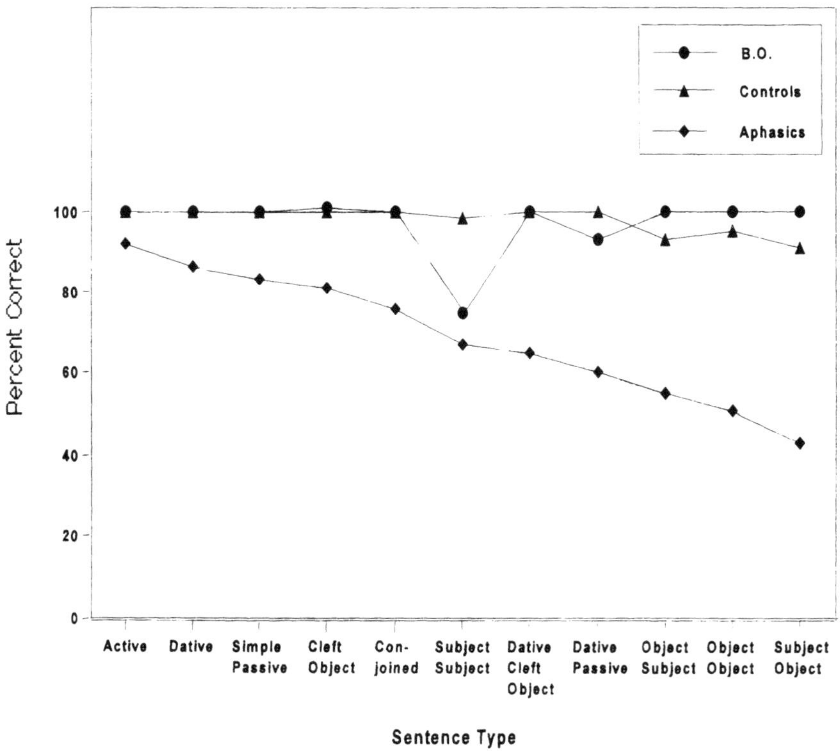

Figure 3. Performance on a sentence enactment test for eleven types of sentences for patient B.O., for a group of age-matched control subjects with no history of brain damage, and for a group of left hemisphere lesion aphasic patients.

In contrast to first-pass language comprehension processes, the STM system would seem to be well suited to aid in second-pass review of linguistic stimuli. However, data from another patient, E.A., suggest that STM may not even necessarily play a role in second-pass or review functions. Martin (1990) tested E.A.'s ability to understand sentences which contained lexical garden paths. In lexical garden path sentences, the preceding context biases the interpretation of a lexically ambiguous word but later context indicates that the other meaning of the word is the appropriate one (e.g., "The lawyer decided to take the case because it was large enough to hold all of his papers."). E.A. performed in the normal range on these sentences, even though her STM span was very limited. This would seem to suggest that a phonological record is not needed for reinterpretation.

E.A. was not tested on sentences that contained syntactic garden paths, and so it might be possible that phonological STM may play a role in the second-pass analysis of these sentences. However, additional data from patient B.O. do not support this conclusion (Waters & Caplan, 1993). In this study, B.O. was tested for comprehension of sentences with syntactic garden paths. In a garden path sentence such as "The boat floated down the river sank," an initial syntactic interpretation is found to be incompatible with a later-arising part of the sentence. Readers (and listeners) generally assign *the boat* as the subject of *floated* in this sentence, and they have considerable difficulty revising this assignment in favor of one in which *the boat* is the subject of *sank*, and *floated down the river* is a reduced relative clause. In order to incorporate all the elements of the sentence and arrive at its meaning, the faulty first interpretation must be revised. According to our criteria, being "garden-pathed" (i.e., misanalyzing sentences such as this one) reflects the operation of first-pass processing of syntax, prosody, and lexical meaning. Recovery from a garden-path sentence is a second-pass process that involves reconsideration of the structures already assigned.

In this study, B.O. and age-matched non-brain injured control subjects were tested in their ability to comprehend three different types of syntactic structures which have been shown in a previous study to result in garden path effects (Waters & Caplan, 1996a). Subjects' comprehension of these sentences was tested with an acceptability judgment task both when the sentences were presented auditorily and in print. With written presentation the physical input remains present and can be reviewed, but with a spoken presentation such input cannot be reviewed in physical form. With speech any look-back requires a memory system. Any difference in performance in these two conditions must thus reflect some feature of the modality of presentation and the obvious candidate for this feature is the impersistence of the acoustic record and the consequent inability to maintain a phonological representation. Because of B.O.'s STM impairment, if STM is used to review input when first-pass processing fails, then B.O. should have extreme difficulty in recovering from an initial misinterpretation of a garden path sentence, particularly with auditory presentation.

If B.O. were to have difficulty with garden path structures, this difficulty could also result from difficulty in assigning the correct structure itself. For instance, in a sentence like "The boat floated down the river sank", the syntactic structure associated with the reduced relative clause interpretation of *floated down the river* is more complex in terms of number of syntactic categories, and their pattern of attachment, than is associated with the interpretation of this structure as a main clause. Alternatively, this difficulty could result from the need to revise the incorrectly constructed preferred structure.

In an effort to determine whether any difficulty that B.O. might have with garden path structures was associated with the assignment of the correct structure itself, or with the need to revise the incorrectly constructed preferred structure, her performance on garden path sentences was compared to performance on two different types of non-garden path sentences. In one type of non-garden path sentence (non-garden path A) syntactic structure was indicated by a syntactic cue in the form of an extra word or words that served as an overt marker that only one reading was possible and therefore prevented the subject from "being led down the garden path" (e.g., "The boat that was floated down the river sank"). The second type of non-garden path sentences (non-garden path B) had identical structures to the garden path sentences, with syntactic structure indicated by the form of the verb in these sentences exactly as it was in the garden path sentences (e.g., "The plane flown across the mountain crashed.").

If B.O. had difficulty with garden path sentences because of difficulty in assigning the correct structure itself, then she should have difficulty not only with garden path sentences but also with non-garden path B type sentences. On the other hand, if she had difficulty with these sentences because of an impairment in revising an initially constructed syntactic representation, then this should be evident in the comparison with both types of non-garden path sentences.

The sentence structures used in this experiment did produce reliable garden path effects in age- and education-matched normal control subjects. Garden path effects for all three structures were evident for these subjects in the time taken to make a judgment about the sentence and in the error data for one of the three types of sentences (those with embedded clauses). Moreover, the magnitude of the garden path effects seen in the control subjects in the reaction time data was much greater in the auditory than in the visual presentation condition. The proportional increase in reaction times on garden path compared to non-garden path sentences for the control subjects in the auditory modality was 1.07, but only .37 with visual presentation. This finding is consistent with the data from another study that demonstrated larger garden path effects with rapid serial visual presentation than with whole sentence presentation (Waters & Caplan, 1996a). Both experiments provide support for the idea that the increased difficulty of garden path structures stems from their increased memory load. In addition, in this study as in the previous one, garden path effects were found in relation to both types of non-garden path sentences tested, suggesting that the difficulty with these structures stems from the need to revise an initially constructed representation, rather than simply from a difficulty in assigning the correct structure.

Most importantly, the data from this study showed that B.O. had no difficulty recovering from garden paths, and in fact showed somewhat less of a garden path effect than did control subjects. Figure 4 shows the increase in percent errors for auditory and visual presentations for B.O. and the control subjects. As can be seen in figure 4, in the auditory modality, B.O. showed 16.6% more errors on garden path sentences than on non-garden path sentences, while the difference for control subjects was 25.8%. With visual presentation the magnitude of the garden path effect was 12% for B.O. and 20% for the control subjects. These garden path effects were seen in relation to both non-garden path A and non-garden path B control sentences, thus suggesting that, as with the control subjects, B.O.'s difficulty with these structures stems from difficulty in revising an initially constructed representation. (B.O. showed very little in the way of a garden path effect on the reaction time measures. Her proportional increase in reaction time on garden path compared to non-garden path sentences was .19 in the auditory modality and .03 with visual presentation, compared to proportional increases of 1.07 and .37 for the control subjects.)

These data, along with the data from patient E.A. (Martin, 1990) on sentences containing lexical garden paths, seriously call into question the notion that the articulatory rehearsal and phonological storage components of STM play a necessary role in second-pass language comprehension processes.

Studies of Patients with Limitations in the Central Executive

Despite the neuropsychological data outlined above, Just, Carpenter, and their colleagues have argued that individual differences in working memory capacity can account for individual differences in first-pass sentence comprehension, as well as individual differences in second-pass processes, such as the recovery from garden paths (Just & Carpenter, 1992; King & Just, 1991; McDonald, Just, & Carpenter, 1992). They have claimed that neuropsychological data from patients such as those described above are not relevant to their theory, since these patients had their impairments in peripheral components of working memory (i.e., articulatory rehearsal and phonological storage buffers) (Just & Carpenter, 1992). Rather, they claim that it is limitations in verbal working memory "capacity," or "computational space", that leads to impairments in language processing. This view leads to the claim that patients who have limitations in the central executive component of working memory should have substantial language impairments. We looked at this question previously with normal elderly subjects who show significant deficits in working memory span scores, but whose deficits are relatively small in an absolute sense. It might be argued that working memory capacity would appear to play a greater role in language processing, however, if one were to test neurologically compromised patients with much lower scores on the Daneman and Carpenter working memory span measure.

One group of patients who have intact functioning of the articulatory rehearsal and phonological storage components of working memory, but impairments on tasks that require central executive functions, are patients with Dementia of the Alzheimer's type (DAT) (Baddeley, Bressi, Della Sala, Logie & Spinnler, 1991; Morris, 1984; 1986, 1987; Morris & Baddeley, 1988; Waters, Rochon, & Caplan, in press). All the DAT patients we have tested have had Daneman and Carpenter spans of one or less even when the stimulus sentences were ones that they had no difficulty in understanding when presented in isolation. Thus, the working memories of these patients are far more reduced than those of normal subjects, such as the elderly subjects described at the beginning of the chapter.

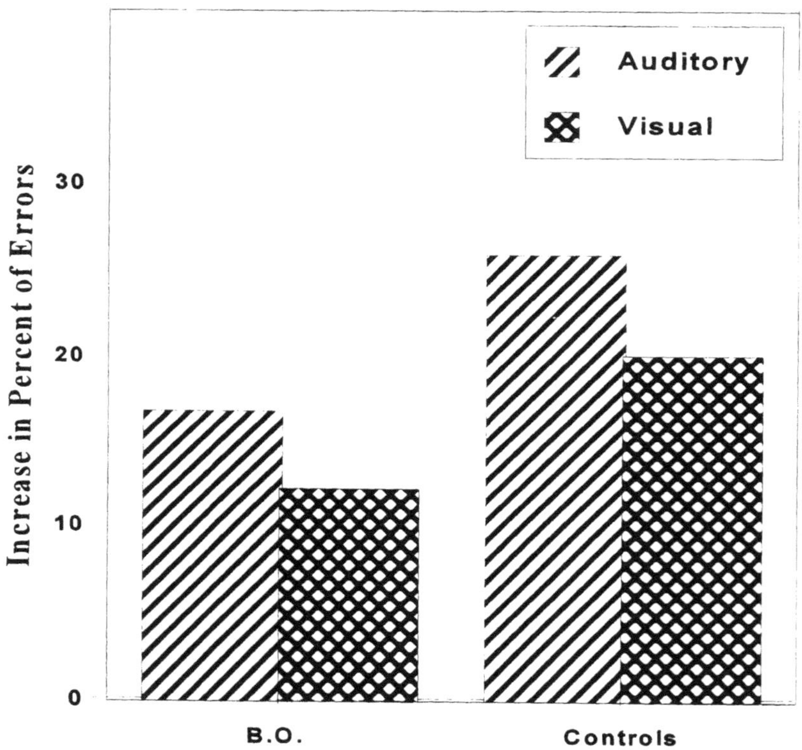

Figure 4. Increase in percentage of errors on garden path sentences compared to non-garden path sentences for patient B.O. and for a group of age-matched controls with no history of brain damage. Data are shown for spoken (auditory presentation) and written (visual presentation) sentences.

Using the logic previously outlined, if the Just and Carpenter theory is correct, DAT patients should have particular difficulty with syntactically more complex sentences. That is, in studies manipulating subject group and syntactic complexity, there should be interactions between group and complexity. Patients with reduced working memory capacity should also have particular difficulty when they are required to perform difficult language comprehension tasks under conditions that further reduce the limited capacity of the central executive (e.g., understanding sentences while holding a digit load in memory or performing a demanding concurrent verbal task). Thus, in dual-task studies, there should be interactions between subject group, syntactic complexity, and load. However, consistent with the data on aging outlined previously, our work with patients with DAT has also failed to consistently produce these results.

Rochon, Waters and Caplan (1994) tested DAT patients and age- and education-matched normal controls for their ability to comprehend nine different syntactic structures using a sentence-picture matching test. The patients were in the early stages of the disease and all were mild to moderately demented. The stimulus materials were designed to contrast sentences that were matched for length and other relevant variables but that differed in syntactic complexity, and sentences that were matched for syntactic complexity but differed in terms of number of propositions. Rochon et al's results showed an effect of Group, with DAT patients performing more poorly than controls, and a Group by Sentence-Type interaction. Analysis of this interaction showed that DAT patients did not perform more poorly than the control subjects on the syntactically more complex sentences, but rather that their performance was poorer than the controls on sentences with two propositions. This pattern of an absence of an effect of syntactic complexity for DAT patients on sentence-picture matching has been replicated in several studies, including those using speeded acceptability judgment tasks (Waters, Rochon & Caplan, 1995; Waters, Rochon & Caplan, in press; Rochon & Saffran, 1995).

Although we have consistently failed to find effects of syntactic complexity in DAT patients, we have, as indicated above, found these patients to be more affected than controls by the number of propositions in a sentence. (We have also found effects of propositional density in some studies for very old subjects over age 80.)

We have argued that the effect of number of propositions arises after the stage of sentence interpretation and reflects an impairment that subjects have with the post-interpretive aspects of language processing. We have found support for this claim in a study with AD patients that manipulated the post-interpretive demands of the sentence comprehension task by manipulating the number of pictures in the array from which subjects must choose on a sentence picture matching task (1 vs. 2 vs. 3 pictures) (Waters, Rochon & Caplan, in press). This study also demonstrated an effect of number of propositions, but not of syntactic complexity, with the effect of the number of propositions increasing proportionally in relation to the number of pictures in the array. This suggests that the effect arises when the subject must hold onto the propositional content of the sentence in order to choose among the alternative pictures.

Patients with Parkinson's Disease (PD) also have impairments in executive functions (Brown & Marsden, 1988; 1991; Lees & Smith 1983; Taylor, Saint-Cyr & Lang, 1987). We tested 17 non-demented PD patients and age- and education-matched elderly controls on a battery of tasks that tapped components of the short-term memory system (articulatory rehearsal and phonological storage), verbal working memory capacity (reading span, self-ordered and externally-ordered number generation), and various aspects of executive functions (Stroop color-word interference, Wisconsin Card Sorting, verbal fluency). Subjects were then tested for the comprehension of sentences differing in syntactic complexity and number of propositions, using a sentence-picture matching task.

Verbal working memory spans were significantly reduced in PD patients compared to controls, but rehearsal and storage functions were normal in span tasks in these patients. The performance of PD patients differed from that of controls on the sentence comprehension task, but once again only on sentences that contained more propositions. These data suggest that, like DAT patients, PD patients do not have impairments in structuring sentences syntactically.

We have also found that the ability of DAT and PD patients to structure sentences syntactically is not affected any more than that of normals under concurrent memory load conditions. In one study, DAT patients performed the sentence-picture matching task outlined above with a no-interference condition, and while retaining a concurrent memory load that was equivalent to their span or one less (Waters et al, 1995). Overall performance was poorer with the digit load, but comparisons of length-matched sentences showed that the concurrent memory load exacerbated the effect of number of propositions, but not the effect of syntactic complexity, in the patient group. We have repeated this study with the PD group described above. As with the DAT patients, the concurrent memory load did not exacerbate the effect of syntactic complexity in the PD group. Once again, these findings are consistent with those in the normal elderly.

The studies just described used untimed accuracy measures of sentence comprehension. They are not subject to the criticism that effects of syntactic structure were missed because of ceiling effects, because some comparisons of sentences that differed in syntactic complexity were made on pairs of sentences on which performance was below ceiling. Nevertheless, latency measures of on-line processing may be more sensitive than an accuracy index. MacDonald and her colleagues used a cross-modal naming task to study on-line processing in DAT patients. They found that DAT patients were as sensitive as age matched controls to grammatical violations and as able as age matched controls to use frequency information and semantic and syntactic contexts to resolve syntactic ambiguities (Lalami et al., 1996; Stevens, Kempler, Andersen, & MacDonald, 1996). The entire pattern of performances suggests that DAT patients have relatively preserved abilities to structure sentences syntactically in sentence interpretation.

Waters and Caplan (1997) report results that combined the use of timed measures with dual task cond itions to examine the ability of patients with DAT to make speeded acceptability judgments to auditorily presented sentences that varied in their syntactic complexity under no interference and under two concurrent tracking conditions. In a dot tracking condition, subjects were required to press the button on a mouse that corresponded to the location of a dot that appeared on the computer screen (left, middle, or right). In a digit tracking condition, a continuous random sequence of the digits "1", "2", and "3" was presented in the center of the computer screen and subjects indicated which digit had been presented by pushing one of three switches on the mouse. DAT and control subjects' error rates were equated on each of the secondary tasks by varying the duration of the dot and digit stimuli and the interval between these stimuli.

The DAT patients showed an effect of syntactic complexity in the reaction time and accuracy measures that did not increase under the tracking conditions. The DAT patients also showed an effect of dual-task condition, but this was not greater for the more syntactically complex sentences. Both patients and controls showed an effect of syntactic structure in the secondary task performance measures, but this effect was not larger for the patients. This experiment thus found that a concurrent task failed to affect processing of syntactically complex sentences more than syntactically simple sentences under very demanding concurrent task conditions in low-capacity subjects, even when sensitive timed measures of syntactic processing efficiency were employed.

These experiments with DAT and PD thus indicate that patients with severely reduced working memory capacity can retain extremely good syntactic processing capability in sentence comprehension. We note, however, that some authors have asserted that sentence comprehension is impaired in patients with DAT (Tomoeda, Bayles, Boone, Kaszniak, & Slauson, 1990; Kontiola, Laaksonen, Sulkava, & Erkinjuntti, 1990; Emery, 1985) and PD (Grossman et al., 1991; Grossman, Carvell, Stern, Gollomp, & Hurtig,1992; Lieberman, Friedman, & Friedman, 1990; Natsopoulos et al., 1991). Examination of these studies, however, suggests that the DAT patients may have performed poorly because of impairments they have with aspects of post-interpretive processing, such as deficiencies in their ability to access semantic knowledge, to enact responses, and to accomplish other post-interpretive requirements of many of these tasks (see Rochon et al., 1994, for a discussion). For instance, real world knowledge is necessary to understand and to respond to questions that are posed in some comprehension tasks (Emery, 1985, 1986) and DAT patients may have done poorly in these tasks because of impairments affecting use of semantic memory even if they understood the stimulus sentences.

Enactment is a response requirement of many of the tasks used (e.g., the Token Test: DeRenzi & Vignolo, 1962), and it requires visuospatial, perceptual and practical abilities that are often abnormal in DAT (Christenson, 1974). Memory abilities are also required in many of the tasks used in existing studies (Hart, 1988). The studies that show little or no sentence comprehension impairments in DAT have tended to use tasks with simpler demands, such as sentence-picture matching (Rochon et al., 1994; Schwartz, Marin & Saffran 1979; Sherman, Schweickert, Growdon, & Corkin, 1988; Smith, 1989; although see Grober & Bang, 1995). The same observations hold regarding studies in which sentence comprehension impairments have been found in PD patients (Grossman et al., 1991, 1992; Lieberman et al., 1990; Natsopoulos et al., 1991). For instance, Natsopoulos et al. (1991) had PD patients match a sentence to one of six pictures. Poor performance on these tasks could therefore reflect problems in handling these task demands.

We conclude this section with a brief note on sentence production in patients with DAT. Although not directly concerned with sentence comprehension, the results of several studies of this function are suggestively similar to those we have reviewed in them domain of comprehension.

Fluent syntactically well-formed speech typically characterizes the conversational output of patients with DAT and has been found in DAT patients in picture description (Hier, Hagenlocker & Spindlier, 1985; Kemper, Anagnopoulos, Lyons & Heberlein, 1994) and sentence construction tasks (Schwartz et al., 1979). This has suggested to many researchers that syntactic abilities are preserved in these patients, at least in the early stages in the illness (Bayles, 1982; Blanken, Dittmann, Haas, & Wallesch, 1987; Hier et al., 1985; Illes, 1989; Irigaray, 1973; Kempler, Curtiss, & Jackson, 1987; Kirschner, 1982; Schwartz et al., 1979). DAT patients have also been found to correct errors of syntax and phonology, but not semantic errors, in anomalous sentences (Bayles, 1982), and to make better use of syntactic than semantic cues in disambiguating spoken homophones and while writing them to dictation (Kempler et al., 1987; Schwartz et al, 1979).

While DAT patients have been shown to produce both oral and written language that is syntactically well structured, the language production of these patients does differ from that of age-matched controls in other important respects. In one study, over 350 DAT patients were asked to write a single sentence and these productions were scored for their length in words and clauses, as well as for the number of propositions produced (Kemper et al., 1993). The sentences were also scored for six categories of grammatic constituents including pronouns, main verbs, secondary verbs, negatives, conjunctions, and questions. Results showed that 89% of the variance in the clinical rating of dementia severity could be accounted for by sentence length in clauses and propositional content. This suggests that the ability to produce propositions in written form is reduced as the severity of dementia increases.

Estimates of these linguistic abilities in early adult life appear to be powerful predictors of cognitive function and Alzheimer's disease in later life. In a longitudinal study, Snowdon et al. (1996) analyzed autobiographies written by 93 nuns when they entered a convent and evaluated the cognitive performances of these women when they were between 75 and 95 years of age (a span of some 58 years). Alzheimer's disease was assessed neuropathologically in a sample of 25 participants who died.

This study showed a stronger and more consistent association between cognitive function later in life and the density of propositions in these early narratives than between cognitive functions and the grammatical complexity of the narratives. Strikingly, low idea density was present in the autobiographies of 90% of women with neuropathologically proven Alzheimer's disease but only in 13% of those without Alzheimer's disease. Further studies have shown that measures of idea density and grammatical complexity are highly stable over the life span (r=.62 to .74) (Kemper, Snowdon & Greiner, 1996). The authors hypothesize that low linguistic ability early in life may be an early expression of Alzheimer's disease neuropathology.

From our point of view, these results suggest a finer distinction. The greater relationship between measures of propositional density and DAT than between measures of grammatical well-formedness and DAT is consistent with the view that these patients are impaired in formulating concepts but are able to use the forms of language to convey the concepts that they do activate. This is a division of function related to language production that corresponds to the one we described between post-interpretive and interpretive aspects of the comprehension process.

Studies of patients with reduced resources for syntactic processing

We may also approach the question of the relationship between working memory capacity and syntactic processing in sentence comprehension from another angle. This approach is to examine the effect of a concurrent memory load on syntactic comprehension in patients in whom there is evidence for a reduction in the resources available for syntactic processing in sentence comprehension.

Patients with aphasia provide such cases. Research into the nature of the sentence comprehension impairments seen in patients who are aphasic subsequent to a left hemisphere stroke has shown that many such patients have disturbances affecting their ability to use syntactic form to determine the meaning of a sentence (Caplan, Baker & Dehaut, 1985; Caplan, Hildebrandt & Makris, 1996; see Berndt et al, 1996, for review). Several aspects of the performance of these patients suggests that one reason for this impairment is a reduction in the processing resources that a patient can apply to this task.

One piece of evidence that favors this resource-reduction view is that factor analyses have shown that a single factor on which all sentence types load accounts for about two-thirds of the variance in many syntactic comprehension tasks in aphasic groups (Caplan et al, 1985, 1996). Second, cluster analyses show that patients tend to be grouped according to their overall level of performance in these tasks, with performance in more impaired clusters showing greater effects of syntactic complexity (Caplan et al, 1985; Caplan & Waters, in press). Finally, some patients have been able to interpret sentences when either of two syntactic features was present, but not when both were found in a sentence (Hildebrandt, Caplan & Evans, 1987). These patterns of performance are consistent with the hypothesis that the problem in syntactic processing in sentence comprehension that is seen in many aphasic patients results in part from reductions in their ability to allocate processing resources to the syntactic comprehension task.

Miyake, Carpenter and Just (1995) see these resource limitations in terms of a general verbal working memory resource pool. For example, they have argued that the processing resource reduction seen in aphasic patients is very similar to that of normal subjects who have reduced working memory capacity for language as measured by the Daneman and Carpenter task. In fact, they have argued that they have been able to simulate the pattern of performance seen on sentence comprehension tasks in aphasic patients, by testing normal college students under concurrent digit load conditions. However, it has been demonstrated that the pattern of performance seen in the college students tested by Miyake et al. is different from that seen in aphasic patients in important respects and does not provide a very good simulation of aphasic performance (Caplan & Waters, 1995). Most importantly, aphasic patients show large effects of syntactic complexity, as well as effects of number of propositions on performance. Re-analysis of the data from Miyake et al. reveals that the college students tested in that study showed effects of number of propositions but not of syntactic complexity. Given that difficulty in interpreting complex syntactic structures is one of the hallmarks of aphasic performance, this is a very important difference. We would suggest, then, that the impairment is in a syntax-specific memory system, and not in a general verbal resource pool (cf., Waters & Caplan, 1996c).

Caplan and Waters (1996) provide a more direct test of Miyake et al.'s theory of aphasic performance by testing the sentence comprehension abilities of aphasic patients under concurrent digit load conditions. If the sentence comprehension impairment seen in aphasic patients stems at least in part from a reduction in the amount of working memory capacity that can be devoted to language comprehension, then syntactic complexity effects should be increased in aphasic patients under a concurrent verbal memory (digit) load condition (i.e., there should be Complexity by Load interactions). On the other hand, if these patients have a reduction in a pool of resources that is separate from that used in other verbally-mediated tasks, such as digit load, then these interactions should not arise. The test, then, is to examine the effect of a concurrent digit load on the sentence comprehension performance of aphasic patients (Caplan & Waters, 1996).

Over 200 aphasic patients were screened to ensure (a) that only patients who showed effects of syntactic complexity on a sentence-picture matching task were tested, (b) that their performance was below ceiling and above chance on that task, and (c) that their abilities to repeat single words permitted them to be tested on a digit span task. Ten patients who met these criteria were selected and they were then tested on a sentence-picture matching task in no-interference and concurrent load conditions.

Although the aphasic patients showed large effects of syntactic complexity when tested on the sentence picture matching test without a concurrent load, these effects were not exacerbated by the addition of a memory load. Their performance on the concurrent memory task was poorer with larger digit loads, but the effect of syntactic complexity was not amplified. In the digit recall data, the patients recalled fewer digits with an increased number of propositions but there was no effect of syntactic complexity. These results provide striking evidence for the separation of the resources used in syntactic processing in sentence comprehension and those required for span tasks.

Conclusions

The studies on brain injured patients we have described here provide important evidence concerning the role of phonological short-term memory and working memory in language processing. Patients with several etiologies of central nervous system disease who have reduced verbal working memory (i.e., DAT and PD patients) have been shown to do well on tests of syntactic comprehension. Where effects of syntactic complexity arise in these groups, the pattern of these effects are comparable to those found in normal subjects. Furthermore, patients who do have impairments in syntactic comprehension (i.e., aphasic patients) do not show increased affects of syntactic complexity under concurrent memory load conditions.

In the studies we cited of healthy elderly subjects with reduced working memory spans, we saw that with language tasks one does not invariably see differential impairment of their performance relative to the young subjects when the complexity of the language materials is increased. Nor does one see age differences in the language tasks magnified by the additional requirements of dual-task studies. Similarly, in our studies of DAT and PD patients involving concurrent verbal loads, we saw that these loads do not disproportionally affect comprehension of syntactically complex sentences for these subjects. In both cases, these results were based on subjects' performance on demanding concurrent tasks, and in both cases the measures included reaction times as well as accuracy. They have documented a domain of retained functional capacity in the midst of demonstrated cognitive and executive limitations. Especially striking are the results for the aphasic patients where there appears to be a reduction in processing resources used for syntactic comprehension, and yet one does not find that a concurrent verbal memory load exacerbates the effect of syntactic complexity.

All of these results are consistent with the view that the resources that are used in language comprehension are not reduced in subjects with reduced verbal working memory capacity. That is, the memory systems that carry language processing appear not to be represented by traditional memory span tasks. As we have shown, even in the case of immediate recall of natural language, correlations between performance and working memory scores are often absent or of a very modest size.

There are, of course, a variety of working memory measures in the literature designed to tap operational capacity (Salthouse, 1988, 1990). The majority of these tasks, however, are focused less on language or language-related activity than the Daneman and Carpenter task. It is thus especially striking that the Daneman and Carpenter span task has shown such variable success in predicting language processing and even language recall in elderly and neurologically impaired individuals.

As one thinks about the operations that are required in the measurements of working memory that we have described, it may not be surprising that these measures are not strong predictors of language processing performance. In ordinary language comprehension, whatever storage of verbal material is occurring, it is usually relevant to ongoing computations. By contrast, in the Daneman and Carpenter task the concurrent memory load that is imposed (i.e., remembering the sentence-final words of the prior sentences in the set) is unrelated to the computations that the sentence processing task requires.

It is the case that a meta-analysis of studies using the Daneman and Carpenter span test does show numerous cases where span scores predict performance on a range of language comprehension and language memory experiments (Daneman & Merikle, 1996). A possible solution to this paradox may lie in the complex nature of the measurement task itself. Most notable is the opportunity for a trade-off on the part of the subject between sentence-final word recall versus processing efficiency on the sentence comprehension portion of the task. Because of this trade-off possibility, perhaps what is needed is a test that offers indices that include both the processing component and the memory component of the task. A preliminary attempt to devise such a metric has suggested that this may be a fruitful approach (Waters & Caplan, 1996b). Indeed, susceptibility to individual differences in strategy use, and session-to-session variability, has been shown to occur even in phonological similarity and word-length effects in putative measures of the phonological and articulatory store (Logie, Della Sala, Laiacona, Chalmers, & Wynn, 1996).

It is important to note that we do not suggest that language processing can be carried out without the support of briefly sustained traces of the sensory input and the products of ongoing syntactic and semantic computations. We see considerable virtue to the short-term memory model proposed by Potter (1993; Potter & Lombardi 1991) that includes both a verbatim trace and a semantic abstraction that are laid down in parallel as speech input arrives at the senses. Perhaps these two types of traces can be flexibly employed, such that an individual can depend more on one or the other given the task demands and complexity of the processing operations. In the domain of aging, for example, there may be a default system preference for an abstract representation. In such cases, infrequent and unfamiliar instances of language processing that place heavy demands on the phonological store, such as comprehension or repetition of left-branching sentences, would show the measurable age differences typically found (Norman et al., 1991). The key here is that of a flexible system that attempts to maximize performance by relying to a relatively greater or lesser extent on memory processes most appropriate to task requirements and subject capabilities. It is possible that such a model may account for many of the apparent paradoxes in data and theory we have outlined here.

Our studies of language processing in normal aging and in brain-injured patients with significantly compromised memory systems are important for understanding the nature of the cognitive deficits seen in these populations. No less important, however, they supply data that seriously constrain models of both the structure of the working memory system, and its role in language processing.

ACKNOWLEDGMENTS

The authors' research is supported by NIH Grants AG04517 (A.W.), AG09661 (G.S.W.) and AG13614 (P.A.T.) from the National Institute on Aging. We also acknowledge support from Grant No. MA9671 from the Medical Research Council of Canada (G.S.L.). The work on brain damaged patients was carried out in collaboration with David Caplan, M.D., Ph.D. We thank Christine Koh for valuable help throughout the preparation of this manuscript, and Kristen Prentice for a careful reading of an earlier draft. Finally, we gratefully acknowledge support from the W.M. Keck Foundation.

References

Abney, S.P., & Johnson, M. (1991). Memory requirements and local ambiguities of parsing strategies. *Journal of Psycholinguistic Research, 20,* 233-250.

Aquino, M.R. (1969). The validity of the Miller-Coleman readability scale. *Reading Research Quarterly, 4,* 332-357.

Atkinson, R.C., & Shiffrin, R.M. (1968). Human memory: A proposed system and its control processes. In K.W. Spence & J.T. Spence (Eds.), *The psychology of learning and motivation: Advances in research and theory* (Vol. 2, pp. 89-195). New York: Academic Press.

Baddeley, A.D. (1981). The concept of working memory: A view of its current state and probable future developments. *Cognition, 10,* 17-27.

Baddeley, A.D. (1986). *Working memory.* Oxford, UK: Oxford University Press.

Baddeley, A. D., Bressi, S., Della Sala, S., Logie, R., & Spinnler, H. (1991). The decline of working memory in Alzheimer's disease. *Brain, 114,* 2521-2542.

Baddeley, A.D., & Dale, H.C.A. (1966). The effect of semantic similarity on retroactive interference in long and short-term memory. *Journal of Verbal Learning and Verbal Behavior, 5,* 417-420.

Baddeley, A. D., & Hitch, G. J. (1974). Working memory. In G.H. Bower (Ed.), *The Psychology of Learning and Motivation* (Vol. 8) . New York: Academic Press.

Baddeley, A.D., Vallar, G., & Wilson, B. (1987). Comprehension and the articulatory loop: Some neuropsychological evidence. In M. Coltheart (Ed.), *Attention and Performance XII* (pp. 509-529). London: Erlbaum.

Barr, R.A., & Giambra, L.M. (1990). Age-related decrement in auditory selective attention. *Psychology and Aging, 3,* 597-599.

Bayles, K. A. (1982). Language function in senile dementia. *Brain and Language, 16*, 265-280.

Berndt, R., Mitchum, C. & Haendigest, A. (1996). Comprehension of reversible sentences in "agrammatism": a meta-analysis. Cognition, 58, 289-308.

Blanken, G., Dittmar, J., Haas, J. C., & Wallesch, C. W. (1987). Spontaneous speech in senile dementia and aphasia: Implications for a neurolinguistic model of language production. *Cognition, 27*, 247-274.

Broadbent, D.E. (1971). *Decision and stress*. New York: Academic Press.

Brown, J. (1958). Some tests of the decay theory of immediate memory. *Quarterly Journal of Experimental Psychology, 10*, 12-21.

Brown, R. G., & Marsden, C. D. (1988). Internal versus external cues and the control of attention in Parkinson's disease. *Brain*, 111, 323-345.

Brown, R. G., & Marsden, C. D. (1991). Dual task performance and processing resources in normal subjects and patients with Parkinson's disease. *Brain*, 114, 215-231.

Bub, J. & Bub, D. (1988). On the methodology of single case studies. *Cognitive Neuropsychology, 5*, 562-582.

Caplan D. (1987): *Neurolinguistics and Linguistic Aphasiology: An Introduction*, Cambridge University Press: Cambridge, U.K.

Caplan, D., & Waters, G. S. (1990). Short-term memory and language comprehension: A critical review of the neuropsychological literature. In G. Vallar, & T. Shallice (Ed.), *Neuropsychological Impairments of Short-Term Memory* (pp. 337-389). Cambridge: Cambridge University Press.

Caplan, D., & Waters, G. (1995). Aphasic disturbances of syntactic comprehension and working memory capacity. *Cognitive Neuropsychology, 12*, 637-649.

Caplan, D., & Waters, G. (1996). Syntactic processing in sentence comprehension under dual-task conditions in aphasic patients. *Language and Cognitive Processes, 11*, 525-551.

Caplan, D., & Waters, G. S. (in press). Determinants of Sentence Comprehension in Aphasic Patients in Sentence-Picture Matching Tasks. *Journal of Speech and Hearing Research.*

Caplan, D., Baker, C., & Dehaut, F. (1985). Syntactic determinants of sentence comprehension in aphasia. *Cognition, 21*, 117-175.

Caplan, D., Hildebrandt, N., & Makris, N. (1996). Location of lesions in stroke patients with deficits in syntactic processing in sentence comprehension. *Brain, 119*, 933-949.

Carpenter, P. A., Miyake, A., & Just, M. A. (1994). Working memory constraints in comprehension: Evidence from individual differences, aphasia, and aging. In M. A. Gernsbacher (Eds.), *Handbook of Psycholinguistics* (pp.1075-1122) . New York: Academic Press.

Caramazza, A., Basili, Koller, & Berndt, R. (1981). An investigation of repetition and language processing in a case of conduction aphasia. *Brain & Language, 14*, 235-271.

Cerella, J. (1990). Aging and information processing rate. In J.E. Birren & K.W. Schaie (Eds.), *Handbook of the psychology of aging* (3rd ed., pp. 201-221). San Diego, CA: Academic Press.

Christensen, A.L. (1974). *Luria's neuropsychological investigation: Text.* Copenhagen: Munksgaard.

Cohen, G. (1981). Inferential reasoning in old age. *Cognition, 9*, 59-72.

Cohen, G., & Faulkner, D. (1981). Memory for discourse in old age. *Discourse Processes, 4,* 253-265.

Cohen, G., & Faulkner, D. (1983). Word recognition: Age differences in contextual facilitation effects. *British Journal of Psychology, 74,* 239-251.

Cole, R.A., & Jakimik, J. (1980). A model of speech perception. In R.A. Cole (Ed.), *Perception and production of fluent speech* (pp. 133-163). Hillsdale, NJ: Erlbaum.

Cole, R.A., & Scott, B. (1974). Toward a theory of speech perception. *Psychological Review, 81*, 348-374.

Connelly, S.L., Hasher, L., & Zacks, R.T. (1991). Age and reading: The impact of distraction. *Psychology and Aging, 4,* 533-541.

Connine, C.M., Blasko, D.G., & Hall, M. (1991). Effects of subsequent sentence context in auditory word recognition: Temporal and linguistic constraints. *Journal of Memory and Language, 30*, 234-250.

Conrad, R. (1963). Acoustic confusions and memory span for words. *Nature, 197*, 1029-1030.

Craik, F.I.M. (1977). Age differences in human memory. In J.E. Birren & K.W. Schaie (Eds.), *Handbook of the psychology of aging* (pp. 384-420). New York: Van Nostrand Reinhold.

Craik, F.I.M., & McDowd, J.M. (1987). Age differences in recall and recognition. *Journal of Experimental Psychology, 13,* 474-479.

Daneman, M., & Carpenter, P.A. (1980). Individual differences in working memory and reading. *Journal of Verbal Learning and Verbal Behavior, 19*, 450-466.

Daneman, M., & Merikle, P. M. (1996). Working memory and language comprehension: A meta-analysis. *Psychonomic Bulletin and Review, 3*: 422-433.

Daneman, M., & Tardif, T. (1987). Working memory and reading skill re-examined. In M. Coltheart (Ed.), *Attention and performance XII: The psychology of reading* (pp. 491-508). London: Erlbaum.

DeRenzi, E., Vignolo, L.A. (1962). The Token Test: A sensitive test to detect receptive disturbances in aphasics. *Brain*, *85*, 665-678.

Dobbs, A. R., & Rule, B. G. (1989). Adult age differences in working memory. *Psychology and Aging, 4, 500-503.*

Emery, O. B. (1985). Language and aging. *Experimental Aging Research (Monograph), 11*, 3-60.

Emery, O. B. (1986). Linguistic decrement in normal aging. *Language & Communication, 6,* 47-64.

Fodor, J.A., Bever, T.G., & Garrett, M.F. (1974). *The psychology of language*. New York: McGraw-Hill.

Foulke, E. (1971). The perception of time compressed speech. In D.L. Horton & J.J. Jenkins (Eds.), *The perception of language* (pp. 79-107). Columbus, OH: Merrill.

Frazier, L., & Rayner, K. (1982). Making and correcting errors during sentence comprehension: Eye movements in the analysis of structurally ambiguous sentences. *Cognitive Psychology, 14*, 178-210.

Gick, M. L., Craik, F. I. M., & Morris, R. G. (1988). Task complexity and age differences in working memory. *Memory & Cognition, 16,* 353-361.

Gordon-Salant, S., & Fitzgibbons, P.J. (1993). Temporal factors and speech recognition performance in young and elderly listeners. *Journal of Speech and Hearing Research, 36*, 1276-1285.

Grober, E., & Bang, S. (1995). Sentence comprehension in Alzheimer's disease. *Developmental Neuropsychology*, 11, 95-107.

Grosjean, F. (1985). The recognition of words after their acoustic offset: Evidence and implications. *Perception and Psychophysics, 38*, 299-310.

Grossman, M., Carvell, S., Gollomp, S., Stern, M. B., Vernon, G., & Hurtig, H. I. (1991). Sentence comprehension and praxis deficits in Parkinson's disease. *Neurology, 41*, 1620-1628.

Grossman, M., Carvell, S., Stern, M. B., Gollomp, S., & Hurtig, H. (1992). Sentence comprehension in Parkinson's disease: The role of attention and memory. *Brain & Language, 42*, 347-384.

Hart, J. (1988). Language and dementia: a review. *Psychological Medicine*, *18*, 99-112.

Hartley, J. T. (1986). Reader and text variables as determinants of discourse memory in adulthood. *Psychology and Aging, 1*, 150-158.

Hartley, J. T. (1988). Aging and individual differences in memory for written discourse. In L. L. Light & D. M. Burke (Eds.), *Language, memory, and aging* (pp. 36-57). New York: Cambridge University Press.

Hier, D. B., Hagenlocker, K., & Schindler, A. G. (1985). Language disintegration in dementia: Effects of etiology and severity. *Brain and Language, 25*, 117-133.

Hildebrandt, N., Caplan, D. & Evans, K. (1988). The man left without a trace: A case study of aphasic processing of empty categories, *Cognitive Neuropsychology*, *4*, 257-302.

Huggins, A.W.F. (1974). On perceptual integration of dichotically alternated pulse trains. *Journal of the Acoustical Society of America, 56*, 939-943.

Illes, J. (1989). Neurolinguistic features of spontaneous language production dissociate three forms of neurodegenerative disease: Alzheimer's, Huntington's, and Parkinson's. *Brain and Language, 37*, 628-642.

Irigaray, L. (1973). *Le langage des dements*. The Hague: Mouton.

Jarvella, R.V. (1970). Effects of syntax on running memory span for connected discourse. *Psychonomic Science*, *19*, 235-236.

Jarvella, R.V. (1971). Syntactic processing of connected speech. *Journal of Verbal Learning and Verbal Behavior*, *10*, 409-416.

Just, M.A., & Carpenter, P.A. (1987). *The psychology of reading and language comprehension.* Newton, MA: Allyn and Bacon.

Just, M.A., & Carpenter, P.A. (1992). A capacity theory of comprehension: Individual differences in working memory. *Psychological Review, 99*, 122-149.

Kahneman, D. (1973). *Attention and effort.* Englewood Cliffs, NJ: Prentice-Hall.

Kemper, S. (1986). Imitation of complex syntactic constructions by elderly adults. *Applied_Psycholinguistics, 7*, 277-287.

Kemper, S. (1988). Geriatric psycholinguistics: Syntactic limitations of oral and written language. In L. Light & D. Burke (Eds.), *Language, memory, and aging* (pp. 58-76). New York: Cambridge University Press.

Kemper, S., Anagnopoulos, C., Lyons, K., & Heberlein, W. (1994). Speech accommodations to dementia. *Journal of Gerontology*, 49, 223-229.

Kemper, S., LaBarge, E., Ferraro, F. R., Cheung, H., Cheung, H., & Storandt, M. (1993). On the preservation of syntax in Alzheimer's disease: Evidence from written sentences. *Archives of Neurology*, 50, 81-86.

Kemper, S., Snowdon, D. A., & Greiner, L. H. (1996). Linguistic ability across the life span: Findings from The Nun Study. Paper presented at the Cognitive Aging Conference, Atlanta, Ga.

Kempler, D., Curtiss, S., & Jackson, C. (1987). Syntactic preservation in Alzheimer's disease. *Journal of Speech and Hearing Research, 30*, 343-350.

Kempler, D., & Zelinski, E.M. (1994). Language in dementia and normal aging. In: F.A. Huppert, C. Brayne, & D.W. O'Connor (Eds.), *Dementia and normal aging* (pp. 331-365). New York: Cambridge University Press.

Kemtes, K.A., & Kemper, S. (1996). Younger and older adults' working memory and on-line processing of syntactically ambiguous sentences. Presented at the Cognitive Aging Conference, Atlanta, Ga.

King, J., & Just, M. A. (1991). Individual differences in syntactic processing: The role of working memory. *Journal of Memory and Language, 30*, 580-602.

Kintsch, W. (1988). The role of knowledge in discourse comprehension: A construction-integration model. *Psychological Review, 95*, 163-182.

Kintsch, W. & Buschke, H. (1969). Homophones and synonyms in short-term memory. *Journal of Experimental Psychology, 80*, 403-407.

Kintsch, W. & Keenan, J. (1973). Reading rate and retention as a function of the number of propositions in the base structure of sentences. *Cognitive Psychology, 5*, 257-274.

Kirshner, H. S. (1982). Language disorders in dementia. In H. S. Kirshner, & F. R. Freeman (Ed.), *The neurology of aphasia* (pp. 187-196). Lisse, Holland: Swets and Zeitlinger.

Konkle, D.F., Beasley, D.S., & Bess, F.H. (1977). Intelligibility of time-altered speech in relation to chronological aging. *Journal of Speech and Hearing Research, 20*, 108-115.

Kontiola, P., Laaksonen, R., Sulkava, R., & Erkinjuntti, T. (1990). Pattern of language impairment is different in Alzheimer's disease and multi-infarct dementia. *Brain and Language, 38*, 364-383.

Lalami, L., Marblestone, K., Schuster, S., Andersen, E., Kempler, D., Tyler, L., & MacDonald, M. (1996). On-line vs. off-line sentence processing in Alzheimer's disease. Presented at the Cognitive Aging Conference, Atlanta, Ga.

Lees, A. J., & Smith, E. (1983). Cognitive deficits in the early stages of Parkinson's disease. *Brain, 106*, 257-270.

Liberman, A.M., Cooper, F.S., Shankweiler, D.P., & Studdert-Kennedy, M. (1967). Perception of the speech code. *Psychological review, 74*, 431-461.

Lieberman, P. (1963). Some effects of semantic and grammatical context on the production and perception of speech. *Language and Speech, 6,* 172-187.

Lieberman, P., Friedman, J., & Feldman, L. S. (1990). Syntax comprehension in Parkinson's disease. *Journal of Nervous and Mental Diseases, 178*, 360-366.

Light, L.L. (1990). Interactions between memory and language in old age. In: J.E. Birren and K.W. Schaie (Eds.), *Handbook of the psychology of aging* (3rd Ed., pp. 275-290). San Diego, CA: Academic Press.

Light, L.L., & Anderson, P.A. (1985). Working memory capacity, age, and memory for discourse. *Journal of Gerontology, 4*: 737-747.

Light, L.L., & Capps, J.L. (1986). Comprehension of pronouns in young and older adults. *Developmental Psychology, 22*: 580-585.

Light, L.L., Zelinski, E. M., & Moore, M. (1982). Adult age differences in reasoning from new information. *Journal of Experimental Psychology: Learning, Memory, and Cognition, 8:* 435-447.

Logie, R.H., Della Sala, S., Laiacona, M., Chalmers, P., & Wynn, V. (1996). Group aggregates and individual reliability: The case of verbal short-term memory, *Memory & Cognition*, *24*, 305-321.

Luterman, D.M., Wesh, O.L., & Melrose, J. (1966). Responses of aged males to time-altered speech stimuli. *Journal of Speech and Hearing Research, 9*, 226-230.

MacDonald, M. C., Just, M. A., & Carpenter, P. A. (1992). Working memory constraints on the processing of syntactic ambiguity. *Cognitive Psychology, 24*, 56-98.

Madden, D.J. (1988). Adult age differences in the effects of sentence context and stimulus degradation during visual word recognition. *Psychology and Aging, 3*, 167-172.

Marmurek, H. H. (1990). The dissociation of impression formation and person memory: The effects of processing resources and trait favorableness. *Journal of Research in Personality, 24*, 191-205.

Marslen-Wilson, W.D. (1984). Function and process in spoken word recognition. In H. Bouma & D.G. Bouwhuis (Eds.), *Attention and performance X* (pp. 125-150). Hillsdale, NJ: Erlbaum.

Martin, R.C. (1987). Articulatory and phonological deficits in short-term memory and their relation to syntactic processing. *Brain & Language, 32*, 137-158.

Martin, R.C. (1990). Neuropsychological evidence on the role of short-term memory in sentence processing. In G.Vallar & T. Shallice (eds.). *Neuropsychological impairments of short-term memory* (pp. 390-427). Cambridge, U.K.: Cambridge University Press.

Massaro, D.W. (1972). Preperceptual images, processing time, and perceptual units in auditory perception. *Psychological Review, 79*, 124-145.

McLeod, P. (1977). A dual task modality effect: Support for multiprocessor models of attention. *Quarterly Journal of Experimental Psychology, 29*, 651-667.

Miller, G.R., & Coleman, E.B. (1967). A set of thirty-six prose passages calibrated for complexity. *Journal of Verbal Learning and Verbal Behavior, 6*, 851-854.

Milner, B. (1966). Amnesia following operation on the temporal lobes. In C. Whitty & O. Zangwill (Eds.), *Amnesia* (pp. 109-133). London: Butterworth.

Miyake, A., Carpenter, P., & Just, M. (1994). A capacity approach to syntactic comprehension disorders: Making normal adults perform like aphasic patients. *Cognitive Neuropsychology, 11*, 671-717.

Miyake, A., Just, M. A., & Carpenter, P.A. (in press). Working memory constrains on the resolution of lexical ambiguity: Maintaining multiple interpretations in neutral contexts. *Journal of Memory and Language.*

Monsell, S. (1984). Components of working memory underlying verbal skills: A "distributed capacities" view. In H. Bouma and D.G. Bouwhuis (Eds.) *Attention and performance X: Control of language processes* (pp. 327-350). Hillsdale, NJ: Erlbaum.

Morris, R. G. (1984). Dementia and the functioning of the articulatory loop system. *Cognitive Neuropsychology, 1*, 143-157.

Morris, R. G. (1986). Short-term forgetting in senile dementia of the Alzheimer's type. *Cognitive Neuropsychology, 3*, 77-97.

Morris, R. G. (1987). Articulatory rehearsal in Alzheimer type dementia. *Brain and Language, 30,* 351-362.

Morris, R. G., & Baddeley, A. D. (1988). Primary and working memory functioning in Alzheimer-type dementia. *Journal of Clinical and Experimental Neuropsychology, 10*, 279-296.

Morris, R.G., Craik, F.I.M., & Gick, M. L. (1990). Age differences in working memory tasks: The role of secondary memory and the central executive system. *The Quarterly Journal of Experimental Psychology, 42A*, 67-86.

Moss, H.E., & Marslen-Wilson, W.D. (1993). Access to word meanings during spoken language comprehension. *Journal of Experimental Psychology: Learning, Memory and Cognition, 19*, 1254-1276.

Murphy, G.L., & Shapiro, A.M. (1994). Forgetting of verbatim information in discourse. *Memory and Cognition, 22*, 85-94.

Natsopoulos, D., Katsarou, Z., Bostantzopoulo, S., Grouios, G., Mentanopoulos, G., & Logothetis, J. (1991). Strategies in comprehension of relative clauses in Parkinsonian patients. *Cortex, 27*, 255-268.

Norman, S., Kemper, S., Kynette, D., Cheung, H., & Anagnopoulos, C. (1991). Syntactic complexity and adults' running memory span. *Journal of*

Gerontology: Psychological Sciences, 46, 346-351.

Obler, L.K., Fein, D., Nicholas, M., & Albert, M. L. (1991). Auditory comprehension and aging: Decline in syntactic processing. *Applied Psycholinguistics, 12*, 433-452.

Paulesu, E., Frith, C.D., & Frackowiak, R.S.J. (1993). The neural correlates of the verbal component of working memory. *Nature, 362*, 342-344.

Perry, A.R., & Wingfield, A. (1994). Contextual encoding by young and elderly adults as revealed by cued and free recall. *Aging and Cognition, 1*, 120-139.

Peterson, L.R., & Peterson, M.J. (1959). Short-term retention of individual verbal items. *Journal of Experimental Psychology, 58*, 193-198.

Poeppel, D. (1996). A critical review of PET studies of language. *Brain and Language*, 55, 317-351.

Pollack, I., & Pickett, J.M. (1963). The intelligibility of excerpts from conversation. *Language and Speech, 6,* 165-171.

Potter, M.C. (1993). Very short-term conceptual memory. *Memory and Cognition*, *21*, 156-161.

Potter, M.C., & Lombardi, L. (1990). Regeneration in the short-term recall of sentences. *Journal of Memory and Language*, *29*, 633-654.

Pratt, M. W., Boyes, C., Robins, S., & Manchester, J. (1989). Telling tales: aging, working memory, and the narrative cohesion of story retellings. *Developmental Psychology, 25*, 628-635.

Pratt, M. W., & Robins, S. L. (1991). That's the way it was: Age differences in the structure and quality of adults' personal narratives. *Discourse Processes, 14*, 73-85.

Riggs, K. M., Wingfield, A., & Tun, P.A. (1993). Passage difficulty, speech rate, and age differences in memory for spoken text: Speech recall and the complexity hypothesis. *Experimental Aging Research, 19*, 111-128.

Rochon, E., & Saffran, E. M. (1995). A semantic contribution to sentence comprehension impairments in Alzheimer's disease. Presented at the Academy of Aphasia, San Diego, Ca.

Rochon, E., Waters, G. S., & Caplan, D. (1994). Sentence comprehension in patients with Alzheimer's Disease. *Brain & Language, 46*, 329-349.

Sachs, J.S. (1967). Recognition memory for syntactic and semantic aspects of connected discourse. *Perception and Psychophysics, 2*, 437-442.

Saffran, E.M. (1985). Short-term memory and language comprehension: Specifying the nature of the interaction. Presented at the Venice meeting on Cognitive Neuropsychology, Venice, Italy.

Saffran, E.M. & Marin, O.S.M. (1975). Immediate memory for word lists and sentences in a patient with deficient auditory short-term memory. *Brain and Language, 2*, 420-433.

Salthouse, T.A. (1988). The role of processing resources in cognitive aging. In M.L. Howe & C.J. Brainerd (Ed.), *Cognitive development in adulthood* (pp. 185-239). New York: Springer-Verlag.

Salthouse, T.A. (1990). Working memory as a processing resource in cognitive aging. *Developmental Review, 10*, 101-124.

Salthouse, T.A. (1991). *Theoretical perspectives on cognitive aging.* Hillsdale, NJ: Erlbaum.

Salthouse, T.A., & Babcock, R.L. (1991). Decomposing adult age differences in working memory. *Developmental Psychology, 27*, 763-776.

Schneider, W. (1993). Varieties of working memory as seen in biology and in connectionist/control architectures. *Memory and Cognition, 21*, 184-192.

Schneider, W., & Detweiler, M. (1987). A connectionist/control architecture for working memory. In G.H. Bower (Ed.), *The psychology of learning and motivation* (Vol. 21, pp. 54-119). New York: Academic Press.

Schwartz, M. F., Marin, O. S. M., & Saffran, E. M. (1979). Dissociations of language function in dementia: A case study. *Brain and Language, 7*, 277-306.

Schweickert, R. (1993). A multinomial processing tree model for degradation and reintegration in immediate recall. *Memory and Cognition, 21*, 168-175.

Sherman, J. C., Schweickert, J., Growdon, J., & Corkin, S. (1988). Sentence comprehension in Alzheimer's disease. Presented at the 18th annual meeting of the Society for Neuroscience, Toronto, Ont.

Shiffrin, R.M. (1993). Short-term memory: A brief commentary. *Memory and Cognition, 21*, 193-197.

Smith, S. (1989). *Syntactic comprehension in Alzheimer's Disease*. Santa Fe. NM:

Snowdon, D. A., Kemper, S. J., Mortimer, J. A., Greiner, L. H., Wekstein, D. R., & Markesbery, W. R. (1996). Linguistic ability in early life and cognitive function and Alzheimer's disease in late life: Findings from The Nun Study. *Journal of the American Medical Association, 275*, 528-532.

Stevens, K., Kempler, D., Andersen, E., & MacDonald, M. C. (1996). Preserved use of semantic and syntactic context in Alzheimer's disease. Poster presented at the Meeting of Cognitive Aging, Atlanta.

Sticht, T.G., & Gray, B.B. (1969). The intelligibility of time compressed words as a function of age and hearing loss. *Journal of Speech and Hearing Research, 12*, 443-448.

Stine, E.A.L. (1995). Aging and the distribution of resources in working memory. In P. Allen and T.R. Bashore (Eds.), *Age differences in word and language processing* (pp. 171-186). Elsevier.

Stine, E. A. L., & Wingfield, A. (1987). Process and strategy in memory for speech among younger and older adults. *Psychology and Aging, 2*, 272-279.

Stine, E. A. L., & Wingfield, A. (1990). How much do working memory deficits contribute to age differences in discourse memory? *European Journal of Cognitive Psychology, 2*, 289-304.

Stine, E. A. L., Wingfield, A., & Poon, L. W. (1986). How much and how fast: Rapid speech processing of spoken language in late adulthood. *Psychology and Aging, 1*, 303-311.

Stoltzfus, E. R., Hasher, L., & Zacks, R.T. (1996). Working memory and aging: Current status of the inhibitory view. In J. T. E. Richardson (Ed.) *Working Memory and Cognition.* New York: Oxford University Press.

Taylor, A. E., Saint-Cyr, J. A., & Lang, A. E. (1987). Frontal lobe dysfunction in Parkinson's disease. *Brain, 109*,

Titchener, E.B. (1910). *A textbook of psychology.* New York: Macmillan.

Tomoeda, C. K., Bayles, K. A., Boone, D. R., Kaszniak, A. W., & Slauson, T. J. (1990). Speech rate and syntactic complexity effects on the auditory comprehension of Alzheimer patients. *Journal of Communication Disorders, 23*, 151-161.

Tun, C.G., Tun, P.A., & Wingfield, A. (1997). Cognitive function following long-term spinal cord injury. *Rehabilitation Psychology, 3,*

Tun, P. A. (1989). Age differences in processing expository and narrative text. *Journal of Gerontology, 44*, 9-15.

Tun, P. A., & Wingfield, A. (1993). Is speech special? Perception and recall of spoken language in complex environments. In J. Cerella, J. Rybash, W. Hoyer, & M. L. Commons (Eds.), *Adult information processing: Limits on loss* (pp. 425-457). San Diego: Academic Press.

Tun, P. A., & Wingfield, A. (1994). Speech recall under heavy load conditions: Age, predictability, and limits on dual-task interference. *Aging and*

Cognition, 1, 29-44.

Tun, P. A., Wingfield, A., & Stine, E. A. L. (1991). Speech-processing capacity in young and older adults: A dual-task study. *Psychology and Aging, 6*, 3-9.

Tun, P. A., Wingfield, A., Stine, E. A. L., & Mecsas, C. (1992). Rapid speech processing and divided attention: Processing rate versus processing resources as an explanation of age effects. *Psychology and Aging, 7,* 546-550.

van Dijk, T. A., & Kintsch, W. (1983). *Strategies of discourse comprehension*. New York: Academic Press.

Warrington, E.K. & Shallice, T. (1969). The selective impairment of auditory-verbal short-term memory. *Brain, 92*, 885-896.

Waters, G.S. & Caplan, D. (1993). Comprehension of garden path structures in a patient with an impairment of verbal short-term memory. Presented at the Academy of Aphasia, Tucson, Az.

Waters, G., & Caplan, D. (1996a). Processing resource capacity and the comprehension of garden path sentences. *Memory and Cognition, 24*, 342-355.

Waters, G., & Caplan, D. (1996b). The measurement of verbal working memory capacity and its relation to reading comprehension. *The Quarterly Journal of Experimental Psychology, 49A*, 51-79.

Waters, G., & Caplan, D. (1996). The capacity theory of sentence comprehension: Critique of Just and Carpenter (1992). *Psychological Review, 103*, 761-772.

Waters, G., & Caplan, D. (1997). Working memory and on-line sentence comprehension in patients with Alzheimer's disease. *Journal of Psycholinguistic Research*. 26, 337-400.

Waters, G. S., Caplan, D., & Hildebrandt, N. (1991). On the structure of verbal short-term memory and its functional role in sentence comprehension:

Evidence from neuropsychology. *Cognitive Neuropsychology, 8*, 81-126.

Waters, G. S., Caplan, D., & Rochon, E. (1995). Processing capacity and sentence comprehension in patients with Alzheimer's Disease. *Cognitive Neuropsychology, 12*, 1-30.

Waters, G. S., Rochon, E., & Caplan, D. (in press). Task demands and sentence comprehension in patients with dementia of the Alzheimer's type. *Brain and Language* .

Waugh, N.C., & Norman, D.A. (1965). Primary memory. *Psychological Review, 72*, 89-104.

Welford, A.T. (1958). *Ageing and human skill.* London: Oxford University Press.

Wickelgren, W. A. (1965). Acoustic similarity and intrusion errors in short-term memory. *Journal of Experimental Psychology, 70*, 102-108.

Wingfield, A. (1975). Acoustic redundancy and the perception of time-compressed speech. *Journal of Speech and Hearing Research, 18*, 96-104.

Wingfield, A., Aberdeen , J.S., & Stine, E.A.L. (1991). Word onset gating and linguistic context in spoken word recognition by young and elderly adults. *Journal of Gerontology: Psychological Sciences, 46*, P127-P129.

Wingfield, A., Alexander, A.H., & Cavigelli, S. (1994). Does memory constrain utilization of top-down information in spoken word recognition? Evidence from normal aging. *Language and Speech, 37*, 221-235.

Wingfield, A., & Butterworth, B. (1984). Running memory for sentences and parts of sentences: Syntactic parsing as a control function in working memory. In H. Bouma & D.G. Bouwhuis (Eds.), *Attention and performance X: Control of language processes* (pp. 351-363). Hillsdale, NJ: Erlbaum.

Wingfield, A., & Klein, J.F. (1971). Syntactic structures and acoustic pattern in speech perception. *Perception and Psychophysics, 9*, 23-25.

Wingfield, A., Lahar, C.J., & Stine, E.A.L. (1989). Age and decision strategies in running memory for speech: Effects of prosody and linguistic structure. *Journal of Gerontology: Psychological Sciences, 44*, 106-113.

Wingfield, A., & Lindfield, K.C. (1995). Multiple memory systems in the processing of speech: Evidence from aging. *Experimental Aging Research, 21*, 101-121.

Wingfield, A., & Nolan, K.A. (1980). Spontaneous segmentation in normal and in time-compressed speech. *Perception and Psychophysics, 28*, 97-102.

Wingfield, A., Poon, L.W., Lombardi, L., & Lowe, D. (1985). Speed of processing in normal aging: Effects of speech rate, linguistic structure, and processing time. *Journal of Gerontology, 40*, 579-585.

Wingfield, A., & Stine, E.A.L. (1986). Organizational strategies in immediate recall of rapid speech by young and elderly adults. *Experimental Aging Research, 12*, 79-83.

Wingfield, A., & Stine, E.A.L. (1992). Age differences in perceptual processing and memory for spoken language. In R.L. West, & J.D. Sinnott (Eds.), *Everyday memory and aging: Current research and methodology* (pp. 101-123). New York: Springer-Verlag.

Wingfield, A., Stine, E.A.L., Lahar, C.J., & Aberdeen, J.S. (1988). Does the capacity of working memory change with age? *Experimental Aging Research, 14*, 103-107.

Wingfield, A., Tun, P.A., & Rosen, M.J. (1995). Age differences in veridical and reconstructive recall of syntactically and randomly segmented speech. *Journal of Gerontology: Psychological Sciences, 50*, P257-P266.

Wingfield, A., Wayland, S.C., & Stine, E.A.L. (1992). Adult age differences in the use of prosody for syntactic parsing and recall of spoken sentences. *Journal of Gerontology: Psychological Sciences, 47*, P350-P356.

Zurif, E., Swinney, D., Prather, P., Wingfield, A., & Brownell, H. (1995). The allocation of memory resources during sentence comprehension: Evidence from the elderly. *Journal of Psycholinguistic Research, 24*, 165-182.

The Other Side of the Error Term - N. Raz (Editor)

Chapter 8
PROBLEM SOLVING, INHIBITION, AND FRONTAL LOBE FUNCTION

Jennifer Dorfman
Rush Presbyterian St-Luke's Medical Center

ABSTRACT

Traditionally, cognitive models of problem solving have not incorporated inhibitory mechanisms, conceiving of human thinking as similar to the computations carried out by a serial computer (e.g., Newell & Simon, 1972). This chapter seeks to demonstrate the importance of inhibition in problem solving by examining subject populations with selective impairments of cognitive inhibition associated with frontal lobe pathology. Studies of three groups with putative frontal lobe dysfunction are reviewed: patients with focal lesions of the prefrontal cortex; schizophrenics; and the normal elderly. It is argued that the basic deficits observed in these groups reflect breakdowns in a supervisory attentional system that modulates problem-solving activity and that is subserved by the frontal cortex (Shallice, 1982). It is concluded that it is time to abandon the computer metaphor of human problem solving and adopt a brain metaphor.

Despite the long focus within neuropsychology on the role of inhibition in higher-order cognition (e.g., Luria, 1966; Milner, 1964), inhibitory processes have not figured prominently in the cognitive psychology of problem solving. Information-processing models based on the computer metaphor have remained popular accounts of human problem solving (e.g., Newell & Simon, 1972) -- due in part to the inherent seriality of the problem-solving process. With the growing alliance between cognitive psychology and neuropsychology, and consequent emphasis on brain-based accounts of human cognition, inhibitory mechanisms have begun to play a more central role in theories of normal cognitive function -- particularly in the domains of attention, language, and memory (see Dagenbach & Carr, 1994; Dempster & Brainerd, 1995, for collections of related readings). The present chapter seeks to demonstrate a similar role for cognitive inhibition in problem solving, by considering the breakdowns in inhibitory processing and problem-solving performance that are linked with frontal lobe pathology.

The chapter is divided into five sections. The first section outlines the general role of inhibitory processes in cognition. The range of inhibitory phenomena is illustrated with examples from selective attention, language, memory, and problem solving. The second section discusses the role of the frontal lobes in cognitive inhibition. The neuroanatomy of the frontal lobes is reviewed, and theories linking the frontal lobes with inhibitory function are outlined. In the third section, the relation between inhibition and problem solving is discussed. Traditional search-based accounts are described which illustrate the basic elements of solving a problem. A neurally-inspired theory linking problem solving with frontal lobe and inhibitory function is then presented. The fourth section reviews problem-solving studies of three subject populations with putative frontal lobe dysfunction: patients with focal lesions of the prefrontal cortex; schizophrenic patients; and the normal elderly. The last section integrates the material discussed throughout the chapter and suggests directions for future research.

The Role of Inhibition in Cognition

Inhibitory mechanisms play a ubiquitous role in the human cognitive system. Automatic processes such as lateral inhibition aid in orienting attention, identifying objects, and selecting responses. At a higher level, controlled inhibitory processes function to coordinate automatic responses and processes with goal-oriented behavior. Inhibition in this latter sense is important in overcoming primary reflexes, screening out distracting stimuli, dampening prepotent response tendencies, and reducing interference from task-irrelevant thoughts. It is this form of inhibition, *cognitive inhibition*, that is the focus of the current chapter.

Cognitive inhibition is strongly associated with selective attention, the ability to respond discriminatively to important features in the environment while ignoring unimportant ones. Screening out irrelevant sensory inputs is of vital adaptive value, in that it permits focus on critical environmental features that may call for immediate action. Consider, for example, a laboratory task of dichotic listening (Cherry, 1953). In such a task, subjects hear different messages presented simultaneously to each ear. They are required to shadow, or repeat back, the message presented in one channel. Subjects generally show little awareness of the message presented in the alternate channel, aside from gross perceptual features. Importantly, however, they are able to process meaning when potentially significant information is encountered, such as their own name; that is, they are able to shift the focus of attention and suppress the shadowed channel. Similar processes are seen in everyday life in situations in which important information must be distinguished from background noise; for example, hearing a child's cry or spotting a dangerous animal.

Cognitive inhibition also plays an important role in linguistic functions. This role spans both comprehension and production, helping listeners to decipher ambiguous utterances and speakers to avoid slips of the tongue. The role of inhibition in comprehension can be illustrated with a paradigm involving recognition of ambiguous words (Simpson & Burgess, 1985). In this paradigm, a homograph such as *bank* is presented, followed by a letter string for lexical decision. Some of the test items are related to the dominant meaning of the homograph (e.g., *money*) and others to the subordinate meaning (e.g., *river*). Whereas priming of the dominant meaning is evident at very short delays and builds over time, priming of the subordinate meaning takes longer to develop and recedes more quickly. This suggests that recognition of ambiguous words involves simultaneously focusing on one meaning and inhibiting others. Similar kinds of effects are evident in sentence comprehension: subjects show sensitivity to context-irrelevant word meanings at short but not long test delays (e.g., Onifer & Swinney, 1981). In language production, analogously, inhibition seems to play a role in selecting appropriate lexical items, syntactic structures, and so on (Dell & O'Seaghdha, 1994).

In memory, inhibition plays an important role in updating the system, facilitating new learning and the development of expertise; it also may function, in a Freudian sense, to avoid threatening or painful memories. This kind of inhibition is known specifically as retrieval inhibition, the loss of access to information that is in fact stored in memory (Bjork, 1989). A classic example is the A-B, A-C paradigm popularized in verbal learning experiments in the 1960s and 1970s. In this paradigm, subjects learn a list of paired associates of the form A-B (e.g., GARDEN-STOVE), followed by a second list in which the stimulus terms are re-paired with different response terms (e.g., GARDEN-DOLL). The general finding is a retroactive interference effect, in which subjects show reduced memory for A-B pairs; that is, memory for A-C pairs interferes with retrieval of A-B pairs. This effect is said to reflect suppression of response sets, in which inhibition of the first list facilitates learning of the second (Postman, Stark, & Fraser, 1968). Inhibition also seems to play a role in the development and use of expertise as well as in memory for serial order, permitting fast access to unitized knowledge structures and dampening activation of lower-order units (e.g., Estes, 1972).

In higher-order cognition, inhibitory processes are important in a variety of ways, including developing and carrying out plans, starting and stopping actions, and adopting flexible problem-solving strategies. In problem solving specifically, inhibition functions to screen out irrelevant details of the problem situation and overcome pre-existing response tendencies. This latter function can be illustrated with the Wisconsin Card Sorting Test (WCST; Grant & Berg, 1948). In this test, subjects are required to sort a deck of cards that vary in terms of the attributes of color, form, and number. They must place each card beneath one of four reference cards based on a pre-established, but unspecified, sorting rule that changes after a certain number of trials. Feedback from the experimenter is given to allow learning of the appropriate rule. Successful problem-solving performance requires the ability to discover the rule, persist in using it across relevant trials, and shift to a new rule during the next block of trials. This latter ability involves suppressing or inhibiting prior rules that are no longer appropriate in the current context. Inhibition is also important in problem-solving situations calling for divergent or creative thinking. For example, fluency tasks, which involve generating diverse ideas and responses, require overcoming conventional or well-established response patterns and fluidly shifting among mental categories. This is also true of insight problem solving, in which the proper solution path is not immediately obvious and problem solvers must restructure a problem to arrive at the solution (see Dorfman, Shames, & Kihlstrom, 1996, for a discussion of the cognitive aspects of insight).

In summary, inhibitory mechanisms play a vital role in many aspects of cognition, including selective attention, language, memory, and, problem solving. Controlled mental processes function to suppress irrelevant environmental and intrapsychic information, working in tandem with automatic processes to accomplish goal-oriented behavior.

Inhibition and the Frontal Lobes

The hypothesis that frontal lobe function is linked with inhibition has appeared in many forms. Writers at mid-century stressed the role of the frontal lobes in, variously, forming successions of conflicting habits (Lashley, 1948), inhibiting response sequences (Stanley & Jaynes, 1949), reducing perseverative interference (Settlage, Butler, & Odoi, 1956), and disinhibiting conditioned reflexes (Brutkowski, Konorski, Stepien, & Stepien, 1956). In the 1962 symposium devoted to the frontal cortex and behavior, many of the participants -- Luria, Milner, and Mishkin among them -- advocated some form of an inhibitory hypothesis (see Warren & Akert, 1964).

Inhibitory function, on these accounts, is linked specifically with the prefrontal cortex (see Figure 1).

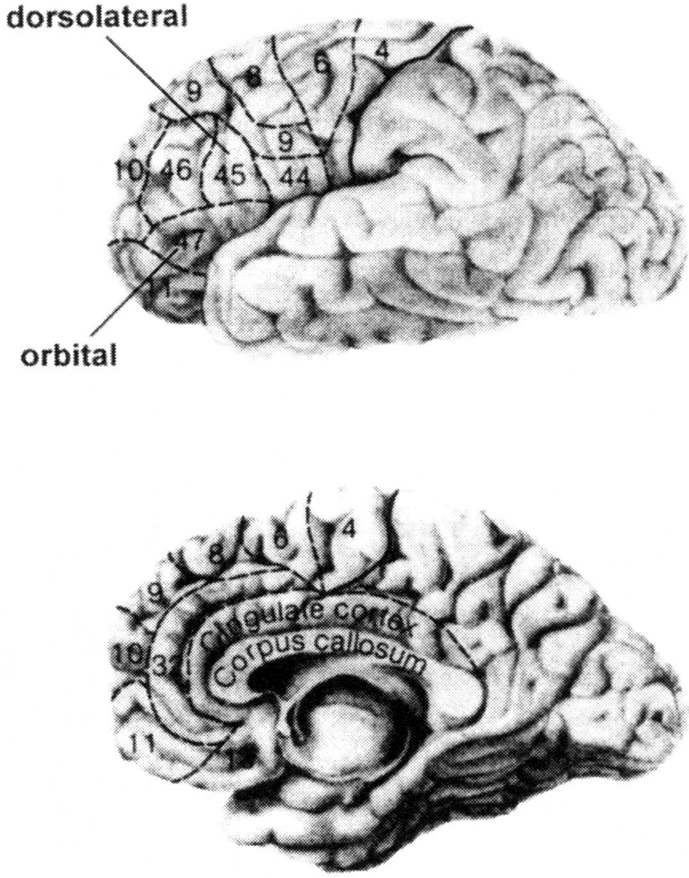

Figure 1. Lateral and medial views of the frontal lobe. From: *Fundamentals of Human Neuropsychology* by B. Kolb and I.Q. Whishaw © 1980 by W.H. Freeman and Company. Used with permission.

The prefrontal cortex refers to the area of the frontal lobes anterior to the premotor and motor cortices and connected directly to the dorsomedial nucleus of the thalamus. This region covers, roughly, Brodmann areas 8, 9, 10, 11, 12, 13, 14, 32, 33, 44, 45, 46, and 47. Anatomically, the prefrontal cortex is well-situated for complex integrative functions, given its rich connections with virtually all areas of the brain (Fuster, 1989; Goldman-Rakic, 1987). The prefrontal cortex receives projections from parietal, temporal, and occipital cortex, as well as from limbic and subcortical structures, positioning it to integrate multi-modal inputs as well as information about internal states. It also is connected to major motor centers, permitting regulation of eye, head, and body movements. The prefrontal cortex is thought to modulate sensory activity in posterior parietal regions; regulation of mnemonic and emotional functions is accomplished by gating output from the hippocampus, amygdala, and other limbic structures. Intimate connections are formed with the neostriatum via several circuits which are linked with higher cognitive functions (see Figure 2; Alexander, DeLong, & Strick, 1986). These frontostriatal circuits funnel information via the globus pallidus and substantia nigra to the thalamus and back to the frontal regions that initiated the circuit. These circuits have been implicated in the cognitive deficits observed in schizophrenia and normal aging, as will be discussed later.

The prefrontal cortex consists of multiple subdivisions that can be distinguished both anatomically and functionally. At the more general level, it can be divided into dorsolateral and orbital aspects. The dorsolateral region, covering much of the superior, middle, and inferior frontal gyri, has traditionally been linked with higher-order cognitive functions. Among its cytoarchitectonic subdivisions are areas 44 and 45 (Broca's area), connected with language production; area 46, associated with spatial memory; area 12, linked with visual memory; and area 8 (the frontal eye fields), involved in oculomotor control. The orbitofrontal region, located on the ventral surface of the brain, has historically been associated with affective and motivational functions. This region may play an important role in autonomic control and the processing of interoceptive and olfactory stimuli. Like the dorsolateral region, the orbitofrontal cortex is thought to play a significant role in executive functions.

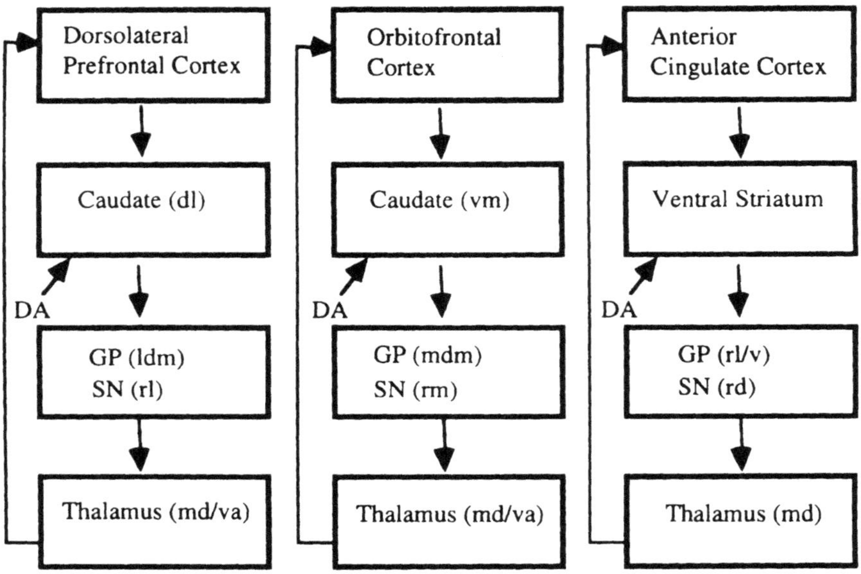

Figure 2. Three frontostriatal circuits described by Alexander et al. (1986). DA = dopamine. GP = globus pallidus. SN = substantia nigra. dl = dorsolateral. ldm = lateral dorsomedial. md = mediodorsal. mdm= medial dorsomedial. rd= rostro-dorsal. rl = rostrolateral. rm = rostromedial. v= ventral. va = ventral anterior. vm = ventromedial.

Although different areas within the prefrontal cortex show some degree of specialization, they may be thought of as components of a larger system with a unified function. Some theorists, in keeping with traditional conceptions, have argued that the principal function of the prefrontal cortex is cognitive inhibition (e.g., Shimamura, 1995; see also Levin, 1984). Others have argued that inhibition is a subfunction of a more global representational or working memory system (e.g.,

Goldman-Rakic, 1987; see also Cohen & Servan-Schreiber, 1992) or a temporal integration system (e.g., Fuster, 1989). In either case, inhibition figures prominently in the computations carried out by the frontal lobes.

Consider, for example, Goldman-Rakic's (1987) theory of prefrontal function. In her theory, different subdivisions of the prefrontal cortex serve as central executive centers for guiding voluntary behavior by representational memory. This involves accessing and holding temporarily on-line symbolic representations of the external world. Goldman-Rakic focuses on one prefrontal region, the principal sulcus (Walker area 46), as a model system for understanding the general functions of the frontal lobes. The functions of this region can be illustrated with the delayed-response task, commonly used in animal investigations of prefrontal function. In this task, the animal observes a morsel of food being placed in one of two wells. After a delay of several seconds, in which the wells are blocked from view, it selects one of the locations and receives a reward if correct. The principal sulcus is said to spotlight spatial signals relevant to the task, represented in parietal cortex, and maintain access to the relevant information during the test delay. This function is disrupted by prefrontal damage: animals with principal sulcus (but not other prefrontal) lesions choose either the first well they see or the most recently reinforced location. Goldman-Rakic notes: "Deprived of access to representational knowledge ... an animal would almost be forced to rely on external stimuli present at the time of response; it would be at the mercy of environmental cues or unlearned and prepotent responses to those stimuli" (p. 378). Lesions to other areas of the prefrontal cortex, similarly, would be expected to disrupt representational memory, and by extension inhibitory processing, associated with the particular stimulus domain in question (e.g., visual, linguistic, interoceptive) -- reflecting differential connectivity between prefrontal regions and other parts of the brain.

Shimamura (1995) has adopted a similar position, but argues that inhibitory function is a primary, not subsidiary, function of the frontal lobes. On his view, constructed within the framework of human cognitive neuropsychology, deficits observed following prefrontal damage reflect disruption of inhibitory processes that filter different aspects of cognitive function. For example, one can think of deficits in selective attention as reflecting difficulty inhibiting irrelevant environmental stimuli. In a similar vein, memory deficits can be seen as involving reduced inhibition of prepotent associations, while problem solving impairments may reflect difficulty suppressing erroneous search or decision paths. Shimamura has argued that tasks which place a great demand on inhibitory function are most likely to be disrupted following frontal lobe damage. For example, he notes that deficits in recency judgment tasks, often taken to indicate an impairment in temporal processing, vanish when subjects are encouraged to encode items distinctively. Diamond, Cruttenden, and Neiderman (1994), similarly, have pointed out that errors by infants in the A-not-B task (a close analogue of the delayed response task) can occur even when hidden stimuli are visible; moreover, infants often look toward the correct location while searching the incorrect one, indicating intact representational memory.

Unlike the foregoing theories, Fuster (1989) views inhibitory function as controlled by specific subdivisions of the prefrontal cortex. He has proposed a hierarchical model of prefrontal function whose global purpose is to form temporal structures of behavior with a unifying goal. This is accomplished via three subfunctions: an anticipatory or prospective function that prepares the organism for goal-related events; a provisional or retrospective memory function that retains event-related information until the goal is achieved; and an interference control function that suppresses interfering stimuli and memories. The first two functions are associated with the dorsolateral prefrontal cortex; the latter, with the orbitofrontal cortex and also with medial frontal regions. Consistent with this framework, Fuster notes that deficits in tasks most clearly associated with inhibitory function, namely go-no go and conditioned differential inhibition tasks, are associated with orbitomedial lesions.

The importance of medial frontal regions in inhibition, particularly the anterior cingulate gyrus, has been underscored by Posner and Petersen (1990) in their description of an anterior attention system. This system may help control what is represented in lateral regions by selecting appropriate responses and suppressing inappropriate ones. The anterior cingulate sends projections to dorsolateral prefrontal cortex and is one of the cortical areas forming the "closed loop" portion of the frontostriatal circuits depicted in Figure 2. Though histologically not part of the prefrontal cortex, the anterior cingulate and related midline areas are often linked with the prefrontal region based on functional or connective criteria (see, e.g., Stanley & Jaynes, 1949; Stuss & Benson, 1984).

In summary, neuroanatomical evidence supports the hypothesis that the frontal lobes play a critical role in cognitive inhibition. Anatomical connections linking prefrontal regions with other brain areas support a modulatory or gating function that screens out irrelevant stimuli and suppresses prepotent response tendencies. Inhibition may serve as the principal function of the frontal lobes, with different subregions specialized for different cognitive operations. Alternatively, it may be a subfunction of a more global representational memory system that functions in all subregions or a hierarchically-organized temporal integration system.

Problem Solving and Inhibition

Traditionally, cognitive theories of problem solving have not incorporated concepts of inhibition. The highly influential theory of Newell and Simon (1972), for example, which grew out of the tradition of artificial intelligence, conceives of human thinking as similar to the information processing carried out by a serial computer. This focus on symbolic processing, at the expense of underlying neural architecture, is evident in the authors' introductory remarks in *Human Problem Solving*:

> This model of symbol manipulation remains very much an approximation, of course, hypothesizing in an extreme form the neatness of discrete symbols and a small set of elementary processes, each with precisely defined and limited behavior. This abstraction, though possibly severe, does provide a grip on symbolic behavior that was not available heretofore. It does, equally, steer away from physiological models, with their concern for fidelity to continuous physiological mechanisms, either electrical, chemical, or hormonal. (p. 5)

The Newell and Simon approach, whatever its shortcomings, remains one of the best articulated accounts of human problem solving. In this section, I will use their theory to frame some of the general issues that are important for a proper understanding of the problem-solving process. Once this groundwork has been laid, I will consider more recent accounts which remain truer to the way in which the brain carries out problem solving, including the important role of inhibition.

Newell and Simon characterized the problem solving process as a search through a problem space -- a metaphor which has now become commonplace in descriptions of human problem solving. A problem space is the internal representation that a problem solver constructs of the critical aspects of a problem. This representation contains a description of the initial state at which problem solving commences, a goal state which the problem solver seeks to achieve, and a set of operations for moving from the initial state to the goal state. One can think of the problem solving process as involving a search through a maze. Finding the appropriate path may be achieved by moving forward; but it also may involve dead ends, backing up, and taking detours.

The task confronting the problem solver is to devise search strategies for tackling the problem. This generally involves what Newell and Simon call heuristic search, or selectively as opposed to exhaustively searching through a problem space. For example, in means-end analysis, the problem solver breaks down a problem into subgoals and attacks each to reduce the difference between the current state and the goal state. The search-based approach is commonly implemented with production system models (see, e.g., Anderson, 1983, 1993; McDermott & Forgy, 1978; Newell, 1973). In these models, information pertinent to solving a problem is represented in long-term memory as a set of production rules, or if-then statements linking conditions with actions. For example, a production rule relevant to solving an arithmetic problem might be: "IF the goal is to write out an answer in the right-most column, and d1 and d2 are the digits in that column, and d3 is the sum of d1 and d2, THEN set a subgoal to write out d3 in the right-most column." The representation of the current problem state, held in working memory, is matched against the conditions of the productions available in the system. If a match is achieved with a single production, then that production is executed. If more than one production is matched, conflict resolution procedures are carried out to select one of the productions. Once the action is carried out, a new representation is constructed of the current problem state.

In their classical forms, production system models did not incorporate inhibitory mechanisms for achieving conflict resolution. Rather, selection of productions was determined by criteria such as the ordering of productions within the system, the recency of the selecting data, the specificity of the conditions of the relevant productions, and production refractoriness. More recent accounts, e.g., Anderson's ACT theory of problem solving (cf. Anderson, 1983, 1993), have implemented neurologically motivated mechanisms of conflict resolution. In the ACT-R model, the most recent incarnation of the ACT framework, conflict resolution is achieved via lateral inhibitory mechanisms that dampen activation levels of competing productions. For example, if a node receives excitatory input from two subpatterns, it also receives inhibitory input from all the other nodes that receive inputs from those subpatterns. Higher-order inhibitory effects may be modeled by generating goal structures that serve as plans as opposed to producing actions directly.

Although the descriptive adequacy of production system models such as ACT cannot be disputed, the models suffer from an important limitation -- the psychological plausibility of their mechanisms. A theoretical framework which provides a more natural architecture for human problem solving is Shallice's schema-based model of thought and action (e.g., Norman & Shallice, 1986; Shallice, 1982; Shallice & Burgess, 1991a; see Figure 3). This framework was inspired by data from patients with localized frontal lobe damage and derives directly from Luria's (e.g., Luria, 1966) account of executive functioning and the frontal lobes. I will use this theory throughout the chapter as a framework for understanding inhibitory effects in problem solving.

Shallice argues that two modes of cognitive processing are important in controlling thought and action, one relatively automatic and the other controlled. The first, contention scheduling, is most important in routine situations. This mechanism involves the selection of highly automatic programs or schemas triggered by cues in the problem situation. A schema is a flexible data structure that stores and organizes past experience and guides subsequent perception and experience. Schemas represent information ranging from individual features; to objects, events, and actions; to sequences or groups of objects, events, and actions. Information processing in a schema-based framework involves determining which schema best fits the incoming data. Selection in contention scheduling involves the mutual inhibition of competing schemas, through lateral inhibitory mechanisms, with selection of the one that is most neuronally active. Problems that invoke over-learned procedures, such as simple arithmetic problems, can be solved via contention scheduling.

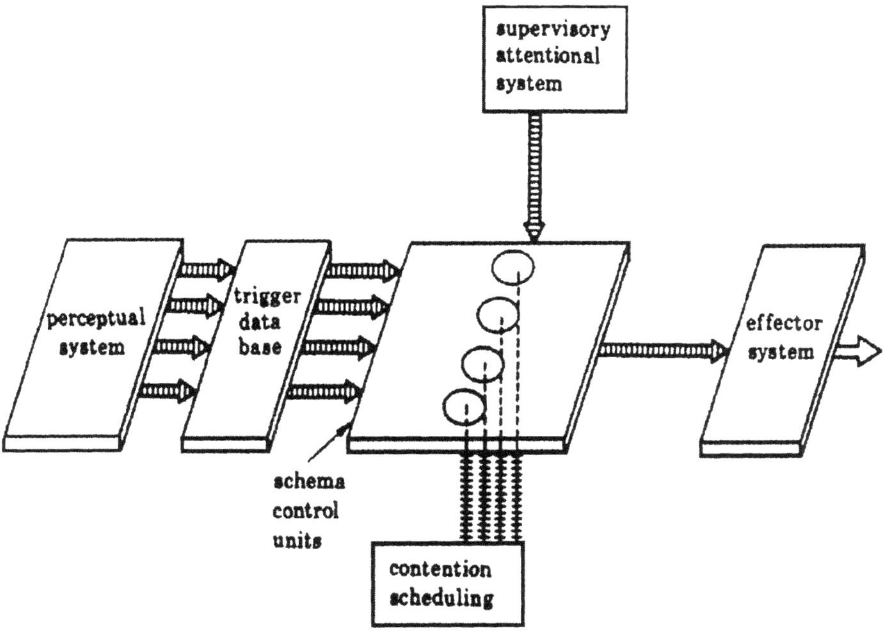

Figure 3. Shallice's (1982) schema-based model of thought and action. Reprinted with permission.

In novel situations, problem solving relies as well on a supervisory attentional system (SAS), which performs a general programming or planning function. The directing activity of the SAS modulates the activation level of schemas, biasing the probability of their being selected. A major component of this activity is inhibitory: the SAS permits the problem solver to suppress irrelevant aspects of the problem situation and prepotent response tendencies. Shallice's framework not only provides a viable alternative to rule-based models, it also provides a natural account of the breakdowns in problem solving associated with frontal lobe damage. As will be described shortly, frontal lobe patients show problem-solving deficits suggestive of a dysfunctional SAS, leaving their performance based on automatic contention-scheduling processes. The problem-solving impairments observed in schizophrenic patients and the normal elderly, similarly, can be thought of in terms of this distinction.

In summary, traditional rule-based models of problem solving, though successful in many ways, fail to provide a neurologically or psychologically plausible framework for human problem solving. Shallice's schema-based model provides a more natural account of the problem-solving process, capturing the role of inhibitory processes that are linked with the intact functioning of the frontal lobes.

Insights from Special Populations

Shallice's approach makes clear the important insights that can be gained from studying subject populations with selective neurological damage. In this section, I consider evidence from three subject populations that may help clarify the role of frontally-mediated inhibition in problem solving: patients with focal frontal lobe lesions; schizophrenic patients; and the normal elderly. In all cases, frontal lobe dysfunction is implicated, whether it be through frank structural damage to the prefrontal cortex or through functional abnormalities in frontal circuitry.

Frontal lobe patients

As Luria (1966) described it, the frontal lobe syndrome is characterized by an inherent contradiction: potentially preserved formal intellect and profoundly disturbed intellectual activity. Patients with focal lesions to the prefrontal cortex (due to injury, disease, or surgical procedures) show little impairment in tests of general intelligence such as the Wechsler Adult Intelligence Scale (WAIS; Stuss & Benson, 1984). Yet they show marked deficits in "executive" functions, including goal-directed behavior, planning, judgment and decision-making, and cognitive monitoring. They exhibit associated deficits in processing temporal and contextual aspects of events, as well as difficulties with attention and motivation.

Many of the symptoms associated with frontal lobe damage are suggestive of impaired inhibitory function. One of the hallmarks of the syndrome, exemplified by the classic case of Phineas Gage, is disinhibition of social behavior -- characterized by lack of restraint and tactlessness, inappropriate affect, obstinancy, and grandiosity. Perseverative and stereotyped behaviors have also long been considered a cardinal sign of frontal lobe damage. For example, frontal patients often respond stereotypically to objects in their immediate environment, as in the case of Lhermitte's (1983) patient who repeatedly put on glasses each time he was handed a new pair. Luria (1966), similarly, describes the case of a patient who was unable to draw a watch after previously drawing a pair of spectacles; when pressed, the patient drew a pair of spectacles with a watch in the center of one lens. Frontal patients also evidence difficulty suppressing on-going responses; for example, repeatedly cleaning a select item or continuously shaking someone's hand.

Experimental studies corroborate these clinical observations. For example, frontal lobe patients show increased interference on the Stroop color-word test, which requires selectively attending to the color a word is printed in while ignoring its meaning (e.g., Perret, 1974). Frontal patients also show increased reflexive glancing on the anti-saccade task, which requires looking in the opposite direction of a cue presented to one visual field (e.g., Guitton, Buchtel, & Douglas, 1985), as well as impairments on a go-no go task involving pressing a button when one light is illuminated and withholding responding when another is displayed (e.g., Drewe, 1975).

Luria (1966) assigns a fundamental role to inhibition in his description of the breakdown in problem solving associated with frontal lobe lesions. He notes:

> Such patients as a rule do not begin to analyze the situation created by the task presented to them. The orienting basis of the intellectual action is either completely omitted or greatly contracted; the individual elements of the task are not compared with one another; and no hypotheses are put forward on their basis, whereby the more appropriate connections would be more likely to arise and the less appropriate, not corresponding to the hypothesis, inhibited. For this reason heuristic connections are no longer stronger than irrelevant, random, or perseverating connections, and the whole process of intellectual activity loses its selective character. (p. 346)

Consider the case of arithmetic problems. Although patients evidence no primary disturbance in arithmetical skill (i.e., knowledge of the category of number or ability to carry out arithmetic operations), their performance breaks down when the task goes beyond the limits of simple and habitual operations. Thus, for example, they have difficulty when a task involves a long series of calculations in which it is necessary to continually switch from one operation to another. In the common clinical test of counting backwards from 100 by 7's, for instance, a patient might replace the required operation with a series of stereotyped responses based on an earlier operation (e.g., 100-93-83-73-63). Another example is a so-called conflict problem, in which the wording of the problem causes a tendency toward an incorrect method of solution. Luria (1966) gives the following example: "A pedestrian walks to the station in 15 minutes, and a cyclist rides there 5 times faster. How long does the cyclist take to get to the station?" In this problem, the word "faster" causes a tendency to multiply; this tendency must be overcome to arrive at the correct solution of 3 minutes.

Milner (1964) has argued that the problem-solving deficits observed following frontal lobe lesions reflect an impairment in the ability to shift response sets in accordance with varying environmental demands. She writes: "The patient with a frontal lobe lesion seems unable to suppress his ongoing response tendencies, whether spontaneous or experimentally induced, or to rid himself of perseverative interference from previous sensory events" (p. 331). Milner marshalled evidence for this view from studies of frontal lobectomy patients using a variety of problem-solving tasks. Some of the most compelling evidence was obtained with the Wisconsin Card Sorting Test. Milner found that patients with dorsolateral prefrontal lesions achieved fewer categories and made more perseverative responses than patients with other frontal or non-frontal lesions (a perseverative response refers to a response based on the previously correct category). Importantly, the patients did not show increases in nonperseverative responses, indicating a selective difficulty in shifting ability; that is, a tendency to perseverate on old sorting strategies that are no longer appropriate. This deficit did not reflect a general failure in abstract thinking, in that patients understood the task instructions, and could often verbalize (in spite of not being able to carry out) the correct sorting strategy. The importance of the dorsolateral region for performance of this task has been corroborated by other behavioral studies (e.g., Eslinger & Grattan, 1993), as well as by functional neuroimaging techniques (e.g., Rezai, Andreasen, Alliger, Cohen, Swayze, & O'Leary, 1993; Weinberger, Berman, & Zec, 1986). WCST deficits have also been reported in patients with orbital and medial lesions (e.g., Drewe, 1974; Stuss, Benson, Kaplan, Weir, Naeser, Lieberman, & Ferrill, 1983).

One can think of these kinds of problem-solving deficits in terms of Shallice's distinction between automatic contention scheduling processes and a frontally-mediated supervisory attentional system. When the SAS is dysfunctional, problem solving proceeds without regard to goals or plans, relying entirely on information available in the problem situation. This can result in impulsive responding, where information in the problem automatically triggers a well-learned response; this seems to be the case in Luria's conflict problems. It also can result in response perseveration and difficulty shifting cognitive set, as in the case of the WCST, in which a response is reinforced experimentally. In either case, contention scheduling processes select highly activated schemas that ordinarily would be inhibited by the supervisory system.

Shallice (1982) provided evidence in support of this framework in a study using a "look-ahead" task similar to the Tower of Hanoi. The Tower of Hanoi, commonly used in artificial intelligence studies, requires the subject to move a stack of disks to a new configuration in a minimum number of moves. The standard version uses three or four disks of varying sizes that are situated on the left-most of three pegs. The subject's task is to transfer the disks to the right-most peg moving only one disk at a time and not placing a larger disk on top of a smaller disk. Shallice developed a variant of this task, the Tower of London, in which three colored beads must be moved from a starting configuration on three uneven sticks to a target position. Some puzzles have two- or three-move solutions which can be achieved by simply working forward. Other puzzles have four-move solutions which require means-end analysis or error correction procedures. Finally, the remaining puzzles have five-move solutions; these problems have conflicting sub-goals and require complex planning. Shallice observed that patients with left frontal lesions performed significantly worse than patients with posterior or right frontal lesions, as measured by the number of problems correctly solved in less than 60 seconds. This was true for all three types of problem, although the difference in performance was greater the more planning that was required to solve the problem. These deficits were not due to a general visuospatial impairment, in that patients performed normally on the block design subtest of the WAIS. They also could not be attributed to impaired short-term memory, as indexed by digit span. The basic deficit was said to reflect an impairment in planning associated with a dysfunctional SAS.

Owen, Downes, Sahakian, Polkey, and Robbins (1990) provided evidence pointing to the dual role of planning and inhibition in performance of the Tower of London. They used a computerized version of the task, in which planning times could be measured separately from execution times. The authors found that patients with unilateral or bilateral frontal excisions required more moves per problem than matched controls. Unlike Shallice (1982), there were no hemispheric differences. Importantly, although frontal patients and controls did not differ in amount of planning time prior to the first move, frontals spent more time thinking during the rest of the problems. This latter result suggests impulsivity on the part of the frontal patients; i.e., a failure to adequately analyze the problem and suppress dominant modes of response.

More direct evidence for the role of inhibitory processing in tower-type tasks has been found in a recent study by Goel and Grafman (1995). The authors used a computerized version of a 5-disk Tower of Hanoi task with a variety of different start states and a goal state requiring stacking all the disks in descending order on the middle peg. They argued that the Tower of Hanoi cannot be solved solely on the basis of planning or look-ahead processes: unlike the Tower of London, it requires a counterintuitive backward move, in which the problem solver must inhibit the global goal of the end configuration and focus on a subgoal. Results indicated that patients with prefrontal lesions performed worse than matched controls, using a standardized score based on accuracy, completion time, and problem difficulty. No differences were observed for patients with left, right, or bilateral lesions. Consistent with the authors' hypothesis, analysis of the individual moves carried out by each subject indicated that poorer performance was due to difficulties in resolving goal-subgoal conflicts.

In a task modeled after everyday problem-solving situations, Shallice and Burgess (1991) provided further evidence for a link between problem solving, inhibition, and the frontal lobes. Patients were required to carry out multiple errands on a city street. Somė of these were simple tasks such as buying a loaf of bread or a package of throat lozenges. Another task required the subject to be at a certain place after 15 minutes. A final task required obtaining a variety of different information (e.g., the name of the coldest place in Britain yesterday, the name of the shop likely to have the most expensive item) and recording that information on a postcard. Subjects were required to abide by a set of specific rules (e.g., staying within certain boundaries or not entering a store without buying anything). There were many instances of what appeared to reflect a defect in inhibition. For example, one patient entered a drug store and refused to make the required purchase, because the store did not stock the brand she liked. Other errors included going into irrelevant shops and entering shops out of bounds. Shallice and Burgess argued that many of the errors on both tests reflected a disruption in the creation or triggering of markers. A marker is defined as a message that some future behavior or event should not be treated as routine; instead, a certain aspect of the situation should be viewed as particularly relevant for action. When the appropriate trigger occurs, ongoing behavior is ordinarily inhibited and the person switches to a different course of action.

The problem-solving tasks discussed thus far have all involved convergent thinking; i.e., thinking which requires discovery of a pre-determined solution. As noted in the section on *The Role of Inhibition in Cognition*, however, there is another kind of thinking in which flexibility and inhibition may be important: divergent thinking. Zangwill (1966) noted that frontal lobe patients, though exhibiting intact performance on standard intelligence tests that tap convergent thinking abilities, show breakdowns in tasks calling for divergent output.

Most of the tasks investigating divergent thinking in frontal lobe patients have been fluency tasks. These tasks require the subject to produce as many instances of a category as they can within a certain time limit. Milner (1964) showed that patients with left prefrontal excisions (sparing Broca's area) showed markedly reduced output on a verbal fluency test requiring the generation of words beginning with a certain letter, as compared to patients with right frontal or left temporal excisions. Many patients adopted the highly inefficient technique of looking around the room for objects beginning with the required letter. A double dissociation was observed, in that left frontal, but not left temporal, patients showed good performance on a verbal memory test. Perret (1974) suggested that word fluency deficits may reflect an impairment in the ability to suppress the habit of using words according to their meaning, similar to what one sees on the Stroop test. In support of this hypothesis, she found disproportionate impairment on both word fluency and Stroop measures in patients with frontal lesions (left frontals performed considerably worse than right frontals); a strong correlation was found between the two measures, particularly in the left frontal group. Patients with right frontal damage show disproportionate impairment on design fluency, a nonverbal analogue of verbal fluency (e.g., Jones-Gottman & Milner, 1977). Both left and right frontal lesions seem to produce deficits on ideational fluency tests. For example, Eslinger and Grattan (1993) showed that frontal patients (with unilateral dorsolateral lesions and, in one case, bilateral medial damage) were more likely than patients with posterior lesions to make incorrect or perseverative responses on a test requiring the production of alternate uses of common objects.

To summarize, frontal lobe patients show problem-solving deficits on tasks as diverse as complex arithmetic problems, conflict problems, the WCST, the Towers of Hanoi and London, multiple errand problems, and divergent- thinking problems. The pattern of errors on these tasks -- difficulty shifting cognitive set, impulsive behavior, and response perseveration -- is suggestive of a breakdown in inhibitory processes linked with a dysfunctional supervisory attentional system. The finding of inhibitory deficits following lesions in a variety of prefrontal loci, together with some regional specificity, suggests that the prefrontal cortex performs a global inhibitory function, but that different prefrontal subregions may be selectively involved in different problem-solving tasks (Goldman-Rakic, 1987; Shimamura, 1995).

Schizophrenics

Since at least the time of Kraepelin and Bleuler, frontal lobe dysfunction has been thought to contribute to the primary behavioral deficits of schizophrenia. In his classic book, *Dementia Praecox and Paraphrenia*, Kraepelin (1919/1971) wrote: "On various grounds it is easy to believe that the frontal cortex, which is specially well developed in man, stands in closer relation to his higher intellectual abilities, and these are the faculties which in our patients suffer profound loss..." (p. 219). Kraepelin viewed dementia praecox as a "destruction of the psychic personality," in which "judgment is lost, the critical faculty, the creative gift, especially the capacity to make a higher use of knowledge and ability."

In contemporary formulations, schizophrenic symptoms may be broken down into two classes: positive and negative. Positive symptoms refer to excesses or distortions of normal functions; these include hallucinations, delusions, and thought disorder. Negative symptoms refer to decreases or losses in normal functions, and include flattened affect, reduced motivation, deficits in social functioning, paucity of speech, and cognitive impairment. A number of authors have noted the similarity between these latter symptoms and the behavioral effects of frontal lobe lesions (e.g., Andreasen, Rezai, Alliger, Swayze, Flaum, Kirschner, Cohen, & O'Leary, 1992; Cohen & Servan-Schreiber, 1992; Frith, 1992; Levin, 1984; Weinberger et al., 1986)

-- providing some suggestion that pathology of the frontal lobes may be involved in schizophrenia. Consistent with this, schizophrenics show disproportionate impairment on neuropsychological tests of frontal lobe function (e.g., Kolb & Wishaw, 1983; Taylor & Abrams, 1984); they also show impairments in smooth-pursuit eye movements, which have been linked with dysfunction in the frontal eye fields.

In addition to these behavioral parallels, there is growing evidence from neuroimaging studies for frontal lobe dysfunction in schizophrenia. Reduced volume of the frontal cortex has been observed in several structural magnetic resonance imaging (MRI) studies (e.g., Andreasen, Nasrallah, Dunn, Olson, Grove, Ehrhardt, Coffman, & Crossett, 1986; DeMyer, Gilmor, Hendrite, DeMyer, Augustyn, & Jackson, 1988), and it has been suggested that a subtle prefrontal lesion may contribute to the positive deficits of schizophrenia by affecting subcortical structures downstream (e.g., Weinberger et al., 1986). However, other structural MRI studies have failed to find evidence of frontal pathology (e.g., Andreasen, Ehrhardt, Swayze, Alliger, Yuh, Cohen, & Ziebell, 1990; Smith, Baumgartner, & Calderon, 1987), raising the possibility that any frontal lobe involvement may be based on functional abnormalities. Early studies of resting regional cerebral blood flow (rCBF) documented a "hypofrontal" pattern of brain activity in schizophrenics; that is, a reversal of the usual finding of increased blood flow to frontal relative to posterior brain regions, an effect which was associated with the severity of negative symptoms (Ingvar & Franzen, 1974). More recent work suggests that reduced blood flow may only occur during the execution of specific behavioral tasks that are thought to challenge the prefrontal cortex (e.g. Andreasen et al., 1992; Weinberger et al., 1986).

The failure of the prefrontal cortex to engage during specific cognitive activity may reflect malfunctioning in circuitry involving dopaminergic projections from the neostriatum (see, e.g., Cohen & Servan-Schreiber, 1992; Early, Posner, Reiman, & Raichle, 1989; Frith, 1992; Levin, 1984; Robbins, 1990; Weinberger et al., 1986). It has long been thought that hyperactivity in subcortical dopamine pathways contributes to the positive symptoms of schizophrenia, the so-called "dopamine hypothesis". Altered dopamine innervation from the ventral tegmentum (perhaps resulting from dysfunction in descending prefrontal projections) may disrupt frontostriatal circuitry involving the ventral striatum and anterior cingulate (see Figure 2). Associated dysfunction in the nigrostriatal dopamine system may disrupt pathways involving the caudate nucleus and dorsolateral and orbitofrontal cortices. Early et al. (1989) have cited evidence suggestive of a particular impairment in the anterior cingulate circuit. Schizophrenics show a constellation of deficits associated with impaired attentional function (linked with the cingulate), including difficulty orienting to the right side of space, loss of control of verbal associations, and convictions of thought and mind control; they also evidence anatomic abnormalities in the cingulate and physiological disturbances in structures that project to it (e.g., the globus pallidus). Dysfunction of the anterior cingulate circuit may produce cognitive impairments by disrupting the ability to control activity in lateral prefrontal areas important for the maintenance of information over time.

One likely behavioral outcome of disrupted frontostriatal circuitry is impaired inhibitory function. Indeed, breakdowns in inhibition have been thought to play a role in schizophrenia since the time the disorder was named. Bleuler (1911/1950) noted:

> It is probable that in the normal psyche there are also inhibitions which prevent the use of disparate associational material and hinder the transition to another theme, except under the influence of special forces... If these inhibitions can be overcome in the normal psyche,

> it is obvious that they can fail completely in schizophrenics ... This in itself may be one of the reasons why the schizophrenic's thoughts are so easily lost in irrelevancies and why such strange associations crop up in his train of thoughts. (p. 361)

Clinical observations suggest that schizophrenic patients show perseverative and stereotyped responses in a number of domains, consistent with a loss of cognitive inhibition. It has frequently been reported that patients repeat the same expressions or phrases, carry out the same movements or actions, or maintain the same position for hours at a time. Kraepelin (1919/1971), for instance, described the case of a patient who added, "We Germans don't have that" to the end of every utterance, and another who threw his roll on the table 100 times. As Bleuler (1911/1950) put it, "The patients are caught in and remain fixed to the same circle of ideas, the same words, the same sentence structures, or, at any rate, return to them again and again without any logical need" (p. 27).

Experimental evidence also points to disrupted inhibitory function. Like frontal lobe patients, schizophrenics show increased interference on the Stroop test (e.g., Wysocki & Sweet, 1985) and reflexive glances in the anti-saccade task (e.g., Thaker, Nguyen, & Tamminga, 1989). They also exhibit language deficits in which they interpret ambiguous words in terms of prepotent meanings (e.g., for the sentence, "The farmer needed a new *pen* for his cattle", schizophrenics are more likely than normals to interpret *pen* as a writing implement (e.g., Chapman, Chapman, & Miller, 1964). Overly literal interpretations of proverbs may also reflect impairments in inhibition, to the extent that patients are unable to suppress the dominant meanings of the component words. Disrupted inhibitory processes are also apparent in the domain of problem solving -- as evidenced by impaired cognitive shifting, impulsive responding, and perseveration. As is the case for frontal lobe patients, these deficits can be thought of in terms of a dissociation between contention scheduling processes and a frontally-mediated supervisory attentional system.

Weinberger and colleagues have provided particularly compelling evidence implicating the frontal lobes in inhibitory deficits in problem solving in schizophrenia (e.g., Berman, Illowsky, & Weinberger, 1988; Berman, Zec, & Weinberger, 1986; Goldberg, Weinberger, Berman, Pliskin, & Hyde, 1987; Weinberger et al., 1986; Weinberger, Berman, & Illowsky, 1988). These studies examined regional cerebral blood flow during performance of the Wisconsin Card Sorting Test. Behaviorially, schizophrenic patients showed the typical frontal pattern of impaired set shifting, as evidenced by increased numbers of perseverative errors and reduced numbers of achieved categories compared to controls. Furthermore, patients often knew their responses were incorrect but carried them out anyway. More telling, patients failed to show increased activation in the (dorsolateral) prefrontal cortex during execution of the task. This effect was present in both medicated and unmedicated patients; moreover, reduced activation was associated with the extent of cognitive impairment. These findings were not indicative of deficits in mental effort or motivation, as illustrated by a failure to find a hypofrontal activational pattern on an equally difficult visual continuous performance task. They also could not be attributed to a general deficit in abstract thinking, in that no such pattern was found during performance of the Raven's Progressive Matrices test. Importantly, the level of prefrontal activation was related to cerebrospinal fluid levels of the dopamine metabolite homovanillic acid, consistent with the dopamine explanation of schizophrenic cognitive deficits.

Studies using the Towers of Hanoi and London provide further evidence for a link between problem solving, inhibition, and the frontal lobes (e.g., Andreasen et al., 1992; Goldberg, Saint Cyr, & Weinberger, 1990; Morris, Rushe, Woodruffe, &

Murray, 1995; Schmand, Brand, & Kuipers, 1992). On the Tower of Hanoi, Goldberg et al. (1990) found that medicated schizophrenic patients took more moves than controls to solve the 3- or 4-disk versions of the test. Patients also made considerably more illegal moves on both tests, evidencing typical frontal impulsiveness. Schmand et al. (1992) found a similar deficit on the 4-disk task, as measured by both number of moves and speed of response. Patients were unimpaired in these measures on the 3-disk version, but did show a disproportionate number of illegal moves. Unfortunately, no data were available in either study relevant to Goel and Grafman's (1995) hypothesis concerning the role of inhibition in the resolution of goal-subgoal conflicts.

An rCBF study by Andreasen et al. (1992) found evidence implicating the medial frontal lobes, including the anterior cingulate, in performance of the Tower of London. Both neuroleptic-naive and chronic unmedicated patients solved fewer problems than controls; moreover, patients failed to show increased perfusion to left medial frontal cortex. Follow-up analyses suggested that the failure to activate frontal cortex was only evident in patients with prominent negative symptoms. This study is important, in that it indicates that hypofrontality is not due to long-term use of medication, a possible confounding factor in many studies of schizophrenia. It also is noteworthy in showing a link between problem-solving performance and the medial frontal lobes, perhaps indicating the importance of an anterior attention system in planning and cognitive inhibition.

More detailed behavioral data on the Tower of London were reported in a study by Morris et al. (1995). This study used a computerized version of the task similar to that used by Owen et al. (1992) in their study of frontal lobe patients. As in that study, patients took more moves than controls and exhibited slower overall response times. Like frontal lobe patients, however, they did not show a difference in the amount of planning time prior to the first move, indicating impulsive responding and reduced cognitive inhibition. These results cannot be attributed to a general impairment in working memory, in that patients showed intact performance on the Corsi spatial span test, indicating that they did not have difficulty holding in mind a sequence of moves.

Performance of schizophrenics may also bear on the role of inhibition in divergent or creative forms of problem solving. It has long been speculated that there may be a link between creativity and psychosis, as evidenced by the frequent reports of creative individuals going insane and psychotic individuals producing highly creative works. Although the strong version of this hypothesis has not held up to scientific scrutiny, there is reason to believe that the thinking patterns of schizophrenics bear some resemblance to those of creative individuals. Dykes and McGhie (1976) present an interesting study that is relevant to this hypothesis. They argue that both schizophrenics and highly creative people show a widening of attention, in which they sample a broader range of environmental input than other individuals. In support of this, they showed that schizophrenics and subjects scoring high on tests of creative thinking produced unusual and idiosyncratic responses on an object sorting test. This test presents subjects with a starting object (e.g., a red paper circle) and requires them to choose other objects that belong with it. An idiosyncratic response might be *cigarettes*, which when lit resemble a red circle. In a related vein, it has been shown that schizophrenics perform better than normals on tests of ideational fluency. For example, Keefe and Magaro (1980) reported that acutely schizophrenic patients were more creative on the Alternate Uses Test than were non-schizophrenic controls. This advantage contrasts with Eslinger and Grattan's (1993) finding of impoverished output on the same test in frontal lobe patients, suggesting a potential difference in divergent problem solving between the two subject populations. It may be that dysfunction in the anterior attention system of the medial frontal cortex is a precondition for heightened ideational fluency.

The increased sensitivity to environmental input observed in schizophrenia, though beneficial in divergent thinking, may impede problem solving that calls for convergent thinking. Dykes and McGhie (1976) showed that schizophrenics, but not highly creative individuals, performed poorly on the Chapman card sorting test, which requires classifying into a single category cards representing common objects; distractor items are also presented which lead the subject to make an improper classification. The authors concluded that schizophrenics have difficulty focusing attention on the central elements of a problem and screening out irrelevant information in conformity with the requirements of the task. Consistent with this view, schizophrenics show impaired performance on verbal fluency tasks that require a constrained search through lexical memory and inhibition of task-inappropriate information (e.g., Kolb & Wishaw, 1983).

In sum, like frontal lobe patients, schizophrenics show problem-solving deficits that implicate impaired inhibitory function and a dysfunctional supervisory attentional system. Increased perseverative responding on the WCST and impulsive responding on tower tasks suggest a failure to shift cognitive sets and inhibit prepotent response tendencies. These deficits may be attributed to dysfunction in frontostriatal circuits and reduced dopamine levels in the prefrontal cortex. The finding of enhanced performance on certain divergent-thinking tasks points to the special importance of disrupted circuitry involving medial frontal regions, particularly the anterior cingulate (Early et al., 1989).

Normal elderly

The notion that inhibitory function may be compromised in normal aging dates back to Pavlov. Neurological noise theories of aging were popular in the 1950s and 1960s, positing a general difficulty in picking out signals against a background of increased ambient neural activity (cf. Gregory, 1959). Inhibitory concepts were also prevalent in psychology, with a number of early studies demonstrating effects suggestive of inhibitory deficits (e.g., Jerome, 1959; Rabbitt, 1965). Over the course of the next several decades, inhibitory approaches were temporarily displaced by processing resource models positing declines in working memory, attentional capacity, or speed of processing (e.g., Cerella, 1985; Craik & Byrd, 1982; Salthouse, 1982). With the publication of Hasher and Zacks' (1988) "new view" of working memory and age-related cognitive declines, however, inhibitory models have once again become a dominant force within cognitive gerontology (see also Dempster, 1992).

Due to conceptual and empirical problems associated with processing resource theories, Hasher and Zacks proposed an alternative framework in which age-related cognitive declines can be thought of as reflecting inefficiencies in inhibitory attentional processes. Their theory, originally proposed in the context of reading and discourse comprehension, focuses on the contents of working memory as opposed to its capacity. They argue that breakdowns in inhibitory processing allow task-irrelevant information to enter working memory, including contextually-inappropriate interpretations of words and phrases, extraneous environmental details, and personalistic memories or concerns. Inhibition also functions to remove irrelevant information that leaks into working memory or that becomes irrelevant with changes in goals or the task situation. In a later paper, Zacks and Hasher (1994) generalized this model to account for age deficits in a variety of cognitive domains, including attention, language, memory, and problem solving.

There is evidence from many tasks supporting the role of inhibition in cognitive deficits that occur with advancing age. Like frontal lobe and schizophrenic patients, older adults show increased susceptibility to Stroop interference, as well as other deficits in selective attention (e.g., Cohn, Dustman, & Bradford, 1984; Hasher, Stoltzfus, Zacks, & Rympa, 1991; McDowd & Oseas-Kreger, 1991). In language, elderly individuals exhibit difficulty inhibiting previously generated inferences that are no longer relevant and show increased verbosity in speech (e.g., Arbuckle & Gold, 1993; Hamm & Hasher, 1992). Memory studies have demonstrated that the elderly exhibit increased intrusions and repetitions in free recall, among other deficits (e.g., Koriat, Ben-Zur, & Sheffer, 1988; Stine & Wingfield, 1987).

The inhibitory hypothesis of age-related cognitive declines gains considerable support from evidence implicating dysfunction of the frontal lobes as one of the hallmarks of cognitive aging. Neuropsychological studies reveal selective impairments in the elderly on tests of frontal lobe function (e.g., Albert & Kaplan, 1980; Daigneault, Braun, & Whitaker, 1992; Mittenberg, Seidenberg, O'Leary, Di Giulio, 1989; Whelihan & Lesher, 1985). In addition, there is clear evidence of structural changes in the frontal cortex (e.g., Haug, Barmwater, Eggers, Fischer, Kuhl, & Sass, 1983; Scheibel & Scheibel, 1975; Terry, DeTeresa, & Hansen, 1987). Some regional specificity within the frontal cortex may be present, with dorsolateral and orbital regions showing more extensive atrophy than medial regions (e.g., Raz, Gunning, Head, Dupuis, McQuain, Briggs, Loken, Thorton, & Acker, 1997). Functional abnormalities in the prefrontal cortex have also been documented in studies of resting regional cerebral blood flow (e.g., Gur, Gur, Obrist, Skolnick, & Reivitch, 1987; Shaw, Mortel, Meyer, Rogers, Hardenberg, & Cutaia, 1984). Finally, there is evidence for reduced dopaminergic activity in both the prefrontal cortex and the dorsal striatum (e.g., Severson, Marcusso, Winblad, & Finch, 1982; Suhara, Fukuda, Inoue, Itoh, Suzuki, Yamasaki, & Tateno, 1991), pointing to dysfunction in frontostriatal circuitry involving the nigrostriatal dopamine system (see Figure 2). One possibility is that cognitive deficits arise due to slowing of psychomotor speed associated with basal ganglia dysfunction, which indirectly affects working memory (including inhibitory) capabilities of the prefrontal cortex (Gabrieli, 1994).

Consistent with pathology in frontal or frontostriatal systems, the elderly show deficits in goal-directed behavior that interfere with problem solving. An early study by Jerome (1962; cited in Botwinick, 1984) illustrates this impairment. In this study, subjects were required to learn complex relations among button-activated peripheral lights to turn on a central light. This involved learning three different concepts (e.g, that one light must be lit for another to turn on) and integrating those concepts. Elderly subjects performed very poorly on the task, repeatedly pressing buttons to receive information they had already acquired. Their performance was characterized by a lack of order or direction, involving "haphazard questioning rather than concentration on a single path to the goal" which "brought information only randomly, making it difficult to distinguish the relevant from the irrelevant." This description recalls Luria's (1966) characterization of the problem-solving deficits in frontal lobe patients, and can be thought of as well as reflecting a dissociation between a supervisory attentional system and stimulus-driven contention-scheduling processes (Shallice, 1982).

Like frontal lobe patients, the elderly show particular difficulties with problem-solving situations that call for flexible thinking and shifting of cognitive set. For example, early studies demonstrated that older adults show impaired performance when different kinds of problems are presented in alternation (e.g., Botwinick, Brinley, & Robbin, 1958). Similar kinds of deficits have been observed on the Wisconsin Card Sorting Test (e.g., Daigneault et al., 1992; Kramer, Humphrey, Larish, Logan, & Strayer, 1994). Elderly subjects exhibit increased perseverative errors and achieve fewer categories than young controls, suggesting an impairment in cognitive shifting. By contrast, old subjects perform equivalently to young in terms of the number of trials required to complete the first category and the number of concept level responses (i.e., correct responses occurring in consecutive runs of three), indicating relative preservation of conceptual ability (Kramer et al., 1994). Mirroring the findings in schizophrenics, Raz, Gunning-Dixon, Head, Dupuis, and Acker (1998) demonstrated a link between perseverative errors and age-related volumetric changes in the prefrontal cortex, as measured with structural magnetic resonance imaging scans (the prefrontal cortex was defined to include dorsolateral and orbital regions). Importantly, no such link was observed for nonperseverative errors.

Hoyer, Rebok, and Sved (1979) provided further evidence for a link between problem solving, aging, and inhibition using a different concept identification paradigm. This study was designed specifically to examine the effects of different amounts of irrelevant information on age deficits in problem solving. Subjects were presented with stimuli that varied according to the dimensions of form (circle, square, of triangle), color (green, red, or yellow), number (two, three, or four), and position (horizontal, vertical, or diagonal). They were given cards containing two such items and a standard card; one of the test items matched the standard card on one stimulus dimension (the relevant dimension). Subjects were instructed to select the test item that was most similar to the standard. Irrelevancy was manipulated by using four different kinds of problems that varied according to the number of irrelevant dimensions (0 through 3). Hoyer et al. found that elderly subjects showed disproportionately longer reaction times and increased errors the greater the number of irrelevant dimensions. Their impairments were particularly pronounced when problems contained two or three irrelevant attributes. Since the amount of relevant information was held constant in this study, these results provide strong evidence for an inhibitory model of age-related deficits in problem solving.

As in the other populations discussed thus far, elderly individuals exhibit problem-solving deficits on the Tower of Hanoi. Charness (1987) found that elderly subjects showed an increased number of illegal moves on the 4-disk task, suggesting impulsive responding and inability to follow task instructions. As was the case in frontal lobe and schizophrenic patients, old subjects spent no more time planning than controls on the first trial of the task. However, they took more time overall to plan legal moves, again suggestive of failure to adequately develop a plan prior to responding. Correlational analyses revealed that the number of illegal moves was related to speed of processing, as indexed by simple reaction time. This may reflect the role of impaired frontostriatal function, with reduced perceptual-motor speed, associated with dopamine depletion in the basal ganglia, affecting the inhibitory function of the prefrontal cortex. Working memory, as indexed by digit span, was not correlated with the number of illegal moves, as in schizophrenia suggesting a primary deficit of inhibition. Detailed analysis of subjects' moves was not carried out, so it is unknown whether or not subjects showed specific difficulties resolving goal-subgoal conflicts, as might be expected on an inhibitory account (Goel & Grafman, 1995).

In addition to impairments in convergent problem solving, the elderly exhibit declines in divergent and creative thinking. It has long been thought that creativity declines in old age, as evidenced by reduced quality and quantity of work in scientists, artists, and other creative individuals (e.g., Lehman, 1953). Alpaugh and Birren (1977) provided evidence suggesting that such declines may be linked with age-related changes in divergent-thinking abilities. In their study, subjects ranging in age from 20 to 83 completed a series of classic divergent-thinking tasks. These included thinking of new uses for objects, making up titles for stories, and producing symbols. A composite measure of creativity showed clear declines over the life span. Importantly, verbal intelligence was comparable across age groups. McCrae,

Arenberg, and Costa (1987) provided both cross-sectional and longitudinal data supporting Alpaugh and Birren's conclusions. Studies of word and design fluency have also documented declines in divergent thinking, as well as increases in perseverative responding (e.g., Daigneault et al., 1992; Mittenberg et al., 1989; Whelihan & Lesher, 1985).

Performance on insight tasks provides further evidence for disrupted inhibitory function in aging. In an early study, Heglin (1956) examined set effects in old, young, and middle-aged subjects on water jar and alphabet maze problems. In the water jar problems, subjects were given three imaginary containers, A, B, and C, of different capacities, and asked to obtain a specific quantity of water. An example is a problem in which jug A contains 21 quarts, jug B contains 127 quarts, and jug C contains 3 quarts, and the required quantity of water is 100 quarts. This problem can be solved via the formula B-A-2C. Subjects were first given a group of problems that were soluble via the same formula. They then received problems that could be solved either with that formula or with a simpler one (e.g., A-C). Finally, they were given problems that only could be solved with a simpler formula. Heglin found that older subjects exhibited stronger set effects on the final problem (i.e., performed worse) than subjects of other ages, consistent with an impairment in cognitive inhibition. Similar results were observed on an alphabet maze task, which required finding a path of words beginning at the upper right-hand corner of a grid of letters and continuing to the lower left-hand corner.

In summary, studies of the normal elderly provide converging evidence for the importance of inhibitory frontal lobe processes in problem solving. Set-shifting deficits, difficulty screening out task-irrelevant information, and impulsive responding are observed in tasks such as the WCST, Tower of Hanoi, and divergent and creative thinking problems. These deficits may arise from structural abnormalities in the prefrontal cortex or may reflect disruptions in frontostriatal circuitry. Associations of problem-solving decrements with changes in psychomotor speed point to the possible importance of a frontostriatal system in age-associated changes in problem solving.

Conclusions and Future Directions

In this chapter, I have considered the role that cognitive inhibition plays in problem solving by examining evidence from studies of frontal lobe patients, schizophrenics, and the normal elderly. In all of these subject populations, frontal cortical dysfunction is implicated, which has considerable negative consequences for problem-solving performance. By disrupting the ability to flexibly shift hypotheses and strategies, as well as suppress task-inappropriate information, frontal dysfunction affects performance on tasks as diverse as the Wisconsin Card Sorting Test, the Towers of Hanoi and London, and divergent-thinking problems. This problem-solving impairment can be seen as reflecting disruption in a supervisory attentional system, leaving intact the relatively automatic processes of contention-scheduling (Shallice, 1982).

For the most part, my discussion has focused on the general role of the frontal lobes in inhibition and problem solving. Due to the limited range of studies that have been carried out to date, little can be said about the relative role of different subdivisions of the prefrontal cortex in inhibitory function. Moreover, differences in problem-solving performance depending on the relative role of focal frontal damage as opposed to frontostriatal dysfunction remain poorly understood. Finally, it is unclear to what extent the inhibitory role of the frontal lobes differs in various forms of problem solving. In this section, I consider directions for future research which may help fill some of these gaps.

In the section on *Inhibition and the Frontal Lobes*, I outlined two possible organizations of inhibitory function within the prefrontal cortex: a global function that operates across subdivisions but on specifically different inputs for each (Goldman-Rakic, 1987; Shimamura, 1995) and a specific function localized to orbital and perhaps medial regions (Fuster, 1989). The evidence reviewed in this chapter is most consistent with the former view. In line with this, one might reasonably suppose that the inhibitory role of the prefrontal cortex depends on the nature of a particular problem-solving task. For example, the WCST may depend primarily on dorsolateral inhibition, to the extent that it requires suppression of previously reinforced sorting strategies in interaction with the hippocampus. By contrast, fluency tasks, which require shifting among pre-existent mental categories, may depend on connections between multiple prefrontal regions (specialized for different kinds of information) and associated posterior cortical sites. Medial frontal regions important for attention, particularly the anterior cingulate, may also contribute to performance in these tasks, working in tandem with lateral areas to select task-appropriate responses and inhibit inappropriate ones. Medial regions may also play a role in tower-type tasks, which require suppressing impulsive responding and following a plan.

These considerations should make clear that there is unlikely to be a monolithic supervisory system that oversees goal-directed problem solving and mediates cognitive inhibition. An important task for future research is to specify subprocesses of the supervisory system and their role in inhibitory function. One way to accomplish this is to employ functional neuroimaging techniques, as in Weinberger and colleagues' investigations of the WCST and Andreasen and coworkers' studies of the Tower of London. Directly manipulating the inhibitory component of a particular task, as in Hoyer et al.'s (1979) study of concept identification, might be a particularly promising approach for future neuroimaging studies. Both neuroimaging and behavioral techniques should also be used to examine in further depth whether inhibitory effects in problem solving are based on a general representational or working memory system (Goldman-Rakic, 1987) or on a system specialized specifically for cognitive inhibition (Shimamura, 1995).

Further studies are also needed to better understand the role of inhibition in a broader range of problem-solving tasks. Better contact with the cognitive psychological literature on problem solving is called for in this regard. For example, it would be interesting to examine interference effects in analogical problem solving, as in Lovett and Anderson's (1994) study of geometry proofs. It is possible that memory for prior problem-solving episodes interferes with subsequent problem solving, and neuropsychological studies may help illuminate the role of inhibition in overcoming these effects. Similarly, given the likely importance of inhibition in insight problem solving, it would be worthwhile to examine this kind of problem solving from a neurocognitive perspective. Smith and Blankenship (1991), for example, have demonstrated a possible role for inhibitory processes in incubation effects that lead to insight. It would be useful to have convergent neuropsychological evidence in support of this hypothesis.

Another important task for future research concerns pinpointing differences in inhibition and problem solving in populations with different forms of neuropathology. The present chapter suggests that there are important similarities among different groups but that there may be important differences as well. For example, focal frontal lobe lesions may produce more severe, yet less pervasive, impairments than disruptions in frontostriatal circuitry. The specific kinds of impairment that are observed in the latter case, moreover, may depend on where in the circuitry a break lies. For instance, schizophrenics may show very different impairments than the elderly, specifically linked with attentional functions, due to involvement of the anterior cingulate. Reduced dopamine levels in the basal ganglia in normal aging, similarly, may produce cognitive slowing that affects problem solving in selective ways. More systematic comparisons of different subject populations, instead of studies focusing on isolated groups, should be carried out in hopes of better understanding the role of inhibition in problem solving. Study of populations other than those considered in this chapter -- for example, patients with Parkinson's disease, obsessive-compulsive disorder, and focal lesions of the basal ganglia -- should also be undertaken.

In conclusion, in keeping with the general theme of this volume, the present chapter highlights the important insights that can be achieved by adopting a neuropsychological approach to the study of human problem solving. It is time to abandon the computer metaphor of problem solving and adopt a brain metaphor.

ACKNOWLEDGMENT

Preparation of this chapter was supported by grant 2P01-AG09466 from the National Institute on Aging.

References

Albert, M.S., & Kaplan, E. (1980). Organic implications of neuropsychologic deficits in the elderly. In L.W. Poon, J.L. Fozard, L.S. Cermak, D. Arenberg, & L.W. Thompson (Eds.), *New directions in memory and aging* (pp. 403-429). Hillsdale, NJ: Erlbaum.

Alexander, G.E., DeLong, M.R., & Strick, P.L. (1986). Parallel organization of functionally segregated circuits linking basal ganglia and cortex. *Annual Review of Neuroscience, 9*, 357-381.

Alpaugh, P.K., & Birren, J.E. (1977). Variables affecting creative contributions across the adult life span. *Human Development, 20*, 240-248.

Anderson, J.R. (1983). *The architecture of cognition*. Cambridge, MA: Harvard University Press.

Anderson, J.R. (1993). *Rules of the mind*. Hillsdale, NJ: Erlbaum.

Andreasen, N.C., Ehrhardt, J.C., Swayze, V.W., Alliger, R.J., Yuh, W.T., Cohen, G., & Ziebell, S. (1990). Magnetic resonance imaging of the brain in schizophrenia: The pathophysiologic significance of structural abnormalities. *Archives of General Psychiatry, 47*, 35-44.

Andreasen, N.C., Nasrallah, H.A., Dunn, V., Olson, S.C., Grove, W.M., Ehrhardt, J.C., Coffman, J.A., & Crossett, J.H.W. (1986). Structural abnormalities in the frontal system of schizophrenia. *Archives of General Psychiatry, 43*, 136-144.

Andreasen, N.C., Rezai, K., Alliger, R., Swayze, V.W., Flaum, M., Kirschner, P., Cohen, G., & O'Leary, D.S. (1992). Hypofrontality in neuroleptic-naive patients and patients with chronic schizophrenia. *Archives of General Psychiatry, 49*, 943-958.

Arbuckle, T.Y., & Gold, D.P. (1993). Aging, inhibition, and verbosity. *Journal of Gerontology: Psychological Sciences, 48*, 225-232.

Berman, K.F., Illowsky, B.P., & Weinberger, D.R. (1988). Physiologic dysfunction of dorsolateral prefrontal cortex in schizophrenia. II: Role of neuroleptic treatment, attention, and mental effort. *Archives of General Psychiatry, 43*, 126-135.

Berman, K.F., Zec, R.F., & Weinberger, D.R. (1986). Physiologic dysfunction of dorsolateral prefrontal cortex in schizophrenia. IV: Further evidence for regional and behavioral specificity. *Archives of General Psychiatry, 45*, 616-623.

Bjork, R.A. (1989). Retrieval inhibition as an adaptive mechanism in human memory. In H.L. Roediger III, & F.I.M. Craik (Eds.), *Varieties of memory and consciousness: Essays in honor of Endel Tulving* (pp. 309-330). Hillsdale, NJ: Erlbaum.

Bleuler, E. (1911/1950). *Dementia praecox or the group of schizophrenias*. New York: International Universities Press.

Botwinick, J. (1984). *Aging and Behavior* (3rd Ed.). New York: Springer.

Botwinick, J., Brinley, J.F., & Robbin, J.S. (1958). Task alternation time in relation to problem difficulty. *Journal of Gerontology, 13*, 414-417.

Brutkowski, S., Konorski, J., Lawicka, W., Stepien, I., & Stepien, L. (1956). The effect of the removal of frontal poles of the cerebral cortex on motor conditioned reflexes in dogs. *Acta Biologica Experimental (Warsaw), 17*, 167-188.

Cerella, J. (1985). Information processing rates in the elderly. *Psychological Bulletin, 98*, 67-83.

Chapman, L.J., Chapman, J.P., & Miller, G.A. (1964). A theory of verbal behavior in schizophrenia. In B.A. Maher (Ed.), *Progress in experimental personality research* (Vol. 1, pp. 135-167). San Diego: Academic Press.

Charness, N. (1987). Component processes in bridge bidding and novel problem-solving tasks. *Canadian Journal of Psychology, 41*, 223-243.

Cherry, E.C. (1953). Some experiments on the recognition of speech, with one and two ears. *Journal of the Acoustical Society of America, 25*, 975-979.

Cohen, J.D., & Servan-Schreiber, D. (1992). Context, cortex, and dopamine: A connectionist approach to behavior and biology in schizophrenia. *Psychological Review, 99*, 45-77.

Cohn, N.B., Dustman, R.E., & Bradford, D.C. (1984). Age-related decrements in Stroop color test performance. *Journal of Clinical Psychology, 40*, 1244-1250.

Craik, F.I.M., & Byrd, M. (1982). Aging and cognitive deficits: The role of attentional resources. In F.I.M. Craik & S. Trehub (Eds.), *Aging and cognitive processes* (pp. 191-211). New York: Plenum.

Dagenbach, D., & Carr, T.H. (1994). *Inhibitory processes in attention, memory, and language.* San Diego: Academic Press.

Daigneault, S., Braun, C.M.J., & Whitaker, H.A. (1992). Early effects of normal aging on perseverative and non-perseverative prefrontal measures. *Developmental Neuropsychology, 8*, 99-114.

Dell, G.S., & O'Seaghdha, P.G. (1994). Inhibition in interactive activation models of linguistic selection and sequencing. In D. Dagenbach & T.H. Carr (1994), *Inhibitory processes in attention, memory, and language.* San Diego: Academic Press.

Dempster, F.N. (1992). The rise and fall of the inhibitory mechanism: Toward a unified theory of cognitive development and aging. *Developmental Review, 12*, 45-75.

Dempster, F.N., & Brainerd, C. (1995). *New perspectives on interference and inhibition in cognition.* San Diego: Academic Press.

DeMyer, M.K., Gilmor, R.L., Hendrie, H.C., DeMyer, W.E., Augustyn, G.T., & Jackson, R.K. (1988). Magnetic resonance brain images in schizophrenic and normal subjects: Influence of diagnosis and education. *Schizophrenia Bulletin, 14*, 21-37.

Diamond, A., Cruttenden, L., & Neiderman, D. (1994). A-not-B with multiple wells: 1. Why are multiple wells sometimes easier than two wells? 2. Memory or memory + inhibition? *Developmental Psychology, 30*, 192-205.

Dorfman, J., Shames, V.A., & Kihlstrom, J.F. (1996). Intuition, incubation, and insight: Implicit cognition in problem solving. In G. Underwood (Ed.), *Implicit cognition.* Oxford, U.K.: Oxford University Press.

Drewe, E. (1974). The effect of type and area of brain lesion on Wisconsin Card Sorting performance. *Cortex, 10*, 159-170.

Drewe, E. (1975). Go-no-go learning after frontal lobe lesions in humans. *Cortex, 11*, 8-16.

Dykes, M., & McGhie, A. (1976). A comparative study of attentional strategies of schizophrenic and highly creative normal subjects. *British Journal of Psychiatry, 128*, 50-56.

Early, T.S., Posner, M.I., Reiman, E.M., & Raichle, M.E. (1989). Left striato-pallidal hyperactivity in schizophrenia Part II: Phenomenology and thought disorder. *Psychiatric Developments, 2*, 109-121.

Eslinger, P.L, & Grattan, L.M. (1993). Frontal lobe and frontal-striatal substrates for different forms of human cognitive flexibility. *Neuropsychologia, 31*, 17-28.

Estes, W.K. (1972). An associative basis for coding and organization in memory. In A.W. Melton & E. Martin (Eds.), *Coding processes in human memory.* Washington, DC: Winston.

Frith, C.D. (1992). *The cognitive neuropsychology of schizophrenia.* Hillsdale, NJ: Erlbaum.

Fuster, J.M. (1989). *The prefrontal cortex: Anatomy, physiology, and neuropsychology of the frontal lobe* (2nd ed.). New York: Raven Press.

Gabrieli, J.D.E. (1994). Contributions of the basal ganglia to skill learning and working memory in humans. In J.C. Houk, J.L. Davis, & D.G. Beiser (Eds.), *Models of information processing in the basal ganglia* (pp. 277-294). Cambridge, MA: MIT Press.

Goel, V., & Grafman, J. (1995). Are the frontal lobes implicated in "planning" functions? Interpreting data from the Tower of Hanoi. *Neuropsychologia, 33*, 623-642.

Goldberg, T.E, Saint-Cyr, J.A., & Weinberger, D.R. (1990). Assessment of procedural learning and problem solving in schizophrenic patients by Tower of Hanoi type tasks. *Journal of Neuropsychiatry, 2*, 165-173.

Goldberg, T.E., Weinberger, D.R., Berman, K.F., Pliskin, N.H., & Hyde, N. (1987). Further evidence for dementia of the prefrontal type in schizophrenia. *Archives of General Psychiatry, 44*, 1008-1014.

Goldman-Rakic, P.S. (1987). Circuitry of primate prefrontal cortex and regulation of behavior by representational memory. In F. Plum (Ed.), *Handbook of physiology - The nervous system, V* (pp. 373-417). Bethesda, MD: American Physiological Society.

Grant, D.A., & Berg, E.A. (1948). A behavioral analysis of degree of reinforcement and ease of shifting to new responses in a Weigl type card sorting problem. *Journal of Experimental Psychology, 38*, 404-411.

Gregory, R.L. (1959). Increase in "neurological noise" as a factor in aging. *Proceedings of the Fourth International Congress on Gerontology, 1*, 314-324.

Guitton, D., Buchtel, H.A., & Douglas, R.M. (1985). Frontal lobe lesions in man cause difficulties in suppressing reflexive glances and in generated goal-directed saccades. *Experimental Brain Research, 58*, 455-472.

Gur, R.C., Gur, R.E., Obrist, W.D., Skolnick, B.E., & Reivitch, M. (1987). Age and regional cerebral blood flow at rest and during cognitive activity. *Archives of General Psychiatry, 44*, 617-621.

Hamm, V.P., & Hasher, L. (1992). Age and the availability of inferences. *Psychology and Aging, 7*, 56-64.

Hasher, L., Stoltzfus, E.R., Zacks, R.T., & Rympa, B. (1991). Age and inhibition. *Journal of Experimental Psychology: Learning, Memory, and Cognition, 17*, 163-169.

Hasher, L., & Zacks, R.T. (1988). Working memory, comprehension, and aging: A review and a new view. In G.H. Bower (Ed.), *The psychology of learning and motivation: Advances in research and theory* (Vol. 22, pp. 193-224). San Diego: Academic Press.

Haug, H., Barmwater, U., Eggers, R., Fischer, D., Kuhl, S., & Sass, N.L. (1983). Anatomical changes in aging brain: Morphometric analysis of the human prosencephalon. In J. Cervois-Navarro & H.A. Sarkander (Eds.), *Brain aging: Neuropathology and neuropharmacology. Vol. 21: Aging*. New York: Raven Press.

Heglin, H.J. (1956). Problem-solving set in different age groups. *Journal of Gerontology, 11*, 310-317.

Hoyer, W.J., Rebok, G.W., & Sved, S.M. (1979). Effects of varying irrelevant information on adult age differences in problem solving. *Journal of Gerontology, 34*, 553-560.

Ingvar, D.H., & Franzen, G. (1974). Abnormalities of cerebral flow distribution in patients with chronic schizophrenia. *Acta Psychiatrica Scandinavica, 50*, 425-462.

Jerome, E.A. (1959). Age and learning -- Experimental studies. In J.E. Birren (Ed.), *Handbook of aging and the individual: Psychological and biological aspects* (pp. 655-699). Chicago: University of Chicago Press.

Jones-Gottman, M., & Milner, B. (1977). Design Fluency: The invention of nonsense drawings after focal cortical lesions. *Neuropsychologia, 15*, 653-674.

Keefe, J.A., & Magaro, P.A. (1980). Creativity and schizophrenia: An equivalence of cognitive processing. *Journal of Abnormal Psychology, 89*, 390-398.

Kolb, B., & Wishaw, I.Q. (1983). Performance of schizophrenic patients on tests sensitive to left or right frontal, temporal, or parietal function in neurologic patients. *Journal of Mental and Nervous Disease, 171*, 435-443.

Koriat, A., Ben-Zur, H., & Sheffer, D. (1988). Telling the same story twice: Output monitoring and age. *Journal of Memory and Language, 27*, 23-39.

Kraepelin, E. (1919/1971). *Dementia praecox and paraphrenia*. Huntington, NY: Krieger.

Kramer, A.F., Humphrey, D.G., Larish, J.F., Logan, G.D., & Strayer, D.L. (1994). Aging and inhibition: Beyond a unitary view of inhibitory processing in attention. *Psychology and Aging, 9*, 491-512.

Lashley, K.S. (1948). The mechanism of vision: XVIII. Effects of destroying the visual "association areas" of the monkey. *Genetic Psychological Monographs, 37*, 107-166.

Lehman, H. (1953). *Age and achievement*. Princeton, NJ: Princeton University Press.

Levin, S. (1984). Frontal lobe dysfunction in schizophrenia. II. Impairments of psychological and brain functions. *Journal of Psychiatric Research, 18*, 27-55.

Lhermitte, F. (1983). "Utilization behavior" and its relation to lesions of the frontal lobes. *Brain, 106*, 237-255.

Lovett, M.C., & Anderson, J.R. (1994). Effects of solving related proofs on memory and transfer in geometry problem solving. *Journal of Experimental Psychology: Learning, Memory, and Cognition, 20*, 366-378.

Luria, A.R. (1966). *Higher cortical functions in man*. London: Tavistock.

McCrae, R.R., Arenberg, D., & Costa, P.T. (1987). Declines in divergent thinking with age: Cross-sectional, longitudinal, and cross-sequential analyses. *Psychology and Aging, 2*, 130-137.

McDermott, J., & Forgy, C. (1978). Production system conflict resolution strategies. In D.A. Waterman & F. Hayes-Roth (Eds.), *Pattern-directed inference systems* (pp. 177-199). New York: Academic Press.

McDowd, J., & Oseas-Kreger, D. (1991). Aging, inhibitory processes, and negative priming. *Journal of Gerontology: Psychological Sciences, 46*, 340-345.

Milner, B. (1964). Some effects of frontal lobectomy in man. In J.M. Warren and K. Akert (Eds.), *The frontal granular cortex and behavior.* New York: McGraw-Hill.

Mittenberg, W., Seidenberg, M., O'Leary, D.S., & Di Giulio, D.V. (1989). Changes in cerebral functioning associated with normal aging. *Journal of Clinical and Experimental Neuropsychology, 11*, 918-933.

Morris, R.G., Rushe, T., Woodruffe, P.W.R., & Murray, R.M. (1995). Problem solving in schizophrenia: A specific deficit in planning ability. *Schizophrenia Research, 14*, 235-246.

Newell, A. (1973). Production systems: Models of control structures. In W.G. Chase (Ed.), *Visual information processing*. New York: Academic Press.

Newell, A., & Simon, H.A. (1972). *Human problem solving*. Englewood Cliffs, NJ: Prentice-Hall.

Norman, D.A., & Shallice, T. (1986). Attention to action: Willed and automatic control of behavior. In R.J. Davidson, G.E. Schwartz, & D. Shapiro (Eds.), *Consciousness and self-regulation* (Vol. 4, pp. 1-18). New York: Plenum.

Onifer, W., & Swinney, D.A. (1981). Accessing lexical ambiguities during sentence comprehension: Effects of frequency of meaning and contextual bias. *Memory & Cognition, 9*, 225-236.

Owen, A.M., Downes, J.J., Sahakian, B.J., Polkey, C.E., & Robbins, T.W. (1990). Planning and spatial working memory following frontal lobe lesions in man. *Neuropsychologia, 28*, 1021-1034.

Perret, E. (1974). The left frontal lobe of man and the suppression of habitual responses in verbal categorical behavior. *Neuropsychologia, 12*, 323-330.

Posner, M.I, & Petersen, S.E. (1990). The attention system of the human brain. *Annual Review of Neuroscience, 13*, 25-42.

Postman, L., Stark, K., & Fraser, J. (1968). Temporal changes in interference. *Journal of Verbal Learning and Verbal Behavior, 7*, 672-694.

Rabbitt, P.M.A. (1965). An age decrement in the ability to ignore irrelevant information. *Journal of Gerontology, 20*, 233-238.

Raz, N., Gunning-Dixon, F.M., Head, D., Dupuis, J.H., & Acker, J.D. (1998). Neuroanatomical correlates of cognitive aging: Evidence from structural MRI. *Neuropsychology*, in press.

Raz, N., Gunning, F.M., Head, D., Dupuis, J.H., McQuain, J.M., Briggs, S.D., Thorton, A.E., Loken, W.J., & Acker, J.D. (1997). Selective aging of human cerebral cortex observed in vivo: Differential vulnerability of the prefrontal gray matter. *Cerebral Cortex, 7*, 268-282.

Rezai, K., Andreasen, N.C., Alliger, R., Cohen, G., Swayze, V., & O'Leary, D.S. (1993). The neuropsychology of the prefrontal cortex. *Archives of Neurology, 50*, 636-642.

Robbins, T.W. (1990). The case for frontostriatal dysfunction in schizophrenia. *Schizophrenia Bulletin, 16*, 392-402.

Salthouse, T.A. (1982). *Adult cognition: An experimental psychology of aging.* New York: Springer Verlag.

Scheibel, M., & Scheibel, A. (1975). Structural changes in the aging brain. In H. Brody, D. Harmon, & J. Ordy (Eds.), *Aging* (Vol. 1, pp. 11-37). New York: Raven Press.

Schmand, B., Brand, N., & Kuipers, T. (1992). Procedural learning of cognitive and motor skills in psychotic patients. *Schizophrenia Research, 8*, 157-170.

Settlage, P., Butler, R., & Odoi, H. (1956). Perseverative interference in monkeys following bilateral removal of prefrontal areas. *Journal of General Psychology, 54*, 255-262.

Severson, J.A., Marcusso, J., Winblad, B., & Finch, C.E. (1982). Age-correlated loss of dopaminergic binding sites in human basal ganglia. *Journal of Neurochemistry, 39*, 1623-1631.

Shallice, T. (1982). Specific impairments of planning. *Philosophical Transactions of the Royal Society of London, Series B, 298,* 199-209.

Shallice, T., & Burgess, P. (1991a). Higher-order cognitive impairments and frontal lobe lesions in man. In H.S. Levin, H.M. Eisenberg, & A.L. Benton (Eds.), *Frontal lobe function and dysfunction*. New York: Oxford University Press.

Shallice, T., & Burgess, P. (1991b). Deficits in strategy application following frontal lobe damage in man. *Brain, 114*, 727-741.

Shaw, T.G., Mortel, K.F., Meyer, J.S., Rogers, R.L., Hardenberg, J., & Cutaia, M.M. (1984). Cerebral blood flow changes in benign aging and cerebrovascular disease. *Neurology, 34*, 855-862.

Shimamura, A.P. (1995). Memory and frontal lobe function. In M.S. Gazzaniga (Ed.), *The cognitive neurosciences* (pp. 803-813). Cambridge, MA: MIT Press.

Simpson, G.B., & Burgess, C.A. (1985). Activation and selection processes in the recognition of ambiguous words. *Journal of Experimental Psychology: Human Perception and Performance, 11*, 28-39.

Smith, R.C., Baumgartner, R., & Calderon, M. (1987). Magnetic resonance imaging studies of the brains of schizophrenic patients. *Psychiatry Research, 20*, 33-46.

Smith, S.M., & Blankenship, S.E. (1991). Incubation and the persistence of fixation in problem solving. *American Journal of Psychology, 104*, 61-87.

Stanley, W.C., & Jaynes, J. (1949). The function of the frontal cortex. *Psychological Review, 56*, 18-32.

Stine, E.L., & Wingfield, A. (1987). Process and strategy in memory for speech among younger and older adults. *Psychology and Aging, 2*, 272-279.

Stuss, D.T., & Benson, D.F. (1984). Neuropsychological studies of the frontal lobes. *Psychological Bulletin, 95*, 3-28.

Stuss, D.T., Benson, D.F., Kaplan, E.F., Weir, W.S., Naeser, M.A., Lieberman, I., & Ferrill, D. (1983). The involvement of the orbitofrontal cerebrum in cognitive tasks. *Neuropsychologia, 21*, 235-248.

Suhara, T., Fukuda, H., Inoue, O., Itoh, T., Suzuki, K., & Yamasaki, T., & Tateno, Y. (1991). Age-related changes in D_1 dopamine receptors measured by positron emission tomography. *Psychopharmacology, 103*, 41-45.

Taylor, M.A., & Abrams, R. (1984). Cognitive impairments in schizophrenia. *American Journal of Psychiatry, 14*, 196-201.

Terry, R.D., DeTeresa, R., & Hansen, L.A. (1987). Neocortical cell counts in normal adult aging. *Annals of Neurology, 21*, 530-539.

Thaker, G., Nguyen, J., & Tamminga, C. (1989). Increased saccadic distractibility in tardive dyskinesia: Functional evidence for a subcortical GABA dysfunction. *Biological Psychiatry, 25*, 45-59.

Warren, J.M., & Akert, K. (1964). *The frontal granular cortex and behavior.* New York: McGraw-Hill.

Weinberger, D.R., Berman, K.F., & Illowsky, B.P. (1988). Physiologic dysfunction of dorsolateral prefrontal cortex in schizophrenia: III. A new cohort and evidence for a monoaminergic mechanism. *Archives of General Psychiatry, 45*, 609-615.

Weinberger, D.R., Berman, K.F., & Zec, R.F. (1986). Physiologic dysfunction of dorsolateral prefrontal cortex in schizophrenia: I. Regional cerebral blood flow evidence. *Archives of General Psychiatry, 43*, 114-125.

Whelihan, W.M., & Lesher, E.L. (1985). Neuropsychological changes in frontal functions with aging. *Developmental Neuropsychology, 1*, 371-380.

Wysocki, J.J., & Sweet, J.J. (1985). Identification of brain-damaged, schizophrenic, and normal medical patients using a brief neuropsychological screening battery. *International Journal of Clinical Neuropsychology, 7*, 40-49.

Zacks, R., & Hasher, L. (1994). Directed ignoring: Inhibitory regulation of working memory. In D. Dagenbach & T. Carr (Eds.), *Inhibitory mechanisms in attention, language, and memory* (pp. 241-263). San Diego: Academic Press.

Zangwill, O. (1966). Psychological deficits associated with frontal lobe lesions. *International Journal of Neurology, 5*, 395-401.

Subject Index

Author Index

Z

www.ingramcontent.com/pod-product-compliance
Ingram Content Group UK Ltd.
Pitfield, Milton Keynes, MK11 3LW, UK
UKHW020226290926
15470UKWH00001B/406

9 780444 825223